The Social Credit Phenomenon in Alberta

ALVIN FINKEL

UNIVERSITY OF TORONTO PRESS

Toronto Buffalo London

© University of Toronto Press 1989
Toronto Buffalo London
Printed in Canada

ISBN 0-8020-5821-3 (cloth)
ISBN 0-8020-6731-X (paper)

♾ \

Printed on acid-free paper.

Canadian Cataloguing in Publication Data

Finkel, Alvin, 1947–
The Social Credit phenomenon in Alberta

(The State and economic life; 12)
Includes bibliographical references and index.
ISBN 0-8020-5821-3 (bound)   ISBN 0-8020-6731-X (pbk.)

1. Social Credit Party of Alberta – History.
2. Alberta – Politics and government – 1935–1971.*
3. Alberta – Politics and government – 1971–
I. Title.   II. Series.

FC3674.2.F56 1989   971.23′03   C89-093317-0
F1078.F56 1989

Cover photo: ,
William Aberhart and E.C. Manning campaigning, circa 1940
(Provincial Archives of Alberta, A2048)

This book has been published with the help of a grant from the Canadian
Federation for the Humanities, using funds provided by the Social Sciences and
Humanities Research Council of Canada.

THE STATE AND ECONOMIC LIFE

EDITORS: Mel Watkins, University of Toronto; Leo Panitch, York University

... metamorphosis
from on... Social C... 1930s and ... ...ment in 1971, the party ... ... reformist organization to a cliqui... ... ...ose main purpose was to hold th...

In thi... ...mation, Alvin Finkel challen... ...cial Credit moneta... ...ally ... ...the early party is best seen a... ...formers, ... working-class social dem... ...mployed, ...ness owners, and farmers ... ...ly by the Depression. In its first term of office, ...was perceived as on ... left, opposed in the 1940 ... ...on by a right-wing coalition.

During ... ...berhart years, and especially after Ernest Manning's accession to the premiership, Social Credit switched its fire from bankers to socialists and the party's rhetoric became extremely right-wing. Manning opposed, on ideological grounds, most of the social programs introduced by the federal government after 1945.

Though patronage was rife, most Albertans regarded Social Credit as righteous because of the leadership of Manning, a radio evangelist. Only Manning's departure from the political scene began the slow process of decay of the governing party.

ALVIN FINKEL is Professor of History, Athabasca University, and author of *Business and Social Reform in the Thirties*.

For Carol and Antony

Contents

Acknowledgments

Portions of this book have appeared in *Prairie Forum, Labour/Le Travail, Studies in Political Economy*, and *Alberta History*. The reviewers and editors of these journals forced me to rethink or sharpen certain arguments. I am grateful to the editors of these journals as well for permission to make use of the materials found in these articles.

Former Alberta Premier Ernest Manning was kind enough to provide unrestricted access to his papers from 1960 to 1968. Although deposited with the Provincial Archives of Alberta, these papers are not yet available for general use by researchers.

The archivists at the Provincial Archives of Alberta, the Glenbow-Alberta Archives, the City of Edmonton Archives, and the Public Archives of Canada provided much assistance.

Financial assistance for the research was provided by both the Social Sciences and Humanities Research Council and the Athabasca University Academic Research Committee.

The various versions of the manuscript were typed quickly and efficiently by members of the Text Processing Unit of Athabasca University and by Myrna Nolan.

The anonymous reviewers chosen by the University of Toronto Press and by Aid to Scholarly Publications provided useful suggestions, and the CFH's grant in aid of publication made the appearance of the work possible. Both R.I.K. Davidson and Virgil Duff of the University of Toronto Press ensured that the manuscript went through the requisite hoops with admirable speed. Michael Carley, director of the Aid to Scholarly Publications program of the SSFC and the Canadian Federation for the Humanities, performed a similar service. Howard Palmer and Bob Hesketh kindly pointed out errors in the manuscript, and copyeditor Dan Liebman tightened up the prose.

Discussions and correspondence over the years with a variety of friends and colleagues shaped the sorts of questions that this book attempts to answer. The late Professor C.B. Macpherson encouraged what is essentially a revision of his earlier analysis of Social Credit. Further encouragement was provided by the late Professor L.H. Thomas, a perceptive scholar of Prairie populist politics. I am also grateful to Harold Chorney, Phil Hansen, Leo Panitch, Don Wetherell, David Elliott, John Richards, and, especially, to my wife, Carol Taylor.

Preface

The Social Credit League dominated Alberta political life from 1935 to 1971 and shaped a political culture that is unique in Canada. Partly because of the personalities and programs of Social Credit itself and partly because of the vagaries of the first-past-the-post system, opposition within the provincial legislature (except after the elections of 1940, 1955, and 1967) became the prerogative of a generally ineffectual handful of members. Charismatic premiers, presenting themselves as champions of Alberta rights trampled upon by a federal government allegedly shackled by central Canadian interests, became the only public face of Alberta political life.

Scholars have attempted to deal with the various phases of Social Credit development in Alberta, and a partisan, journalistic synthesis of the party's history appeared in 1974. The present book represents the first attempt by an academic historian to piece together the continuities and discontinuities of Alberta political life during the Social Credit era and to assess the legacy of that era to Alberta's political present and future.

What emerges is a history which suggests that neither Social Credit's original ascent nor its later conversion to a pro-business, Cold War party was inevitable. Alberta's political culture before 1935 did not crowd out left-wing forces, and indeed many social reformers of working-class and farm backgrounds joined the early Social Credit movement and worked for the election of the party of Aberhart and Manning. Some were attracted by the monetary-reform ideas that were the basis of social credit theory, while others, simply disillusioned with the United Farmers of Alberta and the Canadian Labour party, latched on to William Aberhart's anti-Establishment rhetoric in the belief that he represented the possibility of major social reform. The monetary reformers were well represented in the provincial and federal caucuses, which consisted of hand-picked

Aberhart men and women, while the social reformers loomed large in the party organization and the rank-and-file.

The process by which both social reformers and monetary reformers were eased out of the party forms an important component of this book. So does the character of the government in the Manning years when Alberta, lashing out at the welfare-state consensus forming elsewhere in the country, preached self-reliance and free enterprise, all the while gladly spending its windfall revenues from oil and gas development in the province. With the mantle of religion available to cloak its misdeeds, the Manning regime earned a reputation for honesty and frugality. But while the premier himself, a radio evangelist, was principled, his government and civil service were venal and free-spending.

Lavish public spending, especially on schools and roads, kept Social Credit in office, but because of the government's right-wing ideological outlook, little effort was made to redistribute wealth or aid the province's poor. Restrictive labour laws, user fees for medical services, municipal administration of relief, and neglect of native communities (at least until the mid-sixties) all made worse the plight of those upon whom the market did not smile. The province's growing urban middle classes, meanwhile, were also restive, because they believed the provincial government was too passive in its approach to economic diversification and in its response to the demands for the improved urban services that economic development supposedly required.

Ironically, from 1944 onwards, while the party's legislative position remained impregnable, the edifice upon which it stood was weak. From 41,000 members in its heyday of 1937 the party declined to a collection of a few thousand aging activists mainly activated at election time. Out of touch with the rising middle class and the unionized working class, Social Credit, once a broadly based party of workers, farmers, and small business, became a narrowly based party of rural religious fundamentalists. Only Manning's departure and the arrival on the scene of a new charismatic politician – Peter Lougheed, the Progressive Conservative leader – were necessary to topple the presumed-invincible Social Credit regime. In opposition, this party, deprived of its original purpose and weak and divided, collapsed bit by bit until right-wing extremists claimed it for their own in the 1980s and thereby sealed its doom.

THE SOCIAL CREDIT PHENOMENON

I The Social Credit Phenomenon

A government that styled itself 'Social Credit' ruled the province of Alberta from 1935 to 1971, swept to power by a Depression-born movement for reform and maintained in office by a wartime and post-war prosperity that allowed it to indeed achieve many reforms. Yet the reforms achieved, mainly in the social service and educational areas, appeared to bear little relationship to the party's pre-1935 promises for economic restructuring. And the original radicalism of the Social Credit League later gave way to conservative and often reactionary ideology.

This book explores the changing character of Social Credit and seeks to explain why changes occurred. In so doing, I modify the interpretations of earlier studies of the Social Credit movement, most of which, in any case, go little beyond the early years of the Social Credit administrations. In the view of the present study, the early Social Credit movement was far more radical and diffuse than the monetary crank organization that scholars have depicted, although even the first Aberhart administration had its authoritarian and conservative side.

The view that Social Credit's radicalism was restricted to the monetary sphere has caused scholars to conclude that the shift to conservatism after the death of the first Social Credit premier, William Aberhart, in 1943, was unproblematic. The courts had ruled that a province had no right to tinker with banking and currency, and in the view of many its rulings left Social Credit scrambling for a program. Unsurprisingly, the new Social Credit premier, Ernest Manning, forced to abandon the monetary panaceas of his party, simply concentrated on the provision of 'good government.' His administration, while espousing conservatism, made use of the windfall revenues from oil development after 1947 to outspend most other provinces in the areas of education and social services. In sum, it was not a radical right-wing regime and did not therefore represent a major shift from the earlier Aberhart regime.

Although these studies all contain valuable insights into the psychology and practice of the Social Credit movement, they underrate both the degree and diffuseness of radicalism of the early Social Credit movement and the extremity of the conservatism of the Manning period in which Albertans, if one accepted their provincial government as representative, seemed to lie outside the national consensus which produced a modified version of a 'welfare state' in Canada. The province's political culture had changed from one of large-scale popular participation in the 1930s and throughout the interwar period to one of large-scale political apathy. And the openness to radical ideas of all sorts, which had led earlier Social Crediters to co-operate with Communists and CCFers against conventional political forces, had been replaced by a visceral anti-socialism that placed Social Credit well to the right of the old-line parties against whom Social Credit had once battled from the left. In short, the changes both in Social Credit and in the overall political culture of Alberta were dramatic and cannot be explained away with simple reference to the province's inability to institute reforms in the monetary system.

This book attempts to reconstruct the entire Social Credit period – roughly from the conversion of Aberhart to Social Credit doctrine in 1932 to the party's political defeat almost half a century later – in order to indicate the extent of the changes that occurred both within the movement and within the political culture of the province as a whole. Making use of primary materials, the book outlines the dramatic changes that occurred and attempts to explain why they happened.

The following chapter, chapter 2, examines the political environment into which Aberhart inserted Social Credit and posits the thesis that the early Social Credit is best understood as a loose coalition of reformers rather than as a single-minded (or mindless, as its detractors saw it) movement to tame the financiers. Chapter 3 elaborates this thesis with reference to the Aberhart years in office, demonstrating that the government and, to a greater extent, the movement itself proved open to left-wing influences. Chapter 3 seeks also to repudiate the popular view that the Social Credit organization was little more than a cheering gallery for the government. At the same time, the chapter indicates why disillusionment with the government and party set in early for many party members.

Chapter 4 outlines the breakup of the coalition character of Social Credit and its reconstitution as simply the 'government party.' The shift of the party to the right in the late Aberhart and early Manning years is explained in terms of the exit of the left-minded sections of the early Social Credit movement and the growth outside the party of a left-wing alternative that dissenters could join.

Chapters 5 and 6 examine the Manning years in Alberta, a period largely ignored by scholars of political life. Despite the government's enviable record in certain areas, it was, I suggest, as reactionary as some of its propaganda hinted. Authoritarian and paranoid, the Manning government at times suppressed civil rights, restricted the operations of the labour movement, and proved paternalistic to the poor. Its religious-based fear of collectivism led the government both to oppose most federal programs of a distributive character and, in the name of decentralization, to burden municipalities – particularly the cities – with costs that they could ill afford. At the same time Manning evolved a political philosophy, which he later labelled social conservatism, to justify the government's approach. This philosophy gradually became that of the party as well and, because of the apparent successes of the government, deeply influenced political thinking among Albertans as a whole.

Chapter 7 traces the electoral defeat and subsequent collapse of Social Credit in the post-Manning years. During these years the party was engaged in a fruitless search for an organizing idea that would resuscitate the movement – an especially difficult task after 1971, when its principal opponent was a Conservative government that appeared to espouse Manning's old principles. Finally, chapter 8 seeks to synthesize the experience of the Social Credit years by way of comparison with the history of other so-called populist movements in other provinces and countries.

The book now begins by reviewing the major existing literature on Social Credit and indicating areas of agreement and disagreement with the findings of earlier authors. It should be noted in passing, however, that the major body of work done on Social Credit occurred in the 1950s, when the primary materials available to researchers were skimpy and the direction in which Manning was taking Alberta may still have been uncertain.

Alberta's Social Credit movement-turned-government once inspired a flurry of research. In the 1950s, the Canadian Social Science Research Council sponsored a series of studies on the 'background and development' of Social Credit in Alberta.[1] Although only three of the ten works produced in this series dealt principally with Social Credit, the series as a whole indicated the extent to which the Alberta movement had sparked renewed interest in traditions of unconventional political movements within Canada.[2] At the same time, the early Social Credit movement seemed to become a popular topic for graduate theses, including a political biography of Alberta's first Social Credit premier, William Aberhart.[3]

The early work on Social Credit was largely restricted to the Aberhart period, which ended with the premier's death in 1943 and, not surprisingly, focused on the peculiar monetary theories of Social Credit and the federal-provincial conflicts set in motion by a provincial administration's attempts to control the financial institutions whose fate the British North America Act had confided almost exclusively to the federal government.[4] There was also considerable reflection on the personality of Aberhart himself and the charismatic qualities which allowed him to win massive support for the proposals that economists labelled as nonsense and legal experts pointed out to be unconstitutional.[5]

To C.B. Macpherson goes the credit for first having analysed closely the economic and political theories of Social Credit. *Democracy in Alberta* is not only a lucid critique of the ideas of Major C.H. Douglas, the British engineer who fathered the basic theories of Social Credit, but a brilliant work of political theory that places such ideas in the context of debates on the larger meaning of democracy in the western world.

Although Macpherson's book will likely remain the standard reference on Social Credit theory, his contentions regarding the manifestation of the phenomenon in Alberta have been placed in doubt by many authors. Macpherson emphasizes the role of 'independent commodity producers,' mainly farmers, in spawning a monetary-reform party in Alberta. These people lived in a province in which most people were self-employed and had little contact with either the urban working class or the leaders of the corporations. Thus they developed a world-view from which the main economic players were excluded and only forces external to their environment could be accused of fostering economic injustices. These people had a long history, even before Aberhart appeared on the scene, of blaming their problems on central Canadian financial barons. Feeling helpless before their invisible foes, they gladly surrendered their autonomy of thought to the authoritarian radio preacher who promised to hand them social dividends and fair prices for their products. Their understanding of political economy, owing to their class position, did not allow them to evaluate Aberhart's proposals seriously or to seek to participate as equals in the new social movement that he was launching in Alberta.[6]

Macpherson notes the admittedly authoritarian and cranky views of political organization held by Major Douglas and by his Alberta disciple, Aberhart, with whom he proved largely unwilling to co-operate. Both men advocated government by technical experts, particularly on monetary questions, and regarded the role of the electorate and their elected members as little more than one of expressing a vague general will concerning 'results' expected from the government. The technical experts hired by the legislators, rather than the legislators themselves, would come up with a program to produce the re-sults demanded by the people. Such a view of government obviously would have made both the political parties and the legislature fairly peripheral to the political process, and Macpherson suggests that although in fact the cabinet, rather than experts, took charge under Aberhart, the debasement of both the legislature and political parties implicit in the Douglas theory of social credit did occur.[7]

Macpherson is correct in indicating the important role of self-employed small entrepreneurs in Social Credit and in Alberta political life generally, but subsequent authors have questioned his claims regarding both the character of the farm population and its relative importance within the Social Credit movement. Questions have also been raised about the extent to which Social Credit in Alberta, as a movement and a government, followed Douglas's teachings.

David McGinnis, for example, has challenged Macpherson's view that farmers derived most income from self-employment and were minimally familiar with wage employment, either as employers or as employees.[8] He does none the less largely corroborate Macpherson's view that farmers *perceived* themselves to be independent commodity producers.

It has been suggested by some authors that the social chaos produced by the Depression did cause economic divisions among farmers and rural town residents to be perceived. The social solidarity, once characteristic of small communities, was replaced by economic divisions and increasingly by fierce political divisions as well. Jean Burnet, writing a year before Macpherson's book appeared, noted in her study of the town and surrounding community of Hanna, Alberta, that:

Informal social activities reflected the cleavage. U.F.A. and Social Credit partisanship was so strong that people of different allegiance, even if on adjacent farms in the sparsely settled countryside, stopped speaking to one another and 'neighbouring' ...

Disorganization in the rural communities in the drought and depression years did not show itself only in the division between the U.F.A. and Social Credit. Something resembling class division developed. A few families of wealth, educational aspiration and achievement, and superior standards of housing came to stand apart from the rest of the community.[9]

Macpherson's limited treatment of Social Credit's urban support has drawn as much criticism as his underplaying of conflict within the farm community. John Richards and Larry Pratt, who fault Macpherson generally with a 'consistent tendency toward single-class analysis,' state the criticism starkly:

Neither regional capital nor urbanized labour, each of which has played significant roles in the evolution of the Canadian West, feature at all in Macpherson's study. Thus he passes over in silence such developments as the radicalization of western labour during and after World War I, the considerable influence of the Communist party on the Prairies, especially among East European and Ukrainian immigrants, the movement for a One Big Union, the Winnipeg General Strike, and the bitter and prolonged strikes in the coal mines of Drumheller, Estevan and the Crow's Nest Pass in the early 1930s – none of which is evidence of an insignificant working class or an absence of class divisions within Prairie society.[10]

Indeed, Macpherson was aware of Social Credit's support in the cities (a support statistically confirmed in 1974 by Grayson and Grayson[11]) but attempted to explain such support as a reflection of the quasi-colonial economy of Alberta: an economy ultimately controlled by decisions made by buyers and sellers outside the province. The dependence upon outsiders united Albertans – including those who were not independent commodity producers – behind the political demands of the farmer-based movements. In the 1930s it led them to accept the authoritarian rule of Aberhart.

This study largely corroborates the views of Macpherson's critics that 'single-class analysis,' as Richards and Pratt call it, leaves gaps in the analysis of the social forces that produced the Social Credit party. The urban working class, and particularly the unemployed,[12] were attracted to Social Credit in 1935 and often interpreted the movement's purpose somewhat differently from the interpretation of the 'independent commodity producers.' I argue that workers (as well as other social groups) were attracted, in part, by the promise of participatory democracy in the new movement, a promise that Macpherson establishes was hollow. Despite Social Credit theories that suggested to them another form of behaviour, the party's 1930s activists were unwilling to leave decision-making to the 'experts.' The party in its early years was, as suggested in chapters 2 and 3, vibrant and little willing to restrict itself to a discussion of 'results.' If these activists had not been politically unsophisticated, they might have recognized, with Professor Macpherson, that the chances of making an Aberhart-led, Douglasite government truly reflective of grass-roots thinking were slim. None the less, most of these men and women *were* concerned about democracy, and, within a decade of Aberhart's initial conversion to the Douglasite theories, the majority left the Social Credit party in disillusionment.

The most vivid study of how Aberhart and his followers convinced them to join in the first place is John Irving's classic study, *The Social Credit Movement in Alberta*. Irving is less interested in class analysis of Alberta society in his search for the roots of Social Credit than is Macpherson. Instead he concentrates on a social-psychological analysis of Social Credit. He notes that straitened economic circumstances and a tradition that regarded monetary reform as key to economic stability made Albertans susceptible to a social credit appeal. Their embrace of the movement, he observes – and most contemporary commentators, as well as most Social Credit scholars, would agree – represented a form of 'mass hysteria.'[13]

Irving demonstrates effectively the excessive zeal and intolerance of Social Credit activists and their devotion, at least in the early years, to William Aberhart. He notes:

The phenomenon of dynamic interaction between leader and led was especially apparent in the process of coming to a decision to go into politics. If Aberhart had said to the people, 'Don't go into politics' they would have accepted his advice. It is significant that he never made such a categorical statement; equally significant that he hesitated for a year before publicly accepting direct political participation as the goal of the movement. It should be stressed that during most of this period of indecision he was subjected to constant pressure from both the people and the secondary leaders to take the movement into politics. At the same time, like a cat playing with a mouse, he asked the people repeatedly to tell him what to do.[14]

Although one should not underestimate either Aberhart's shrewdness or the gullibility of his followers, this study attempts to examine the features of Social Credit's rhetoric and program that attracted masses of people to a monetary-reform party. Aberhart might have indeed been able to exercise the type of persuasion which Irving attributes to him in 1935, but I suggest that such persuasive power began to fade once Aberhart became premier and could be judged by deeds as well as words.

No doubt, as Irving suggests, Aberhart's skills as a preacher proved invaluable in mobilizing Social Credit's early support. Subsequent writings, however, have questioned his claim that 'in its inception, the Social Credit movement may be best understood as an extension of an already existing religious movement. Similarly, political participation may be interpreted as continuous with the religious and educational activities of the social movement.'[15] The religious factor in Aberhart's appeal should not be underestimated, but Irving's portrayal of Social Crediters as mainly attracted by religious fervour is somewhat undermined by his own evidence. A 1974 study of electoral statistics by Grayson and Grayson also calls for caution regarding the role of religion, particularly fundamentalist religion, in explaining Social Credit support. They note: 'It is clear that over-all support for the Social Credit party is different than might have been expected. The percentage of religious fundamentalists, contrary to what Clark and Irving had to say, in urban areas at least, accounted for very little of the variance. On the basis of this evidence it might be concluded that the economic appeal of Social Credit was more important than its religious appeal in urban areas.'[16]

The 'economic appeal' was partly the result of a left-wing thrust in the early Social Credit movement. This thrust is acknowledged in the third major work of the fifties on Social Credit: Mallory's study of the constitutional battles in the courts between Aberhart's Alberta and the federal government led by the Liberal prime minister, Mackenzie King. But the point is mentioned only in passing, in a discussion of the government's increasing conservatism in the early forties. Mallory indicates correctly that wartime prosperity blunted popular enthusiasm for root-and-branch reform and allowed the government to concentrate on day-to-day administration rather than on long-term reform. He also notes that the Social Credit leaders, always partial to conspiracy theories in the explanation of events (as Macpherson demonstrates well), embraced in the early forties the view of a secret financier-socialist alliance against Social Credit and free enterprise.[17] But he underestimates the size of the socialist threat to the Social Credit regime in the early forties, emphasizing the external character of the threat that Manning and company decried. As noted in chapter 4, the CCF enjoyed a larger membership than did Social Credit, and while the two left-wing parties won only 30 per cent of the vote in 1944 and a derisive two seats out of fifty-seven, the momentum in favour of the left scared the leaders of Social Credit. Indeed the wartime prosperity, which allowed Social Credit to move rightwards and still retain the reins of power, left many Albertans unpersuaded that collectivist reforms were passé. The election of 1944 to some extent represented a last-ditch effort by reformers, now locked out of Social Credit, to revive the fighting spirit that Social Credit had once represented.

The histories of the early Social Credit movement produced in the 1950s appear to have satiated scholarly interest in the subject for several decades. No major new work on Social Credit in Canada appeared for many years. A biography of Aberhart appeared from a vanity press in 1970, written by his daughter with the aid of an agronomist. It was unabashed hagiography and included little new information about the Social Credit movement or the Aberhart government.[18] Unfortunately, the one major thesis regarding Social Credit which appeared a year later received little attention. F. Richard Swann's 'Progressive Social Credit in Alberta' detailed some of the progressive legislative achievements of the first Aberhart government.[19] Although the thesis offered little explanation of the progressive character of a regime that later turned reactionary – and indeed failed to deal with the failures of the government, which kept forces to the left of Social Credit alive – it suggested that some rethinking of the character of the early Social Credit movement was necessary, as was closer attention to why the movement changed so dramatically in the Manning years. A documentary collection by L.H. Thomas[20] and essays by David Elliott[21] later confirmed the view that much progressive legislation had been passed in the early Social Credit years, and indeed some authors began to see similarities between the CCF and Social Credit in the formative years of the two parties. Ironically, however, because the view persisted that Social Credit must always have been a conservative force on the whole, apparent similarities between the CCF and Social Credit were seen to suggest that the former movement was less radical than had once been thought rather than that the latter was somewhat more radical than earlier scholarship indicated. This literature is reviewed in chapter 8 which suggests that there were indeed similarities, but the seeds of the future direction taken by each movement were planted early on, and the directions diverged dramatically.

If little of interest on Canadian Social Credit appeared in the sixties, a provocative thesis on the movement in the United Kingdom did appear in 1968. John Finlay's 'The Origins of the Social Credit Movement,' which later formed the basis for a book,[22] challenged C.B. Macpherson's characterization of the British founders of Social Credit as a uniformly reactionary, authoritarian lot. Finlay stressed that Social Credit was a philosophy of wealth redistribution which had contradictory strands and therefore appealed to very different groups. While Macpherson emphasizes Social Credit's support from middle-class groups, Finlay observes that it proved equally attractive to left-wingers in the British Labour party and especially to the Independent Labour party (ILP), the influential left-wing affiliate of the Labour party. He sums up the odd assortment of groups of individuals and organizations attracted to Social Credit: 'In the religious sphere the juxtaposition was that of Anglo-Catholic and Quaker-Theosophist; in the political it was the I.L.P. and Fascists; while the general intellectual interest spanned Ezra Pound (who could with justice be called a Fascist) and C.M. Grieve (who was a member of the Communist Party) and embraced support of early Nazi Germany and that of Republican Spain.'[23] As we shall see, in Alberta as well, the vague philosophy of using social credit dividends to redistribute income appealed to diverse groups and diverse instincts, creating a movement whose ultimate political direction was not clear in the thirties.

Work by David Elliott and by Larry Hannant in the 1980s suggested a reawakened interest in Alberta's early Social Credit party, including an interest in the groups that participated in the movement and the ideas that attracted them. In a biography with Iris Miller as well as in several articles, Elliott examined the relationship between Aberhart's religious views and his political views. Unlike Irving, who regarded Aberhart's political views after 1932 as a natural outgrowth of his fundamentalist beliefs, Elliott suggested that the adoption of an interest in political events changed Aberhart's religious outlook. Although he still considered himself a fundamentalist, his religious teaching began to sound much like the 'social gospel' preached by essentially secular preachers within the mainstream Protestant churches – preachers whom Aberhart had once rejected for allegedly abandoning the literal teachings of the Bible.[24] Elliott's writings strongly suggest a social-democratic tendency in Aberhart's thinking, although ultimately he regards Aberhart as an erratic authoritarian who fits uneasily in the categories of either left-wing or right-wing politics.

Larry Hannant documents the strong attraction this party held for working-class people who once had identified with socialist or at least social-democratic politics. Unfortunately, he virtually dismisses the importance of his own insight by strongly suggesting that many working-class activists for Social Credit must have been police agents, presumably because, in his mind, Social Credit ulti-mately embodies a set of ideas objectively opposed to working-class interests.[25] The work of Swann and Elliott, as well as the evidence in chapters 2 and 3, suggests that even if this supposition were ultimately true, there was no reason for workers to believe it in the 1930s.

If the Aberhart years have received scholarly attention because of the government's attempts to introduce radical financial schemes, the Manning years (1944–68) have been largely without interest to scholars because of the half-heartedness with which Manning approached monetary issues. Although he maintained Social Credit rhetoric about the need for monetary reform, Manning made only one real attempt to introduce a provincial social credit scheme and gave no indication of a desire to do battle with Ottawa as Aberhart had done when the courts struck down the legislation. Apart from this one effort at monetary reform, Manning ran a conservative administration – hardly surprising, from Macpherson's point of view. Stripped of its money-printing panaceas Social Credit was not a radical movement, and so it was natural that once the courts forced it to leave banks alone, it would prove bereft of any other ideas for social reform.[26] As I have indicated, more recent works suggest that the overall reform impetus in the early Social Credit movement and government was stronger than Macpherson recognizes. So the dramatic shift to conservatism requires some explanation.

Journalist John Barr's *The Dynasty: The Rise and Fall of Social Credit in Alberta* is the only work that deals at any length with either the transition from Aberhart to Manning or the Manning years. But Barr, a Social Crediter of the post-Manning period, gives almost twice as much space to the two and a half years of Harry Strom's rule (1969–71) as to the twenty-four Manning years. His position as executive assistant in the Strom years to Education Minister Robert Clark[27] no doubt shaped his priorities in his discussion of the post-Aberhart years. In any case, whether because of faulty research or because of Social Credit partisanship, Barr's discussion of the Manning years is shallow and full of errors and distortions. He emphasizes the reformism of the Manning years and fails to analyse closely any of the government's programs. From Barr's viewpoint, the conservative rhetoric of the government notwithstanding, Manning provided the province with a liberal administration; unions' public complaints about labour legislation were only ritualistic, native people had their concerns attended, and opposition criticisms of government–oil industry relations were completely wrong-headed.[28] Barr provides no references for such questionable conclusions in his largely impressionistic, journalistic account, and his grasp of even the basic facts of the Manning era must be questioned. He attributes to the Social Credit League a membership perhaps four times greater that it really enjoyed,[29] and he reduces the many scandals that confronted the government in 1955 – and cost it dearly in votes and seats that year – to one rather unimportant incident.[30] Unfortunately then, the one book that purports to provide an overview of the Manning years must be used with care. Still, Barr no doubt has valuable insights into the Strom years, during which he was a government insider.

Another Social Credit official, Owen Anderson,[31] produced a PhD thesis in 1972 that provided an empirical analysis of the membership of the later Social Credit party. This work is somewhat contradictory, stating at one point that 'even after years in office the Alberta Social Credit Party maintained a tradition of participation by the rank and file membership that is unusual for Canadian political parties,'[32] but at another that the party became 'highly electoral in orientation, in many cases holding only annual meetings when there was no electoral activity, as contrasted to the former frequent and regular meetings and activities.'[33] Nevertheless, Anderson's account provides useful materials on the thinking of the Social Credit membership of the Strom period, as I note in chapter 7.

The existing literature on Social Credit, as noted earlier, provides a starting-point for discussions of the Social Credit record and attempts to determine the extent to which continuities and discontinuities mark the development of Alberta political life. Fortunately, there is now also a wealth of primary materials available to the researcher of the Social Credit era. The premiers' papers, except for those from the short Strom period, are available for public viewing, as are the records of the Social Credit League. Most government department papers for the Social Credit years are also public, and the papers of a variety of second-string political figures of the Socred years – including cabinet ministers, MLAs, and leading opposition figures – are open to public scrutiny. What follows is largely the product of a reading of these sources, although an obvious debt is owed as well to existing work on Social Credit and, more generally, on reform movements as a whole.

2 Alberta Society at the Time of Social Credit's Appearance

A short three years elapsed between William Aberhart's conversion to Social Credit doctrine and the Social Credit League's provincial election victory in 1935. But such a victory would have been unlikely had the ground both for social credit and for reform more generally not been sown for many years in the province by agrarian and labour reformers. And the broad base that the Aberhart-led organization boasted would have been equally unlikely had that organization not been, in the minds of its members, democratic and open. The political atmosphere of the early thirties – before Social Credit's entry on the scene – was supercharged, and potential recruits for a new political organization were readily available. This chapter examines the economic and social conditions that had created reformist and radical movements in Alberta before the thirties and assesses why the social movements created earlier were found wanting in the thirties. It suggests that Social Credit's appeal did not lie in its defence of capitalism, reformed only by currency reform, as an alternative to socialism, but in its initial implacable hostility to big business generally and its staunch support for a variety of social reforms also supported by socialists. Above all, this chapter suggests that the socialist groups themselves largely failed to provide an alternative to that movement.

Social Credit appeared to many to be the logical inheritor in 1935 of the province's reform tradition. Although ultimately some of the structural features of the Social Credit League worked to undermine democracy in the movement-turned-party, there was much about the organization that reflected traditions both of radicalism and of democracy in Alberta.

Alberta was still primarily a rural province when Social Credit began to organize. Only about three Albertans in ten lived in population centres of 1000 or more, with 70 per cent of these urbanites accounted for by the two major cities,

Edmonton and Calgary. Twenty-three other centres shared the remaining non-rural dwellers.[1] The cities experienced slow growth between the wars, and the rural-urban balance remained almost constant between 1921 and 1941.[2] Farmers and farmers' sons made up about 48 per cent of the gainfully occupied population,[3] although many of these agriculturists, as David McGinnis observes, depended for some and often most of their income on seasonal off-farm employment.[4]

Although there were almost 100,000 farms in a province of 772,000 people,[5] there were also just short of 10,000 non-farm business units, most of them in the service sector.[6] The 1931 census indicated that, even as the Depression struck, 47 per cent of employed Albertans were non-agriculturists. Of these, just under half worked in the service, trade, commercial and financial sectors. Manufacturing accounted for only 11.5 per cent of non-farm jobs, and mining for 7.1 per cent.[7] Even in Calgary, the major manufacturing centre in the province, manufacturing accounted for only one job in seven.[8] In short, much of non-farm employment in the province was simply generated by the farm sector; economic diversification had not really occurred.

Another characteristic of the Alberta economy, apart from its dependence on the health of the agricultural sector, was the small size of most operations outside of the transportation and coal-mining sectors.[9] In all sectors, most firms would have been small enough to allow – theoretically – for personal paternalistic relations between owners and employees.[10] Only the 800 employees of the Canadian Pacific Railway's Ogden Shops in Calgary, the workers in a handful of food-processing establishments, and the employees of the governments of Alberta, Edmonton, and Calgary worked for corporate employers with personnel departments to deal with workers.

But employer-employee relations were often tense. In the coal mines, there was a history of employer authoritarianism and worker militancy. Safety standards in Alberta were laxer than in other jurisdictions, except perhaps British Columbia, and pay rates were unstable.[11] During the 1920s and 1930s, strikes intended to improve conditions and lockouts intended to resist change cost workers millions of days lost[12] without, however, much changing conditions.[13] Employer resistance to minimum wages, which initially applied only to women,[14] also indicated that small employers, with their smaller margin of manoeuvre, were not necessarily preferable to the large corporations whose huge profits gave them some scope to meet union demands. The union movement, enrolling about 20,000 workers in 1931,[15] was heavily concentrated in mining, railways, and construction. Edmonton and Calgary saw municipal workers enjoying union status, but in the private-service industries there was only limited unionization of workers.[16]

For Alberta's urban dwellers, almost as much as for the rural dwellers, the question of indebtedness was a sore point. An urban boom at the turn of the century in Edmonton and Calgary sent land values soaring, pushing up the cost of housing. Workers who bought houses at inflated prices before 1914 saw the value of their homes descend as the Alberta economy went into a tailspin following the completion of the railway-building that had fuelled the earlier boom. Then mortgage interest rates rose during the war, confronting home-owners with the ignominy of paying several times over for homes whose value fell well below the mortgage principal. Large numbers of the population simply abandoned their homes to seek rental accommodation, all the while cursing the bankers who had given the coup de grâce to their dreams of owning their own homes. The bitter fact was that because of the earlier profiteering by the land speculators, such dreams had always been precarious.[17]

For the farmers, of course, the solution of simple abandonment of their homes and land meant also the abandonment of a livelihood. But the debt load that they carried forced many of them under. Mortgages on farms carried, on average, 8 per cent annual interest payments, and farm machinery was sold on time with interest payments of 7 to 10 per cent.[18] While their incomes barely allowed most farmers to keep up interest payments before the Depression, the majority were in trouble when Alberta's farm products in the early thirties drew only a bit more than one-third of their 1927 price.[19]

The debt problem was also a serious one for both levels of government in the province. Both the provincial government and the municipalities had spent lavishly – and, in the case of several railway projects, corruptly – to build the infrastructure needed by pioneer communities.[20] The dispersed character of farm settlement, the result of Dominion land policies and accompanying land speculation,[21] made these expenditures higher than they ought to have been for a small population. When the Liberals left office in 1921, the provincial debt was $95 million. It rose slowly to $117 million during the first nine years of UFA administration,[22] which despite overall parsimony spent generously to relocate thousands of unsuccessful farmers left stranded by the collapse of farming in the southwestern dry belt. The UFA also spent millions reimbursing its creditors.[23] Afterwards, the costs of Depression relief and reduced provincial revenue pushed indebtedness up to $160 million before the UFA left office.[24] The result was a perceived inability on the part of the UFA either to increase relief costs or to declare a frontal assault on the financial companies.[25]

Although the federal government contributed 30 to 40 per cent of relief costs in Alberta during the Depression, its programs changed annually, causing the provincial government to shift much of the blame for both its growing indebtedness and its inability to meet relief demands to the senior level of government.[26]

The government's concern about its debt, however, met with little sympathy from desperate workers and farmers. The Depression in Alberta was not as severe as in Saskatchewan, where drought engulfed most of the province, and indeed the burden of relief on the public purse in Alberta was no greater than the Depression average for Canada.[27] But such was the severity of the Depression in Canada that in this 'average' province 15 per cent of Edmontonians and 13 per cent of residents of Calgary and Lethbridge were on relief in 1933. More city residents would have been on relief rolls had not large numbers of single, homeless men been relegated to relief camps.[28] Several camps were established by the federal government under the control of the Department of National Defence and several more were operated by the provincial government along the same lines: five dollars pay per month, bed and board in return for work performed, such as ditch-digging and road-building. In all camps, complaints of overcrowding, poor food, and isolation were general.[29]

In the cities, married men on welfare received small vouchers for rent and for food, and single unemployed men and women ate in quickly established food kitchens. Both groups were required to perform work for the municipality in return for meagre relief.[30] Some people stayed out of the relief system entirely by living in makeshift homes constructed from cast-off materials. The 'cavemen' along the river banks in Edmonton, for example, somehow survived Edmonton's cold winters by digging coal from the frozen ground on the hillsides to bring some warmth into their nondescript shelters. Selling crêpe-paper handicrafts and willow baskets to earn food money, they provided all their other needs by visiting garbage dumps and by gathering wood floating down the river in the spring.[31]

Most of the jobless, however, could not be so resourceful, and for those with families, in particular, relief provided the only hope for sufficient income for survival. If one was an immigrant who had not yet become a Canadian citizen, one risked deportation by merely applying for relief. More than 2500 men and women were indeed deported because they lacked sufficient income to support themselves. And many central Europeans who were not deported were simply cut off the relief rolls in Edmonton.[32] Those who did receive aid complained of the government's parsimony and regimentation.[33]

Even those who were employed in Alberta, such as the miners, were often in dire straits. Coal prices had been declining even in the prosperous 1920s, and pitched battles between miners and employers had occurred in that decade. In the thirties, further pay cuts as well as fewer hours of work created grinding poverty in mining communities.[34]

Some of the urban poor were placed by the provincial government on marginal farms, but few could make a real living in this way and more than half had left these farms when the Depression was over.[35] In the meantime they joined the province's farmers as a whole in wondering what the government would do to make farming viable for Albertans.

All of these groups – farmers, miners, unemployed workers – protested the poverty to which the Depression condemned them. If the 'cavemen' represented the embodiment of the frontier spirit of the west about which a great deal of mythology exists, the responses of the vast majority reflected even more deep-seated collectivist political reactions in Alberta. Fluctuating resource prices, unstable wages, and debt, as noted, had characterized the provincial economy before the Depression and, as we shall see, influenced political culture. This chapter looks now at the history of reformist movements in the province before the arrival of the Social Credit movement in 1933 and assesses why these movements seemed like spent forces by that time.

The United Farmers of Alberta formed the most important reformist organization before the Depression. Originating in 1909 as an economic movement, it restricted its political role to lobbying governments for legislative changes beneficial to farmers. Governments in Alberta from the province's incorporation in 1905 to 1921 meant the Liberal party. The Liberals, despite Macpherson's characterization of Alberta as essentially a one-class province of independent commodity producers, were led almost exclusively by urban employers and lawyers of substantial means.[36] The later UFA entry into politics can be seen as a revolt not only against the party system and against 'eastern-controlled' parties but against class-based government in which the smallest but most influential social class in the province monopolized political as well as economic life. The first political manifestation of a farmers' revolt against the domination by the urban economic elite occurred in 1917 with the entry in the provincial elections of candidates of the Non-Partisan League,[37] in which William Irvine had played a major role. Irvine is a key figure in the history of Alberta radicalism, having played a major part not only in the founding of the NPL and the provincial Labour party, but in the turn of the UFA to politics, and, later, in the founding of the CCF.[38] The league, inspired by the Non-Partisan League administration that governed North Dakota from 1916 to 1922, called for grass-roots control over the individual MLA.[39] After winning two of the four seats it contested in 1917, the league's ranks grew to six thousand by 1919, swelled because of farmers' anger at the wartime Union government's seemingly weak efforts to control profiteering.[40] Although historians stress the league's hostility to partyism, it ought to be noted that the NPL's economic program was fairly radical, particularly in its insistence on the need for public ownership of natural resources, banks, transport and communications firms, 'flour mills, packing houses and farm machinery manufacturing and insurance.'[41]

The league's insistence on public ownership reflected the farmers' doubts about the abilities of independent commodity producers to survive in a competitive capitalist economy. Farmers could not control the prices received for their products sold on international markets. But public ownership of food-processing plants would provide farmers with a say in the prices charged for their products sold within the country. Equally, public ownership of farm machinery firms, banks, railways, coal mines, and insurance companies would give farmers a chance to limit their input costs. The public-ownership program, as noted later, also appealed to urban labour, and William Irvine was a link between the political movements of farmers and workers.

Most NPL members were also members of the larger UFA, and their pressure as well as the growth of a national farmers' political movement helped convince UFA president Henry Wise Wood to set aside his opposition to a UFA electoral presence. While rejecting the NPL's emphasis on public ownership, Wood accepted its anti-partyism. He called for the institution of 'group government,' by which he understood representation on the basis of occupational groupings rather than on the basis of residence-based constituencies.[42] He never offered any program for conversion of the existing parliament into a 'group government' parliament, but the theory seemed to serve in any case as a sufficient excuse for the UFA, as the major representative of one of the groups (farmers), to enter the electoral arena. With 38,000 members in 1921, the UFA proved up to the challenge of winning the first election it had contested.[43]

The group government idea proved particularly attractive to the former NPLers, who now actively threw in their support behind the UFA entry into politics. Enthused William Irvine in 1920: 'When the representatives of the various industrial groups meet around one common government table, each with his, or her, responsibility, both to the group and to the nation as a whole, cooperation will open the door to a new era of Canadian liberty. Then, and only then, will economic problems be admitted, faced and settled on a basis making for the well-being of all. Which will Canada choose? Class domination through party government with red revolution at the end, or class organization, class representation and class cooperation for national harmony? As I see it, there is no other alternative.'[44] The UFA embrace of 'group government,' however, did not find much resonance in other provinces. And within Alberta the operations of the UFA government and the 'group government' concept were not exactly coterminous. On the one hand, most of those elected on the UFA ticket in 1921 were farmers, and with the significant exception of J.E. Brownlee, wealthy lawyer and premier from 1924 to 1934, most of the MLAs throughout the fourteen years of UFA power were farmers.[45] The lawyers and businessmen had been largely pushed out from the seats of political power. In line with the group government idea, the first UFA premier invited one of the four elected Labour representatives to join his cabinet; in 1926, however, when Labour elected six members, no such invitation was forthcoming.[46]

But on the other hand, the UFA government quickly established that it saw itself as a government like any other. Its members were not the delegates of the farmers in their constituencies, free to support whatever their constituents demanded. Instead they were members of a caucus of a political group that was a party in all but name. The UFA government proved unresponsive to the resolutions passed by UFA constituency groups and provincial conventions, preferring to rely upon the views of 'experts' in the formulation of government policy. As UFA members came to realize that their direct influence on the conduct of the government and on the votes of their local MLAS was negligible, membership declined precipitously.[47] None the less, the government appeared impregnable, challenged only by the Liberals, a party which in opposition even more than in government appeared to be a lawyers' party with a limited popular base. The party split its operations in 1932 to create a provincial wing concerned with the provincial elections and a federal wing to contest federal elections. It hoped in this way to strengthen its position in provincial elections by alleviating suspicions of federal Liberal involvement in the provincial party's affairs. By 1937, however, the two wings of the party in Alberta had reunited.[48]

The UFA government became increasingly conservative, particularly as the Depression gripped the province. Concerned about the province's indebtedness, it appeared timid in the face of creditor actions against owners of farms, businesses, and homes. Its funding and administration of relief, in conjunction with the municipalities, appeared less than generous,[49] and its willingness to deport unemployed immigrants[50] and to suppress demonstrations and strikes[51] indicated a reactionary side to the administration.

While the UFA government in the 1930s became indistinguishable from other conservative administrations in the country, the UFA organization, a shell of its former self, took a sharp turn to the left, reflecting the continued influence of the former NPL group in the movement. Robert Gardiner, the member of parliament for Medicine Hat and a convert to J.S. Woodsworth's brand of democratic socialism, had succeeded Henry Wise Wood as UFA president in 1931. At the organization's annual convention a year earlier, delegates declared that the government policy on natural resources should be: 'development in accordance with the principles of public ownership and second, proper conservation to make these natural resources of value to succeeding generations in this province.'[52] And in 1932 the statist orientation of the party activists (if the UFA can be, against its will, labelled a party) was even more evident in a resolution that defined the organization's goal as: 'A community freed from the domination of irresponsible financial and economic power, in which all social means of production and distribution, including land, are socially owned and controlled either by voluntary organized groups of producers and consumers or in the case of the major public services and utilities and such productive and distributive enterprises as can be conducted most efficiently when owned in common – by public corporations responsible to the people's elected representatives.'[53]

The majority of the federal members of the UFA shared such views.[54] Several had been elected as joint UFA-Labour members in seats with an urban or mining-area component,[55] and others had moved leftwards perhaps because of their participation in a caucus with several persuasive socialist exponents. As a caucus they had, for some time, made common cause with the small Labour group led by J.S. Woodsworth.[56] It was the combination of Labour and UFA members that hatched the idea of a new national political party, which later took the name Co-operative Commonwealth Federation. The first organizing meeting for the CCF was held in Calgary in August 1932, and a year later the party's Regina Manifesto outlined the CCF's short-term reformist aims and its long-term aim of a society in which production for profit would be replaced by production for use, in part by state expropriation and democratic operation of the major industrial corporations in the country.[57] The UFA affiliated with the CCF at its 1933 convention.[58]

This was heady stuff, and contrary to some scholars' reports – based on the hazy memories of contemporaries[59] – the left turn increased rather than decreased UFA membership.[60] Interest in the new CCF sent large crowds to meetings at which CCF spokespersons explained the party's objectives.[61] Chester Ronning won a by-election in Camrose in October 1932 on a UFA-CCF ticket. Amelia Turner, an executive officer of the UFA running on the CCF ticket, received 12,307 votes against 14,128 for a candidate supported by both old-line parties in a Calgary-wide by-election in January 1933. One year later she actually bettered her performance.[62]

But there was an air of unreality in the socialist fervour emanating from the leaders of the UFA organization. After all, the UFA government, which supposedly originated from the same organization as the socialist prophets, was anything but socialist. There were good grounds to question whether the UFA's affiliation with the CCF was meaningful. The CCF was a rather amorphous collection of affiliates, none of them subjected to any central direction in the early days of the party; and while the national CCF and its local affiliates could make all the fine pronouncements they wished, they could not budge the UFA government. Despite the 1930 UFA resolution on resources, the provincial government, which won control over provincial revenues that year, followed a laissez-faire policy.[63] An attempt by G.G. Coote, one of the more moderate UFA federal members, to convince the government to lower interest rates by taxing at 100 per cent all interest above a government-specified maximum fell on deaf ears.[64] So did an attempt by a CCF-leaning MLA to issue scrip to pensioners.[65]

A CCF-supporting farmer who was planning to vote Social Credit provincially in 1935 indicated in a letter to Coote why radical farmers were disillusioned with the UFA and confused by the CCF's willingness to accept the UFA as its Alberta affiliate rather than as a reactionary political enemy to be organizationally combated: 'If there is no place in our provincial politics for our CCF program of reform,' he wrote, 'then to my mind it is not such a disaster for our provincial political organization to be defeated which we are sure it is going to be ... Our members are refusing to pay their dues because they say it is just for a political party to fight the things we want done.' He added significantly that the sights of reformers in the province were on Edmonton rather than on Ottawa because Albertans no longer believed that a national majority of MPs committed to the reforms advocated by the UFA federal members would ever occur: 'We know well enough that the dominion government is the place the reforms we want must finally be brought about. But we have sent you men there for fourteen years and we know you have worked hard for our cause and to help educate the other members and provinces along the lines of social justice ... but the other provinces have not seen fit to do what we have done, and it is beginning to look to us as if we would pass from the scene of action before we will accomplish our purpose unless we give them an object lesson by showing them what we can do for ourselves.'[66]

The 'what we can do for ourselves' that the farmer had in mind was the establishment of some form of social credit in the province. His notions about social credit may not have originated so much with Aberhart as with the spokesmen for the UFA to whom, as his letter indicated, he was planning to turn his back. It has generally been accepted by earlier scholars of Social Credit that members of the federal wing of the UFA, particularly William Irvine and Henry Spencer, popularized social credit ideas in Alberta well before Aberhart was won to Douglas's ideas and thought to build a political program around the ideas.[67] Indeed Irvine and others in the UFA group had been regarded by many Albertans as social crediters first and socialists second. While they believed that the rapacity of the banks was simply one facet of the exploitation inherent in the capitalist system, they tended to focus their attack on the financial institutions. In this regard they both reflected and reinforced the views of their constituents, who perceived themselves as the victims of monopolies such as the banking system and the railways but regarded such institutions as perversions of the capitalist economic system rather than its core element. Henry Spencer, for example, admitted that federal UFA members like himself, who embraced social credit theory at the same time as they pledged allegiance to the more radical analysis of the Regina Manifesto, were somewhat opportunist. Writing to a friend, he observed: 'As you say, I supported the Douglas theory thinking that while it was not the goal, it might be an easier step towards the economic freedom which we are working [sic] than by a direct socialization which might be hardest to meet with general public support. It was a plan I felt might be our economic salvation along with public ownership of our great national resources and natural monopolies.'[68]

But Spencer and Irvine and other radicals in the UFA accepted that the provincial government had no constitutional power to develop a meaningful social credit program.[69] Although these men were discouraged by the conservatism of the provincial UFA administration, they concentrated their efforts on the promotion of national solutions via the CCF. But the grass roots wanted reforms in the foreseeable future, and that meant the need for change provincially. A similar problem faced the UFA's urban ally in the CCF, the Canadian Labour party.

The Canadian Labour party seemed, on the surface, a more logical choice for affiliation with the CCF than did the internally divided UFA. While the left-leaning NPL group in the UFA had always vied with more conservative elements associated with Wood and Brownlee, the provincial Labour party had always been avowedly a thoroughgoing socialist outfit. Like the farmers' movement, the labour movement had been reluctant to sponsor a political organization before the First World War, but grievances against the wartime government and a growth in union numbers contributed to a growth of workers' radicalism. There was anger over conscription, war profiteering, and the federal government's clampdown on radicals. Large-scale worker participation in the general strikes in Edmonton and Calgary in sympathy with the Winnipeg strikers in 1919 demonstrated the new militancy. These strikes lasted four weeks and strengthened worker solidarity as reflected in the mass picnics and parades sponsored by the union movement over the next decade and a half.[70]

The creation of an Alberta branch of the Dominion Labour party in January 1919 was another reflection of the increased militancy of Alberta workers. The new party adopted as its own the radical program adopted for post-war Britain by the British Labour party. This program, according to Edmonton's labour paper, called for the gradual socialization of industry, the allotment of 'surplus wealth for the common good,' a 'revolution in national finance,' and guarantees of minimum incomes for all citizens.[71] Four Labour party members were elected provincially in 1921, and Alex Ross, who had been elected initially in 1917 as a candidate of Calgary's Labour Election Committee, was invited to join the cabinet.[72] Although no Labour members were invited to join the cabinet after

Ross was narrowly defeated in 1926, the Labour party leadership continued to promote friendly relations with the UFA.

Friendly relations were more the result of opportunism than of principle. Although the two groups could use the 'group government' idea to justify co-operation, there were growing policy differences between the socialist Labour party (which had become part of the Canadian Labour party in 1921)[73] and the conservative wing of the UFA, which controlled the government. But in mixed urban-rural seats, the two parties depended on one's standing down in favour of the other to assure election. This need was particularly true federally, where the larger seats made it less likely that a seat would be entirely industrial or entirely agricultural. As the official organ of the Alberta Federation of Labour explained:

If it is seen to be advisable to cooperate in elections, as was done in East Calgary in the case of William Irvine, MP, such cooperation should not compromise the position of either group. Mr. Irvine, it will be remembered, is the Labor representative. He is only answerable to Labor and is not subject in any way to any other organization. The cooperation was a cooperation of voting strength only. The same applies to Robert Gardiner, the UFA member for Medicine Hat, who was supported by Labor. It should be freely admitted that in East Calgary, the farmers had no candidate because they doubted their ability to elect one, and their support was given to Labor as the group that more nearly represented the economic position of the farmers. The same applies to the reverse situation in Medicine Hat.[74]

The co-operation between the Labour party and the UFA, however, became less popular within the former organization as the provincial government proved less and less responsive to labour's demands. The Communists, who were an affiliated body within the Labour party until their expulsion in 1929, were particularly opposed to the CLP's co-operation with the UFA government.[75] Indeed the Communists and the trade union establishment were at odds throughout the eight years that they remained in a loose coalition within one party, and the Communist expulsion was accompanied by a general hardening in attitudes by the trade union establishment. The party was increasingly suspicious of prospective new entrants and became, to all intents and purposes, the political vehicle of a small clique of union leaders. Increasingly inactive except at election time, even its activists reported a growing 'prejudice' that the party was no more than 'a machine organized by certain dominating influences to catch votes.'[76]

The Labour party none the less remained, until the Social Credit onslaught of 1935, a key political force in the cities, particularly in municipal elections. In both Edmonton and Calgary, from 1920 to 1935, one-third to one-half of the municipal councillors were elected on the Labour ticket, and their representations assured higher relief rates in the two cities during the Depression than existed in most other Canadian cities.[77] From 1932 to 1934, Labour also controlled the mayor's chair in Edmonton.

But the Labour party largely abandoned the Depression unemployed to the organizing efforts of the Communists. The suppression by the Labour mayor Dan Knott of the 'Hunger March' organized by Communist-led groups in December 1932 indicated the alienation of the Labour party from the unemployed groups, and a three-week strike by unemployed activists in 1934 demonstrated the unemployed's increasing lack of confidence in the Labour municipal group.[78] Like the UFA leaders, the Labour leaders seemed to have become increasingly conservative. Their joining the CCF could have brought new blood and fresh idealism into their movement, but the Labour leaders continued to be suspicious of those outside their number and resisted, for example, attempts by radical Labour alderwoman Margaret Crang to form an unemployed section within the party.[79]

Interestingly, despite the disillusionment with the UFA and the Labour party, large crowds turned up for organizing meetings of the CCF. The socialist alternative was not rejected out-of-hand by Albertans in favour of Social Credit, which in any case did not form a separate party until 1935. Rather the socialist alternative, the CCF, negated itself by tying its fate to two increasingly discredited organizations instead of establishing itself as a new grass-roots party without ties to existing parties. Urban interest in the CCF as such was demonstrated by the new party's near-win in the Calgary-wide by-elections of 1933 and 1934 in which Amelia Turner served as the party's candidate. But in the Calgary by-elections, as in Camrose, the CCF candidates were not forced to confront the contradiction between the socialist policies they advocated and their affiliation with the same organization as the reactionary government of the province. The entry of Social Credit on the provincial scene made such a confrontation essential if the CCF were not to be stillborn.

But few socialists, either in the Labour party or in the UFA, seemed willing to confront this dilemma. As the Social Credit movement gathered momentum, the instinct of those members of the two CCF affiliates who had not bolted to the new organization seemed to be to draw in their horns. Thus, no repudiation of the UFA government by the CCF occurred; nor was there any attempt to unseat conservative-sitting UFA members in favour of radicals.

In January 1935 the Provincial Council of the CCF, composed of equal representation from the UFA and the CLP, confirmed the unwillingness of the two parties to make a fresh start. It announced simply that:

Whereas, the United Farmers of Alberta and the Canadian Labour Party are affiliated with the CCF, and in pursuance of the affiliation are cooperating in holding joint conventions for the nomination of candidates in the federal field; and

Whereas it becomes necessary to clarify the relations between the two organizations in provincial affairs; and

Whereas in the Province of Alberta the predominant occupational grouping in each constituency lends itself to the nomination of either a Labour or a Farmer candidate; therefore be it

Resolved that this Council recommend to the Canadian Labour Party and the UFA that the two groups contest the forthcoming provincial election as separate entities.[80]

The CCF refused to provide a new political alternative to Albertans. Others, however, had already come forth to take up the challenge.

The Communist party, although its formal Alberta membership was never likely more than a thousand,[81] enjoyed a great deal of influence among farmers and workers in the years before the Social Credit victory, and, as we see in the next chapter, for a decade thereafter. It is pointless to speculate how many votes this party might have garnered had Social Credit remained outside the electoral arena at a time when the CCF seemed stillborn in Alberta. With Social Credit in the picture, the CPC managed to poll only 5771 votes, or less than 2 per cent of the vote, in the 1935 provincial election, although it did substantially better in mining regions and farming districts with large east European populations.[82]

Unfortunately, for the Communist party, many of its ardent supporters were immigrants who had not yet received Canadian citizenship (and who, in many cases, because of their Communist connections, never would).[83] But if few Alberta electors were prepared to vote for a party that called itself Communist and enjoyed close (some felt slavish) ties with Stalin's Soviet Union and the Comintern, many were prepared to follow its lead in extra-parliamentary organizations. With the UFA and the Labour party concentrating largely on the parliamentary arena, the Communists enjoyed a fairly free rein in the organization of unemployed unions. Although none of the unemployed groups was completely Communist-led, the Communists played a large role in most of them, and while spontaneous militancy would have likely occurred without the presence of Communist 'agitators' (the government's view of causation notwithstanding), the presence of party-trained organizers ensured that militancy had an organized expression. Relief strikes, demonstrations, petition campaigns, and the like were energetically and carefully organized by dedicated Communists who usually found little difficulty in selling their ideas to unemployed and underpaid workers and to farmers facing bankruptcy.[84] Communism as a philosophy no doubt remained an unsaleable commodity in Depression Alberta, but the Communists won much support when they focused on immediate demands rather than on wholesale calls for restructuring the economy or organizing bloody revolution to achieve a classless society. Their success demonstrates the fallacy of implying that Aberhart acted as a pied piper, drawing to the streets an inert mass of desperate people who had suddenly found the light. Many of these people had been in the streets well before they heard of Aberhart.

Indeed the size of rallies, which the daily press and the Labour press labelled Communist, compared favourably with those held by Social Credit in the months approaching the 1935 election. It should be stressed that the Communists always involved other individuals and groups in organizing these activities and that participation might have been smaller if the Communists, like their opponents, advertised their activities as party-led. In November 1932, for example, twenty-five hundred single jobless men demonstrated in Calgary for the closing down of the community kitchen and the granting of cash allowances to the single jobless. Police broke up the demonstrations and later raided Communist party headquarters in Calgary, arresting seven men.[85] Twelve thousand people participated in the Hunger March in Edmonton, earlier alluded to, despite police attempts to keep non-residents of the city from entering Edmonton to take part in the march. That event resulted in forty arrests and some drawn-out trials.[86]

Then, in March 1933, seven thousand married unemployed men in Calgary struck against a cut of 20 per cent in relief payments. Two months later, after a series of rallies attracting up to five thousand people, and a series of delegations to city council by wives of the unemployed men, the council reversed its earlier decision to cut the relief rates.[87]

The next two years witnessed drawn-out relief strikes in Edmonton.[88] There was also a strike of restaurant waitresses in the city, demanding only the enforcement of minimum-wage provisions, which succeeded largely because of mass picketing of the offending employers by the unemployed.[89]

In the coal-mining regions, the Mine Workers Union of Canada, led by Communists, was a militant force against wage cutbacks. Its role in the Crow's Nest Pass strike of 1932, a classic employer-miner confrontation in which the provincial authorities brought in the RCMP to aid the employers' side, was rewarded with the election of a Communist-led 'united front' group on the Blairmore town council from 1933 to 1939.[90]

Not all the activities initiated by Communists were related to immediate economic issues. The International Committee against War and Fascism, a product of international communism's turn after 1934 towards greater co-operation with non-Communist opponents of fascism, drew an audience of fifteen hundred in Calgary in 1934 for one of its discussions.[91]

In all the above events, the Workers' Unity League, the Communist-controlled trade union central, and the unemployed organizations with strong Communist participation took the lead. On the farms the Communists played a lesser role through the Farmers' Unity League, the rural counterpart of the Workers' Unity League, which was influential in the regions where east European farmers predominated. The FUL organized mass resistance by farmers against bailiffs' attempts to dispose of the property of creditor-harassed farmers.[92]

Although the Communist presence did not win that party the number of recruits it hoped for, it kept rank-and-file militancy at a boil and paved the way for a more respectable electoral party to mobilize at the polls people whom Communists had mobilized on the streets. The UFA government's repression of the organized efforts by reliefers and bankrupt farmers to improve conditions, and the apparent aloofness of the Labour party, added to the discredit of these two organizations.[93] A new political organization with a charismatic leader would receive a respectful audience in these circumstances. Social Credit had William Aberhart.

The story of William Aberhart's conversion to Social Credit has been explained elsewhere. There has also been a great deal written to demonstrate that Aberhart did not truly understand the Douglas theory of Social Credit and produced a political program that was at odds with many key features of Douglas's ideas.[94] There were overtones of tax-the-rich, rigid controls over the operation of the free market, and hatred of big corporations – including non-financial corporations – in Aberhart's rhetoric and specific proposals. In the view of this study, the issue is not whether Aberhart understood Douglas's theory; clearly he did not.[95] The real issue is why he deviated from Douglas in the left-leaning manner that he did. The answer would seem to be that, despite being steeped in fundamentalist religion, Aberhart had absorbed some of the political rhetoric of radicalism that was characteristic of the Alberta environment into which he inserted his social credit crusade.

Whether the radical rhetoric was cynical on Aberhart's part, we do not know. But as mentioned in chapter 1, Aberhart, the radio prophet of 'born again' fundamentalism – with salvation available only to those who were reborn in love of Jesus and a total devotion to his testament, literally accepted as the Word of God – had become a social gospeller. He did not cast aside his fundamentalist religious beliefs, but he did not allow them to prevent him from taking positions on secular issues that were identified with social gospellers and generally anathema to fundamentalists.

Aberhart, born in a farmhouse near Seaforth, Ontario, in 1878, had emigrated to Calgary in 1911 to accept a position as a high school principal. Four years later he became principal of the city's newest high school, Crescent Heights, and he remained in that post until he became premier in 1935. A rotund, physically imposing man – six foot two inches and over 250 pounds – he had seemingly boundless energy and began to play an important role in the religious life of Calgary within a few years of his arrival in the city. Initially he participated in the Presbyterian church, the church of his father, but gradually he shifted to the Baptists, becoming the revitalizing force of the Westbourne Baptist Church.[96]

A popular lay preacher at Westbourne church, Aberhart was largely responsible for organizing the Calgary Prophetic Bible Conference in 1918, whose official propaganda claimed it was formed by 'earnest men of different denominations for the purpose of discussing the fundamental doctrines of the Word, more especially those connected with the Second Coming of the Messiah.'[97] The conference, which met weekly on Sunday afternoons to hear addresses by Aberhart and his followers, attracted continually larger audiences until, by 1923, it was meeting in the 2200-seat Palace Theatre.

The success of the conference led to the opening in 1925 of the Calgary Prophetic Bible Institute as a rival to existing seminaries. Referring to themselves as 'fundamentalists,' the executive of the institute, of which Aberhart was principal, said they were 'convinced that many of the theological seminaries or colleges are disseminating Modernism and infidelity in all their various destructive forms. They realize that the time must come in the very near future when churches here and there throughout this great West, will be calling for fundamental Bible preachers who will be able to teach them the Word of God that liveth and abideth forever.'[98] That year the Bible Conference began radio broadcasts on Calgary's 50,000-watt radio station, CFCN, with Aberhart as the major broadcast figure. It was in his role as radio preacher that Aberhart became widely known throughout the province. His radio show was estimated to reach about 300,000 people, up to 65 per cent of whom lived in Alberta.[99]

As noted in chapter 1, there is some debate about how great a role Albertans' growing predilection for fundamentalist Christianity played in establishing Social Credit in Alberta. Fundamentalists did not vote for Social Credit in 1935 in significantly greater numbers than did other Albertans. None the less, it is likely, as Irving suggests, that Aberhart's reputation as a preacher provided credibility to the new movement. Many adherents of main-line churches formed part of Aberhart's radio audience, and even if they did not agree with Aberhart's religious views, he won widespread respect for his adherence to convictions and for his spellbinding oratorical skills.

The listeners to the radio show provided Aberhart with his earliest political audience when in late 1932 he began injecting social credit doctrines into his radio sermons. The addition of politics to the show indeed attracted additions to Aberhart's audience. Irving notes, for example: 'The religious background of the Social Credit movement was never far to seek, but during the autumn of 1933 it became apparent that not everyone who had become enthusiastic over Douglas's proposals was equally well disposed towards Aberhart's specifically religious doctrines. In fact the original study group in the Institute had contained a number of intellectuals who had little or no interest in religious matters.'[100]

David Elliott suggests that these non-fundamentalist supporters of Social Credit were the majority of the movement. And Larry Hannant demonstrates that working-class activists, none of whom was identified with Aberhart's religious movement, formed a large portion of the original Social Credit study group, whose members 'fanned out through the province dispensing the Social Credit gospel.'[101] This was a secular gospel for these people, and the attraction of the Social Credit views peddled by Aberhart was, for most supporters, political rather than religious. No doubt Aberhart's demagogic style, used with equal effect to propound religious views and political views, was essential to the rapid take-off of the Social Credit movement. More important, however, was that both the organization that he established and the principles it upheld represented, to a large extent, continuity with the early years of the farmer and labour political movements. C.B. Macpherson notes that, at bottom, Social Credit was authoritarian: 'From the beginning, Aberhart's organization was strongly centralized, in contrast with the U.F.A. His headquarters, not a delegate convention, decided and announced that candidates would be run in every constituency, issued the draft platform and instructions to the constituencies, limited the agenda of constituency conventions, and laid down the procedure for nominations ... The social credit political theory and the inspirational quality of Aberhart's leadership, which demanded and received the complete submergence of his followers' wills, combined to put any problem of the popular control of the legislature out of sight, or at least in abeyance.'[102]

Indeed, if the Alberta electorate were more politically sophisticated, the authoritarian features of Social Credit might have given them pause. But superficially at least the Social Credit League's structure was democratic, and its members had reason to regard it as at least as democratic as the UFA or the Labour party. Initially, it should be noted, the 'Aberhart organization' was merely an informal network of study groups whose purpose was to study Douglas's ideas and discuss ways of pressuring politicians to implement social credit proposals. As the study groups proliferated, a central council was established in Calgary, containing representatives from each recognized study group. Although Aberhart may largely have ignored the council, it was this representative body which organized the two conventions in 1935 (one for the area Red Deer and north, the other for the area south of Red Deer) that turned Social Credit into a political party and vested it with a constitution.[103]

The basic unit of the Social Credit League, according to the constitution established in 1935, remained the local study group. Any group of ten or more individuals within a constituency who had gathered to study and support social credit principles could apply for membership in the league. A group was expected to meet regularly and to choose a delegate to a zone assembly that was to meet not less than once every three months. Zone assemblies in turn would elect delegates to an annual constituency convention, which would pass resolutions to be forwarded to a divisional conference. Finally, the resolutions from the divisional conferences would be voted upon by constituency delegates to an annual league convention. Each single-member constituency was to elect one delegate to the league convention, and the multi-member constituencies of Calgary and Edmonton each received six delegates – equal to the number of legislative seats allocated in Alberta to each of the two major urban centres.[104]

The structure of the Social Credit League, then, gave apparent control to the rank-and-file just as did the structure of the UFA. And, as noted in the next chapter, clubs, zone assemblies, constituency association meetings, and provincial conventions all provided forums for views not always appreciated by the Social Credit government.

It is, none the less, true – although only informally – that Aberhart and his lieutenants largely controlled the process that led to Social Credit's electoral victory in 1935. Formally, party conventions did determine that the league would contest every seat and did issue the platform. The platform was the one with which Aberhart provided them, but it in turn reflected the programs that the rank-and-file had been calling for in local meetings – and included such planks as socialized medicine, which had no currency in Social Credit thought or in Aberhart's political speeches.[105]

The truly undemocratic feature of Social Credit's handling of the 1935 election, although it received approval by both conventions, was the method of candidate selection. Aberhart persuaded the delegates that political opportunists would be seeking Social Credit nominations and that only grilling by himself and advisers could determine whether a proposed candidate would serve the best interests of the Social Credit cause. He therefore proposed – indeed, insisted – that constituencies merely draw up a list of three or four acceptable nominees. These nominees would be interviewed by a board headed by Aberhart, and one would receive the nod.[106] Thus, the claim that the candidates for Social Credit in 1935 were hand-picked Aberhart men and women has some credence. The Social Credit organization included men and women of many backgrounds, including many left-leaning individuals formerly associated with the UFA and CLP, but this variety was somewhat muted in the candidate-selection process. Only nine farmers and a handful of workers were chosen as candidates since Aberhart preferred small businessmen and professionals (particularly teachers) as candidates – there were as many teachers as farmers in the first Social Credit caucus. Thus the legislature after 1935 reflected the profile of the province less well than did the legislature of the UFA period.[107] Perhaps more significantly Aberhart, who never publicly indicated his criteria for candidate selection, chose fairly conservative individuals whose appetite for reform, unlike that of the rank-and-file (as seen in chapter 3), did not extend beyond monetary changes.

But the character of the study groups indicates that the movement attracted support from broad sections of the Alberta population and particularly from the poorest sections. It would appear that most mining towns and relief camps had active Social Credit groups before the 1935 election and that the larger workplaces in Calgary, including the Ogden rail shops and the Burns meat-packing plant, were well supplied with activists.[108] The Labour Temple in Calgary was second only to Aberhart's Bible Institute as a favourite place for Social Credit meetings, and although few of the leading unionists in the city supported Aberhart's program, rank-and-file trade groups for Social Credit sprouted.[109] Altogether, 32,000 of Alberta's 760,000 people were formally enrolled in the Social Credit League at the time of the election.[110]

The organization's propaganda in 1935 indicated both the presence of working-class activists and the league's desire to appeal for the votes of workers, the unemployed, and desperate farmers (at the same time that Aberhart was ensuring that mainly solvent small businessmen would represent the league in the legislature).

The *Social Credit Chronicle*, the semi-official newspaper of the Social Credit groups,[111] emphasized the class character of the movement as well as the contradictory politics of Social Credit. The newspaper called for an end to relief camps and supported the right to demonstrate of the On-to-Ottawa relief camp trekkers who were violently dispersed by the RCMP in Regina on 1 July 1935 on orders from the federal Conservative government of R.B. Bennett.[112] The *Chronicle* reported on meetings sponsored by workers' groups, and it printed workers' testimonies not only about how social credit could improve things but about how treacherous owners and managers proved to be. A 'woiking girl,' for example, outlined in detail the rough life of a single girl working in the downtown department stores, 'you know the big millionaire outfits.' She earned only 'six bucks a week' and had to cope with the lecherous, slave-driving managers: 'a whip, two guns and a big slouch hat and you'd think it was Uncle Tom's Cabin all over again.'[113]

Such accounts emphasized rank-and-file Social Credit hostility not only to banks but to big employers in general. Indeed, the *Social Credit Chronicle* regarded big capital as the enemy. One front-page article in September 1934, although it largely dealt with monetary reform, began: 'In the final analysis, the important point is the ownership of the machinery. Under our existing system the machinery of production is in private hands. Men and women are hired at the lowest possible wage, to operate the machinery and produce goods for the sole purpose of creating profits for the owner of the machine.'[114] The same issue contained an editorial that claimed that Social Credit's ultimate goal was the over-throw of the power of the capitalists: 'How many of these capitalistic lions will support Social Credit? Not one of them. How many of them will try and obstruct the bringing in of Social Credit principles? Everyone of them. They know that if ever Social Credit is adopted in Alberta it will not only be the beginning of a new era, it will be the overthrow of their power ... Let the supporters of Social Credit stand firm on this issue, let Alberta take the lead in showing the country that the people have broken away from the old yoke of the capitalistic system.'[115]

Such anti-capitalist views, however, while commonplace in the *Social Credit Chronicle*, did not prevent the publication of such headlines as 'No Breadlines with Mussolini.'[116] Although Social Crediters were not fascists, their leaders apparently did not have sufficient political sophistication to recognize that fascism restricted rights of ordinary workers, farmers, and small businesses in ways that Social Credit's avowed principles could not justify. Germany's Nazi regime was, in fairness, denounced as a tool of financiers and industrialists,[117] but the importance of the article on Italy should not be minimized.

The overall left-of-centre views of the Social Credit newspaper were echoed by left-wing–sounding rhetoric from Aberhart himself. As mentioned, Aberhart did not abandon existing reformist political discourse in Alberta, which emphasized issues of social justice and class division, in favour of a complete concentration on the monetary question. In fact it was when he strayed from monetary issues that he sounded least like the generally right-wing Major Douglas. Aberhart's *Social Credit Manual*, which was widely distributed throughout the province during the 1935 provincial election, reflected his party's confusion about the extent to which the state should be involved in economic life, but it leaned to the left. The manual's opening comments indicated that the party rejected the traditional views of political economists that the market-place rather than the state must act as the guarantor of economic justice. The party's 'basic premise,' it claimed, was that 'It is the duty of the State through the government to organize its economic structure in such a way that no bona fide citizen, man, woman or child shall be allowed to suffer the lack of the base [sic] necessities of food, clothing and shelter, in the midst of plenty or abundance.'[118] The state, it argued, should not confiscate the wealth of the rich and distribute it to the poor.

Party doctrine recognized individual enterprise and ownership, but the party also believed the state must outlaw 'wildcat exploitation of the consumer through the medium of enormously excessive spreads in price for the purpose of giving exorbitant profits or paying high dividends on pyramids of watered stock.'[119] It could prevent such exploitation by systematically controlling prices 'for all goods and services used in the province' and fixing minimum and maximum wages for each type of worker.[120] This was hardly a prescription for saving a market-based free-enterprise economy, although it substituted state regulation of pricing for the socialist solution of state ownership of industry. Yet it went far beyond Douglas's call for the state merely to publish a list of 'just prices' which an informed public rather than the state would pressure businessmen to accept.[121] Aberhart indeed envisioned that the state would fix and enforce the 'just price' after such prices were determined by 'a commission of our best experts from every sphere of life.'[122]

The notion of the 'just price,' it might be added, was in line with the Non-Partisan League's goal during the First World War of adjusting the market-place so that farmers' input costs were controlled to balance farm prices. The NPL, however, had argued that extensive socialization of industry was required to achieve parity between farmers' costs and farmers' returns.

Aberhart also rejected Douglas's view that the purpose of Social Credit would be to raise everyone's income rather than to limit the incomes of the rich. Although Aberhart believed that social credit dividends rather than wealth confiscated from the rich would provide the new income for the poor, he promised that a Social Credit government would 'limit the income of the citizens to a certain maximum.' This would be done because 'no one should be allowed to have an income that is greater than he himself and his loved ones can possibly enjoy, to the privation of his fellow citizens.'[123]

In radio announcements during the 1935 electoral campaign Aberhart implied that the maximum incomes allowed would not be especially high. In one announcement he observed that $52 million of income in Alberta had been subject in 1932 to Canada's modest income tax. This tax was paid by single persons whose incomes exceeded one thousand dollars and by married men with incomes over two thousand dollars. Yet Aberhart referred to all income above these figures as 'surplus income of the province' and asked: 'Why do we allow 20 per cent of our bona fide citizens to be in privation and want while we have a surplus income of $52,000,000? As a matter of fact, if this surplus income had been distributed by an unearned increment levy, we would be able to provide for the base necessities of food, clothing and shelter for twice the number of unemployed that we have in the province.'[124] Aberhart's antipathy to big business was also apparent in his promise to break up the large oil companies' control of the oil industry and to allow new entrants into the field. Although he resisted the calls for nationalization of big business which the CCF emphasized, he appropriated the CCF's phrase, 'fifty big shots,' to describe the country's ruling economic clique.[125]

It was these 'big shots,' he assured his audiences, who accounted for most of the opposition to Social Credit's plans. The major plank in Social Credit's platform was the 'social dividend.' The league conventions of 1935 did not establish the size of the dividend but simply called for 'basic dividends to secure the base necessities of food, clothing and shelter.'[126] Aberhart made clear in his speeches, however, that the initial dividend would likely be twenty-five dollars per adult per month, with smaller allowances, to be paid to the parents, for each child in a household.[127]

Some of the money for these dividends was to come from 'monetization' of the province's resource wealth, a fuzzily explained concept that seemed to imply the issuing of cheques based on the yet-to-be-exploited resource wealth of the province. Inevitably, since a province could not create new money to cover these cheques, monetization meant incurring increased public debt, although Aberhart avoided this issue.[128]

Dividends would also be paid in part from income raised by a turnover tax to be assessed on every sales transaction within the province. The enforced 'just price' would ensure that the cost of this tax would not be borne mainly by the consumers, who were, after all, the recipients of the tax.[129] Such a method of raising the money for the dividends was more likely to be constitutional for a province to implement than the printing of new money, proposed by Douglas, which clearly only a federal government could do. But it could only raise the ire of businessmen, who would pay the tax, and of Douglas, who regarded it as completely contradictory to his pro-capitalist theories.[130]

There were certainly more than 'fifty big shots' in Alberta who opposed Social Credit. The party that would one day become the darling of multinational oil companies was, in its origins, anathema to the large corporate interests in the province and even to many smaller businessmen who had managed to weather the Depression.

During the election of 1935, business opposition to Social Credit was largely undertaken by a group known as the Economic Safety League, which served as a surrogate for local boards of trade. As J.H. Hanna, secretary of the Calgary Board of Trade, commented to his counterpart in Drumheller, direct opposition to Social Credit by the boards would be regarded with suspicion because 'those who take so readily to such schemes as Social Credit look upon our organization as having the capitalistic viewpoint.'[131] But the league, nominally headed by Dr

William Egbert, a former lieutenant-governor, with Jesse George of Drumheller, a prominent mining figure, serving as secretary,[132] may have had a negative impact. Commenting a few days after the election, the *Edmonton Bulletin*, which supported the Liberals in the election, charged that Social Crediters started a whispering campaign that the league was a stalking horse for the old-line parties: 'Its grotesque campaign methods and lavish expenditures gave credence to this campaign as its radio and publicity material was considered of the most reactionary kind, while the fact that its membership was anonymous, as was the source of its funds, gave Mr. Aberhart and his followers a priceless opportunity to point to it as being a glaring example of financial control from the East.'[133]

Eventually, several boards of trade themselves did openly oppose Social Credit before the election campaign was over. The boards in Edmonton, Calgary, Drumheller, Stettler, and Medicine Hat, among others, despite their professed non-partisanship, went on record as opposed to Aberhart's plans. The Calgary board claimed that the Aberhart programs 'must necessarily involve crushing taxation entirely beyond the capacity of the people of Alberta to pay.' Monetization of resource wealth was said to be 'impracticable and impossible.' As for the just-price proposal, 'any attempt to fix just prices can only result in incredible confusion and paralysis of business to the detriment of every producer and consumer.'[134]

But J.H. Hanna was not surprised that a majority of Albertans paid such warnings little heed: 'We should keep in mind that the majority of the people who support these new and radical plans blame the so-called capitalist class for their troubles and are prejudiced against Boards of Trade because they believe they are the servants of the capital class and are not interested in the welfare of the people generally. I am not satisfied that it is simply the promise of twenty-five dollars per month, though many no doubt have been lured into supporting Social Credit on that account.'[135]

As well as opposition from organized business, Social Credit faced implacable hostility from an influential sector of the business community: the newspapers. Among daily newspapers, the Calgary *Albertan*, whose circulation in southern Alberta was dwarfed by that of the *Calgary Herald*, was somewhat supportive of, or at least neutral towards, the Aberhart movement. The *Herald*, both Edmonton newspapers, the dailies in Lethbridge and Medicine Hat, and many rural weeklies attacked Social Credit viciously as a chimera which, if placed in power, would wreck Alberta's chances for economic recovery.[136]

Business opposition, which would prove a restraining force on Social Credit once it took office, also caused some retrenchment from hard-line positions taken by Aberhart before the election. In an early Social Credit pamphlet, Aberhart, attempting to show workaday Albertans that those already privileged would benefit less from across-the-board social dividends, claimed that a Social Credit government would require life insurance policy holders to transfer the cash surrender value of their policies for Social Credit bonds. There was no need for a life insurance industry, argued Aberhart, if citizens were guaranteed social dividends from the state. Under pressure from the life insurance industry, however, which began a scare campaign among policy holders – some of whom presumably were not so rich as to be beyond the Social Credit appeal – Aberhart disclaimed his earlier proposal.[137]

In general, however, Social Credit attracted the support of the poor and was rejected by the better-off, even in rural areas, although a minority of small businessmen also supported the party.[138] In Claresholm, for example, the president of a men's club in which businessmen predominated observed: 'We are composed of a membership of about 75, perhaps 60 being businessmen or associated in a business or profession and perhaps 15 being farmers, retired farmers, etc. I think 75 per cent are opposed to Social Credit including myself and all our executive. Among the affiliated legion members, many of whom are in poor condition financially the percentage of those supporting Social Credit would be considerably greater. There are I think four merchants, one lawyer, one dentist and one medical man here supporting Social Credit.'[139]

Of course, not only the rich opposed Social Credit. The leaders of the labour movement opposed Social Credit proposals as well, at times echoing business's view that the Aberhart forces, even before their election, were scaring away private investments that would have created jobs for Albertans.[140] Such a critique, however, sounded hollow in the mouths of supporters of a group – the CCF – that called for state ownership of major industries. More serious, from labour's point of view, was Aberhart's call for the government to fix wages as well as prices. While Aberhart claimed to be supportive of the union movement, union leaders wondered what purpose unions could serve if they were not able to negotiate the wages of their members.[141]

The labour leaders, it should be emphasized, could hardly be said to be opponents of monetary tinkering as such. For years their official organ had run columns by William Irvine supporting Douglasite social credit ideas. And in 1933 a special committee of Calgary council, with a Labour majority, recommended, in line with the thinking of Labour members generally, the issuing of scrip (or 'revenue anticipation certificates') to act as the equivalent of money in payment of a portion of the city's debts and part of the salaries of civic employees. The business community was aghast at the proposal and questioned its legality.[142] The scrip supporters eventually retreated in Calgary, although several rural municipal councils did indeed issue scrip in the 1930s for purely local use.[143]

The opposition of the business and labour establishment proved of little avail in stemming the Social Credit tide. On 22 August 1935 Albertans elected a Social Credit majority government. Social Credit carried fifty-six of sixty-three provincial seats, while the Liberals took five seats and the Conservatives two. The UFA lost all of its seats, as did the Labour party.

Social Credit's share of the popular vote was a hefty 54 per cent, although that figure, unlike Socred's sweep of seats, indicated that Albertans were in fact divided down the middle by the Aberhart movement. But the anti-Aberhart vote was splintered. The Liberals, who remained the official opposition, had 23.1 per cent of the vote while the once-mighty UFA won the support of only 11 per cent of voters. The Conservatives picked up few votes outside the two major cities but managed to win one seat in each of the two cities, despite receiving only 6.4 per cent of the provincial vote. Indeed the Liberals, as well, despite a respectable showing in the rural constituencies north of Edmonton, won only one seat (Grouard) outside the two major centres.[144]

Social Credit's support was high throughout the province, although many of the northern Alberta seats witnessed close Social Credit–Liberal or occasionally Social Credit–UFA contests. As we shall see, Social Credit strength would continue to be greater in southern Alberta than in northern Alberta. The two major cities, where Social Credit strength would later attain similar levels, did, however, provide quite a contrast in 1935. In Aberhart's home base, Calgary, the Social Credit League candidates had 58.6 per cent of the vote while in Edmonton they enjoyed the support of a more modest 38.7 per cent of voters. The league's delays in carrying its campaign to the capital city perhaps explain the weaker penetration of the movement in this city by 1935 than in Calgary.

The foregoing has emphasized Social Credit's initial class appeal to workers, farmers, and small businessmen in Alberta and its rejection by successful businessmen and the establishment within the farm and labour movements. Little has been said of its appeal to sentiments of regional alienation. Interestingly, such an appeal was largely indirect at the outset. Before the 1935 election, Social Credit orators, particularly Aberhart, rarely made use of the traditional western political rhetoric regarding tariffs and freight rates. The solutions they presented to economic problems – social dividends, just prices, maximum incomes – bore a universalist stamp, and no indication was given that the Douglas theories, which after all were British in origin, were best applied to one context than another.

None the less, regional disillusionment might be read into the obvious fact that the financial institutions being attacked all had their headquarters outside the region. Equally, the acceptance of the Aberhart view that the province should institute social credit as against the Irvine-Spencer (and, to an extent, Douglas) stress on the federal sphere was less an indication of constitutional ignorance than of disbelief that a federal government committed to Albertan reform views of economic restructuring would ever be elected.

At least indirectly, then, a majority of Albertans thumbed their noses at the British North America Act and voted for a party that promised to deliver more than the constitution would permit. When federal intervention subsequently scuttled that party's efforts, as we see in chapter 3, many Albertans were angrier with the federal government, which asserted its constitutional rights, than with the provincial government, which had attempted to go beyond its constitutional rights. Thus, regional feelings provided a card that Social Credit could play, for political effect, when the time came.

In conclusion, the early Social Credit movement can be seen as providing continuity with an earlier radical tradition in the province. That tradition, because of the pioneer nature of the province and the resultant dependence of individuals and government upon loans from financial institutions, had always focused in part, although never exclusively, on the issue of monetary reform. The traditions of reform and radicalism in the province had witnessed large-scale mobilization of workers and farmers before the arrival of Social Credit. The Social Credit party, elected to power in 1935 and regarded as a quasi-religious crusade by some, had fewer members than the UFA, elected in 1921, which no one regards as a victim of mass hysteria. The Social Credit rallies and picnics involved no more and often fewer participants than did the relief demonstrations organized by the Communists. And the structure of the Social Credit organization resembled the democratic structure, on paper, of the UFA and the Labour party, whose leaders had, to an increasing degree, flouted party decisions.

The early Social Credit organization is best seen as a confederation of loosely connected study groups, largely composed of workers, farmers, and not especially successful small businessmen, united only by a common disillusionment with existing political organizations and support for the basic Aberhart proposals. Although, as we shall see in the next chapter, such a coalition of forces proved unstable once Aberhart took office, it is important to underscore this coalition character of Social Credit. The notion that 'independent commodity producers,' who formed the bulk of the Alberta population, provided the only impetus for Social Credit is disproved both by the large-scale working-class support for the party and by the hostility of the successful small businessmen of the province, not excluding the government of the United Farmers of Alberta. And the support of many individuals who rejected Aberhart's religious views limits the usefulness of seeing Alberta Social Credit as merely an extension of

Aberhart's religious movement. Aberhart's message found a resonance with a mass audience, but it was an audience that had already been politically aroused before its members heard of William Aberhart and Social Credit.

Eventually Social Credit governments would shunt the reforming impetus that had originally put them in power, but it would be reading history backwards to imply that the Aberhart movement was elected as an anti-socialist, right-wing force. Few Alberta voters in 1935 could be so far-sighted as to know that the administration they were electing, after a short burst of reform energy, would prove as reactionary as any provincial administration this country has known. Chapter 3 explores that short burst of reform and the role played by various social actors in encouraging and discouraging change.

3 The Schizophrenic Period: Social Credit's First Term, 1935–1940

The first Social Credit administration, from 1935 to 1940, had two personalities. One was reform-minded and anti-corporate; the other was economy-minded and appeasing towards the corporate sector. The reform-minded personality was shaped both by the monetary reformers and by the more amorphous grass-roots movement of reform-minded people who formed the mass base of the Social Credit League. The economy-minded personality reflected pressures from the Alberta and Canadian 'establishments' and the approaches of key members of the government, including Aberhart. When the electorate voted in 1940, it was as yet unclear which of these two personalities would dominate future Social Credit directions, but there were ominous warnings that the reform impulse had gone from the government and would no longer be tolerated by the party. This chapter begins with an outline of the key events of the first Aberhart administration.

Aberhart took office in September 1935, only to find that the treasury was bare. A loan from the outgoing Bennett Conservative government in Ottawa tided the new Alberta administration over while R.J. Magor, an actuary recommended by the 'sound finance' men of eastern Canada whom Aberhart had pilloried during the election, was appointed to advise the government on cost control. Magor's recommendations led to the tabling of a conservative budget in 1936, which cut expenditures and raised taxes that hit ordinary citizens.[1] While the government's supporters and critics alike wondered how such a budget could be squared with Aberhart's election promises, Aberhart was also engaged, as he had been since the election, in negotiations with Douglas to come to Alberta and work up a plan to implement social credit in the province. Douglas's quixotic personality proved an unbridgeable obstacle in this regard, and the employ of Magor gave Douglas sufficient cause to be incensed at the heresies of his confused Alberta disciple.[2]

Aberhart none the less took several steps in 1936 to limit financiers' power, if not to implement social credit in the form of social dividends. In April the government unilaterally announced that it would repay its loans at only half the interest rate that the bond holders were then receiving. Aberhart earlier had refused federal orders to allow a Dominion loans council to supervise provincial borrowings even though the cost was an end to future federal loan guarantees to Alberta. The government meanwhile began a short-lived, ill-conceived experiment with scrip money issued by the province in partial payment of wages and debts. In the face of merchant opposition, this program evaporated before the end of 1936.[3]

Enabling legislation for the eventual issuance of social credit did appear in 1936, but the mechanisms for producing the promised dividends were left in abeyance. Despite Aberhart's pre-election promise that his government would issue credit dividends within eighteen months, 1937 opened with no dividends in sight.

At this time, a caucus insurgency forced Aberhart to stop dawdling. He appointed a Social Credit board, composed of insurgents and two acolytes of Douglas, shipped out from Britain. The board drew up a plan for controlling the province's financial institutions, throwing in the press to boot, all as an apparent prelude to the establishment of social credit. But none of the social credit legislation passed in 1937 or 1938 was, in fact, constitutional. The lieutenant-governor, acting on behalf of the federal government, refused assent, and challenges in the courts upheld the federal position that the province was attempting to legislate in areas exclusive to federal jurisdiction, specifically the areas of banking and currency.[4]

While the court decisions left the program of 'social credit' in disarray, the Social Credit government laboured on, attempting to appease both its monetary and social reform factions without at the same time going too far in offending the business interests who kept a constant barrage of criticism aimed at the government. The government's opponents on the right united in an attempt to oust Aberhart's administration, which had been weakened by four cabinet resignations in 1936 and 1937. Meanwhile, left-wing critics of the government abandoned the shells of the UFA and the CLP to provide an organized alternative to Aberhart. None the less, the Social Credit regime, shaken by its failure to deliver on key election promises in 1935, managed to win a provincial election in 1940. But while it retained a comfortable if much-reduced majority of seats, the party's vote total was only a tad greater than that of its right-wing opponent, the so-called People's Leagues or Independents. The government, thanks to a program of reforms, had survived the first electoral test of its performance without having ever issued a single social credit dividend. This chapter looks now at these reforms and the positive, or reform-minded, face of the Aberhart administration.

The first session of the legislature under Aberhart opened early in 1936 and passed several pieces of legislation that were denounced as 'fascist' as well as 'socialist' by the Calgary Board of Trade, which was not known for precision in its use of either term. Among the offending items of legislation were Canada's first male minimum wages (minimums for women in Alberta had existed since 1920), compulsory membership of teachers in the Alberta Teachers' Association, motor vehicle licences for all drivers, and legislation restricting various trades to licensed individuals.[5] While male minimum wages and restricted entry into trades offended employers, they won the government considerable support among the working people in the party's rank and file. Also popular was the removal of fees at the provincial tuberculosis hospital.

The government's achievements in the health and education sectors were impressive, considering the straitened circumstances of the provincial treasury. Hospital beds were increased, tuberculosis expenditures were doubled, state expenditures for needy polio and cancer patients were initiated, and maternity grants to needy mothers were instituted. As the government claimed in its election literature in 1940, there was reason to believe that Alberta was making 'steady progress toward state health for all.'[6]

The granting of a monopoly over teachers to the ATA in 1936 was followed by the granting of security of tenure to teachers the next year along with the setting up of an independent tribunal to rule on cases of teacher dismissal. A contributory pension plan for teachers, which the ATA had campaigned for fruitlessly with the UFA administration over many years, was established in 1938. The ATA was, unsurprisingly, pleased with the results achieved for its members by the principal-turned-premier and named Aberhart an honorary life member, also establishing a scholarship in his honour.[7] As well, the government overcame the resistance of the local school-boards to establish larger, more efficient school units and made steps in the direction of greater equality in the mill rates paid by rural residents for the support of schools.[8]

Just as the government's educational reforms often raised the hackles of the rural establishment, its economic reforms usually drew fire from the business community. Organized business had been leery about the Department of Trade and Industry Act passed by the United Farmers of Alberta administration in 1934.[9] This act allowed businessmen in a particular industry – manufacturers, wholesalers, or retailers of a product – to combine to write a 'code of fair practice' for the industry, which could include price-fixing and the setting of production quotas; the code regulations would be enforced by the government.[10] Although the legislation proved generally attractive to small business, it was greeted with hostility by large retailers and wholesalers who claimed that it would keep small, inefficient firms afloat at the expense of the consumer. The

UFA attempted unsuccessfully to win consensus for codes before imposing them and ended up implementing few. But Social Credit proved more daring. Within a year of taking office, it had established codes for retailers, wholesalers, and a variety of service industries. These codes included price schedules, hours of work for employees, hours of operation for firms, and proscriptions against such practices as offering loss leaders. The codes, warmly greeted by small business, were attacked by large firms, which claimed correctly that they made the government, rather than the market-place, the arbiter of prices and business practices.[11]

The opposition to 'codes' was mild in comparison to the opposition to the Licensing of Trades and Industry Act passed in October 1937. The act gave the minister of trade and industry sweeping powers to determine who could operate a business in the province. The minister could 'provide for the registration of all persons engaged in or employed in any business or any description or class thereof so designated and prohibit the carrying on of that business or the engagement in that business of any person who is required to be licensed and who is not so licensed.'[12] The minister could impose on firms in particular industries whatever licence fees he regarded as appropriate and could prohibit licensed firms from engaging in operations other than those which they had been authorized to perform. Stiff fines could be imposed against violators of the act's provisions, and a licence could be cancelled if a firm or individual contravened more than once the Department of Trade and Industry Act, one of the Minimum Wage Acts, the Hours of Work Act, or the Tradesmen's Qualification Act.

Predictably, boards of trade, in which the small businessmen who supported Social Credit appear to have lacked influence, unanimously opposed the legislation; so did the provincial branch of the Canadian Manufacturers' Association.[13] A legal challenge to the Licensing Act, launched by a Calgary automobile dealer with financial aid from boards of trade,[14] stalled the government. The Honourable Mr Justice Howson, who had been leader of the provincial Liberal party during the 1935 provincial election, ruled in favour of the dealer because the attorney-general's department had made technical mistakes in its drafting of the legislation.[15] The legislation was redrafted and reintroduced, and a second appeal by the car dealer was dismissed by a justice of the Alberta Supreme Court. The federal government, meanwhile, had rejected business pleas that the legislation be disallowed.[16]

The provincial government then fulfilled the business community's worst fears by giving itself the absolute right to broadly regulate all industries. A provincial marketing board was established in 1939 with the power 'to buy and sell and deal in any goods, wares, merchandise and natural products, or any of them whatsoever, either by wholesale or by retail, or both by wholesale and retail, and to act as a broker, factor or agent for any person in the acquisition or disposition of any goods, wares, merchandise or natural products, and for the purpose to do and transact all acts and things which a natural person engaged in a general mercantile business had the capacity or the power to transact.' The board was also given the sweeping power 'to engage in any or all of the following businesses, namely manufacturing, producing, processing, handling or distributing of any goods, wares, merchandise or natural products,' and in the process 'to acquire by purchase or otherwise any land or other property required by the Provincial Board for the purpose of or incidental to any such business.'[17] The Edmonton Chamber of Commerce warned ominously: 'The full exercise of such powers will transform Alberta into a corporative state; the partial exercise without any safeguards which do not appear in the bill, will endanger democratic freedom and private enterprise, and discourage investment in all lines of industry.'[18] And the Toronto *Globe and Mail* claimed 'the project is a long step on the road to state socialism, to the regimentation of Canadian farmers and other primary producers.'[19] The frustration of the government's efforts to restore prosperity by monetary tinkering had led to a re-awakening of its interest in the 'just price,' and the result was a piece of legislation that would have enabled a socialist government to nationalize and operate any industry it wished. Social Credit preferred to leave businesses under private ownership and later professed total opposition to public ownership and regulation, but in the late thirties it was prepared to consider a giant leap to the left, as the Marketing Act demonstrates. Government officials had at least toyed with the idea of establishing a complete enough control over industry to yield the funds needed to provide the chimerical social dividends that had proved so alluring to the electorate in 1935.

Pressure for government operation of industry in order to achieve just prices had come from the Social Credit caucus in 1938, when the legislature passed a resolution calling on the government 'to give consideration to taking over the wholesale and retail distribution of petroleum products in the province and/or to undertake a thorough inquiry into the spread between the field price of crude oil and the wholesale and retail prices for refined petroleum products with a view to bringing about a reduction in the consumer price of the said products.'[20]

Alfred W. Farmilo, the secretary-treasurer of the Alberta Federation of Labour, recorded notes of a meeting in July 1937 with the powerful emissaries to Alberta of Major C.H. Douglas, the founder of Social Credit. G.F. Powell and L.D. Byrne were the two men hired to the Social Credit Board, which, as noted earlier, was established as a sop to the insurgent MLAs in 1937. Both men were interested in finding ways that the government could secure the funds to begin paying social dividends. As Alfred Farmilo wrote: 'He [Powell] then said do you not think productive industry could be controlled in a manner similar to the pools and cooperatives. We then discussed the possibility of the Province of [sic] setting up an institution similar to the Savings Department into which the flow of currency or money might be diverted through the control of industry. Powell looked over to Byrne, and asked if he had considered this phase and the answer was in the affirmative. It would therefore be as well to keep in mind that the treasury department may eventually be used along these lines.'[21]

In practice, there was no drastic attempt undertaken to control industry in order to marshal savings. A rather more modest program of treasury branches was established 'to provide the people of this province with the facilities for conducting their exchanges of goods and services through institutions under their own control.'[22] This description meant simply that a provincial savings bank network was set up. In the first year of operation alone, thirty-six branches were established, and more than 31,000 accounts opened. The government also established a provincially operated state fire insurance agency to insure government operations and compete with private insurers for the public's business. The narrow scope of these efforts might, however, suggest that the Marketing Act represented a symbolic concession to a restless rank-and-file and a symbolic snub to the federal government for its efforts at scuttling Social Credit legislation. None the less, the treasury branches, like the Marketing board, the codes, and the Licensing Act, demonstrated the interventionist character of the Social Credit administration. Some of the legislation disallowed by the courts also demonstrated this character: the Reduction and Settlement of Debts Act in 1936 and the Home Owners' Security Act of 1938 would have allowed provincial boards to reduce unilaterally the interest that financial institutions charged homeowners, farmers, and small business.[23]

The Aberhart government also proved more willing that its predecessor or any other government in western Canada to provide land for the dispossessed and desperate Métis of the Prairies. The Métis Population Betterment Act of 1939 established six Métis colonies in which 320 acres of land were allotted per Métis family and schools and health care were provided. Although ultimately the government failed to aid the Métis in establishing a viable economic base, initially its actions showed a willingness not to leave the Métis to the disposition of market forces and the recent settlers of northern Alberta.[24]

On the whole, then, the free-enterprise side of Social Credit was rather muted during the party's first term in office. Using language that, as Social Credit rhetoric, would not survive his time in office Premier Aberhart thundered against his opponents in the business community who opposed licensing. He told a Bible Institute audience:

We are hearing a great deal of bally-hoo about liberty ... Some bray about liberty in a time of the greatest economic bondage in history. Why are we so easily beguiled by fine phrases? What liberty have many of you regarding occupation? What liberty have you to use the press? ... liberty begins in the freedom of the individual from selfish control or exploitation on the part of another or others ... Tell me what profession today is not licensed. Lawyers, teachers, and preachers are all licensed. It does not interfere with their liberty in the slightest, except to protect the public ... Surely it is evident that a license is for the purpose of preventing wrong and injustice when it touches the welfare of others, rather than curing faults already done.[25]

The government's support of the weak against the strong, as indicated later, was, however, inconsistent. But to the extent that it championed workers and farmers against business interests, the administration enjoyed the enthusiastic support of its own very large grass-roots Social Credit organization.

The Social Credit League enrolled some 32,000 individuals in its clubs across Alberta at the time of the 1935 election. That number rose to almost 41,000 in 1937, before beginning a decline to 24,000 by the time of the 1940 election.[26] Each club was affiliated with a zone assembly which in turn formed part of the constituency organization. Representatives from the constituency organizations attended provincial conventions, which set policy for the party. Historians have tended to underrate the importance of the grass-roots Social Credit organization because, in Social Credit philosophy, experts, not party members, determined the details of policy. Members were expected only to demand 'results' such as a social dividend. In practice, however, if the general membership of Social Credit were even aware that Major Douglas's theory accorded them so minor a role, they ignored his teachings. Social Credit clubs, constituency associations, and conventions all sought to influence the details of government policy and strayed well beyond monetary policy in their search for solutions. Furthermore, Social Credit groups sought to achieve broader alliances for social change than those encompassing party members. An olive branch was extended to socialists and communists for collaboration against common enemies of the disadvantaged classes.

Resolutions passed at provincial conventions provide perhaps the best barometer of the views most widespread in Social Credit ranks. Aberhart's response to several of these resolutions also indicates that, while ideologically he may not have opposed the social-democratic tenor of the conventions, in practice there were well-defined limits to his willingness to effect reforms. As an example, a successful resolution at the 1938 convention called for free textbooks for Alberta's primary and secondary students. But, on his copy of the resolutions, Aberhart scribbled: 'This is impossible under the present financial system.'[27] Another resolution resolved 'that we request the Government to immediately formulate a scheme of state medicine and hospitalization and state insurance to cover time lost while sick.' Aberhart noted: 'favourable as soon as financially possible.'[28] Adequate relief 'for all who need it,' requested by the convention, received the comment: 'cannot be done under present financial system.'[29]

From the province-wide conventions, there were few calls for state ownership of industry. But there was general support for the type of policies that would later be implemented by the CCF in Saskatchewan only to be denounced by Ernest Manning as socialist tampering with the rights of individuals. State medicine, which would be viciously denounced by Social Credit from the mid-forties onward, was supported by every convention from 1937 to 1940. The 1938 convention called in addition for 'state insurance to cover time lost while sick.'[30] Other resolutions included a call for producers' marketing boards controlled by producers' representatives, with livestock to be regulated immediately (passed in 1939) and the eight-hour day in industry (passed in 1937).[31] Perhaps most indicative of the tendency in the early Social Credit movement to distrust the workings of private industry, as well as of the banking system, was the early league's stand, supported by Aberhart, that conscription of wealth should precede conscription of manpower – a position which the CCF shared. As a resolution passed by the 1940 convention expressed it, the party members 'are opposed to profiteering out of the sale of armaments and also opposed to profiteering out of the sale of foodstuffs, clothing and the necessities of life. Be it therefore resolved that conscription of capital and finance must precede any other form of conscription that the exigencies of war may make.'[32]

The need for close state supervision of industry, and for the strengthening of producers' rights relative to those of processors, was made clear in a number of resolutions, passed in the 1930s, which would have been soundly defeated in the 1950s when, as we shall see, both the party's mass character and the positive evaluation of state intervention had disappeared. For example, the resolution in 1939 calling for the livestock marketing board stated that the free-market system 'tends to place all profits of the livestock industry in the hands of distributors.'[33] And a resolution in 1937, calling for a provincial price spreads investigation, declared that adequate purchasing power for primary producers and wage earners was impossible 'when our industries handling and processing these products and employing this labour are taking a large portion of the profit, through market control and price manipulation.'[34]

Social Crediters also sought a revamping of the tax system so that no direct taxation of farmers and working people, specifically via property taxes, would be levied. A resolution passed at the league convention in 1938 stressed the class unfairness of existing taxation and, in effect, proposed class-restricted legislation as a solution:

... the farmer or the working man can not pass the burden of direct taxes to the consumer, and further that owing to the successive drought in some districts, frost and hail in others, and in the case of the working man, loss of employment through depression years, thus depriving thousands of their homes each year through the process of the Tax Recovery Act.

Therefore be it resolved that we condemn such a system of taxation that deprives ageing people of their homes after a lifetime of toil, and ask the Provincial Government of Alberta to abolish direct taxation on farm and working men's homes, and this legislation be brought in at the next session of the Legislature, and that any loss arising out of such be made up out of net income.[35]

Interestingly, Aberhart noted on his copy of the resolutions: 'Government is considering a change in the basis and nature of taxation.'[36] If that were so, however, the results never saw the light of day.

Although the resolutions discussed above shied away from the socialist emphasis on public ownership of industry, they indicate a desire on the part of early Social Crediters to use state intervention in favour of workers and farmers. Social Credit's emphasis on the lack of purchasing power as the fundamental problem of the capitalist system led to acceptance of the reformist aims of both the labour movement and the organizations of urban unemployed.

Not unexpectedly, the demands that surfaced at the level of the local constituency organizations and study clubs were even more radical. Calls for nationalization of banks, resource industries, and even some manufacturing firms came from more left-minded Social Credit groups,[37] although such demands never became party policy. The more evident impact of the left within Social Credit was in the area of local alliances with Communists and CCFers, particularly in the cities and the mining districts. The Communist party, which had used the epithet 'fascist' to denounce Social Credit in 1935, decided afterwards that it could not afford overtly hostile relations with a party composed largely of the same workers and farmers that it sought to attract to its bosom. It adopted a policy of critical support of Social Credit in the hopes that when Aberhart failed to deliver the promised goods, disillusioned Social Crediters might turn to the Communists for a new political home.[38]

In Communist strongholds, such as Blairmore, meetings to support the Aberhart administration united Communist and Social Credit ranks. An example is a 1938 meeting in Beaver Mines, addressed both by Enoch Williams, the Communist-leaning mayor of Blairmore, and two Social Credit MLAs, which passed a resolution calling on 'all progressives' to 'close their ranks in a united front.' The president of the zone assembly wrote Aberhart that local Social Credit members and supporters friendly to communism made the holding of such meetings essential. '... it was in deference to the wishes of a number of our supporters who are not or only a few of them members of the group that we called the meeting on the platform of support for your government by progressives of any party. These people have a leaning towards communism ever since they belonged to that party when miners. I feel we ought to do all in our power to promote friendly cooperation and to eliminate suspicion, jealousy and cross purposes.'[39]

The way rank-and-file Social Crediters tended to promote such 'friendly cooperation' in the cities was through formal and informal electoral alliances. In 1936 the CPC was able to secure the joint Social Credit–CPC nomination of Margaret Crang for a city-wide provincial by-election in Edmonton. A 'united front' meeting in which both parties participated nominated Crang, who was a member of neither party. She was a left-wing Labour party alderman, and the Communists had hoped to secure CCF–Labour party endorsation for her nomination as well. The Labour leaders, however, aware that their cosy relationship with the UFA eventually discredited the Labour party, wanted no part of an alliance with Social Credit, especially one that might slow efforts to build a provincial CCF on the ruins of the UFA and Labour. The Edmonton CCF (which consisted of the Labour party and a few CCF clubs) expelled Crang from its organization and ran a rival candidate on a more clearly socialist platform than Crang, obligated to support the Aberhart government, outlined. The split vote on the left ensured a win by the Liberal candidate, the candidate of a united right.[40]

There were, however, Communist-leaning elements and others within the CCF who favoured the united-front strategy. In 1937 the united-front forces within the CCF successfully argued for unity in policies and candidates of the three parties in the Edmonton and Calgary municipal elections. Only the opposition of the old-guard in Labour prevented such fronts from being created in 1938.[41] Social Credit in the cities, however, remained open to the unity concept and co-operated informally with the Communists in that year's civic elections. Indeed a Communist alderman, Patrick Lenihan, was elected in Calgary in 1938 with Social Credit votes.[42] Orvis Kennedy's election in a federal by-election in 1937 on the Social Credit ticket resulted from a joint Social Credit–Communist campaign, and the victory photograph showed Communist leader Leslie Morris holding Kennedy's hand in the air as the two stood on the running-board of a car.[43]

Aberhart opposed close Social Credit–Communist links. He had been happy enough to involve Communists in the government's campaign in 1937, as a prelude to the passage of major pieces of legislation to implement social credit, to sign up citizens' pledges of 'unity for results,' the results requested being twenty-five dollars per month in social dividends.[44] But he opposed other forms of Social Credit–CPC unity and railed against the municipal pledges to which Social Crediters, in alliances with Communists, committed themselves.

Aberhart made clear, for example, his rejection of the municipal platform of his party in Calgary in 1938. He wrote Ethel Baker, secretary-treasurer of the Calgary provincial constituency association (Calgary and Edmonton formed single constituencies, each with five seats), which in 1937 enrolled more than 10,000 of the league's 41,000 Alberta members, to register his disapproval. The platform pledged, for example, 'to help and develop trade unionism in every way in the City of Calgary.' Commented Aberhart: 'This is a pure labour plank to which Social Credit could not wholly subscribe. The beliefs of trade unions are not altogether in harmony with the program of Social Credit.' To the platform call for a 'humanizing of relief rates and relief rules; clothing allowance to be increased,' Aberhart retorted: 'This will give the person who supports it very great difficulty in carrying it out.'[45] The Calgary Social Crediters, however, ignored Aberhart's misgivings and stuck to this platform during the municipal election.[46]

Rural members of Social Credit, like their urban counterparts, supported non-monetary reforms and at times made alliances with socialists and Communists. As noted earlier, party conventions had supported producer-controlled marketing boards. Social Crediters were also behind the establishment of the Alberta Farmers' Union (AFU), a rival to the United Farmers of Alberta. The AFU manifesto adopted by the founding convention in 1939 announced that the organization intended to 'initiate a policy of direct action in the way of non-buying of machinery strike and the non-delivery of grain strike … In other words to adopt the same methods as the organized labourers, and withhold our production from the industrial set-up the way they withhold their services from the industrial concerns for whom they work, and a definite, direct way of protest against the lowering of their living standards.'[47]

Such a stance reflected a far more militant posture than the UFA adopted. Many Social Credit farmers regarded the UFA as too cautious and objected to its leadership's continuous stream of anti–Social Credit rhetoric.[48] The AFU's early leadership included a large contingent of east Europeans, and many of the early members were sympathetic to Communism as well as to Social Credit.[49] Their views on the efficiency of militancy in obtaining results were reminiscent of the attitudes of the Communist-led Farmers' Unity League in the early thirties.

As the disagreement between Aberhart and the Calgary Social Crediters indicated, the left-wing drift of the membership did not always have a resonance within the government, despite the reformist thrust of the Aberhart administration. Particularly on the issue of relief, a fairly wide rift developed between the leaders and the rank-and-file, rather reminiscent of the gulf between the UFA government, on the one hand, and the desires of UFA and Labour party members in the early thirties on the other.

The Provincial Unemployed Married Men's Association, which had led several of the large relief strikes in Edmonton and Calgary, probably summed up best the frustration of the unemployed with Social Credit's failure to alter UFA relief policies significantly. In a letter to all Social Credit MLAS, the association wrote:

Had you been a candidate in a time of prosperity, would you have been elected? It was the unemployed, the farmers on relief, those crushed by debt, those on starvation wages, those who had sympathy for the unfortunate, who elected you.

The department of Government that comes in closest contact with those who are unfortunate, is the Department of Relief. The Commissioner of relief should be carefully chosen by your party, and he should be a member of your party.

The present Commissioner of Relief was appointed by the former UFA government. He is unduly harsh and arbitrary. As long as he remains in charge of relief your Government stands undermined in the eyes of the unemployed ...

The man you appoint might not be able to relieve the suffering of those on provincial relief; that must be done by you as legislators. But he will have the confidence of the unemployed. They can trust him, because as a loyal Social Crediter, he will have their welfare in his hands.[50]

The unemployed as a whole obviously felt that Social Credit principles included respect and compassion for the unemployed and questioned why UFA hangovers and UFA policies dominated relief in Alberta under Social Credit rule. Social Crediters questioned the government's handling of relief as well and were not content to voice the criticism simply through the agency of non-partisan organizations such as the Unemployed Married Men's Association. Social Credit clubs and constituency organizations as well as the provincial conventions denounced government relief policies and the attitudes of provincial relief authorities.

The Social Credit party, as noted in chapter 2, had committed itself before its election in August 1935 to the closing down of relief camps. It had also, of course, committed itself to issue social dividends of at least twenty-five dollars per adult per month, a figure which would have been a fortune to those on relief. The dividends did not materialize, and although the federal Liberal government in 1936 eliminated the camps earlier established by the Bennett government, the provincial camps remained in operation during Social Credit's first term in office. In late 1936 when it was clear that the government had no plans to abolish camps, one group of relief camp Social Crediters proposed an alternative: keep the camps but pay the inmates a living wage – forty dollars a month before deductions – with twenty-five dollars per month to be held in trust for each man until he left the camp.[51] The plan was ignored. The opening of the 'rest camps' for older unemployed men caused widespread unrest in Social Credit ranks. A divisional convention of the Social Credit constituencies of Calgary and Edmonton unanimously requested that 'the order from the Honourable Dr. Cross of the Bureau of Relief and Public Welfare to Mr. Eady, Superintendent of the Department in Calgary, to the effect that all unemployable men over fifty years of age at present eating in the kitchen be compelled to go to so called rest camps be immediately rescinded and thus help in great measure to unite our forces instead of dividing them.'[52]

Leading officials of the Relief Department in the UFA period remained in place under Social Credit, and the conservative chairman of the provincial Relief Commission, A.A. Mackenzie, strongly continued to influence the direction of relief policy. In a letter to the minister of health and relief, Dr W.W. Cross, for example, Mackenzie persuaded the government not to close the soup kitchens for the single unemployed. Responding to Cross's request for his views on the demand from Calgary unemployed groups that single homeless men receive negotiable food vouchers rather than soup kitchen tickets, Mackenzie said: 'This is a matter of policy and I would be glad to have the Government's direction.' But then he added:

I would point out, however, that during our recent visit to Calgary, when you changed the policy in respect to returned men, that 112 new applicants applied for relief under the new policy, who would not accept relief in the dining hall. This would indicate that they managed to exist without relief but are quite prepared to accept cash, and we had no evidence that these men were not entitled to relief, but were aware that they had existed previously and made no complaints.

The additional cost of a negotiable voucher over feeding in the dining halls is in excess of $1300 per month.

If a negotiable voucher was issued to all single men they would immediately flock here from all parts of Canada.[53]

The soup kitchens, in fact, were not closed down. The government, following the lead of the Relief Department, abandoned its early notions that the unemployed must be given more purchasing power to stimulate the economy. Instead, it attempted to reduce relief costs as much as possible by removing as many people as possible from the relief rolls. In an attempt both to cut relief expenditures and to appeal to rural voters, the government in October 1937 announced that farmers could hire single reliefers for five dollars per month – the same rate paid in the stigmatized relief camps. A reliefer would be assigned to a farmer; if he refused to accept the job, he would be cut off the relief rolls.[54]

The farm relief scheme was opposed by the organizations of the unemployed and by the trade unions. The Calgary Trades and Labour Council called for generous cash relief for the unemployed 'until work at trade union rates of pay and conditions is provided.'[55] More than three hundred young men demonstrated their opposition while their representatives attempted unsuccessfully to convince the government to reverse itself on the farm relief scheme. Many of the men had been cut off relief for refusing to go to the farms, and thirteen were arrested during the demonstration.[56]

Just as the government did not budge from its position on the farm relief scheme, it proved immovable on its policy about relief camps, once again influenced by the opinion of relief officials. In 1937 many men left camps to protest conditions and sought either to be posted to other camps or to go on relief in the cities. Relief official F.J. Buck wrote Dr Cross:

The present situation has developed through a number of men who were dissatisfied with employment now offered for single men in work camps, and who left their employment, or who were discharged from camps as agitators, and now request that they be placed in other camps. As there are in Edmonton and Calgary between 2500 and 3000 men who have not had the opportunity of employment in the work camps, any opportunity that may develop to place men in camps should be provided for these men prior to any consideration given to those who quit such camps. Honourable Mr. Maynard (in charge of relief) has full knowledge of the situation and dealt with it before he left for Ottawa.[57]

Maynard 'dealt with' the situation by issuing an order that men who had left camps would not be able to get meals in the soup kitchens. The government would listen to no one who argued that this was an unjust course of action. Cross wrote Aberhart that he had refused to meet with a Co-operative Commonwealth youth movement delegation of the single unemployed because 'I understand that this delegation's sole purpose was to persuade me to provide for these people in the kitchen.'[58]

The government not only did not abolish existing camps, but it opened new ones. In 1938 Minister of Relief Dr W.W. Cross announced the opening of two 'rest camps' for unmarried unemployed men over fifty years of age. Within a year there were charges from several quarters that the old men in the 'rest camps' were mistreated. An elderly Social Credit supporter, Sam MacDonald, proclaiming the continued support of the men in the camp for Social Credit despite everything, wrote Aberhart on behalf of the men to counter the 'glowing reports' of the relief department inspectors regarding conditions at the Evansburg 'rest home': 'Here is one man who frightened, worked as hard as he could, and was laid up for three days with a swollen testicle. While another lay dying without priest or minister, then placed in a plain board box was taken up and buried without benefit of Clergy ... [The food is] heavy and starchy, totally unfit for an aged man's [stomach].'[59] MacDonald added detailed complaints about the small quantities of nutritious food and noted that the men slept nine or ten to a hut in which bedbugs crawled in the bunks. The complaints were referred by Aberhart to Cross who referred them to Mackenzie, who was responsible for the camps. Mackenzie wrote Cross that he had inspected the camp and found it to be fine. He also claimed to have affidavits from some men at Evansburg indicating they were happy to be there (but MacDonald had written that such testimonials were easily extracted from old men by intimidation). Finally, to discredit MacDonald, Mackenzie wrote that he had learned that MacDonald had worked in railway camps and was known there to be an 'agitator.'[60] But although Aberhart received an anonymous letter from a camp inmate corroborating MacDonald's accusations,[61] no impartial investigation was carried out to determine whether MacDonald or Mackenzie was correct. The department officials' view prevailed.

Social Crediters viewed the continued callousness of relief officials with disbelief and joined the unemployed organizations and labour in calling for a change. Unhappiness with Mackenzie and his officials was general among urban Social Crediters. A typical resolution passed by a Social Credit study group was approved by the Central Social Credit Club in Calgary, the city's largest and most active club: 'Resolved that we request Dr. W.J. [sic] Cross, Minister of Health and Relief, to replace as soon as possible, all obstructionists in his department who are in our opinion not working in accordance with Social Credit principles, particularly A.A. Mackenzie, Chairman of the Relief Commission.'[62] The club president noted further that: 'We feel when this is done it will be possible to discipline the rest of the personnel in this department who are guilty of petty persecution and lack of courtesy to the public.'[63]

Lack of courtesy on the part of the Relief Department officials was a common complaint of Social Credit groups calling for the dismissal of Mackenzie and other department officials. The King Edward Social Credit group in Edmonton claimed that the attitudes of provincial relief officials encouraged municipalities to violate the Bureau of Relief and Public Welfare Act, a UFA act which established eligibility and minimal levels of assistance for the unemployed.[64]

Aberhart did not dismiss Mackenzie and other leading officials of the Relief Department. Indeed he and his minister would not engage in debate with Social Credit clubs and unemployed groups on the subject of staffing the Relief Commission. Their motivation in retaining these officials could not have been respect for the nonpartisanship of the civil service. The Social Credit government sacked many civil servants whom it regarded as hostile to social credit theories and replaced them with party activists.[65] Aberhart believed that partisanship should play a role not only in the hiring of top officials but even in the hiring of labourers, stenographers, and truckers.[66] Clearly, Mackenzie and his associates were retained because the government was won over to their views. Amidst the general clamour against the administration of relief in 1938, the Social Credit Board wrote the party's MLAS: 'Rather than condemn the Minister and the officials of the Department, we should marvel at the efficiency with which they handle relief with the all too inadequate supply of money at their disposal.'[67]

The board believed that anger should be directed against the banks rather than the Relief Department: 'The banks have been given a monopoly in the past, over the control of the one thing which alone can relieve the distress of the masses, "Money." The people should demonstrate in an orderly yet audible manner against financial domination. Each demonstration should be definite enough to cause plenty of concern to Ottawa and the financial institutions.'[68] But Social Crediters, to the board's chagrin, directed their anger with policies concerning the unemployed to the Social Credit government rather than to the banks. There were defections from the party and increasing divisions between the leadership and the rank-and-file. Unpopular removals of some families from the relief rolls in Lethbridge in 1937, for example, led to a demoralization of the local party organization that contributed to a provincial by-election defeat in a seat won by the party in 1935. The Lethbridge constituency association wrote Aberhart that many Social Crediters were angry with the government because Mackenzie had cut off about 30 people from relief for having earned a little extra money on road work: 'The Vice-president of the group at Coalhurst states that this money was used to buy winter clothes for their children. The Vice-president feels this is a very poor move at this time as it is unjust and unfair besides creating much hardship and ill feeling.'[69]

Even after the by-election defeat, with a clear signal from the local electorate about the government's responsiveness to local complaints, nothing changed. The constituency secretary-treasurer, noting that most of the party membership in Lethbridge consisted of unemployed people, charged that attempts by the constituency president to have various relief cases resolved had all been in vain and 'it makes one wonder whether the constituency officers are just figureheads who serve no useful purpose.'[70]

The barrage of resolutions and letters from Social Credit groups demanding revision of relief policies brought increasingly testy replies from Aberhart. Early in 1938, for example, a Calgary study group noted that people were still waiting for the government to take steps towards lowering the cost of living. The group added that it was 'strongly opposed to any reduction in the relief grant on the part of the Provincial Government.'[71] Aberhart responded by calling the letter 'an uncalled for insult' and added: 'The group who could pass such a resolution, I am satisfied, has not the best interests of Social Credit at heart, or they are not keeping in touch with what is being done. It is just that type of letter we receive from our bitterest opposition, and I would like to tell the West End Social Credit group of Calgary that I have no time to read any further such letters from it.'[72] He had no kinder words for a single unemployed Edmonton Social Crediter who opposed the farm scheme: 'I sometimes wonder if the single unemployed men in the cities do not forget that there are many families in the outlying districts of the province who are suffering greater privations than they. We would be very happy to give the unemployed men in the cities better treatment, but this cannot be done at the expense of the welfare of those who are in need in other parts of the province.'[73]

The anger of the rank-and-file with relief policies was reflected in resolutions sponsored by urban constituency associations and passed by the provincial conventions in 1937 and 1938. The convention in 1937 demanded the closing of the soup kitchens and the immediate reinstatement of former relief recipients when destitution forced them to reapply. It also called for the naming of a government official with the power to order immediate provision of relief by the province to those in need for whom responsibility was in dispute.[74] A resolution passed in 1938 again called for direct relief for the single unemployed as the alternative to soup kitchens and non-negotiable bed tickets. The resolution, sponsored by the Calgary and Edmonton constituencies, claimed that the conditions under which the single unemployed lived had become 'worse than they ever were, and are gradually getting worse.' It also noted that Saskatchewan and British Columbia, which 'have the same quota of men on relief as this province,' paid direct relief, 'leaving no excuse for the treatment of the men in this Province.'[75]

Once the Depression eased, the government might have been expected to become more susceptible to the rank-and-file pressure that was beginning to deplete Social Credit ranks. The number of Albertans receiving relief was still 61,235 in April 1939,[76] or about 8 per cent of the provincial population. But as mobilization for war occurred, the numbers dropped dramatically to 39, 565 in April 1940.[77] By March 1941 the Employment Service claimed only 4473 unplaced applicants.[78] None the less, the Alberta government and the Relief Department continued to follow tight-fisted policies. The Unemployed Association of Calgary charged in November 1939 that provincial relief officials are 'using every conceivable means to force relief recipients to join the army'[79] and claimed that the province was instituting a back-door conscription of manpower before there was conscription of capital and finance.

The Edmonton constituency association, frustrated by continued government indifference to the view of party members, attacked the revised Relief Act of 1939, which tightened existing regulations for eligibility to relief: 'The Alberta Provincial Welfare Act, as enacted by our Social Credit Government in 1939, does not in our opinion give the average relief recipient a fair deal, particularly in cases where a recipient is temporarily employed, in these cases his exemptions are shamefully out of proportions to what a working man should be allowed to spend.'[80] But the Alberta government had little time for rank-and-file Social Crediters' opinions about how to broaden the scope of the Welfare Act. In September 1940, relief for the employable unemployed was cut off altogether, ostensibly because jobs were going begging for workers. One United Mine Workers' local challenged this view. 'Many men,' commented a union local official, 'are being sent away daily with the familiar words "nothing doing." ' But Aberhart was unrepentant. He responded: 'There is no desire on our part to cut off legitimate relief but we do feel that when people from other provinces are coming in here and getting work our able-bodied men should not expect to receive relief when they will not make any effort to get a job. I am given to understand that transportation to any job is given by our relief Department.'[81] This was a vastly different statement from Aberhart's claim in 1935 that the state should issue dividends that would cover the cost of necessities for every citizen, 'whether he works or does not work.'

The rank-and-file campaign against the government's handling of relief produced the greatest rift between leaders and led in the Social Credit League. Workmen's compensation was another issue that caused division between the Aberhart administration and the ordinary working people who composed the party's rank-and-file in urban and industrial areas. The government received dozens of complaints about the parsimony of the Workmen's Compensation Board, and it proved as unresponsive on this issue as it did on relief policy.[82] Such government indifference to rank-and-file complaints contributed greatly to the apathy that caused many reform-minded members to leave the party between 1937 and 1940. This exodus later helped tip the balance in favour of the party's abandoning ideological ambivalence and taking a lurch to the right because it magnified the strength within the overall party of those who had been attracted to Social Credit for religious reasons or purely because of its monetary policies.

Aberhart was made aware that members were leaving because of the government's inconsistency in its support of the interests of ordinary workers.

But his petulance, of which we have already seen several examples, made matters worse. For example, in September 1938 he receive word from the secretary of a Social Credit group in one of Edmonton's working-class river valley groups that members were leaving to such an extent that four study groups were in danger of dissolving. At a recent meeting, the secretary noted, a variety of objections to government policy had been raised: 'For example, when the Compensation Act was under review by the legislature, the committee in charge of the bill was much more impressed by the CPR and lawyers representing the Manufacturers' Association than by the organized workers of the province. Other legislation reveals more or less the same tendency.'[83] The author enclosed 'a couple of articles I happened to read today and to all intents and purposes they cover most of the objections brought up at our meeting.' The articles were from the Communist organ, the *Clarion Weekly*, and written by Jan Lakeman, Edmonton's best-known Communist.

Aberhart's response indicates clearly how unwilling he was to respond to legitimate complaints from below. He wrote, in part:

It is just such letters that are most dismaying to me.

It is so vague and indefinite that I hardly know what is meant and at the same time it indicates that I cannot count on any support from that quarter.

If that is all I can count on the groups you are mentioning, what is the use of my bothering ... Attached to your letter was a page or two of the worst propaganda that I have read for some days. Surely our Social Crediters know how utterly false and unfair this paper is.

The attacks upon our Compensation Committee and your own Relief Committee are so ridiculous and so far fetched that I am more than surprised to think any of our supporters should be disturbed by it.

I hardly know what can be done about these things.[84]

But if Aberhart could dismiss so brutally the rank-and-file criticism, he could not so easily ignore complaints – of a different nature – that came from his hand-picked MLAS.

The government, as noted earlier, did little during its first eighteen months in office to follow through on its election promises to institute social dividends. Only the insurgency of a large group of Social Credit back-benchers forced its unconstitutional attempts to control financial institutions in the province. The insurgency has been detailed elsewhere, but some aspects of the challenge to Aberhart ought to be highlighted because they help explain the shift away from Social Credit's early radicalism to the conservatism of the Manning period.

In the first place, it should be noted, the evidence suggests that most of the Social Credit rank-and-file opposed the insurgency. Although we have seen that the party members, particularly in the cities, relief camps, and mining districts, had many complaints about government failure to live up to election promises, there seemed only marginal concern about its slow progress regarding the issuing of social dividends.[85] The party as a whole was not as fixated about launching an attack on financiers as the caucus was, a perhaps not unsurprising situation considering that Aberhart personally played so large a role in choosing the Social Credit candidates and was generally concerned that his caucus, although ironically not his cabinet, consist of men and women devoted to the Douglas ideas.

Perhaps the major outcome of the insurgency was the creation of the Social Credit Board and the hiring of two Douglas disciples, G.F. Powell and D.L. Byrne, as the board's experts. It was they who drew up the ill-fated social credit legislation. The overall impact of their activities was to obliterate the democratic and radical aspects of the early Social Credit movement in favour of creating an authoritarian party and government. Acting as a direct funnel for Major Douglas to the Alberta government, they convinced the government to accept Douglas orthodoxies that previously had been ignored or at least fudged. In particular, they emphasized the view that ordinary people could play no real role in determining government policy, something Social Crediters learned painfully through the government's indifference to convention resolutions. Perhaps so authoritarian a character as Aberhart needed little push towards such a view, but the Douglas experts provided him with a theoretical basis for his unwillingness to acquiesce to the demands of rank-and-file Social Crediters – or of Albertans in general. The role of the electorate in Douglas's view was simply to demand that the government provide them with material prosperity. The mechanisms by which it would do this were to be left solely in the hands of government-appointed Social Credit experts.[86]

In practice, the government placed itself in the hands of its 'experts' only with regard to monetary legislation, which was – as Aberhart, by his dithering before the insurgency, seemed to know – outside its legislative competence. Ultimately the cabinet rather than the Social Credit Board would reign supreme, but the net effect was, as C.B. Macpherson correctly indicates, a debasement of the powers of the legislature and of the influence of political party organizations.[87] With the sorry episode of the board and its sham monetary legislation, however, also came a comic opera political period in Alberta which, by its climax, had dissipated much of the interest and activity in politics that characterized the province before the Second World War.

Powell and Byrne, anxious to apply Douglas's theories in which the electorate did little more than express a Rousseauian general will, which their elected legislators would embody by their votes and the experts by their programs, set loose a program of covenants or pledges. The members of the legislature were to pledge themselves to support the work of the board (although the wording was vague enough that it was unclear whether the MLAs had agreed to support the social credit proposals before seeing them);[88] as for the population at large, they were to sign pledges of 'unity for results.' The pledge read as follows:

1. I know that Alberta is naturally one of the richest places in the world.
2. That there is plenty of employable idle people.
3. I demand that these be encouraged to produce, with the aid of our many idle and partly idle machines, such goods as will justify the issue of a dividend of $25.00 a month to every bona fide citizen and secure to them a lower cost of living.
4. And I will only give my support to a candidate for any office who will vote consistently against any party who opposes this my policy.[89]

Collection of signatures for this vacuous pledge became the government's main goal for Social Credit supporters, and the Communists joined in the signature-collecting campaign. Some 360,000 signatures, representing perhaps 70 per cent of the province's adult population, were collected. But the signatures were meaningless even as a signal of support for the government. Many people feared that if they did not sign they would be left off the lists of recipients for any social dividends that the government might issue, and so some signed although they regarded the idea of social dividends as hare-brained.[90]

Seven members of the Social Credit caucus refused to sign the pledge to the Social Credit Board although only one of them, Attorney-General John Hugill, declared himself opposed to the province's attempting to implement a social credit scheme.[91] Hugill, a Calgary lawyer and former alderman, had opportunistically agreed to step on the Social Credit bandwagon in 1935 and claimed afterwards, rather disingenuously, that he had received Aberhart's assurance that no legislation to implement social credit that was *ultra vires* provincial jurisdiction would be legislated.[92] When the Social Credit Board's proposed legislation was placed before him, he offered his viewpoint as a lawyer that it was all *ultra vires*. He was forced to resign from cabinet, and Aberhart himself assumed his portfolio.[93] Once outside of cabinet, Hugill became a bitter foe of the administration.[94] He was not alone: four of the nine original members of the Aberhart cabinet had resigned their portfolios before the end of 1937, the others being C.C. Ross, minister of lands and mines; Charles C. Cockcroft, provincial treasurer; and William Chant, minister of agriculture.[95] All except Chant had been recruited by Aberhart as candidates, despite their coolness to social credit monetary theories, because they were respected citizens who would bring needed expertise to the cabinet.[96] Their departure left a government with little expertise, advised by a board of 'experts' whose proposed legislative program was of dubious economic soundness and of clear unconstitutionality. It was a government increasingly concerned about pledges of unquestioning loyalty and increasingly closed to criticism.

Unsurprisingly, then, the government accepted the board's proposal for the inclusion of an 'Accurate News and Information Bill' as part of the package of laws to implement social credit presented to the legislature in October 1937. This bill, for which the lieutenant-governor reserved assent, would have forced all newspapers in Alberta to print 'when required to do so' by the chairman of the Social Credit Board 'any statement furnished by the Chairman which has for its object the correction or amplification of any statement relating to any policy or activity of the Government of the Province published by that newspaper within the next preceding thirty-one days.'[97]

This censorship bill demonstrates the increasingly authoritarian character of the Aberhart regime. It was true, it should be noted, that the major newspapers of the province opposed virtually everything the government did. Virtually every reform instituted was made to sound more draconian than it actually was. The conservative views of the owners and editors often interfered with the objective presentation of news reports, although perhaps not to the extent that the government claimed. In many cases, the papers simply concentrated on the very real chaos and confusion in government ranks and required few embellishments to make the government look bad.

But the government was not powerless in getting its message across. The Social Credit party had a membership of almost 41,000 in 1937, a potential propaganda army if the government had been willing to work more closely with its rank-and-file. There was also one newspaper which did give general support to the government, the Calgary *Albertan*. Indeed, shortly after the government's election, the *Albertan* became briefly the 'official organ' of the Alberta Social Credit League.[98] The newspaper had been in financial trouble before arranging to become a Social Credit vehicle, and the change in editorial policy doubled its circulation to about 27,000 copies sold daily.[99] The Social Credit League, by arrangement with the owners, attempted to have its members buy a majority of the *Albertan* shares and vest their control in the league. But party members were not wealthy, and this share-buying campaign proved a disappointment.[100] In any case, although the *Albertan* gradually drifted away from its self-proclaimed role as 'official organ' of the Social Credit movement, it remained editorially favourable to the government.

But opposition to the government from both left and right was mounting, and much of the rank-and-file seemed to agree with left-wing critiques of the government's performance. As the first electoral test of its performance approached, Aberhart sought to broaden the base of his party's support.

Having lost its battle to license the banks in Alberta, the provincial government sought to rally Albertans against federal interference in provincial affairs. Its opportunity came with the establishment by Mackenzie King in 1938 of the Royal Commission on Dominion-Provincial Relations. The Alberta government denounced the members of the commission as centralizers and refused to meet with them.[101] None the less, it presented a detailed submission of the province's case with regard to dominion-provincial relations, not to the commission but 'to the highest court in the land – the Sovereign People of Canada.'[102]

The Case for Alberta repeated familiar western complaints about tariffs and freight rates as well as the eastern-controlled banks. Interestingly, Aberhart had said nothing of these matters during the 1935 election, preferring to run on a positive campaign of reform rather than use western alienation as a vehicle to achieve power. Western alienation, none the less, no doubt played an indirect role in electing Social Credit as it had played a direct role in the earlier election of the UFA. The insistence of the UFA in 1935 that social credit policies could only be instituted federally left many voters cold because they had no faith in the federal government and could not believe that a government sympathetic to their interests would be installed in Ottawa.

Now, however, Social Credit openly tapped the deep reserve of resentment towards Ottawa within the province. The result was an incoherent report. On the one hand, The Case for Alberta demanded that the federal government assure 'a nation-wide minimum standard of living for all areas.'[103] But on the other it called for a loose alliance of the ten provinces such that 'policy (in particular policy in the economic sphere) shall be decided by the people of the provinces concerned, except in regard to matters affecting the relations of the Dominion with other countries, in which case it should be decided by the people of all provinces collectively.'[104]

The report was clearer in its condemnation of financial institutions for creating the severe debt problems facing western Canadians and demonstrated that, at least with regard to financial institutions, Social Credit remained radical. Life insurance companies, for example, were blasted for claiming that reduced interest rates would affect the returns on investments these companies would have available to pay policy holders. Argued The Case for Alberta: 'The Government of Alberta believes that life insurance companies have misrepresented their position to the public generally. Do they expect the people of Canada to believe that policy holders should thrive at the expense of our impoverished farmers and city dwellers by taking from them their entire surplus income for interest charges, by evicting them from their homes for non-payment of exorbitant interest, by depriving them of the necessities of life and education for their children and by relegating them to a status removed from serfdom only by name?'[105]

The report called on the federal government to make long-term mortgage loans available at an interest rate of 2 per cent,[106] a demand inconsistent with the call for federal government powers to be reduced to a nullity although perhaps consistent with the call for greater income equality across the country. Government thinking on the extent of federal intervention required in the economy was fuzzy at the time. At the same time as one section of *The Case for Alberta* was calling on the federal government to concentrate on Canada's international relations, Health Minister W.W. Cross was re-creating the long-standing Social Credit call for a massive federal works program to replace the dole. 'From time to time,' he wrote Dominion Labour Minister Norman Rogers, 'we have pointed out that the problem of relief is a national one; that the country as a whole should assume the major portion of the responsibility.'[107]

Clearly, unhappiness with federal disallowance of the social credit legislation rather than a philosophical commitment to decentralization motivated the tone of *The Case for Alberta*. In any case, Aberhart knew that the province's report to the 'sovereign people of Canada' would not in itself impress the federal government sufficiently to cause it to relent against further disallowances of provincial legislation. He decided to take 'the case for Alberta' to the Saskatchewan electorate in that province's 1938 provincial election. His hope was that the election of a Social Credit government in Saskatchewan would force the federal Liberal government to moderate its opposition to Alberta's attempts to control financial institutions within the province.[108]

But the plan backfired. Social Credit organization outside Alberta was weak, and the attempt to spread its appeal beyond the province was carried out in a ham-fisted manner. In April 1938 a convention was held to form a western Canadian Social Credit Association. The executive chosen consisted of four Alberta cabinet ministers and a member of the federal Social Credit caucus, also an Albertan. Among other powers, this executive was empowered to sit in on the selection of Social Credit candidates in all four western provinces.[109] This arrangement was ironic because a convention of the Social Credit constituency associations in southern Alberta that year called for constituency associations alone in future to make the choice of candidates.[110] It is symptomatic of Aberhart's increasingly undemocratic frame of mind that he not only ignored grass-roots opposition to an undemocratic practice in Alberta but saw no problem in compounding it by extending the authority of himself and his key associates to other provinces.

The Alberta-run Social Credit election effort in Saskatchewan provided only two Social Credit seats in a fifty-five–seat house. Interestingly, however, Social Credit's vote of 15.5 per cent was only 2.5 per cent behind that of the CCF, which managed nevertheless to win ten seats and hold on to its official opposition status.[111] The Social Credit revolution had been stopped at the Alberta-Saskatchewan border.

Aberhart, however, did not give up the idea of winning national support for social credit ideas. He had been pleased when W.D. Herridge, brother-in-law of R.B. Bennett and former Canadian ambassador to Washington, called on the 1938 Conservative convention for economic and monetary reform 'to stabilize production upon its maximum level and to raise purchasing power to that level.' The Conservatives had rejected such Keynesian rhetoric, but Aberhart wrongly read into Herridge's words support for social credit notions.[112]

In March 1939 Herridge launched the New Democracy movement at a presentation in Ottawa attended by the CCF and the Social Credit MPs, among other political notables. Herridge sought to unite all reform forces in the country within one electoral united front.[113] Although the program of his movement was vague, he emphasized the federal government's role in establishing and maintaining prosperity. The federal government would establish national minimum wages and guarantee all citizens sufficient income 'to meet all contingencies such as unemployment, sickness, crop failures.' A 'just price structure' and federal assumption of all relief costs were also promised.[114] There was not a word about decentralization and the rights of provincial regimes.

That did not worry Aberhart and the federal Social Credit members, whose commitment obviously was to social credit principles rather than to provincial rights. If indeed a federal government could be elected that would implement a program of social credit, the Social Credit leaders would apparently forgo their arguments favouring a feeble federal government.

On 30 June 1939, two days after Herridge announced his platform, Aberhart met with the federal Social Credit members and subsequently announced that Social Credit would align itself in the next federal election with the New Democracy movement.[115] Both Herridge and the Social Credit MPs seemed anxious to win the CCF over to the new movement as well,[116] indicating that, despite Aberhart's reticence about the rank-and-file embrace of coalitions with the CCF and Communists, he was not dead set yet against alliances with socialists.

The CCF, in any case, proved hostile to an alliance with Herridge and Social Credit. Ultimately, apart from Aberhart and Social Credit, the New Democracy movement failed to attract significant personalities or political forces to its banner. The Herridge-Aberhart collaboration faltered once Canada entered the Second World War on Britain's side in September 1939. Herridge favoured conscription for the war effort, a position which ensured that New Democracy would win no votes in Quebec. Aberhart, as noted earlier, insisted on conscription of wealth before any conscription of manpower and indeed saw no need for conscription at that time. This dispute was not resolved before the 1940 election. The federal Social Credit candidates in 1940 none the less styled themselves as New Democracy candidates, and ten of them were elected from Alberta. The party lost five Alberta federal seats and two in Saskatchewan, and New Democracy won no seats outside Alberta.[117] The attempt to ally Social Credit with a broader movement had failed. Indeed, as the federal results showed, Social Credit support in Alberta was slipping. The provincial results in 1940 demonstrated the same trend.

The Social Credit government faced a double threat in the provincial election of 1940. First there was the threat from a united right whose votes had been scattered among the Liberal, Conservative, and UFA candidates in 1935. Secondly there was the threat from the left in the form of the CCF, which had insufficient support to make it a potential government but conceivably could take enough votes away from Social Credit to allow the right to take power.

The unity on the right demonstrated the fear and loathing of a substantial section of Alberta's organized business and professional communities for the Aberhart regime. The poor showing of opposition parties in terms of winning seats has spawned questionable theories about the single-mindedness of Albertans and their contempt for parliamentary procedures in which a strong opposition is beneficial.[118] But even a superficial survey of votes per party as opposed to seats per party shows that most Alberta elections demonstrate nothing of the kind. Instead they simply reveal the weaknesses in the first-past-the-post system in producing representative legislatures. The United Farmers of Alberta won their various impressive seat majorities in 1921, 1926, and 1930 with less than 40 per cent of the vote. And Social Credit's fifty-six seats in a sixty-three–seat legislature in 1935 were won with 54 per cent of the vote.[119] Most of the remaining vote went to Liberal, Conservative, and UFA candidates campaigning against one another on barely distinguishable platforms.

In the 1940 election, the establishment forces in Alberta politics proved that when like-minded groups worked together it was possible to run an election in Alberta whose outcome was not predictable at the outset. The party leaders, left to their own devices, might never have achieved unity. The Liberal leaders in particular seemed reluctant to sink the party's identity in a collaborative effort with the Conservatives.[120] The federal leaders of these parties, not surprisingly, were even more reticent to support a coalition whose existence suggested that there were no substantial differences between the two main federal parties.[121] But rank-and-file pressure weakened the leaders' resistance. Businessmen who regarded Aberhart as a socialist menace to their uninhibited profit-making had no time for partisan duels, the result of which could only be the re-election of the hated Social Credit party.

The movement for unity of the free-enterprise forces started in Calgary, where a majority of the business and professional classes were particularly opposed to the activities of the Aberhart government.[122] In both Calgary and Edmonton, businessmen affiliated with the Conservatives and the Liberals had two decades' experience of working together on the municipal level to prevent Labour majorities.[123] In the early thirties, the desire to limit Labour's electoral gains had also produced coalition candidacies in several Calgary provincial by-elections.[124] Hence it was only natural that in the face of a new and hated adversary regarded at the time as a left-wing threat, an attempt to achieve unity would be attempted once more. A People's League, consisting of Liberals and Conservatives as well as anti-Aberhart individuals affiliated with no party, was established in Calgary in 1936. The *Calgary Herald*, ferociously opposed to Aberhart, called the league a spontaneous creation of citizens irate about the shenanigans of the Social Credit administration.[125] Social Credit propagandists, by contrast, claimed that the bankers' conspiracy had hatched the league.[126] Neither claim was exactly accurate. There is no evidence to suggest, on the one hand, that the headquarters of the banks in eastern Canada played any role whatsoever in its formation. On the other hand, it was not ordinary Calgarians who set up the league but the substantial leaders of the business community, a group of men who were often conspiratorial in their attempts to reduce their tax burdens.[127]

The movement to establish people's leagues that would nominate Independent, anti-Aberhart candidates without regard to candidates' normal political affiliations quickly spread to the other urban centres. In Edmonton as in Calgary, a clear attempt was made to nominate a slate in which Liberals and Conservatives enjoyed fairly equal representation.[128]

The leagues were also set up in the rural areas, where right-wing members of the UFA joined Liberals, Conservatives, and unaffiliated conservative business-men and professionals in a move to unseat Social Crediters. But the weaker representation of successful middle-class people in these areas and concomitant-ly of organizations of either the Liberal or Conservative parties made most of these peoples' leagues rather small outfits.[129]

The Independent candidates lacked a common platform or a recognized leader. While many assumed that Calgary Mayor Andrew Davison, an Independent candidate in the city, would likely be the premier should the Independents win an absolute majority of seats, he held no formal leadership position. Indeed the Independent candidates, much like the UFA candidates in 1921, were constituency candidates only loosely connected with candidates in other constituencies.

But the Independent campaigns across the province were similar in their thrust. Independents wanted an end to social experimentation and a return to business-like, frugal government in Alberta. They could point to deleterious effects of Social Credit policies. Fear of Social Credit's debt legislation had, allegedly, produced something of a capital strike in the province, causing investors to hold back planned building projects and financiers to withhold loan money from provincial businessmen.[130] Certainly it was clear that while other provinces enjoyed a small building boom thanks to subsidized loans to home-builders under the Dominion Housing Act, in Alberta not a cent had been loaned under the program.[131] Overall, the Independents directed their message to those who had suffered least because of the Depression and feared that Social Credit's radicalism would limit business opportunities and result in higher taxes on those with means. But those who had benefited from Social Credit's economic interventionism feared the Independents' intentions regarding social programs, the 'codes' that protected small businesses, and the programs to protect farmers against creditors.[132]

The CCF, by contrast, presented itself to the little man as being even friendlier than Social Credit. Indeed its detailed platform strongly resembled the resolutions of Social Credit conventions in 1937 and 1938. It called for a provincial works and housing program to reduce unemployment and 'adequate relief pending the assumption of the responsibility by the superior (federal) government'; free school textbooks; fully socialized medical services; and taxation based on ability to pay. The program also called for 'progressive socialization of natural resources, industries and services such as electric power, oil production and distribution, packing plants or any other property or service the public ownership and operation of which is necessary for the common good.'[133] In this regard the CCF program stood clearly to the left of Social Credit's program because, while the Marketing Act of 1939 allowed the government to socialize any industry where the public good demanded such action, there had been no indication that the government had its eyes on any particular industry or company.

The CCF's main support came from the labour leaders who had previously founded and supported the Labour party. Organized labour's relations with Social Credit were rocky. Although Aberhart's government was the first in Canada to pass legislation ensuring the right of workers to organize, the labour leaders regarded the legislation as too weak to be meaningful. They also found, as did the premier's critics within his own party, that the authoritarian Aberhart regarded their very proposing of legislative changes as presumptuous meddling in the government's affairs.[134] The Industrial Conciliation and Arbitration Act of 1938 raised labour's hackles because of its provisions imposing conciliation and compulsory (but not binding) arbitration when requested by either party to a dispute. Strikes were made illegal until conciliation and arbitration had been completed, and the AFL lambasted the government for handing a gift to employers who would, in the AFL's view, use the conciliation-arbitration procedure to stall for time to hire scabs.[135]

But CCF organization in 1940 was weak despite the increasing disillusionment of many of the Social Credit rank-and-file. The party was held back by its affiliation with the discredited UFA and Canadian Labour parties. Only in 1939 did the UFA withdraw from politics, leaving its right wing free to join with the people's leagues and its left wing to form CCF clubs. The CLP continued a rather somnolent existence until 1942.

In 1939 the provincial CCF held a convention and elected Chester Ronning, the former UFA-CCF MLA for Camrose and former principal of Camrose Lutheran College, as leader. But the party was poorly organized in 1940 and able to nominate only thirty-four candidates for the fifty-five legislative seats. It earned a respectable 11 per cent of the vote, although it failed to elect a single member.[136]

As the *People's Weekly*, the CCF's virtual house organ, commented after the election, 'the progressive voters of the province are remaining loyal to the government they elected in 1935 and the turn to the CCF will only come when it is seen that the Aberhart policies, or lack of policies, are not beneficial to the province.'[137]

For most voters, including disillusioned Social Crediters, the choice was between a reformist Social Credit administration and a business-oriented, conservative administration led by the Independents. Many Social Credit voters from 1935, of course, had switched to the CCF; even more apparently simply did not vote, since the traditional high voting abstention rate, broken temporarily in 1935, was re-established. But most working-class voters, and less successful farmers and small businessmen who did vote, chose to remain loyal to the government despite the record of undelivered promises. The alternative of the people's leagues frightened many into voting Social Credit rather than voting CCF or staying home.

The economic turnaround resulting from the onset of war also helped Social Credit. Although the government remained stingy to those on relief, the absolute numbers of people on relief had dropped dramatically. Social Credit's economic and social legislation had benefited working people and farmers who were not on relief and the party promised more reforms in its 1940 platform, particularly in the direction of providing 'state health for all.'[138]

Aberhart was aware, however, as the election campaign began, of the decline in his party's support. It was particularly apparent in his own seat, Okotoks–High River, which he had won handily in a by-election immediately after the 1935 election. (He had been unwilling to run as a candidate in 1935 until a legislative majority for his party was assured.) In this mixed-rural–oilfields seat, Aberhart experienced the twin forces of opposition that characterized every urban and industrial area's reaction to his administration: business antipathy to the government's interventionism on the one hand, and popular disillusionment with the government's timidity on the other. Imperial Oil, the major oil company in Turner Valley, as well as the smaller independent producers resented the government's conservation legislation, which built upon UFA legislation also opposed by the oilmen.[139] The oilmen also joined Alberta businessmen in general in opposing the government's social credit experimentation. Newspaper reports warned local workers that oil investors would not invest more money in Turner Valley until the government's attitude to investors changed.[140]

The workers might have been expected to resent the attitude of the employers; the oilfields had given Social Credit five of every six votes cast in their midst in 1935, and active Social Credit groups were at work in the valley in 1935 and 1936.[141] But these groups found their local MLA, despite his high office, rather impervious to their complaints. When they complained that Imperial Oil was ignoring Social Credit legislation making six days a week the maximum work week in the oilfields, the prickly premier told them to complain to the Labour Bureau and to stop complaining to him.[142] When they complained that nothing was being done to deal with local epidemics, he replied that he had appointed a doctor to investigate and could do no more.[143]

His constituents, tired of his testy responses to their complaints, circulated a petition in 1937 calling for his removal as the local MLA. Aberhart's government had passed a recall act, but the premier promptly had the legislation ditched. He blamed financiers and oil companies for the recall campaign, and there is no doubt that the oil executives, supported by the *Calgary Herald*, sought to embarrass the premier, although it is unproved that they organized the recall campaign.[144]

But Aberhart knew that his troubles in his home constituency went beyond the opposition of the vested interests. By 1939 the Social Credit study groups in the oilfields had largely collapsed. Total Social Credit membership in the constituency in January 1939 was only 136, down from 384 the previous year. Aberhart scribbled grimly on the note containing the membership figures: '4.11 per cent of 1935 votes.'[145]

In the end, the premier was forced to beat a retreat and run in the multi-member Calgary constituency where he could be assured of a victory despite declining

Social Credit support. His decision was shrewd: the Independents had an easy victory in Okotoks–High River.[146]

Despite the loss of his former seat, Aberhart was able to hold on to enough support to win the election. His party ran on its record and judiciously made no mention of its handling of relief or of the sorts of issues that put Okotoks–High River beyond its reach. It also downplayed its failure to produce social dividends although, of course, it blamed this failure on the federal government; it made no commitments to future attempts to implement social credit legislation.

The government did, however, pledge itself to further programs of government interventionism, although in a cautious manner. Farmers were promised collective-marketing schemes and steps towards the removal of land taxes. Workers were promised ability-to-pay taxation and better working conditions and fewer hours of work, although this was to occur 'with the best interests of both employers and employees and with due regard to further industrial development.'[147]

The election results indicated the strength of Aberhart's right-wing opponents, especially in view of the leakage of reformist votes to the CCF and of the high rate of voter abstentions. In no region of the province did Social Credit win 50 per cent of the vote, and in the two major cities combined its vote had fallen from 48 to 35 per cent of the total.[148] Indeed the Independents won only a few thousand votes fewer than Social Credit across the province: Social Credit won 132,869 of 308,864 votes cast (43 per cent) while the Independents received 130,603 votes (42.3 per cent); the CCF trailed with 34,316 votes (11.1 per cent). But the near-tie in the popular vote was not reflected in seat totals. Social Credit's relative strength in the over-represented rural areas, where gratitude for debt legislation and social policies was greatest and relief had been less contentious as an issue, provided the government with a lopsided margin of thirty-six seats to nineteen for the Independents and one each for a Liberal and an independent Labourite in Edson.[149] For the next four years, however, Alberta would have an opposition of respectable size.

The experience of Social Credit's first term in office demonstrates that, contrary to what earlier scholars of the party claimed, Alberta was bitterly class-divided and the Social Credit party attracted the support of the have-nots and the bitter opposition of the haves. Only the authoritarian character of the government itself eventually effected a split among the have-nots, driving more left-leaning workers and farmers from its ranks. It is not the case that most Albertans who flocked to the Social Credit cause accepted an authoritarian ideology and an authoritarian leader. As the government proved itself increasingly conservative and closed to grass-roots criticism, internal party critics became more vociferous, and by 1940 many had simply refused to participate within the Social Credit organization. As will be seen in chapter 4, Social Credit's loss of the mass character of its party produced changes in the character of both the party and the government.

4   The Transformation:
Social Credit during the War

During its first term in office, Social Credit had proved to be a reformist party of government whose reform program horrified the business community but often disappointed its own members and supporters as too timid. As the party began its second term in office, there was every reason to believe that it would continue to be interventionist. But by the time the next election occurred, in August 1944, the Social Credit administration had become a staunch opponent of many forms of government intervention once favoured, either in action or in rhetoric, by party leaders. The party had also become more violent in its opposition to socialism, once never mentioned at all, than in its opposition to bankers and profiteers. The causes of the Social Credit transformation from a reformist party opposed to the bankers to a conservative party opposed to socialists are explored in this chapter. Also explored are the reactions of Social Credit supporters as well as other Albertans to the reconstructed Social Credit party.

William Aberhart remained Social Credit leader and premier until his death in May 1943. When he was re-elected in March 1940, the path he wished to follow was somewhat uncertain. With the federal government and the courts ready to swoop down on any provincial measures that had an impact on financial capital, his ability to chart a reformist path consistent with social credit ideology was restricted. (But then Aberhart, as noted in chapter 2, had a rather idiosyncratic view of social credit which allowed him to espouse reforms dear to workers and farmers that had no place in Douglas's eschatology.) By 1940, however, rebuffed by Ottawa and constantly in touch with Douglas's ideas via the Social Credit Board, Aberhart appears to have become more of a Douglasite than he had been in 1935. Certainly his scribblings on his 1938 copy of Social Credit convention resolutions, mentioned in chapter 3, showed that he regarded the existing monetary system as a complete barrier to – or at least as a sufficient excuse against – new social programs.

None the less, Aberhart still believed that the forces of finance capital could be defeated and that their defeat would unleash the state's ability to provide advanced social legislation. In 1941, at Aberhart's instigation, a national organization called the Democratic Monetary Reform Organization of Canada was established to proselytize Canadians about the virtues of social credit ideas. The establishment of the DMRO marked the end of the stillborn New Democracy movement, within which Social Credit found its monetary reform ideas playing second fiddle to more general programs for economic redistribution.

The DMRO would serve to co-ordinate the activities of the Social Credit electoral organizations in the various provinces,[1] but like the Social Credit electoral organization in Saskatchewan in 1938, the DMRO appeared mainly to be an extension of the Alberta government. Aberhart served as its president from its founding until his death,[2] and the organization reflected his thinking at the time. Having had enough of the obstreperous Social Credit groups with which he had been forced to deal during his first term of office, Aberhart established rituals for the refurbished social credit movement which seemed more appropriate to an authoritarian religious sect than to a democratic political movement. The 'ritual of the Alberta Monetary Reform Groups' prescribed blow-by-blow agendas for group sessions, and its details extended to the seating arrangements for a meeting and indeed the shape of the room: 'The meeting place of every Group is arranged in the shape of a double "V." This signifies that a double Victory must be gained. The one is international, against the External Foes of Democracy – the totalitarian forces seeking complete dominion over the world in general. The other is Financial or National, against the unseen and internal enemies of economic security and democratic freedom.'[3]

There were some bizarre features in this new Social Credit ritual, particularly the inclusion of officers in monetary reform groups who were called 'senior libra, junior libra, master pilot, inside custodian, senior watchman, junior watchmen.'[4] Among other peculiar rituals of a monetary reform meeting would be one in which 'the senior Libra explains the significance of the suspension from scales in the centre of our room of the seventh sign of the Zodiac.'[5] Lest it be thought, however, that the fundamentalist Aberhart had become completely a star-worshipper, each meeting also included prayers to the God of the Bible from whom 'we desire to learn how to distribute the abundance that Thy great Providence has given us.'[6]

While anyone familiar with the above rituals might be pardoned for dismissing Aberhart as a crank, the Democratic Monetary Reform Organization was not pinning its hopes for reform exclusively on the heavens. A junior watchman, asked by the president to 'suggest some of the means which could be used to distribute additional purchasing power,' was required to say: 'Additional purchasing power could be issued by means of non-contributory Old Age Pensions, Mothers' Allowances, Educational Grants, Health Services, Price Discounts, Bonuses, Social Dividends, and so forth.'[7]

So broad a program of government reforms, to be financed by the issuing of new currency, went well beyond the limited Douglas prescription of social dividends and indicated that Aberhart, while no longer as much the social credit heretic as in 1935 (talk of maximum incomes for the rich and complete state control of all pricing was no longer heard), was an unlikely leader for a free-enterprise crusade. Indeed, the leaders of business continued to regard the Aberhart government with undisguised hostility and to label it as socialist. In the middle of 1941, with rather poor grace, the secretary of the Edmonton Chamber of Commerce attributed the government's re-election a year earlier to Alberta's 'very large foreign population that will believe anything' including the 'fatuous policies' of Aberhart and company.[8] Not to be outdone, the secretary of the Calgary Board of Trade complained: 'It is evident that the Government's interpretation of the theory of social credit is merely one of an autocratic state socialism. Since the present government took office, provincial credit has been destroyed and business credit greatly restricted.'[9]

Aberhart sought no compromise with his detractors who represented the substantial firms operating within the province. He responded to newspaper reports of the views of the two major business organizations in Alberta by castigating his opponents as enemies of all reform and not simply of social credit: 'It is unfortunate and yet not surprising that the organizations from whom the attacks originated have been consistently and bitterly opposed to any movement of social or economic reform. Dependent as they are, however, upon the good will of the banking institutions and subject to the undemocratic controls of the present money system, their attitude is not unexpected.'[10] The resentfulness of the Alberta establishment towards Aberhart was also demonstrated when, in 1941, the university's senate, which normally rubber-stamped the president's list of honorary degree recipients, took the unprecedented move of narrowly voting down the honorary degree to be bestowed on Aberhart. The inclusion of Aberhart's name on the list of those to be honoured had been public knowledge, and Aberhart had prepared his acceptance speech. He was hurt by the senate's action, an action which caused an embarrassed president, Dr W.A. Kerr, to resign. Members of his government, as usual unaware of the limits of their powers, wanted reprisals against the university, but Aberhart, despite the blow to his pride, calmed them down.[11]

Aberhart gave a cold shoulder to his opponents in the business community and professions. But he was concerned about the increasing indifference to his party of ordinary Albertans. The precipitous membership decline between 1937 and 1940, prompted by the government's disdain for the views of its members, became an avalanche after the 1940 election. Despite Macpherson's assessment that Social Crediters agreed to submit their wills to those of their leaders, as Douglas's theory called for, the members were indeed rambunctious and refused to stay in the party once it became clear that the government gave no special consideration to their views. The attempt to impose the above-mentioned authoritarian rules for monetary reform clubs met with little favour; and although the more loosely structured study groups of the past were not suppressed, they had all but disappeared by 1943.[12] Indeed, party membership in May 1944 was only 3576,[13] compared with 24,000 at election time in 1940 and 41,000 at the party's peak of popularity in 1937.

When Aberhart received the 1942 membership figures, he fretted that 'without a strong organization we cannot hope to combat successfully the powerfully entrenched forces of Finance.'[14] He accepted that the organization was so weak that it could not hold an annual delegate convention that year but instead would sponsor a conference open to every Social Crediter; it was a modestly attended affair.[15]

Perhaps a greater openness to criticism on Aberhart's part might have reversed this decline in the party's mass base. But as the proposed ritual of the monetary reform groups indicated, Aberhart was becoming increasingly dictatorial. His letters became pricklier than ever. When the Alberta Motor Association proposed, in non-confrontational language, that gasoline tax and motor licence revenues be earmarked for highway construction and maintenance, an indignant premier not only dismissed its views but unilaterally reduced the association to the level of its Calgary branch: 'We have answered this type of resolution so many times that it seems to us we are wasting time and paper in replying further to them. We do not believe that the Calgary Branch of the Alberta Motor Association has any right to direct this Government in what it should do with its unexpended revenue.'[16]

Aberhart also exhibited an increased unwillingness during his last years to entertain left-wing views. He had never been particularly comfortable with notions of public ownership, although his first administration had established publicly operated treasury branches and state fire insurance, and the Marketing Act of 1939 had established the principle that, in the public interest, the government could nationalize firms.

Late in 1940, the president of the Calgary Social Credit Association, G.M. Whicher, encouraged Aberhart to consider 'operating a large [flour] mill under government auspices' to counter the power of the large corporations which controlled all mills at the time and 'dictated' the price of flour. Whicher, who also regarded direct government involvement in the farm-implements industry as 'advisable and even necessary' for the same reason, claimed the Spiller's Mill at Calgary 'might be purchased at a very small rate on the dollar.'[17] Aberhart's response was open-ended: 'We are not in a position yet to undertake the manufacture of flour or to buy a mill as large as Spiller's. I question, therefore, very much whether at the present time we would care to proceed along this line. At a later date if an opportunity demands it we might consider something of that sort.'[18]

Two years later, however, 'something of that sort' was not worth much consideration in Aberhart's view. He was responding to a party member in Stettler who wanted answers to criticisms raised by a local Social Crediter who had deserted the party to form a CCF group. One criticism was that the government was leaving natural resources completely in private hands. Aberhart responded dismissively: 'Now regarding the developing of the natural resources by the Government directly, I am sure that the efforts of the British Columbia Government has [sic] proved the folly of such a venture. It is usually a waste of money.'[19]

Aberhart had also changed his mind about maximum incomes. Indeed he appears to have forgotten by 1942 his claims seven years earlier that any income over $2000 per year was an unearned increment that should be taxed at 100 per cent. Writing to the Social Crediter who wished to refute CCF arguments about his government's conservatism, he rejected criticisms of his $10,500-per-year premier's salary: '... at no time did I ever make the statement that a Premier or anyone else should not receive more than $3000 a year. Why should the Premier of a Province, who handles greater business than any other private corporation [sic] could possibly handle be paid one-third or one-half of what other companies can well afford to pay.'[20]

Aberhart had not only become more conservative in his economic views, he had also softened his resistance to federal encroachments in areas of alleged provincial rights. The Social Credit leader's defence of provincial rights had, in any case, been a product of the federal disallowance of social credit legislation in 1937 and 1938 rather than a long-term, deeply held conviction. But the Alberta government's emphasis on provincial rights from 1937 to 1939, including its refusal to meet with the commissioners of the Royal Commission on Dominion-Provincial Relations, along with its call for conscription of wealth before there was conscription of manpower, did not bode well for Alberta-federal co-operation when war broke out in September 1939. In practice, however, Aberhart, although convinced that modern wars were brought into being by financiers and war profiteers, accepted the federal government's wartime emergency powers. While suspicious that Mackenzie King was using the wartime emergency as a pretext for expanding federal authority, Aberhart was unwilling to give the least hint of wishing to frustrate the war effort.[21]

Shortly after his re-election, Aberhart gave proof of his willingness to co-operate with the federal government when he relented on the issue of unemployment insurance. His government and party had not, in any case, opposed the proposed federal unemployment insurance scheme on grounds of provincial rights but on economic grounds. Social Credit supported non-contributory unemployment insurance.[22] Indeed, the party agreed more generally that programs of 'insurance' should be non-contributory. Non-contributory programs, it was argued, would add purchasing power to the economy whereas contributory programs, in which people paid either premiums or taxes to qualify, took purchasing power out of the economy. But although this viewpoint had considerable currency among radicals both inside and outside Social Credit, the labour movement feared that resistance to an imperfect unemployment insurance scheme could simply result in there being no scheme at all. Aberhart's willingness to concede on this point demonstrated some toleration on his part and opened the door to less hostile relations between the Alberta Federation of Labour and the government.[23]

Perhaps aware that his government could no longer rely on a solid party base and had to seek at least some institutional support outside party ranks, Aberhart began to court the labour leaders he had once rebuffed because of their associations with the Labour party / CCF. Fred White, the long-time president of the Alberta Federation of Labour as well as leader of the Labour legislative caucus from 1926 to 1935, left Alberta in 1941 for Winnipeg and a position as Prairie regional director of the new Unemployment Insurance Commission.[24] White had been a provincial CCF candidate in 1940 and a feisty opponent of Social Credit. After his departure, more conservative forces came to dominate the AFL, and Aberhart soon revived the UFA's practice of naming a labour representative to the Workmen's Compensation Board. Alf Farmilo, the AFL secretary-treasurer, was appointed in 1941.[25] Other appointments of labour figures to government boards followed, and labour leaders spoke increasingly positively of the Board of Industrial Relation's rulings on maximum hours and minimum wages, and even more so of the Tradesmen's Qualification Act of 1939, which restricted new entrants into the trades.[26] At Aberhart's death in 1943 the federation leaders could, in all sincerity, telegram his successor, Ernest Manning, of their grief 'over the loss of a beloved leader and personal friend.'[27]

Aberhart's courtship of the major provincial labour federation at the same time that his government was becoming more conservative was, no doubt, partly an attempt to undercut the growing provincial strength of the CCF. At the same time that interest and membership in Social Credit were declining, the CCF, in line with a general trend in its favour nationally, was taking off in Alberta. With Elmer Roper as CCF president, the Canadian Labour party was finally convinced in January 1942 to give up its separate existence as a CCF affiliate and to fuse with the umbrella organization 'to form a single political party to be known as the Co-operative Commonwealth – the Alberta Farmer-Labour Party.'[28] The last CCF link with a discredited past was broken.

In April 1942, the CCF won a city-wide by-election in Edmonton. Roper was the party's candidate and he benefited from Alberta's transferable ballot system. The Social Credit candidate had placed third on the first ballot in city voting to the CCF and Independent candidates, whose vote totals were close. The transfer choices of the Social Crediters thus became crucial, and to the concern of a government whose mass base was slipping, a large proportion of Social Credit first-ballot voters had marked second choices; of these, more than two-thirds had given their seconds to Roper.[29]

The radicalism of the urban Social Crediters, discussed in chapter 3, perhaps makes such a result unsurprising, but rumblings of Social Credit defections to the CCF from the increasingly depleted rural ranks of the party were also being heard. The Social Credit Board report to the caucus in 1942 reported on the board's travels across the province and indicated that socialist propaganda was everywhere making headway and would have to be countered by the government and Social Credit League.[30] Two former Social Credit MLAs from rural areas had indeed joined the CCF in 1942, and one MP, Percy Rowe from Athabasca, had defected as early as 1938. The switch in party affiliation of A.C. MacLellan, former member for Innisfail, was least surprising. A railway worker and long-time officer of a railway brotherhood,[31] he had identified with labour's complaints that Social Credit was timid in its programs to benefit working people. MacLellan claimed, in a letter to *People's Weekly*, that Social Crediters in his district were 'rapidly changing to the CCF.'[32]

A more surprising defection was that of Edith Rogers, the former member for Ponoka. Rogers was one of the party's major campaigners in its early years and was responsible for initiating the establishment of study groups as the base for a province-wide Social Credit movement.[33] She had been one of the Douglasite insurgents of 1937 and had seemed more interested in monetary reform than in the general social critique put forward by the CCF. She even had reason to be personally vindictive to the CCF, whose second-ballot votes had elected her Independent opponent in a close contest in Ponoka in 1940.[34] But instead she threw herself headlong into the activities of her new party and served on the membership and organization committee of the CCF in Edmonton.[35]

The CCF in 1942 had 2500 members, only about one thousand fewer than Social Credit.[36] Perhaps more worrying to Social Credit's leaders was that even with the departure of the hotheads who had swelled the league's ranks over the 40,000 mark in 1937, the league did not have a membership who clearly delineated their party's monetary radicalism from the socialism of the CCF and the Communists. So, for example, while Edith Rogers may have decided that her socialistic views were incompatible with Social Credit membership, Leona Barrett, another leading woman member of the party, soldiered on. Barrett, a former president of the United Farm Women of Alberta, the women's auxiliary of the UFA, was the only woman on Aberhart's five-person province-wide advisory committee, which had the final say (in consultation with constituency delegates) over candidate selection in 1935. But by 1942 she was so radical that MLA R.D. Ansley wrote Aberhart: 'I had planned on seeing Mrs. Barrett also on the Mirror trip as she is Vice-President of the Lacombe Constituency. But from others at both Mirror and Lacombe I was informed that she had been greatly influenced with the accompanied propaganda which came of Russia's entrance in the war. Of course she is still actively associated with the league. But as she and I have had very hot personal arguments on socialist philosophy in past years I thought it unwise for me to go out of my way to discuss matters with her at this time.'[37]

Mrs Barrett was not the only prominent Social Crediter whose views were too pink for a party leadership increasingly concerned about the CCF threat and the need to distinguish Social Credit from the socialists as well as from the old-line parties. Mrs R. Hurlburt, a Calgary school trustee elected on a Social Credit ticket to the board in 1942, wrote Aberhart a proposal in 1942 for a national housing program. The federal government would make credit available to local authorities to build standardized homes for which purchasing families would pay no more than 20 per cent of their income over a set period to buy. Those who lost their jobs would have their payments deferred as long as they remained registered with the Unemployment Insurance Commission.[38]

Aberhart referred the scheme to the Social Credit Board's expert adviser, L.D. Byrne, who was aghast that an elected Social Crediter could propose a scheme that was 'socialistic in concept and does not envisage any fundamental change in the social structure.' Although Byrne himself had entertained eclectic views of reform several years earlier, he now lambasted the deviations from Douglas's views obvious in Mrs Hurlburt's proposal. The proposal, he noted, stressed standardization, bureaucratic supervision of wages, and, worst of all, it legitimated the Unemployment Insurance Commission 'and employment as an objective of the economic system' rather than creation of purchasing power.[39]

Another heresy to Douglasism still common among Social Crediters in Alberta was the belief that the government should operate industries where monopolies existed or where private enterprise was not doing a good job. The Calgary constituency president's view that the government should go into the flour-milling and implement businesses was previously mentioned. The Crow's Nest Pass Social Crediters, probably influenced by the strong Communist organization in their area, went even further, urging on the government in 1941 'the necessity of opening up factories for the necessities of life, seeing that present factories are not cooperating with the Government.'[40]

The presence of such left-leaning views led many of the members, unsurprisingly, to be puzzled by the split in progressive forces in the province between Social Credit, the CCF, and the Communists (who, forced underground during the early years of the war, were allowed to re-emerge in 1942 using the name Labour Progressive party). In Calgary, where Social Credit–CCF–Communist co-operation at the municipal level had occurred in the thirties, it was natural that there would be concern that division on the left would aid the Independents, who were strong in that city. (In the minds of many Social Crediters in the early forties their party remained a progressive party.) In June 1943, with a by-election likely to fill the seat of the late Premier Aberhart, one of the Calgary Social Credit groups called for 'a joint conference between CCF, Labour Progressive and Social Credit for purpose of putting up a joint candidate' who 'could run as a People's candidate' against the joint candidate of the old-line parties.[41]

Other requests for a Social Credit–CCF entente during elections were being heard from Social Crediters and CCFers alike as well as from people sympathetic to both parties.[42] Reverend Warwick Kelloway of Calgary, for example, wrote Aberhart in 1941 to support CCF–Social Credit co-operation in an upcoming federal by-election in Edmonton East, the seat that Orvis Kennedy had won because of Communist–Social Credit co-operation and CCF neutrality in the 1937 by-election but that had reverted to the Liberals in 1940 when the CCF nominated a candidate. Kelloway echoed the views of many uninterested in the details of differences between Social Credit and CCF, saying he was 'one who doesn't much care how social security is achieved, so long as it is by peaceful, honest and constructive means.' Kelloway noted that 'most persons I meet, of either party, favour some form of co-operation by which, while we may keep party identity, we shall not oppose each other any more at the polls.'[43] He added, however, that people believed Aberhart did not favour such co-operation.

They were correct. Aberhart resented the competition that the CCF had provided his party for the progressive vote in 1940[44] and was increasingly concerned to differentiate Social Credit ideology from socialist ideology, especially as his own views were drifting to the right. But it would be mainly after

Aberhart's death that the Social Credit League engaged in a virulent anti-socialist campaign which ended all possibility of re-creating the party as the umbrella reform group that it appeared to be in its early stages.

Two men must share the credit or blame for giving Social Credit a decisive turn to the right before the 1944 provincial election: Major Douglas and Ernest Manning.

Major Douglas had directly influenced the thinking of only a minority of Alberta Social Crediters, many of whom had only contempt for Aberhart's watering-down of the guru's ideas and his eclectic reformism. But, as the insurgency revealed, the caucus counted more than its fair share of Douglasites, and the establishment of the Social Credit Board assured that Douglas would enjoy a pipeline to the Alberta cabinet and caucus, particularly via his acolyte, L.D. Byrne.

Douglas had always regarded the financiers of the world as conspiratorial and implied, from the early stages of his writings, that a Jewish cabal controlled finance and, thus, the world. His classic explanatory book of Social Credit makes liberal use of the Czarist forgery, *Protocols of the Elders of Zion*, to demonstrate how easily a small group could take over the world by monopolizing its finances.[45] While *Social Credit* pretended to use the Protocols purely for illustrative purposes rather than as a real document, Douglas's message was clear enough to his followers. When Louis Even prepared his picture-book propaganda piece, *Salvation Island*, for the edification in the late thirties of Canadian Social Crediters, the villain of the piece was unsurprisingly a long-nosed Jewish financier named Oliver Glucksterlingmann. Glucksterlingmann washes up on a deserted island to enslave, via credit, five virtuous independent small business-men who had washed up before him.[46] The island, free of either bosses or workers, accords with the world view of Social Credit theory which C.B. Macpherson attributes to Social Credit: that of a world of independent commodity producers untroubled by class distinction and held back from paradise on earth only by a tiny group of conspiratorial Jewish bankers bent on world domination. All the evidence suggests that only a minuscule group of Alberta Social Crediters in the thirties saw the world in such terms.

The conspiracy theories of the Douglasites in the thirties linked Jews and financiers. But, by the early forties, Douglas, aghast at the limited success world-wide of his campaign to free people from the money power, enlarged the conspiracy. The Second World War to him was a sham: Jews, Nazis, Communists, socialists, and financiers were all part of one integrated conspiracy to enslave mankind.[47] It was a mad enough theory but it found a welcome reception among his Alberta followers, including Aberhart and his successor,

Ernest Manning. Neither Aberhart nor Manning appears to have subscribed to Douglas's notion that the conspiracy had an ethnic character, but both accepted the view that there was an international conspiracy to fool people into not adopting the social credit solution to their woes.

Unlike Douglas, Aberhart did not explain all key international events in terms of the unfolding of the conspiracy's plans. He was content, for example, to attack in late 1942 the plans of William Beveridge in Britain for a post-war welfare state on the grounds that they called for the redistribution of existing wealth rather than the creation of new wealth.[48] (This was, of course, the same criticism that the Douglasites levelled against him in 1934 and 1935; the fact that, both in the unemployment insurance debate and regarding the Beveridge plan, Aberhart made use of it suggests that his social credit orthodoxy was growing with the passage of time.) But in response to British and American plans in 1943 to establish the International Monetary Fund to create accepted international rules for national monetary policies, Aberhart, at death's door, adopted the tone of the Douglasites. It was an 'audacious and evil conspiracy by the Money Powers to set up a World Slave State,' he thundered.[49]

Aberhart's thinking in the last years of his life 'seemed to be more and more dominated by the delusions of Douglas, Byrne and the Social Credit Board.'[50] The board's annual reports stressed the Douglasite conspiracy theories and warned that socialist propaganda was winning adherents in Alberta. Aberhart wished to counter the socialist message, and his radio addresses and pamphlets in 1942 featured all-out attacks against state involvement in the economy, outside the financial sector. Such attacks were consistent enough with Douglasite theory but at odds with the Aberhart government's record during its first five years in office.

According to his biographers, however, Aberhart, while he began cross-Canada broadcasts in early 1943 on post-war reconstruction, 'had no economic plan, knew of none which would work, and was only grasping at straws; he had little sense of direction now.'[51]

On 23 May, at the age of sixty-five, Aberhart, a life-long abstainer from alcohol, died of cirrhosis of the liver, a disease that is sometimes associated with overwork. Aberhart had worked tirelessly throughout his adult life for the religious and political salvation of his fellows. His death marked the end of a colourful chapter in Alberta's political history.

The right-wing path along which Aberhart was likely to have taken the party and government, had he survived, seemed clear enough in the last years of his life. It was a path that Ernest Manning, the new premier, seemed anxious to tread. Manning's take-over of the premiership at Aberhart's sudden death in May

1943 was a foregone conclusion. He had been Aberhart's religious protégé and his closest associate in cabinet. He was regarded by Aberhart, who had two daughters, almost as a son.

Manning was a Saskatchewan farm boy for whom the installation of a radio antenna on Christmas Day in 1924 proved a life-shaping event. In the fall of the next year he began to pick up CFCN, Calgary's powerful radio signal, which every Sunday at three brought him Aberhart's radio broadcast. When Aberhart set up the Prophetic Bible Institute in 1927, Manning was in the first group of students. During his second and third years at the institute, Manning lived in the Aberhart home. After graduation, the Aberhart devotee became a teacher at the institute and played a role in the management of the organization's business affairs. It would be the only work outside of politics that he would perform until he was in his sixties.

Manning followed Aberhart into politics, becoming a key Social Credit organizer and platform speaker before the 1935 election. Elected as an MLA for Calgary, Ernest Manning joined Aberhart's first cabinet as provincial secretary; he was only twenty-seven years old. Aberhart assigned numerous cabinet duties to his protégé, including, in October 1935, the portfolio of Trade and Industry, a position for which he had no qualifications. As a pamphlet biographer hired by the Social Credit League in 1958 had to admit, Manning 'had had no experience in city labour, and his only business experience had been managing the Bible Institute.'[52]

Despite this handicap and despite the business community's antipathy to the Aberhart administration, the diminutive Manning, as thin as Aberhart was fat and as measured in tone as Aberhart was bombastic, proved a success with that community. His political career had been almost cut short by a bout of tuberculosis brought on by overwork in November 1936 and his return to work after only three months of rest was greeted with some relief by the business people who seem to have regarded him as a force for moderation in an administration that they saw as loony and dangerous.[53]

Manning repaid their respect by adopting, over time, views largely consistent with those held by the business community as opposed to labour groups. For example, while labour had long campaigned for limitations on employer rights to hire and fire people at will, particularly because such rights were often used to dismiss and to blacklist trade unionists, Manning opposed interference with employers' rights to hire and fire. When a hospital worker wrote Aberhart to complain that a friend had been fired simply for becoming ill, Manning, to whom Aberhart referred the letter, answered plainly: '... as to one of your friends who became ill and was discharged and whom your employer refuses to reinstate, we regret to advise that there is little that can be done in this regard, as there is nothing which will compel an employer to engage a person they did not wish to have working for them. Upon reflection I am sure you will realize that employers must be left free to engage whom they desire, just the same as workers are free to choose their own employment.'[54]

Manning, although his government had introduced maximum-hours legislation for certain categories of work, also believed that employers' views should be listened to when exceptions to maximum-hours legislation were requested. This was particularly true regarding workers in the petroleum industry. Although Social Credit oil workers' groups had campaigned for shorter hours of work in the industry and for the spreading around of the work, Manning took the companies' side. In a draft of a letter for Aberhart to send to a Social Credit supporter who in 1942 revived the old complaints about hours of work in Turner Valley, Manning wrote: 'It is regrettable that in the nature of the work of maintaining oil production in Turner Valley, particularly during war time, some of the employees have to stay steadily on the job rather than to be free of responsibility as is possible in other categories of labour. In our investigations in the past, however, it has been found that, generally speaking, the men are satisfied with both the nature of their work and their remuneration for the exceptional working conditions necessary in their particular type of employment.'[55]

Manning, a man passionately devoted to the Bible, must have been upset by the tone of the letter asking for adjustments in hours for oil workers. The writer was obviously both religious (his letter began: 'Greetings in the name of our Lord Jesus Christ') and a Social Crediter ('We are praying for you that God will give you strength and wisdom in our fight ... against the wicked forces of evil'). Yet the letter writer lambasted oil companies and was under the illusion that the federal government was using the wartime emergency to make the Social Credit administration kowtow to big business's wishes.[56]

Manning sought to attack the ideological flabbiness that allowed many Social Credit members and supporters to equate finance with big business generally and Social Credit with socialism. It was this fuzziness, after all, that was leading to constant attacks by Social Crediters against private enterprise and was increasing demands for Social Credit co-operation with the CCF and even the Communists. Manning, following Douglas, began to expose the socialists as being in a conspiratorial alliance with finance and therefore as mortal enemies of Social Credit. Although, like Douglas, Manning could present no concrete evidence for such a fantastic view, he propounded it incessantly and presumably in good conscience. So, for example, in response to the Calgary Social Credit group that proposed a united front of Social Credit, the CCF, and the LPP in the by-election to fill Aberhart's seat, Manning responded that the Social Credit League could not 'unite with the advocates of state totalitarianism' if it wished to gain support from democrats. Moreover:

In the past the present financial dictatorship established itself through control of financial institutions until it was able to dominate all phases of our economic life but people generally, at least in this province, have become wise to this form of dictatorship ... finance is today seeking to strengthen its dictatorship by subtlely [sic] advocating the doctrine of a supreme state. In other words it is determined to strengthen its now shaky position by augmenting its present control by the establishment of dictatorship in another field, namely that of Government. This is the ultimate end of all forms of socialism, including the CCF. That is why it is so important that people be made to realize that the socialistic doctrines of a supreme State are, in principle, identical with the doctrines of financial dictatorship which the rank and file of many socialistic parties claim to be fighting. Because of the clever subtlty [sic] of the International Planners of both financial and State dictatorship the socialistic move is, if anything, a greater threat today to true democracy than the actions of those who continue to champion the already established financial dictatorship.[57]

But Manning was not content to restrict himself to windy exposés of the financier-socialist conspiracy. Again following Douglas, he began to associate Nazism with socialism, although he avoided Douglas's extreme claim that the Nazis were actually part of a scheme with the financier-socialist alliance to use a sham war as a cover for an international take-over. Typical of Manning's comments linking the CCF with Nazism was this one in a letter to a CCFer, who apparently unaware of the new dispensation in Social Credit thought, had naively written to suggest CCF–Social Credit electoral co-operation: 'It is an insult to suggest to the Canadian people who are sacrificing their sons to remove the curse which the socialism of Germany has brought in the world that their own social and economic security can be attained only by introducing some form of socialism in Canada. The premise embodied in your proposed resolution, namely, that there is such a thing as democratic Socialism, contradicts itself in that it attempts to associate together two concepts of life which are diametrically opposed and opposite.'[58]

Manning was joined by other members of the cabinet and caucus as well as by the Social Credit press in expounding the new view that the socialists were even a greater menace to liberty than were the financiers and that the two were, in any case, united in their efforts to enslave the ordinary people of the world, whose only real salvation lay in the issuance of social credit. Alf Hooke, a former chairman of the Social Credit Board who became provincial secretary in 1943, proved particularly vicious. A leader of the insurgency in 1938 and a Douglas follower, Hooke came even closer than Manning in negating the differences among democratic socialism, communism, and the so-called 'socialism' of national socialism. During the Throne debate in February 1944, Hooke said: 'I wonder if this is what our boys are fighting for? They are being told today by many spokesmen in Canada that socialism is the answer to their problems. If this is so, Mr. Speaker, why send them to Europe to fight against it? Why don't we tell them that international finance, their worst enemy, is backing the philosophy of socialism.'[59]

The implication, whether Hooke intended it or not, was that international finance, the supposed supporter of socialism, was a worse enemy of the common soldier than was Nazism. Hooke, like other Social Crediters, seemed to feel no burden of proof on his shoulders to prove the improbable link between socialists and the bankers whose assets socialists usually threatened to nationalize or, at least, subject to rigorous controls. Instead, the standard Social Credit argument was that the socialists and financiers had covered their tracks well and a compliant press refused to expose them in any case. A.V. Bourcier, the caucus's legislative whip, was reported by the party's organ to have enlightened the legislature in the following manner: '[Bourcier] said it could be proved that the Socialist movement and the CCF were connected with a group of men behind the scenes "who never are seen in the full light of day," who control international finance. He said the group sponsors true socialism, as set forth in the text books prepared by the top ranks of the party and not intended for the rank and file. Asserting that the Socialists advocate international government, and were not advocating that alone, Mr. Bourcier said, "it is being advocated behind closed doors on Wall Street and newspapers and magazines are full of the propaganda."'[60] This rhetoric was ridiculous and could be likened to the Nazi Big Lie technique. But the Nazis lied consciously to attain their ends and even regarded lying as a political virtue. Alberta's leading Social Crediters, meanwhile, probably because of their devotion to Major Douglas, were genuinely deluded. There is no record of a conscious conspiracy on their part to trump up charges against their left-wing opponents, and indeed their campaign against the CCF was always conducted on the level of extreme generalities.

The logic of their position, however, was leading them to regard almost all forms of government interventionism as anathema, an ironic position considering the variety of interventionist pieces of legislation they had placed on the books during Aberhart's first term of office. A government and party which had been labelled 'socialist' by the Calgary Board of Trade were about to prove the board wrong. The change in attitude to social insurance programs was particularly striking. At one time, Social Credit favoured universal health, unemployment, and old age insurance, although, like the Communists and socialists in the early thirties,[61] it demanded that the state make the programs available without collecting contributions from taxpayers in the first place. Its reasoning was somewhat different from that of the traditional left, however. While socialist advocates of non-contributory insurance were mainly concerned with wealth redistribution (although the question of increasing purchasing power in this manner did not elude them), Social Crediters concentrated on the benefits of added purchasing power. By 1944, however, the Social Credit League's official organ was not only castigating the faulty economics of contributory insurance but indeed was fastening on the compulsory features of proposed insurance programs to find, once again, Nazi-like intentions on the part of non-social credit reformers:

It is now generally recognized that all these Compulsory Contributory State Insurance Schemes such as this, which form the basis of the Beveridge and Marsh plans emanated from Germany under Bismarck, the father of Prussian militarism, modern Nazi-ism and the doctrine of the Supreme State. The British Empire is fighting Germany because of the menace of the poisonous system which its masters are seeking to impose on the world. Yet we find that while brave men are giving their lives in this titanic struggle, small minded bureaucrats, imbued with the same Satanic lust for power that infects the Nazi hierarchy are attempting to trick us into totalitarianism by back door methods.[62]

Not even all of the elected Social Credit members, despite the large number of Douglasites in their numbers, quite grasped their party's rightward lurch. In 1943, for example, one federal Social Credit member, Victor Quelch, said in the budget debate: 'I am of the opinion that the only fair and sound way to deal with the whole question of effective control is to nationalize the chartered banks of Canada.'[63] He was corrected by the caucus leader, John D. Blackmore, who in line with the new Douglasite orthodoxy of the league told the House of Commons: 'It is a fundamental stand of the Social Credit movement that the productive system of the country in every respect should be in private hands, that by maintaining it in private hands, the greatest degree of motivation will be obtained. We favour the individual ownership of the means of production. If the chartered banks, which loan money for commercial purposes, are to be looked upon as a part of the productive system, then in order to be logical, we must have the commercial banks in private hands.'[64] One MLA, C.A. Reynolds of Stettler, bolted from the caucus and not only sat as an Independent Social Crediter but seconded the socialist resolutions put forward by CCF leader Elmer Roper,[65] who previously could count only on Angus Morrison, the Labour MLA from Edson, to perform that function. On the whole, however, the elected members appear to have found little difficulty in espousing the new party line.

The struggle against socialism did not have the same resonance among the people of Alberta as did the struggle against finance. By the time of the 1944 election, Social Credit membership had risen to less than 8000.[66] That was only a third of the membership at the time of the previous election and less than a fifth of the peak membership in 1937 of 41,000.[67] Membership in Calgary was only 414, under 9 per cent of membership of 4706 in 1937, making the party more rural-based than it had been in its beginnings. The Edmonton membership of 522 was more in line with the city's relative strength of membership in 1937, but the decline in Lethbridge was on a par with the decline in Calgary. Ironically, the largest constituency organization in the province was to be found in Vegreville, where 678 people had paid party dues by 31 July 1944, but where the CCF came about as close in rural Alberta to knocking Social Credit off as it did anywhere.[68]

Nor did those who remained in the party yet seem to have entirely gotten the point that socialism, not banks, was now the major enemy. The 1944 provincial convention of the league called for a provincially owned bank and for universal old-age pensions of fifty dollars per month at age sixty to replace the existing means-tested pension of twenty dollars per month at age seventy. The delegates didn't trouble themselves with how the pensions would be financed, perhaps unaware that in the opinion of their leaders financing by any form of taxation of an insurance program was pocket Nazism.[69]

The government's survival did not, as it turned out, require a mass movement. Fortune was smiling on the new Manning administration in several ways. In the first place, the wartime economy had restored a measure of prosperity to Alberta. Total provincial income, only $146 million in 1933, at the nadir of the Depression, had risen to only $185 million in 1936.[70] By 1942 the gross value of agricultural products alone was a record $346 million, a figure $34 million higher than the previous record set in 1927. The value of the grain crop had increased from $83 million in 1941 to $215 million in 1942. Natural resource revenue, meanwhile, hit a record $46 million.[71]

The good economy alone might have caused hesitation among many voters to change the government. But both the weakness of the official opposition and the administration's own legislative performance strengthened resistance to change horses in midstream, particularly on the part of the conservative-minded in the province.

The 'Independent' opposition, despite having won almost as many votes as Social Credit in 1940, had no recognized leader and only a vague program. It was opposition to Social Credit radicalism that had brought the Independents into being, but as that radicalism dissipated, they found little to unite them. The resistance of the federal parties, especially the Liberals, made any real fusion of the right-wing forces (excluding Social Credit, which in 1940 was still seen as on the left) impossible, and strong constituency organizations proved difficult to maintain once the 1940 election was over. The Independents changed house leaders annually and developed no themes in their timid opposition to the Aberhart and Manning regimes. By 1944, the main threat of 1940 had become almost a political nonentity. While the term 'Independent' was used to describe a variety of candidates in 1944, most of them had no great bones to pick with Social Credit and much of their fire was concentrated, as was Social Credit's, on the socialist CCF.[72] These attacks no doubt simply strengthened Social Credit's claim to be the chief bulwark against socialism and pulled most of the right-wing vote, hoarded by the Independents in 1940, into the Social Credit column. From 42 per cent of the vote in 1940, the Independents fell to only 17 per cent in 1944; and although the proportional-representation system allowed them to maintain three seats from the two big cities, they ran poorly in almost every rural seat and won no rural ridings.[73]

The fear of the left among businessmen and the newspaper editors had caused an about-face in attitudes towards Social Credit on the part of conservatives in the province. Manning's whole-hearted rejection of socialism and his apparent renunciation of Aberhart's interventionism were greeted warmly by Social Credit's former enemies, many of whom had, in any case, regarded Manning all along with far less hostility than they regarded his former boss. The *Edmonton Journal* and *Calgary Herald*, while they could not bring themselves to giving an out-and-out endorsement of the party they had once castigated, nevertheless called on voters to give their second-choices to Social Credit after marking their first-choices for Independents. Editorials at election time reviewed the government record favourably.[74]

Many businessmen agreed with the newspapers' strategy of making one's ballot one-two for the Independents and Social Credit, and some believed that Social Credit should receive first choice. As one oil executive wrote another: 'I think that you are making a mistake in opposing the Social Credit members as our main objective should be to defeat the CCF and not split the vote between Independents, Liberals, Conservatives, Labor, etc. I might say that the writer and anybody he has any influence with will vote first choice for the Social Credit candidates and the second choice will be for the Independents.'[75]

But Social Credit could rely on more than new-found business support in 1944. A section of organized labour was now, as indicated previously, on Social Credit's side. In 1940, organized labour had been formally neutral in the provincial election although the CCF candidacy of AFL president Fred White suggested where the sympathies of at least some of the organization's leaders lay. In 1944 the AFL remained neutral again, but statements by some of its leaders suggested fairly strong support for Social Credit. Social Credit was able, for example, to grace its election literature with this statement of support by long-time AFL official Carl Berg, who had also been elevated to the position of vice-president of the Trades and Labour Congress: 'Alberta is singularly fortunate in having a government that has done more to work for and with labour than any other government in Canada. We are pleased to say the relationship between our organizations and the government have been very pleasant. The door is always open for consultation with this government.'[76]

In reality, there was little in common between rank-and-file labour opinion and the new anti-statism of the Social Credit leaders. In 1940 labour's rank-and-file,[77] in common with Social Credit's rank-and-file,[78] had called at its convention for conscription of wealth during wartime; wartime profiteering was regarded as unacceptable by both rank-and-file unionists and Social Crediters. By 1944 neither group at its convention dealt with war profiteering. But both groups expressed an interest in social insurance that was at odds with the new views of Manning and company, inspired by Major Douglas.[79] And the trade unionists attending the AFL convention in 1944 did not share Manning's antipathy to state interventionism, calling on the government to pass 'legislation that will outlaw any plan or scheme of bonuses and speed-up methods.'[80]

But the rank-and-file unionists showed that conservative and jingoist sentiments also had their grip on ordinary workers. Anticipating Social Credit legislation later that year limiting the expansion of Hutterite colonies, the AFL members called on the provincial and federal governments to set a date after which Hutterites and Mennonites refusing to join the war effort would no longer be eligible to receive title to land. As for the Japanese-Canadians victimized by the federal government, with many of them relocated to southern Alberta to serve as cheap labour in the sugar-beet fields, the sympathy seemed to be with the oppressors rather than the oppressed. They were condemned because their labour 'competes with our own race for employment,' and the federal government was asked to promise to remove them from Alberta at war's end and to halt all further settlement of Japanese people in Canada.[81] As it did in the case of Hutterites, the Manning government responded to such racist sentiments with racist resolutions. The legislature had earlier passed a resolution asking 'that the Japanese be kept under constant federal supervision to prevent espionage or sabotage, that any costs involved should be the responsibility of the Dominion and that the Japanese be removed from the province at the end of the war.'[82]

But racism alone did not endear ordinary Albertans to the Social Credit government. It had a record of achievement during its second term that won it many friends. Aided by increased tax revenues that resulted from a rebounding economy,[83] the government increased school grants from $1,451,000 in 1935–6, its first year in office, to $2,086,798 in 1943–4. Health services had been expanded dramatically. During Social Credit's first term of office subsidized treatment had been established for needy tuberculosis, cancer, and polio patients as well as for maternity cases; by 1944, the province provided all Albertans with free treatment in these four areas.[84] In 1942, a flat supplement of five dollars per pensioner per month was introduced by the province to top up the minuscule federal pension for needy persons over seventy. Only in Nova Scotia, with a sliding scale that went up to ten dollars, could a pensioner hope for a larger supplement. Indeed, only British Columbia matched the Alberta supplement; in Saskatchewan, a pensioner received only $1.25 above what he or she received from the federal government.[85]

Much of the provincial government's attention was focused on the farmers, a focus rewarded by Social Credit's carrying every rural seat in the provincial election of 1944. The Marketing Act, while it did not become a vehicle for provincial operation of farm machinery and milling operations as some had hoped, was used to establish mechanisms for farmers to pool together to buy materials and to ship products. According to Social Credit propaganda, this arrangement resulted in many farmers saving from 15 to 35 per cent in the purchase costs of replacement parts for tractors and farm machinery and in others obtaining weed control solutions, hardware, and labour-saving devices via the board's facilities 'virtually at cost.'[86]

Other farm legislation provided for provincial loans to municipalities to aid needy farmers, for the establishment of a debtors' assistance board to act as an intermediary between creditors and debtors, and for the turning of some of the province's demonstration farms into agricultural schools.[87] All in all, Social Credit had a solid if unexciting record to take to the electors in 1944 along with a message of the dark fate that would befall Alberta if the socialists won election.

The CCF and the Communists, both tarnished by Social Credit in 1944 as near equivalents to Nazism, had used the same smear tactic against Social Credit in the past.[88] It had not had much effect and it is doubtful whether the inflated, irresponsible rhetoric of Social Credit in 1944 – as opposed to the government's record, the fact of renewed prosperity, and the new-found love of the administration by conservatives – limited the left's advance at that time. The war was still on, the Soviet Union was still an ally, and there was no cold war to add to the made-in-Alberta propaganda against socialism in all its forms. In any case, the left in the form of the CCF and LPP (including a Communist candidate in the

Pincher Creek–Crow's Nest Pass riding who ran under the 'Labour Unity' banner) harvested 30 per cent of the vote. But Alberta, like all Canadian provinces, assigns seats on the basis of contests in constituencies rather than on the basis of a portion of the provincial vote. It is this policy that makes Alberta appear to be a single-minded province. The left's large vote translated into a mere two of fifty-seven legislative seats. Social Credit meanwhile took fifty-one seats with 52 per cent of the vote, and the Independents with 17 per cent took three seats (the remaining seat going to a Veterans and Armed Forces representative who affiliated with none of the legislative groups).[89]

For the CCF, its failure to transfer a hair's breadth less than 25 per cent of the popular vote into more than 3 per cent of the legislative seats proved a crushing blow. The party had achieved spectacular growth during the war as socialist ideas had gripped many Albertans, a perhaps-unsurprising phenomenon in a province where both the Non-Partisan League and the Canadian Labour party had won support twenty-five years earlier on socialist platforms and where the UFA and Social Credit organizations, if not the governments that bore their names, showed keen interest in state intervention to redistribute wealth and bring the business sector to heel. Party membership rose from 2500 in 1942 to 12,000 at the time of the 1944 election, giving the party 4000 more members than the government party. Much of party recruiting concentrated on disaffected Social Crediters of whom, as we have seen, there were many in Alberta.[90]

Elmer Roper, the Edmonton MLA, succeeded Chester Ronning as CCF leader in December 1942 (Ronning, of course, went on to become Canada's major link with Mao Tse-Tung's Communist regime in China), the latter having failed narrowly on two occasions to regain the Camrose seat that he lost in 1935. Roper, unlike Saskatchewan CCF leader T.C. Douglas, made no attempt to soft-pedal socialism in favour of a left-wing populist message similar to that provided by Aberhart in Alberta in 1935. In March 1944 Roper gave his Social Credit opponents ample opportunity to deplore the evils of socialism when he brought the following resolution before the Alberta legislature:

Whereas all wealth comes into being as the property of those who own the means by which it is produced; and

Whereas the exploitation of the natural resources of the nation for private profit, and the private ownership of the principal means of wealth production, distribution and exchange, has resulted in gross inequalities and inefficiencies in the economy of Alberta and Canada; be it therefore

Resolved that this legislature is of the opinion that future development of the natural resources of the province should be by public ownership and that the whole future economic development of the province should, as far as practicable, be on the basis of social ownership of the principal means of production and distribution.[91]

Such a hard line might have seemed inappropriate in a province where the once-reformist provincial government was denouncing any state action that represented compulsion against certain individuals or groups. But the old desire for a strong state to limit the powers of the big banks and industrial concerns was not completely dead in Alberta. At the Alberta Farmers' Union convention in 1943, 250 delegates called for government ownership or at least total control of all essential war industries, 'parity' prices for farmers' products (prices that reflected farmers' costs, or, as Social Credit once called them, 'just' prices), a government guarantee of land tenure, and the appointment of a tribunal to write down the principal on farm debts and reduce interest.

But with 8800 members, the AFU at that time represented only a small percentage of Alberta farmers.[92] As for labour, the apparent defection of the AFL from the CCF to Social Credit, always under the guise of neutrality, limited the effectiveness of Roper's claims that Social Credit had become reactionary. The industrial unions affiliated with the Canadian Congress of Labour were less enamoured with the government. The CCL had been formed in 1940 after the Trades and Labour Congress and its provincial affiliates – after three years of pressure from the American Federation of Labor – expelled the Canadian sections of unions affiliated with the breakaway Congress of Industrial Organizations. (The congress was a union central composed mainly of organizations expelled from the American Federation of Labor in 1936 for establishing industrial unions where craft jurisdictions were held to be appropriate by the federation.)[93] The CCL-affiliated unions, particularly the United Mine Workers, were unhappy with the increasingly close Alberta Federation of Labour – government relationship. They regarded Alf Farmilo, the government's choice as a labour representative to the Workmen's Compensation Board, as unsympathetic to the claims of industrial workers, particularly miners.[94] But the CCL unions pointedly ignored the 1944 election, partly because Communist influence in the UMW made unlikely endorsement of the CCF as labour's party (as had happened in Ontario), and partly because the CCL unions were just too weak and uncoordinated in Alberta to play a significant political role. In any case, the CCF could claim in June 1944 only a derisive 357 members affiliated via the unions, all of them in Alberta Federation of Labour affiliates.[95]

CCF and Communist electoral strength were also weakened by a failure of these parties to achieve an electoral understanding, however informal. The Communists' strength was greatest in the mining communities, particularly in the polyglot Crow's Nest Pass area where the party's hold over left-wing miners was demonstrated by the CCF's inability to establish even a constituency organization.[96] The Communists also continued to enjoy significant support among farmers of eastern European background.[97]

Meanwhile the Labour Progressive party sought, both nationally and provincially, an entente with the CCF. Some Alberta CCF leaders, notably provincial secretary William Irvine, believed that, because of the preferential voting system in Alberta, an informal coalition between the CCF and the Communists might be possible along the lines of the informal understanding developing among supporters of Social Credit and the Independents. CCFers and LPPers would run against each other in a constituency but agree to ask their supporters to give their second preferences to the other party of the left. The national CCF, however, opposed any co-operation with the LPP. After arguing for a more conciliatory stance, the Alberta CCF, loyal to the national organization, accepted a national council decision rejecting any co-operation with the Communist party in its new guise. Although CCF national secretary David Lewis complained that some CCF groups in Alberta continued to work too closely with Communists, the provincial leadership abided by the national party's decision and refused any arrangement with the LPP in the provincial election of 1944.[98]

The result was that Communist supporters generally refused to mark second choices for CCFers and vice versa. There were four seats where the combined CCF-LPP vote was greater than the Social Credit vote: St Paul, Vegreville, Willingdon, and Pincher Creek–Crow's Nest. In all four seats, the Independents failed to nominate candidates, leaving Social Credit a free hand in areas where the left's gains were worrisome to conservatives. But a majority of Communist ballots in the first three ridings named above contained no second choices; in the fourth riding, where the former mayor of Blairmore, Enoch Williams, a Communist, was the Labour Unity candidate, most CCF voters who cast a second ballot cast it for Social Credit.[99] No doubt slanderous charges by the Communists against Roper during the election, retracted afterwards under threat of a lawsuit, helped to poison relations further between the two groups.[100] But the sad result was that the left's 30 per cent of the vote, which might have translated into six seats – five CCF and one Communist – produced only two seats, a psychological blow that created a feeling of defeatism in CCF ranks and probably in Communist ranks as well.

There were those who suggested that the CCF 'blew' its chances in 1944 in Alberta by running a clearly socialist campaign. Morris Shumiatcher, a Saskatchewan CCF activist who would eventually become a right-winger and desert that party, criticized Roper's emphasis on nationalization. In an article in *Canadian Forum* Shumiatcher admitted that the relative prosperity of Alberta, the weaker state of its co-operative movement, and the achievements of the Social Credit administration in public works and education made Alberta a tougher nut to crack than Saskatchewan. But he also observed that, while the Saskatchewan CCF could draw upon a large co-op movement and a fund of resentment against the federal Liberal government which hurt the provincial Liberal government's standing as well, the reform-oriented campaign of the Saskatchewan CCF in 1944 could have been replicated in Alberta and yielded the party more seats. Instead there had been 'too much abstract theory and not enough live ammunition to hit the electoral bull's-eye squarely.'[101]

Elmer Roper responded by noting that Social Credit had convinced many Albertans that their health and education programs could not be improved upon. The CCF had therefore chosen not to run a reformist campaign but one that challenged Social Credit's frantic defence of private enterprise: 'If we had won with such a campaign we would have claimed a clear mandate from the people to carry out the fundamental aim of our movement, which is public ownership of what by every logical and moral right should be public property. I don't think I'd want to be a member of a CCF Government without such a mandate.'[102]

The provincial election of August 1944 marked the end of any left-wing pretensions on Social Credit's part. Other parties now represented radicalism in Alberta, and Social Credit, buoyed by the economy and by conservative fears of CCF victory, had become the voice of the status quo. It is interesting to observe in this regard the evolution, or perhaps devolution, of Social Credit's attitude to women and the family. Alberta, it should be noted, had long had a strong women's movement. Its government granted suffrage to woman in 1916, only months after the government of Manitoba had done the same, because of strong pressures from farm women's groups. The first female members of a legislature in the British Empire – Louise McKinney, a Non-Partisan League candidate, and Lieutenant Roberta MacAdams, an armed forces representative – were elected from Alberta in 1917 as was the empire's first female cabinet minister (Irene Parlby, a member of the UFA cabinet from 1921 to 1935). The 'persons' case, in which women demanded the right to be recognized as persons within the meaning of the law and therefore to be eligible to hold senatorships, was initiated by Emily Murphy, the province's first female magistrate, along with four other prominent Alberta women: Parlby, McKinney, Henrietta Muir Edwards, and Nellie McClung, the former Manitoba suffragette who was elected as a Liberal MLA in Alberta in 1921.[103] The United Farm Women of Alberta campaigned, although without success, to have equal division of properties when marriages collapsed and equal rights over farm property during the period of a marriage.[104] More successful, at least on paper, was the campaign that produced the Sex Disqualification Removal Act of 1930. The act stated plainly: 'A person shall not be disqualified by sex or marriage from the exercise of any public function, or from being appointed to or holding any civil or judicial office or post, or from entering or assuming or carrying on any civil profession or vocation, or for admission to any incorporated society.'[105]

One might not expect that the fundamentalist radio preacher Bible Bill Aberhart would be sympathetic to women's emancipation, yet he insisted that social dividends would be paid to individuals, female and male, rather than the male 'heads of family.' In his *Social Credit Manual* in 1935, he responded to those who asked if this would not 'make the women too independent': 'Economic security is the right of every citizen, male or female. Women were never intended to be slaves, but helpmates. There would, no doubt, be more wholesome marriages consummated [if women had independent incomes]. They would not need to marry for a meal ticket.'[106] This was hardly a penetrating analysis, but it did at least indicate some questioning of traditional family relationships. Aberhart also enlisted the speaking talents of several women orators, particularly Edith Rogers and Edith Gostick, to proselytize the Alberta masses.

But after the election the dividends that would emancipate women did not appear. Aberhart also failed to include either Rogers or Gostick, the only two Social Credit women elected, in his cabinet, although Rogers in particular was recognized as sharp, articulate, and hard-working.[107] Irene Parlby had been a cabinet minister throughout the UFA period in office and it could thus be argued that Aberhart was less supportive of women in politics than were his predecessors. In 1938 the government established a women's extension program in the Department of Agriculture, and its explanation of the tasks of this program suggested that the government reflected the ideas of the time regarding the proper role for women. It would set up 'home-makers' clubs,' train women to prepare wholesome food, and expand consumer consciousness. It would encourage handicrafts, to enrich farm life and to allow women to produce articles for sale 'to augment the family's income during times of stress.' The significant exception to this collection of aids to women wishing to perform their traditional roles successfully was 'executive training which is a valuable attribute for all people at the present time.'[108]

Women could forget, however, about using that training in the performance of a government job. In March 1941 the civil service commissioner, sending a copy of his letter to the premier, made clear to a complainant that the man was incorrect in stating that married women whose husbands held down good jobs were working for the government. 'May I assure you that this is not permitted in the Government Service. The only married women that [sic] are permitted to work are those whose husbands are cripples and are unable to do any kind of employment, or if the husband is not crippled but is sick or temporarily unable to gain employment. Then a woman is given only temporary employment until such time as the husband becomes employed.'[109] Such a practice took Social Credit several steps backward from its concern in 1935 to end women's position of economic servitude. Indeed it would seem that the government was consciously violating the spirit, if not the letter, of the Sex Disqualification Removal Act of 1930.

Social Credit's change-over from a radical broad-based monetary reform party associated with the left to a cadre party of right-wing paranoids may seem unsurprising if we remember that the theories of Major Douglas were somewhere in the picture from the beginning. Although the mass following of the party may have twigged on to any of a variety of Aberhart's radical promises, Aberhart's hand-picked MLAs and MPs were more in tune with the central tenets of Douglas's thought. As Douglas's paranoid tendencies increased and the attack on all forms of statism became central to his notions of breaking up the vast conspiracy against the adoption of social credit ideas, the leading Alberta Social Crediters also became apostles of the right. Their new right-wing clothes did not suit most of the party's original members, but the party's establishment opponents liked the new Social Credit look. An apparent realignment had occurred in Alberta's politics in 1944, with much of Social Credit's 1940 support moving to the CCF and the Communists and much of the right-wing vote shifting from the Independents to Social Credit.[110] Yet the businessmen and the bankers were not really part of the Social Credit party, however they may have voted. The Social Credit members of the legislature remained mainly lower-middle-class people, and with the workers and the unemployed who had swelled the party's ranks in the thirties now largely gone the party itself appeared to be mainly a lower-middle-class affair. Could such a government and party truly represent the interests of big business even if the leaders had committed themselves to a struggle against socialism? In exploring this question, chapter 5 examines Social Credit behaviour during the Cold War.

5 A Hot Economy and a Cold War: Social Credit, 1945–1960

Within little more than a decade, Social Credit had been transformed from a mass, eclectic movement for social reform led by monetary reformers to a relatively small government party that enjoyed considerable support from various sectors of the Alberta population for its judicious combination of right-wing rhetoric and social service and road-building programs. The combination of a buoyant post-war economy, fuelled after 1947 by fresh oil and gas discoveries, and the U.S. inspired Cold War allowed Social Credit to maintain successfully a combination of mild social reformism and strident anti-socialism to render ineffective the disunited if numerically significant political opposition that it faced. Increasingly, the outlines of what Manning would call 'social conservatism' in the 1960s began to emerge. This chapter looks at the emergence of Social Credit ideology in the Manning period and discusses its consequences for Alberta. I suggest that although the Manning government was responsible for many advances in education and social services, ultimately the legacy of this period was a failure to diversify the provincial economy and the creation of a cultural climate in which government often ignored basic human rights.

The economic recovery that started during the Second World War became the first stage in a sustained economic boom in Alberta that lasted, with relatively minor occurrences of downswings, until 1982. Economist Eric Hanson noted in 1952: 'Because of favourable price-cost relationships in agriculture and because of the investment boom generated by the discovery of oil and sustained agricultural prosperity, provincial income has risen almost fourfold since 1936.'[1]

Albertans as a whole had never had it so good, economically speaking, and the province's prosperity obviously provided its government with a great deal of leeway. Aggregate personal income in the province, which had fallen to $146 million in 1933 from a high of $350 million in 1927, rose to the 1927 level in 1942 and then more than doubled by 1950 to reach a figure of $907 million.[2] The last figure is somewhat reduced if one thinks in terms of constant dollars and dollars per resident since both inflation and a population increase had occurred after the Second World War. And although studies undertaken in the mid-sixties under the government's aegis indicated the presence of substantial groups of Albertans who had been largely untouched by the province's new-found wealth, the economic gains of the average Albertan were considerable none the less.[3]

The discovery of substantial oil reserves in central Alberta, beginning with the Leduc oil strike in February 1947, provided the province with its major ticket out from its previous 'have-not' status. By the end of the period of Social Credit rule in 1971, the oil and gas industries directly accounted for almost 40 per cent of all value added in the province.[4] Royalties from oil and gas gave the Alberta government the highest per capita revenue in the country. In the fiscal year 1955–6, for example, Alberta took in $225 per provincial resident as against a Canadian average of $125. Only British Columbia, another resource-rich province benefiting from post-war resource demands, came close; its per capita revenue was $200. More than half the Alberta revenues came from oil and gas royalties.[5]

The increased provincial revenue allowed the provincial government to pay off the debts that had hung like a millstone over pre-war governments. Anxious to create a favourable climate for investors in the province, the Manning government ignored past Social Credit broadsides against bondholders and agreed to establish a joint debt reorganization committee with the Alberta Bondholders' Committee in 1945. This committee worked out arrangements acceptable to both the provincial administration and its creditors.[6] Manning was determined, however, that the province should never be humiliated again by creditors. The province adopted a pay-as-you-go fiscal policy, accumulating annual surpluses instead of debts. This course of action was made easier by the province's huge petroleum revenues. As we shall see, however, the size of its surpluses – in 1946, the surplus was 26.8 per cent of the total budget although most years it was closer to 10 per cent[7] – caused critics to complain that the province was retaining revenues that it could use to help growing municipalities with necessary capital outlays.

The municipalities were indeed growing as Alberta became increasingly an urban province. The populations of Edmonton and Calgary, respectively, rose from 98,000 and 93,000 in 1941 to 281,027 and 249,641 in 1961, whereas total provincial population less than doubled from 760,000 to 1,332,000 in the same period. In the period from 1951 to 1956, 75 per cent of the population increase for Alberta was accounted for by the two big cities. The seven smaller cities in the province accounted for much of the rest, and their proportion of total provincial population had risen from 5 to 7-1/2 per cent between the 1946 and 1956 censuses.[8]

The agricultural portion of the population was declining. Although 48 per cent of the population lived on farms in 1941, only 21 per cent lived on farms twenty years later. Indeed, by 1961 the total rural population, defined as persons living outside of agglomerations of one thousand or more people, was only 37 per cent of the total.[9]

The farmers who remained in 1961 had far more land and machinery than did their counterparts a generation earlier. The percentage of farms of 160 acres or less dropped by 40 per cent between 1946 and 1961 and the number of combines tripled while tractors doubled. Marginal production was disappearing, and although that meant greater prosperity for the farmers who remained, it also meant that the farms could employ and support fewer people.[10]

If the farms provided few new employment opportunities in the post-war period, the total number of farm residents had fallen only about 20 per cent from 1941 to 1961. The coal mines experienced a more disastrous situation. With the industry faced by competition from new energy sources and unable to convince the federal government to continue subsidies so that Ontario buyers would purchase Alberta coal, Alberta's coal mines gradually shut down.[11] The number of miners, which had peaked at 10,000 in 1921, had fallen to 8500 in 1946, 7000 in 1952, and a mere 1146 in 1966.[12] For the government, the loss of the coal-mines may not have appeared so tragic: the province's most militant workers had been idled. The government proved less than generous in pensioning off the older miners and in aiding the younger ones in the transition to new occupations.[13]

The province also neglected those who depended on the rate set for the minimum wage to keep them from absolute poverty. The minimum wage rose, for example, only 10 cents from 1947 to 1953, from 55 to 65 cents.[14] But this was a period of skilled labour shortages in Alberta – even before the take-off of the energy sector[15] – and average wages during those six years rose from 79.6 cents per hour to $1.40 per hour.[16] In other words, in 1953 the average wage-earner made 115.7 per cent more than the minimum wage whereas he (and rarely she) had earned only 44.7 per cent more than the minimum in 1947. This achievement was cold comfort for those who remained at the minimum; the gap between their earnings and the pay of workers with skills then in demand had increased immensely. But so large a growth in average wages helps to explain why a conservative political climate could reign throughout the fifties.

Unemployment did not disappear during this economic boom. There were 30,000 unemployed persons in Alberta in early 1954, of whom 27,000 lived in the two big cities.[17] Some of this unemployment was seasonal; in 1957, for example, there were 26,000 unemployed applicants in February but only 15,000 in June. In 1958, as a recession gripped North America, high inventories held by Alberta manufacturers led to lay-offs and a rise in the unemployment rate.[18] But the official rate of unemployment in the fifties rarely exceeded 5 per cent, although the rate was deflated by the failure to count seasonal farm workers and, more important, the native population, which comprised about 5 per cent of Alberta's population and was largely side-stepped by the boom.

The evidence of unemployment, while of concern to the labour movement and the unemployed themselves, was not great enough to make job creation by government a major issue. Alberta's population was growing and its economy was buoyant enough to allow Ernest Manning to espouse a right-wing philosophy of government without stirring up tremendous hostility from ordinary Albertans. The small farmers, the unemployed, and the miners, the radical forces of the thirties, had all been marginalized.

The defeat of the Axis powers had no sooner been accomplished than a falling-out emerged between the two largest Allied powers, the United States and the Soviet Union. The two countries clashed over territorial and trade issues, but above all, at least at the level of rhetoric, they collided on ideological grounds. Their philosophies of economic and political organization appeared incompatible, and the resulting mutual distrust made settlement of economic and territorial issues impossible. A Cold War of hostile rhetoric was set in motion alongside hotter clashes in battle between clients and supporters of the two new superpowers. The Cold War did not give way, as many feared, to a third world war, but it did provide the rationale for an unprecedented arms build-up which, added to the work required to reconstruct Europe after the war, fuelled the western industrial economies.[19]

In Alberta, as we have seen, violently anti-socialist rhetoric had become Social Credit's stock-in-trade even before the war ended and the Cold War began. Socialism was linked with Nazism because of its alleged idolization of a 'Supreme State.' Because of Social Credit's origins, however, the villainy of socialism was also made to appear part of a conspiracy with the hated bankers, who played no role in the demonologies established by the Americans during the Cold War. The importance of the bankers to Social Credit demonology declined somewhat after the war as the province paid off its debts, but none the less the concentration on the monetary system as the source of difficulties in an otherwise flawless capitalist system endured.

Indeed, troubled by the dwindling numbers of party activists and afraid that the public would regard the Social Credit League as just another small-'c' conservative movement,[20] the Manning government made one last attempt to establish provincial control of monetary policy. In 1946 it introduced the Alberta Bill of Rights, a 'charter of freedom' for Albertans. Part One of the bill enumerated basic freedoms that Albertans should enjoy. These included such freedoms as freedom of religion and freedom to hold property ('so long as he conforms to the laws in force in the Province'), which were not in question. But it also claimed that Albertans under nineteen were entitled to educational and medical benefits and Albertans over sixty had entitlement to pensions and medical benefits. Those in between had the right either to 'gainful employment' or, if that was unavailable, 'a social security pension.'[21]

Part Two of the bill provided the usual Social Credit monetary solution to the lack of purchasing power which Manning claimed was the sole way the government could guarantee the social benefits promised in Part One. 'For every dollar's worth of goods produced there must be made available to the consuming public a corresponding amount of Purchasing Power,' said Manning. To make this purchasing power available, the Bill of Rights proposed to create a board of credit commissioners whose task was to ensure 'that the credit expansion is sufficient to assure that the people of the Province will at all times have one dollar of purchasing power for every one dollar's worth of goods they produce.'[22] These new dollars would provide the revenue source for the social programs promised in Part One of the bill.

Although the government insisted that it was controlling credit rather than currency, and thus was not simply re-implementing the struck-down legislation of 1937, the Bill of Rights, like the 1937 legislation, required financial institutions to 'carry on the business of dealing in credit in the province,' as Attorney-General Lucien Maynard put it.[23] Unsurprisingly, the courts ruled once again that the government was exceeding its constitutional powers. The Alberta Bill of Rights became a dead letter.[24]

Manning made clear, however, that he did not intend to seek the social aims of the bill by other means, such as a redistribution of wealth via taxation. Ignoring his predecessor's admittedly confused position on the issue, Manning rejected notions of maximum incomes fixed by statute and of an unearned increment hidden in the incomes of the rich. He told the Saskatoon Canadian Club in August 1946 that neither redistribution of income nor subsidies to business would create more purchasing power for Canadians: '... let us not delude ourselves into thinking that the mere redistribution of the national income increases the aggregate by one five cent piece. That, I submit, is the great weakness and inadequacy of the multiplicity of post-war social insurance schemes being propagated today. The majority of them are based on the false premise that post-war economic security can be assured by a simple process of redistributing an inadequate over-all consumer income.'[25]

According to a provincial resolution in March 1948, after the Privy Council had ruled the Alberta Bill of Rights *ultra vires* the British North America Act, federal tax proposals were all marred by this redistribution myth. But probably more important politically, the Alberta government called on Ottawa not only to monetize the nation's wealth, the usual Social Credit remedy for economic ills, but to provide the provinces with sufficient income 'to pay adequate old age pensions at a reduced age,' 'to provide adequate medical and health services,' and 'to expand the construction of national highways and other public projects that will tend to develop the national economy.'[26]

The demands made on the federal government in this resolution, placed before the assembly in a provincial election year, were so progressive that the two CCF members felt compelled to support the resolution despite the preamble which fetishized monetary questions and rejected redistributive notions dear to the socialists.[27] Rhetorically, at least, Social Credit, while embracing the right's opposition to redistribution of income, rejected the usual right-wing view that social programs could be financed only through redistribution of income.

This resolution, however, indicated that Social Credit had effectively thrown in the towel on attempts to establish social credit provincially. Henceforth the provincial party's efforts on behalf of the national Social Credit party would be the 'social credit' side of its character; the provincial government would be a Social Credit government in name only. The national party had been established in 1944 to replace Aberhart's Democratic Monetary Reform Organization, which had failed to take off. The first national leader was Solon Low, a schoolteacher from southern Alberta who had served as Aberhart's provincial treasurer from 1937 until Aberhart's death in 1943. Low had remained at the Treasury during Manning's first year and was also given the education portfolio.[28]

But if social credit was now less a preoccupation of the provincial government than a talking point aimed at bolstering the national party, it none the less marked the thinking of government leaders and a section of the league rank-and-file. The Douglasite notions of conspiracies did not disappear, and in the Cold War atmosphere of the times the league and the government could feel free, to some extent, to parade paranoid views. Federal leader Solon Low, according to Howard Palmer, 'reasoned that he would be opposed to the world plotters no matter what their race or religion, but the majority of them just happened to be Jewish.'[29] John Blackmore, the federal member for Lethbridge, following Douglas's views, was 'notorious for his anti-semitism' and Norman Jaques, MP for Wetaskiwin, was a virulent Jew-hater.[30] With such support for Douglas's views of the Jewish-Communist-Nazi-banker plot in the federal caucus, it was unsurprising that the party's national organ, the *Canadian Social Crediter*, edited by John Patrick Gillese, was filled with anti-Semitic sentiments. Within the provincial administration, Education Minister R.D. Ansley and Social Credit Board technical adviser L.D. Byrne parroted the Douglas line.[31]

Manning set out to rid the party of people whose views reminded the public of the Nazis rather than their opponents. He made clear to the national executive of the Social Credit party his view that the *Canadian Social Crediter*, under Gillese's editorship, was 'a definite detriment.'[32] When that failed to budge the executive, he used strong-arm tactics, threatening to dissociate publicly the Alberta government from the views of the Social Credit national organ. Only then did the national executive agree to fire Gillese.[33] But obviously it was Manning's prestige that had moved the executive, not a sharing of his views that there was something wrong with a 'publication which contains little but negative and destructive criticism flavoured with "Jew-baiting" and of a nature that tends to stir up discontent and discord instead of uniting the people of Canada in a positive, constructive crusade for social and economic justice and political and economic freedom.'[34]

Manning fired Ansley and Byrne in February 1948. As C.B. Macpherson notes, Byrne's position was in any case redundant once it was admitted that the province had no jurisdiction in monetary matters. For years Byrne's major duty had been the propagation of the Social Credit faith; once he had used his position to push Douglasite views not in accord with Manning's, his goose was cooked.

Manning publicly rejected Douglas's anti-Semitism and his attacks on parliamentary democracy, and his campaign against the Douglasites led to the dismissal from the league of those unprepared to toe the new line in which Jews were not to be mentioned as part of the conspiracy and Douglas's hare-brained, anti-democratic political theories as opposed to his economic nostrums were to be firmly denounced.[35] Among those who left the league in anger against the new line and the dismissals were former caucus whip A.V. Bourcier, MLA Norman James, MP Norman Jaques, MLA Patrick Ashby, and Gillese. Ron Gostick, son of former MLA Edith Gostick, was another prominent anti-Semite who left the party.[36]

The breakaway Social Crediters formed a new group of Douglasite Social Crediters which, like the group that had originally opposed Aberhart's aberrant views in 1934 and 1935, had no political relevance. They continued unabated their attack on the alleged Jewish conspiracy. When attacked by Solon Low, who had removed unfavourable mentions of Jews from his rhetoric in accordance with the Manning dictum, the Douglasites demurred. Norman Jaques claimed in a letter to the *Edmonton Journal* that he and his associates were not anti-Semites and were directing their hostility not against all Jews but against 'a cutthroat gang of thugs known as International and Political Zionists.'[37] This line of argument was, at the time, put forward not only by Douglasites but by open neo-Nazis.

At the 1948 provincial Social Credit convention, the Douglasites had attempted to get their views aired, but convention chairman Orvis Kennedy, a close Manning associate, ensured that they did not.[38] Most members seemed eager in any case to support the leader and remove the taint from the party which allowed some of its opponents to brand it as a Nazi party in disguise. Some, however, were unhappy and one wrote the *Edmonton Journal* dramatically: '... since the Sovietization of this [Social Credit] League has come in the open and the Convention has been bludgeoned into acquiescence, I feel there is no course open to me but that of dissociating myself from the said League.'[39]

The departure of the Douglasites left Manning in complete control of the party and government. In a sense, he had used their views to push out the socialist-leaning elements of the party and to end all talk of a coalition of Social Credit and the CCF. Now, however, that the Douglasites' public views had become too extreme, he used them as the lever to push them out of the league. But he did not renounce all their views, and indeed while Social Credit for a period did not attack Jews, it continued to view the world in conspiratorial terms and to govern accordingly.

There is no doubt in my mind at all, that world communism operates in a very definite program designed to extend communist philosophy and the communist concept into every nation of the world and particularly to undermine the democratic nations by communist propaganda. And one of the methods which they use is to agitate industrial unrest which, because of its effect on the productivity of a nation, produces public discontent. And socialism and communism, and this we said earlier is really largely a matter of degree, has a vested interest in social unrest because they always exploit the hardships and the poverty of unemployment, and adverse social conditions, to the attainment of their political objectives.[40]

This linkage of labour unrest with a world-wide communist conspiracy was made by Ernest Manning in an interview a year after he had stepped down as Alberta premier in 1968. It indicates that although Manning could not abide out-and-out racists and extreme anti-democrats within the Social Credit movement, he had not fundamentally altered the views he expressed in the 1944 election. A quarter-century had toned down Manning's opposition to bankers sufficiently that he had become a director of the Canadian Imperial Bank of Commerce, but his conspiratorial view of his left-wing opponents was unchanged. Not only were labourites, socialists, and communists part of a conspiracy, but:

Now this isn't only a matter of agitation of unrest in industry and disrupting the industrial complex of nations. This same effort, along different lines, is evident, in my view, in news media, which are very heavily slanted, as a general rule favourably slanted, to socialistic philosophy. This isn't by chance, it's because communism has been smart enough to see ... that there are always a goodly number of men in that field who are sympathetic to the socialistic and even communistic philosophy. You even have the same thing, to varying degrees, in the field of education. It isn't by chance that you find these [sic] agitation of Marxism and so forth in many of our universities. It isn't by chance.[41]

Such views were paraded regularly by Social Credit in the post-war period. Wetaskiwin MP Norman Jaques, although he was later one of the Jew-baiters pushed out of the party, spoke for most of the party establishment when he charged in 1945 that Communists had infiltrated the CBC 'as they have every other organization.' To prove his point, Jaques used the standard line of evidence that Manning had used the year before to tar the CCF with communism as well as Nazism: lack of concrete evidence (which of course simply proved there was a conspiracy).[42]

The United Nations was another favourite target of Social Credit, and indeed the Alberta government was also contemptuous of the International Monetary Fund and other supranational organizations that emerged in the latter stages of the Second World War and in the immediate post-war period. This hostility placed Social Credit to the right of the Liberals and Conservatives, who ironically had so few years earlier combined in Alberta to fight the 'socialist' Social Credit menace. Provincial Secretary Alf Hooke, the cabinet member who apart from the eventually disgraced Ansley seemed most consumed by the need to fight 'the conspiracy,' moved a government motion in April 1945 that placed the Alberta government on record as opposed to giving the United Nations any real power. Each member nation, the motion stated, must retain complete economic and military sovereignty. The government also rejected the establishment of any international organization which compromised national sovereignty '(a) by investing it with control of the country's economy through centralized financial control under a gold standard system as proposed by the Bretton Woods Conference; and (b) by conferring upon it control over Canada's armed forces and international relations, as proposed by the Dumbarton Oaks Conference.'[43]

The CCF and the Independents opposed the government's motion, proposing a substitute motion which, in Social Credit eyes, simply confirmed the view that the Alberta government's opponents were wrapped up in the conspiracy to establish a 'World government' under banker-socialist control. The substitute motion, in line with popular Canadian thinking of the period, stated that 'the power to make war is one which no nation should be permitted to exercise, and to guard against the occurrence, the sovereignty of all individual nations in this respect must be transferred to an international organization democratically representative of all the nations, great and small, and endowed with the permanent powers necessary to maintain the peace and to provide economic justice and equality of opportunity among the peoples of the world.'[44]

The paranoia of the Alberta government had serious consequences for civil liberties in the province as well as for government economic and social programs. Although the government could not do much about the allegedly Communist-infiltrated CBC, thanks to court decisions that had recognized federal control over broadcasting, its constitutional control over civil rights did extend to films shown in the province. Film censorship had existed in Alberta from the UFA period, when its main goal was to prevent salacious material from being shown to Albertans. Hooke announced in 1946 that the government also wished to ban 'communist propaganda' films. It therefore extended censorship laws to cover 16 mm films which, it was alleged, often contained communist material.[45] The United Farmers of Alberta, the Alberta Farmers' Union, the Alberta unions belonging to the Canadian Congress of Labour, the CCF, and of course the Labour-Progressive party opposed the government's extension of censorship to cover political material.[46] Manning, for his part, without dissociating himself from Hooke's statements of the reasons why 16 mm films were to be reviewed by the provincial Board of Film Censors, insisted in letters to concerned individuals and organizations that the government had no intention of attacking free speech.[47] Indeed, protection of the right to disseminate one's ideas had been included in the Alberta Bill of Rights.

In practice, however, Hooke had told the truth about the government's intentions. Within a year several 16 mm films had been banned for political reasons, including a British Information Office film that gave unreserved support to the United Nations and warned strongly against race hatred.[48] Over the years, the Alberta Board of Film Censors would ban several films that featured mild social criticism, including *The Wild One* and *The Blackboard Jungle* in the mid-fifties.[49] The government decried the CBC's decision in the early sixties to air both of these subversive movies and – reflecting its own willingness to dictate to the provincial radio station, CKUA (a UFA legacy) – was irate at the federal government's refusal to order CBC to remove the offending programs from the air, at least in Alberta.[50]

The government's doubtful commitment to free speech was not only reflected in its attitude to films but also in its attitude to employers' rights. In a series of amendments to the Alberta Labour Act of 1948, the government made it illegal for anyone to participate in the organization of a union on an employer's premises without the employer's permission.[51] The government seemed unperturbed when a year later the pro-government Alberta Federation of Labour reported that, as a result of the legislation, 'employees have also been forbidden to talk union business during their lunch and rest periods.'[52] In general, Social Credit labour legislation reflected the government's belief that much of the labour movement was tied to the famous 'Supreme State' conspiracy which linked communists, socialists, bankers, United Nations supporters, etc.

The government's major consideration in labour matters after the war was the need, in its view, for uninterrupted production of goods and services. For this reason it even ran the political risk of denouncing the Alberta Farmers' Union's thirty-day-non-delivery-of-grain strike in 1946. The AFU was pressing the federal government for parity pricing for farm products, an old farmers' stand-by that had had Aberhart's enthusiastic support and was not, in fact, criticized by Manning. The strike, in which northern Alberta farmers were particularly active, increased AFU membership from 20,000 to 32,000.[53] Manning made clear, however, his view that whatever the goals of the strikers, their tactic was wrong-headed because it limited production and thus post-war economic recovery.[54] The former AFU executive secretary, H.E. Nichols, who had resigned in 1945, became the provincial director of agricultural research and denounced the strike as CCF-inspired,[55] although in fact the strike tactic had been approved in an AFU manifesto in 1939, when the organization was generally regarded as a Social Credit competitor for the UFA.[56] As for Manning, he publicly suggested that the Communists were behind the strike.[57] Ironically, Manning's major institutional support for opposition to the strike came from the United Farmers of Alberta, the organization whose political wing Social Credit had defeated eleven years earlier to form a government, which did not appreciate the rivalry of the militant AFU.[58]

The government's fear that productivity in the urban areas would also be affected by strikes was somewhat alleviated by the labour movement's lack of militancy. According to the Social Credit League's own literature, 1944 had been strike-free in Alberta while 1945 witnessed only one strike, involving thirty workers on strike for ten days. In 1946 there were only three short work stoppages.[59] In 1947, however, a national packinghouse workers' strike, led by a CCL affiliate, the United Packinghouse Workers of America, closed down the major packers in Alberta from late August to late October. The reaction of the cabinet was vociferous. Workers were urged to cross the picket lines.[60]

Premier Manning told a large audience that 'expanded and uninterrupted production of goods in this country is being deliberately sabotaged by industrial and distributing combines and by those who deliberately are fomenting industrial unrest in furtherance of those philosophies which make capital of distress.'[61] The view that strike leaders did not represent rank-and-file workers was also expressed by Public Works Minister W.A. Fallow, who described union members as 'helpless men and women browbeaten by a few' whose activities formed part of 'an effort to impose labour totalitarianism.'[62] And Socred MLA James Hartley, echoing Manning's view of a conspiracy, claimed: 'In days gone by labour organizations were run to benefit working men, today they are operated for anti-Christian organizations.'[63]

Socred paranoia about the 'conspiracy' may not have been the government's sole motive in lashing out so strongly at this time against the labour movement. This was, after all, the year of the Leduc oil strike and Manning's government was determined that the large oil companies have the impression that Alberta was a safe place to invest. From CCF leader Elmer Roper's view, the tirades against labour were meant as 'assurance to the big business interests to which the Alberta Government is now irrevocably committed.' At the same time, claimed Roper, the government hoped to convince the farmers that labour, rather than the 'fifty big shots' once denounced by Aberhart, was the enemy.[64]

The CCL unions were puzzled by the government's attitude. There had, after all, been a recent purge of Communists from the CCL.[65] In a letter that suggested the government was misinformed (rather than deliberately lying, as the CCF leader was claiming), the CCL unions noted:

It is our opinion that you have endeavoured to convey to the public of the province the impression that all labour unions are wrapped up in one inseparable parcel and led by professional fomentors of industrial unrest, and by inference take their orders from foreign countries – even as far distant as Moscow.

We feel that you, as the Honourable Premier of this province, should be better informed. Only last week our organization, the CCL, and its Canadian CIO affiliated unions has by convention denounced Communism in all its forms.

We further feel that you should be aware of the democratic means provided by CCL-CLO unions in respect to the calling of strikes.[66]

The CCL represented about 12,000 workers in 1947, mainly miners and packinghouse workers.[67] Yet it is obvious from the above-quoted letter that the CCL unions were on the defensive against the premier's attacks. Part of their attitude was determined by the split in the labour movement and the apparent desire not to alienate potential members towards the larger Alberta Federation of Labour. The AFL's conservatism in this period has been documented by its official historian, Warren Caragata,[68] and is exemplified in this statement by the one-time-syndicalist-turned-socialist-turned–Social Credit supporter Carl Berg. Berg was vice-president of the Trades and Labour Congress of Canada as well as an executive member of the AFL, and he addressed the Calgary Trades and Labour Council in August 1946 as follows: 'In spite of the many blunders made by Governments, the many inequalities and injustices that do now exist, and while not in any way condemning those who have been forced to resort to strike action, I cannot, now any more than I did in War-time, agree that this is the time to throw our industrial machine and economy out of gear, and into complete chaos through strikes ... strikes will only further retard our building, housing and reconstruction programs, increase the scarcity of commodities, and thus increase prices as well as decrease the flow of supplies to a suffering world.'[69]

Faced with a divided labour movement, the larger part of which was led by conservatives, the Manning government moved fairly quickly after the packing-house strike to ensure through legislation that the province's labour movement would never represent much of a threat and would never scare away potential investors unwilling to place money where the dreaded conspiracy had poisoned the atmosphere. In March 1948 a sweeping rewrite of the Alberta Labour Act, an act passed only the year before, was presented to the legislature. The 1947 legislation consolidated various existing pieces of labour legislation and made reductions in the legal maximum hours of work without overtime pay.[70] The rewrite of the act made both unions as corporate entities and union leaders as individuals responsible for the actions of their members, imposing steep fines against violators of the act. The amended act declared null and void existing collective agreements where a judge ruled that an illegal strike had occurred. And union rights to organize were curtailed. Finally, to ensure that any future meat-packing strikes could be forestalled, meat packing was added to coal mining as an industry which the cabinet could, at any time, remove from the provisions of the act and place under the provisions of the Industrial Disputes Investigation Act, which had built-in stalling mechanisms even more harsh than those of the Alberta Labour Act.[71]

Although the CCL unions and many AFL unions opposed the new legislation,[72] they were able to sway only three Social Credit MLAs to join the five of six opposition MLAs voting against the government's amendments to the Labour Act.[73] The unions, however, were well out of the militant stage they had experienced in the period after the First World War and to a lesser extent in the 1930s. There were no large demonstrations against the government's action, nor was there any real campaign to change it once it had been proclaimed. Instead, the CCL unions restricted themselves to working for the CCF in the 1948 provincial election.[74] The AFL did nothing.

A year later, however, the AFL, still loyal to the government, complained about the impact of the new act. One complaint was that employees' rights of free speech were being impinged upon. Worse, the steep fines in the act had put teeth into the stalling procedures against strikes that had been in place in Alberta since the passage of the Industrial Conciliation and Arbitration Act of 1938.[75] The near-certainty that unions would not dare to strike while conciliation and arbitration dragged on now led, in the AFL's view, to 'some pre-arranged plan' by employers to resist settlements and force almost every contract negotiation to go through the laborious machinery provided by the government for disputes resolution. The AFL's solution to this employer offensive was a conservative one, which the federation admitted was 'something out of the ordinary to be coming from the Labour movement.' The federation suggested that decisions of boards of arbitration be binding; this procedure would achieve the common government-AFL goal of preventing strikes.[76] But as it turned out, employers had no wish to have arbitration awards imposed when there was no guarantee that such awards would favour their side, and the government was not willing to act against the wishes of employers to achieve this particular goal.

The moderation of the trade union movement in Alberta in the 1950s was encouraged by the malaise of its once most militant section: the coal miners. A strike by 7000 miners in 1948, which accounted for more than 99 per cent of person-days lost to strikes during that year, proved the miners' last hurrah. After the 1948 strike, markets for Alberta coal began to dry up. It was in 1948 that the CPR began its policy of 'dieselization,' which the CNR soon followed. 'A 13,000-ton market had disappeared.'[77] While the Alberta government pressed the federal government unsuccessfully for a national coal policy to wrest the Ontario and Quebec markets from American producers, it balked at UMW and Industrial Federation of Labour in Alberta (IFLA) proposals to encourage the establishment of new industries in the coal-mining areas so as to save these communities. It also ignored UMW warnings of the impact on the coal industry of natural gas exports, and even the members for the seats that included coal mines – Drumheller, Edson, Rocky Mountain House, and Crow's Nest Pass – voted in favour of gas exports. Coal-mining employment fell from 8865 in 1948 to 3443 in 1956.[78] The Manning government did little to help the affected miners. 'Not until April 1954 did the provincial Coal Miners' Rehabilitation Act authorize the expenditure of $100,000 to meet the transportation costs of miners who had found work in other areas, but little was done for those without jobs.'[79] Although no one in the government said so publicly, it seemed there was little desire to maintain communities that grouped some of the province's most militant workers. Better to humble them and scatter them.

But while labour peace reigned in the province,[80] the Social Credit offensive against labour as part of the Communist conspiracy continued. On the heels of U.S. Senator Joe McCarthy's public relations success in pulling numbers out of a hat and matching them to particular institutions as a count of hidden

Communists, Municipal Affairs Minister C.F. Gerhart announced in early 1951 that five to six hundred Communist spies were planted among Alberta's working people. The Industrial Federations of Labour of Alberta, the provincial umbrella group of the CCL unions, took this remark as a broadside against them, although Gerhart had been studiedly vague regarding the whereabouts of these alleged spies. Again, however, the union leaders seemed anxious to play the government's game. Rather than calling the minister a liar and challenging him to put up evidence or shut up, the IFLA stressed that 'we have gone to great lengths to eradicate from our organization any subversive elements.'[81] In other words, they too recognized limits on free speech in the union movement and would not chastise the government for implying that some workers had no right to their views but only for implying that such workers had not already been silenced by the leaders.

Indeed, the IFLA leaders showed gratitude for any sign that the government recognized their unions as legitimate, as this excerpt from a letter in 1952 from the Federation to Manning indicated: 'The Federation is honoured that your government extended to the President of the Industrial Federation of Labour of Alberta, Canadian Congress of Labour, an invitation to attend the State Dinner at which their Royal Highnesses were present. We wish to thank you for the opportunity to have representation at this important event, realizing that your government recognizes this labour organization as a responsible, loyal and essential part of our society.'[82] Yet such fawning was in vain. Social Credit was implacably suspicious of collective organization, especially on the part of workers, and although no one in the government ever suggested that unions should not exist, it became a Social Credit stand-by that union power must be curbed or else the famous conspiracy would win out. The *Canadian Social Crediter*, for example, reporting in 1955 on the fusion of the American Federation of Labor with the Congress of Industrial Organizations (the latter led by Walter Reuther and once led by John L. Lewis), claimed: 'With the recent amalgamation of the two great branches of the labour movement in the States, Reuther's power makes John L. Lewis look like a ballet dancer. When the situation is consolidated, we'll see a corporate state south of the border with all its vast potential for evil. Men and women by the millions will be subject to blanket directives from "The Boss." Indeed liberty as we all want it can become a tinkling cymbal … tinkled only on May Day.'[83]

The government-appointed Board of Industrial Relations appeared to share this dim view of big unions. It demonstrated hostility to alleged union inflexibility regarding collective agreement provisions and appeared sympathetic towards the free-and-easy pattern that applied when company unions sat across the table from management. It proved particularly happy to certify and support company unions in the growing energy sector. As an example, at one meeting in 1957 the board rejected union charges of intimidation in an organizing drive where the activists had been fired and the board-reorganized company union, after eight years of official status, had no written contract whatsoever. At the same meeting, board chairman Kenneth Pugh demonstrated the government's pro-employer bias when he reacted against a union complaint of a contract violation by ignoring the violation as such and chiding the union's inflexibility regarding its contract: 'Are you suggesting the company should employ a third man and have the three of you sitting around doing nothing until some machinery wants repairing? When the employees refuse to do what the employer wishes, it impairs collective bargaining.'[84]

The Alberta Federation of Labour charged that in 1957 and 1958 the certification of company unions by the board had become an epidemic and that in some cases not even a vote had been taken. In virtually all cases the company unions had appeared only after a trade union attempted to organize a firm, and in the AFL's view the employee associations or company unions were company-dominated via supervisory staff personnel.[85]

Ten years earlier the labour movement had received assurances that despite the tightening of the screws implied in the changes to the Alberta Labour Act, 'only trade unions and organizations can be certified as bargaining units' and 'an individual who might be subject to the influence of the employer cannot be appointed as a bargaining agent.'[86] Few in the union movement now believed such assurances. With the deaths and retirements of most of those who once had sought to win labour influence with the Social Credit movement, the AFL's attitude to the government had soured. The merger of the AFL and the IFLA in 1956 strengthened the anti-government attitude. Above all, however, Social Credit's hostility to unions made labour an enemy of the Alberta government.[87]

Despite its representation of more than 35,000 workers in 1960, however, the AFL seemed a weak organization that had adopted a stance of militant opposition to the government but had lost the will and perhaps the ability to mobilize its members to pressure the government. The government, despite Alberta's almost strike-free record, moved in 1960 to weaken the union movement even further. Amendments to the Labour Act further restricted labour's ability to organize. Information picketing (that is, handing out information) outside an employer's premises for the purpose of organizing employees was forbidden, and certification was denied to a bargaining unit that had signed up any members as a result of such picketing. All members of professions related to the medical, dental, architectural, engineering, and legal fields were prohibited from unionizing altogether, while the pro-employer Board of Industrial Relations received the power to exclude from unionization those whom it believed performed supervisory functions or enjoyed a confidential relationship to management.

Those still allowed to join unions were to be forbidden from taking job action to protest hirings of non-union employees and from engaging in secondary picketing. The minister of labour received the right to declare an emergency and end a strike where 'life *or property* [emphasis mine] will be in serious jeopardy.'[88] Obviously, the lack of labour militancy had not caused the government to soften its view of labour's participation in the communist conspiracy, which had become a priori in Social Credit thinking. It is indeed arguable that labour's timid behaviour convinced the government that it could take preventive action to ensure the impotence of the labour movement without paying a political price.

While the Cold War attitudes of the Manning government dealt blows to the labour movement, they were a welcome breath of fresh air to Alberta's business community. The major provincial business organizations, such as the Edmonton Chamber of Commerce, the Calgary Board of Trade, and the provincial branch of the Canadian Manufacturers' Association, not only did not see unionization as a worker's civil right but were constantly calling for ever more restrictive legislation regarding unions.

The attitude of the business groups towards organized labour was demonstrated by submissions to a Board of Industrial Relations inquiry into working conditions in 1949. Labour was accused by the Calgary Board of Trade of getting salary increases by means of 'political pressure out of all proportion to their numbers, restriction and obstruction on the job.' Further, labour was attempting to obtain legislative changes 'to establish controls over employers' and 'to spread their authority to the employers of small groups of employees in business, not only in the cities but also in the rural areas.'[89]

Four years later the Alberta Associated Chambers of Commerce and Agriculture called for employers to have the right to demand a vote of unionized employees as to whether they wished to remain in a union at the expiry of each contract.[90] In general it seemed the government could not do enough, from the employers' point of view, to put the labour movement in its place.

The business community, which as late as 1941 was branding Alberta's Social Credit government as socialist, gave it a clean bill of health a decade later on more than its handling of organized labour. In 1956, for example, the Edmonton Chamber of Commerce, whose earlier hostility to Social Credit we have seen, praised government policies in a submission to the Board of Industrial Relations: 'The prosperous condition of the province is, in large measure, due to the fact that the Government and the Boards of Government have supported free enterprise, and have followed the positive policy of the minimum of interference with business.'[91] Indeed, beyond union-bashing, the government did in fact follow a policy of a 'minimum of interference with business.' It was a policy which Larry Pratt and John Richards, somewhat less favourably disposed to Manning and company than was the 1950s business community, regarded as the policy of 'passive rentiers.'[92] Social Credit seemed largely content to sit back and collect royalties from energy companies small enough to leave the companies with huge profits but big enough to allow the government to provide the social services and build the roads that ensured Social Credit's continuous re-election with huge majorities.

Richards and Pratt note that, while the legislature of 1938 was threatening to place the wholesale and retail distribution of petroleum products under provincial operation, there was no talk a decade later of government ownership or even close control of any phase of the energy industry. Aberhart had established a commission to investigate the energy sector in 1938 and appointed as its chairman Alexander McGillivray, an Alberta Supreme Court judge who had previously been a city lawyer and provincial Conservative leader. Unsurprisingly, the McGillivray commission gave the industry a clean bill of health and proposed regulation of the industry on the model of the American oil states, which emphasized prevention of over-production.[93]

The Oil and Gas Conservation Board, created in 1938, was given the job of preventing over-production but proved timid in its dealings with the major oil companies, particularly Imperial Oil, the dominant firm in the province. In 1950 it began to follow the American practice of prorationing. Prorationing meant the acceptance of a policy of cartelization on the part of a government that continued rhetorically to oppose the establishment of monopolies.[94]

But, according to Richards and Pratt, the government regarded its position vis-à-vis the oil companies as weak. Alberta was capital-short, short of technical expertise, and far from markets, and its energy resources might simply be left in the ground if the mostly American multinationals were not largely allowed to dictate terms on the development of the industry. Such a situation would have been disastrous, in Manning's view, since he was sceptical of the province's ability to industrialize and believed that a rapid development of the province's energy resources was the province's best chance to shake its former poverty and, incidentally, of course, to ensure the longevity of a government no longer supported by a large and enthusiastic grass-roots movement.[95]

Publicly, of course, the government supported an economic diversification that went beyond the extraction of resources. In the early fifties, for example, as it became clear that the government was about to agree to large-scale sales of natural gas for export from the province, the CCF and Liberal members of the opposition denounced a policy which they alleged would hamper Alberta's own industrial take-off: better to keep the gas in the province and sell it cheaply to industrialists establishing in Alberta. Manning scoffed at this advice, claiming that the by-products extracted from gas to be exported would enable the petrochemicals industry to establish in the province.[96]

But in a sense it may matter little whether Manning believed that the province was ripe for industrialization or not. His antipathy to state involvement in business left him unwilling to consider using the state as a potential organizer of capital and expertise to start new industries in the province. As for providing state subsidies to prospective new firms, we have seen already that he rejected this approach as equally bankrupt as redistributive policies in the creation of new wealth.

The government did pass legislation in 1946 that set aside $100,000 from general revenue 'and up to' five million dollars to be raised in debentures for loans to those wishing to establish new businesses. And via the Alberta Research Council it initiated a modest amount of research, particularly regarding oil sands development, which was of interest to prospective investors.[97] On the whole, however, the Manning government was simply uninterested in involving the state directly in the process of economic development. It was often enthusiastic about proposed industrial projects but was unwilling to back them financially. So, for example, when a firm manufacturing seismographic instruments inquired in 1952 about the province's interest in having the company set up an Alberta branch, Manning wrote its vice-president that the government would provide the company 'wholehearted support.' He hastened to add, however, that 'it should be clearly understood that the company would be prepared to raise its own finances and stand on its own feet.' Similarly, a year earlier an insulation manufacturer in Vancouver was surprised at the cabinet's rejection of loans despite enthusiasm on its behalf from officials of the Department of Industries and Labour, a favourable Dun and Bradstreet rating, and a previous history of securing loans from the federal Industrial Development Bank.[98]

The government was complacent about the province's success in achieving diversification. A. Russ Patrick, the provincial secretary, told the 1960 provincial convention that manufacturing in Canada had increased by 137 per cent since 1947 while in Alberta the increase was 210 per cent.[99] He neglected to note the limited base from which Alberta's expansion, relative to Canada's, had occurred. But even had the province's performance been more dismal, it is unlikely that the government would have changed its non-interventionist policy much. Social Credit ideology of the Manning period simply didn't allow for much collectivist meddling in the economy. Nor was it simply a question of government tight-fistedness. Social Credit also steadfastly opposed the establishment of marketing boards, the costs of operation of which could be charged back to producers.

In the thirties, of course, rural Social Crediters were staunch supporters of marketing boards, which they saw as a vehicle to achieve a just price for their products. In the fifties, the Alberta Federation of Agriculture, the umbrella farmers' pressure group, still regarded marketing boards as a key aim. But attempts to get the government to establish boards met a hostile response.[100] The *Canadian Social Crediter*, indeed, attacked such boards as anti-democratic, apparently seeing little in common between marketing boards, which would aid many farmers, and the Oil and Gas Conservation Board, which aided the small number of oil producers: 'You can't get more money from consumers without purchasing power ... With regard to the compulsion factor ... If a group of individuals think they can improve their condition in any way by getting together and forming a co-operative society, they are at perfect liberty to do so. However, they must also be willing to concede the same freedom to those who do not see eye to eye with them, to refrain from joining up. To try to compel others to belong to a "cooperative" organization is not only a negation of terms, it is an outrage on democracy itself.'[101]

This new antipathy to price controls, so in contrast to Aberhart's emphasis on 'just prices,' also extended to urban housing rents. In late 1949 the federal government, which had begun to control rents during the Second World War as part of its wartime anti-inflation policy, announced that the next year it would hand over to the provinces power to control rents. The Alberta government decided to end controls and to establish an appeal board on a limited-term basis to adjudicate 'during the transition period' when landlords and tenants could not agree on rents. The government now praised 'natural economic laws' which, it claimed, if left unimpeded would act as a stimulus for the building of homes and apartments (presumably by pushing rents up, although Premier Manning carefully avoided saying so). Somewhat unaware (or unconcerned) about the relative powers of each side in a tight housing market, Manning claimed that 'the desirable goal in this matter is a return as quickly as possible to a free economy, in which landlords and tenants will determine rentals by mutual agreement, entirely free from government interference.'[102]

The impact of the end to rent controls could, of course, have been lessened had the province acted to ensure an increase in accommodations. It was under pressure to do so not only from expected sources such as the CCF and the unions but also from the Canadian Legion. The legion's provincial executive secretary noted that there were 1542 applications for low-rental houses in Calgary and only thirty-five houses soon to become available; in Edmonton the situation was 'much worse.' He called upon Manning to establish a provincial committee on housing, but the premier was adamantly opposed to a committee whose existence would imply provincial responsibility in the housing field. An attempt by the Edmonton legion the following year to interest Manning in the housing situation met much the same response.[103]

Manning also rejected demands eight years later from the unions that the province sponsor house-building and slum clearance projects to spur employment at a time of rising unemployment. Replied Manning: 'lower rental type housing and slum clearance programs are matters, which in our opinion, come entirely under the jurisdiction of the Government of Canada and the Alberta Government does not plan any projects in respect to these two latter programs.'[104]

The Social Credit government, with its pay-as-you-go policy and its belief in the 'natural economic laws,' was not about to embark on expensive programs to create work. It saw no reason either why the province's municipalities should not guard their pennies closely.

The dramatic growth in population of the major municipalities in the province led to organized pressure on the provincial government to share some of the province's new wealth with the junior level of government, which remained dependent upon property tax for the revenues it could collect for itself. The cities argued that they needed larger guaranteed revenues if they were to plan in advance the infrastructure required for an increasing population. But they faced the Social Credit government's distrust of social planning, not to mention its desire not to be faced with choices of taxing more steeply or going into debt. The municipalities, their eyes jealously peeled to the province's collection of oil royalties, campaigned for a portion of the energy largesse. The 1955 convention of the Social Credit League passed a resolution rejecting such grants to municipalities and expressed the view that such requests were motivated by crypto-socialist ideologies. Said the resolution:

Whereas there is continual pressure being exerted on the Provincial Government to make increasing grants to municipal governments of monies derived from the administration of Alberta's natural resources, which are really the property of the people of Alberta, and not of its various governments, and

Whereas this [is] a tendency towards the centralization which is encouraged by socialism, and tends to build up the power of governments rather than building up the power of the people; while democracy implies legislation in the interest of the individual citizens, which does not necessarily mean in the interests of governments elected by the people, and it is not desirable that any government should have the spending of large amounts of money in the form of grants, for the collecting of which it is not responsible; and which grants should always be less in percentage than the amounts which said governments collect by direct levy;

Therefore be it resolved that we heartily endorse the proposal suggested by Premier Manning that any surpluses derived from the administration of Alberta's natural resources be paid to the citizens of the province as individual participation dividends rather than continuing [sic] to increase grants to municipalities.[105]

The distrust of governments evident in this resolution demonstrated Social Credit's ideological reluctance to accept that urbanization unavoidably required municipal authorities to spend vast sums planning new neighbourhoods, expanding transportation facilities, providing recreational facilities, and finding shelter and food for the urban poor. As the resolution indicated, Manning planned a payout of monies from oil royalties to individuals rather than to municipalities. In 1957 the Oil and Gas Royalties Dividend Act set aside one-third of all energy royalties to issue 'annual citizens' dividends' to all adult Albertans meeting a residency requirement.[106] But continued municipal pressures led in 1958 to a change of policy: a third of energy royalties were placed in a municipal assistance fund to be divided among municipalities proportionally by population.[107] A year later, the government suspended the Oil and Gas Royalties Dividend Act,[108] and the ultra-individualist philosophy espoused at the 1955 Social Credit convention appeared to have been abandoned. But government policy was changing in degree rather than in kind. The Manning administration had been and remained reluctant to accept responsibilities for urban problems. Its complete refusal after 1950 to involve itself in the housing problem was one example of this reluctance.

Relief policy was another source of friction. The Aberhart government, at odds with majority opinion in the Social Credit League, particularly in the cities, in 1940 removed itself entirely from the field of unemployment relief. When the war ended and unemployment rose, the cities protested the province's unwillingness to take any responsibility for unemployment relief. In early 1946 Calgary initiated a concerted municipal campaign to force the province to pay 80 per cent of the costs of municipal relief and 100 per cent of the costs of relief for residents of a municipality who had resided there for less than seven years. British Columbia had followed such a policy during the war, it was noted, as well as paying half the costs of medical services to recipients of old age pensions, mothers' allowances, and relief allowances. Calgary argued that it was facing 'a state of emergency ... with many applications for assistance being made to the Relief Department of the City of Calgary.'[109]

Calgary's position was supported by Edmonton and Lethbridge and indeed by most municipalities of any size in the province.[110] But it took the province more than three years to relent – partially – and set the provincial share of unemployment relief at 60 per cent.[111] It did not increase its share to 80 per cent until 1958, by which time the federal government was repaying the provinces for a large share of welfare payments under the Unemployment Assistance Act of

1956.[112] Pressure from the cities for the province to pay 100 per cent now that federal dollars paid much of the province's old share proved to no avail. The 80 per cent figure remained in place when Social Credit was defeated in 1971.

The cities were particularly unhappy with the province's unwillingness to assume various costs. A report prepared for the Union of Alberta Municipalities by the Citizens' Research Institute of Canada in 1954 noted that per capita revenues of the province's cities had grown by less than 60 per cent from 1946 to 1953 while those of municipal districts had risen 175 per cent; yet operating costs for the cities were increasing faster than in non-urban districts because of the costs involved in providing services to an increased concentration of population. The institute argued for special grants to the cities to make up the shortfall.[113]

Pressured by the opposition parties,[114] whose urban base was stronger than their rural support, as well as by the urban business organizations,[115] the government in 1954 established the Royal Commission on the Metropolitan Development of Calgary and Edmonton. When the commission reported in 1956, it called for district planning authorities for the Calgary and Edmonton areas, whose task would be to adopt district general plans 'in respect to those matters which are essential to the orderly development of the region.' The report suggested no special grants for the cities, but it did call for what eventually became the Municipal Assistance Fund to be established to ensure that cities got the share of the fund that their size of population merited. Annexation of certain areas near the two major cities was also proposed as was provincial assumption of all costs related to highways through the cities, as was already in effect in towns and villages.[116]

The province adopted the major recommendations of the commission, thereby blunting somewhat the opposition claim that the government was building up reserves at the cost of the municipalities, particularly the cities. But the province never really accepted the requests from municipalities for more funds as legitimate and always behaved as if it were caving in to public pressure. A.J. Hooke, minister of municipal affairs at the time, told the 1960 Social Credit convention why the province continued to question municipal complaints:

Do we have to be so hasty in getting everything we need at once? How can municipalities get money to meet expenses and at the same time lower taxes? People think that if the Government pays, it is free, but any money that the Government has belongs to the people, and once spent cannot be spent for anything else. Some people think it can be done by borrowing; but the 'day of reckoning' always comes. Others couldn't care less about the management of their affairs, as evidenced by the poor turn-out for municipal elections. For services for municipalities – no matter what is asked for-you are the people who pay the bills. Pay cash-pay once: borrow and you pay twice over.[117]

The expression of such homilies may have had some support in Alberta in 1960, but it is unlikely that Social Credit would have been as popular as it was if its public face were solely that of opposition to state economic planning and to municipal overspending. Indeed, as noted, by the late fifties Manning was prepared to make concessions to the municipalities. But it was in the areas of social spending and highway building that the government tended to win the hearts and votes of Albertans.

Most of the province's operating budget in the Social Credit years went into health, education, public welfare, and highway expenditures. With revenues continually rising and standing at 80 per cent more per capita in 1955–6 than for the provinces as a whole, the Alberta government was able to spend generously in the areas where its philosophy did not hold that a government presence played into the hands of the conspiracy, with goal of a Supreme State. In education, for example, Alberta was the leading spender per capita in 1957, shelling out $90 per capita against a Canadian average of $60 (a figure made less impressive, however, by the fact that Alberta took in overall $225 the year previous per capita against a Canadian average of $125: Alberta's proportion of educational spending as part of its budget was thus below the Canadian average). Of $123 million spent in operating costs in 1955–6 (the government also spent $99.6 million on capital projects), education absorbed $37.8 million, public welfare and health $48.2 million, and highways and bridges $15.7 million. That left, apart from $9.8 million for general governmental expenditures, $3.2 million for the administration of justice, and $2.7 million for agriculture, only $5.8 million for all economic programs outside agriculture, including research and development expenditures.[118]

Social Credit had put in place an enviable program of health, education, and social welfare programs. It was particularly generous in its treatment of pensioners. Until 1952, only pensioners without means received a federal pension at age seventy. Alberta, along with British Columbia, 'instituted flat supplements of five dollars a month for all pensioners' in 1942. By 1950 the supplement had reached ten dollars in both provinces, with no other province matching the generosity of the two westernmost provinces.[119]

The new federal pension in place on 1 January 1952 provided all persons over seventy with a pension without having to submit to a means test. Those in the sixty-five to sixty-nine age group now became eligible for a means-tested pension. Alberta, as well as British Columbia, now paid its supplement to those over sixty-five who met a means test qualification. To the embarrassment of the Alberta CCF, the CCF government of Saskatchewan, never as wealthy as the Alberta government, provided penurious supplements to that province's old people. In the mid-fifties, for example, while Alberta and British Columbia hiked their supplements to fifteen dollars per month, Saskatchewan could only provide a sliding scale ranging from two-and-a-half to ten dollars.[120]

Beginning in 1947 the province also provided free hospital and medical treatment to old-age pensioners, as well as to the blind and to recipients of mothers' allowance. The province also began to pay half the costs involved for municipalities caring for the aged and infirm in approved homes.[121]

The provincial government also subsidized municipal health schemes, but here as in other areas such as relief spending it was unwilling simply to declare a provincial responsibility and free the local government from a financial burden. Legislation in 1946 established health insurance districts in which a board, consisting of physicians and consumers, negotiated with municipalities the provision of services covered in the act and the cost to each insured resident of the services. A ten dollar maximum per adult was established. Among the services that would be included were medical, surgical, and obstetrical benefits, hospitalization costs, and nursing, pharmaceutical, and dental benefits. No scheme could be approved without a local vote in which 60 per cent of those voting had to indicate approval of the agreement.[122] While these schemes were user-pay, the province did pay half the costs of hospitalization to municipalities above a one-dollar-per-day flat fee charged to patients; the municipalities paid the other half.[123] The CCF compared this scheme unfavourably with Saskatchewan's free-hospitalization plan, initiated in 1948, but Manning insisted that some charge to the patient must be levied to prevent people from needlessly occupying hospital beds. As we note in the next chapter, this viewpoint resulted in a federal-Alberta conflict when a federal hospitalization scheme implemented in 1958 required provinces to provide free hospitalization to receive the full federal grant available to provinces for hospitalization purposes. The province did, however, assume the full costs for maternity cases and for tuberculosis and cancer patients.

The government defended its refusal to assume fully the costs of most services and its decision to leave the operation of services to local governments and boards on the grounds that it opposed centralization. Just as it opposed 'world government' and had argued for greater provincial powers relative to the federal government in *The Case for Alberta*, it argued that municipal governments were best equipped to deal with local concerns.[124] The result, however, was that many individuals, particularly those applying for relief, had to deal with the caprices of local officials, not to mention the municipalities' desire to avoid placing someone on welfare when part of the funds for relief came from the municipal treasury. Many individuals wrote to Manning to complain of their treatment at the hands of local officials. But he could do little under the self-denying ordinance that the province had placed upon itself.[125] The plight of such people was ironically perhaps made more acute by the province's overall prosperity: the organizations of the unemployed and of desperate farmers, which in the thirties had interceded on behalf of people having difficulties with the authorities, no longer existed. The poor were on their own in dealing with the authorities, and, in the rural areas at least, it seems that charitable attitudes to the down-and-out were by no means widespread.

The major area in which the government was seen as not doing enough, according to a poll commissioned by the Social Credit League in 1956, was education.[126] Concerned about its image in this area, the government established a royal commission to examine all areas of education and to make recommendations.[127]

The commission found that there was widespread concern in the province that too few skilled, highly educated people were being trained in Alberta. The business community, which was not noted for its desire to have governments spend more on social services, supported spending money to keep more children in school longer. The Canadian Petroleum Association, the chambers of commerce, and spokespersons for the province's manufacturers all agreed that business needed fewer unskilled workers than once had been the case.[128] The manufacturers, noting the increased demand for highly skilled workers and for junior and senior management personnel, called 'for a reduction in pupil-teacher ratios in classrooms, more and better qualified teachers, better materials of instruction, greater efforts to capitalize on the interests of pupils as means of raising the general level of academic attainment, for the purpose of equipping more young people for job efficiency in an age of machines.'[129]

The commission, for its part, claimed that the school system as then constituted was not allowing pupils to achieve their potential. It recommended broader course offerings, a better-educated, better-paid teaching force, lower pupil-teacher ratios, and an expanded curricular effort on the part of the Department of Education so that teachers were aided in providing challenging, interesting materials to students. It also called on the government to turn the agricultural colleges into community colleges offering advanced training in a variety of areas.[130]

One commission member, J.S. Cormack, wrote a dissenting report accusing the commission of swallowing modernist notions of education in which professionals (the teaching staff and Department of Education officials), rather than parents through their local school-boards, controlled education.[131] His pitch against centralization certainly echoed the usual Social Credit view of things. But Manning went along with the majority report, which addressed the issues that concerned not only the business community but most Albertans, if the 1956 poll was to be believed. Local control was less important to people than was the provision of an education that would enhance their children's chances of finding good employment in their adult lives. The view that the requirements of society and particularly of employers had changed to make a respectable education necessary for their children had gripped Albertans, and a sense of unease about the existing system was pervasive, if only perhaps because the drop-out rates at all levels remained high. In the 1959 provincial election Manning committed his government to most of the royal commission's recommendations and announced plans to spend $350 million over five years on education, mainly in grants to municipalities. This was a huge sum for that period, even by Alberta standards, and Manning felt the need to promise that it would be spent without abandoning the Social Credit pay-as-you-go principle.[132]

Opposition parties had a difficult time in Alberta from 1944 onwards. For the CCF, the provincial election that year proved a high point; as for the Independents, who had almost topped the Social Credit vote in 1940 and formed the official opposition in 1944 with three seats (against two for the CCF, which had half again the Independent vote), the 1944 election marked a further step on their road to collapse.

Defeatism overtook the CCF after the party proved unable to win more than two seats in 1944 despite gaining 25 per cent of the vote. Party leader Elmer Roper attempted to minimize the defeat by noting that the party had more than doubled its 1940 vote and had drawn to its ranks many former Social Credit League members. As it became clear that Manning had transformed Social Credit into a reactionary, pro-capitalist party, Roper cheerily predicted, those who had supported Social Credit's early radicalism would flock to the CCF, leaving Social Credit exposed as the new face of the old-line parties in Alberta.[133] Instead, working-class disillusionment over the individual worker's inability to have an impact on Social Credit policy or party matters produced a depoliticization of working class and public life generally in Alberta.

The new prosperity of the province also aided Social Credit. The poor farmers and the unemployed who had backed radicalism in the thirties were now better off, and while they may have resented the relative wealth of others, they feared the consequences of abandoning the Social Credit regime. Long-time CCF party president and later provincial secretary Nellie Peterson years later recalled that CCF organizers in the countryside soon learned that the poor farmers were a hopeless cause for the socialist recruiter.[134] The failure of the non-delivery-of-grain strike in 1946 to achieve its goal of parity prices dealt a telling blow to the Alberta Farmers' Union, and this organization soon evaporated.[135] Meanwhile, the larger of the two rival union federations in the province, the Alberta

Federation of Labour, remained supportive of the government, although its enthusiasm did begin to wane by the time of the AFL-IFLA merger in 1956.

The CCF continued for a period to concentrate its fire against the government's plans to allow development of the oil industry to fall entirely into the hands of the private sector, which in this case was largely American. The party, after considerable debate, moderated its 1944 position of total government control over resources in favour of a 50 per cent position for the government in the development of oil and gas.[136]

But the party began to focus its sights on a more popular candidate for nationalization: Calgary Power, the electrical distribution monopoly in the province (outside of Edmonton, which had public power from an early date). Manning, totally opposed to public ownership of utilities despite their monopoly status, neutralized the Calgary Power issue by allowing a referendum on Calgary Power's nationalization to take place in conjunction with the 1948 provincial election. He was not entirely clear that the government would abide by the referendum if the pro-nationalization forces won, but in any case 139,991 voters opposed nationalization while 139,840 supported it. In thirty-four of the forty-seven seats outside the two big cities, the pro-public operation option carried the day. But Calgary's vote of 11,478 for nationalization against 26,325 opposed ensured continued private operation of the utility.[137]

The CCF attacked the government's anti-labour record as well as its censorship policies in 1948, but to no avail. The party's vote fell by about 14,000 votes, leaving the CCF with only 19 per cent of the vote. The Communist vote had fallen to about 0.5 per cent of the total, so that the total left vote was more than 10 per cent down from the 1944 election.[138] CCF membership had fallen from 12,000 in 1944 to below 4000, and the party now claimed openly that Albertans no longer really wanted radical change.[139]

While the CCF held second place in the popular vote in 1948, it was the Liberals who began to emerge as an alternative to the government. Led by J. Harper Prowse, who had been elected as an armed forces representative in 1944, the Liberals, with only thirty-two candidates, captured almost 18 per cent of the vote and two seats.[140] The provincial Liberal party organization had collapsed in 1942, but a convention attended by seventy people in Red Deer in 1945 announced both its rebirth and its severing of ties with the Independent movement – ties that had earlier limited the possibility of an autonomous Liberal existence on the provincial level.[141] Prowse, chosen leader at a convention in 1947, found that the business community was reluctant to support the revival of the Liberals. The businessmen liked the Manning regime and feared that two strong pro-capitalist parties in the running might strengthen CCF electoral chances.[142]

None the less, while Social Credit won fifty-one of fifty-seven seats in 1948, and won 56 per cent of the popular vote, the Liberals had adopted a critique of the government from the non-socialist left, which would increase that party's support levels over the next two elections.

One part of the critique was that the government was not serious in its claims to want to diversify the economy. In 1952 the Liberals took essentially the same line as the CCF in opposing exports of provincial gas surpluses, arguing that cheap gas supplies within the province could be used as an inducement to entice manufacturers to come to the province.[143] This position put the Liberals at odds with their former Conservative allies in the Independent movement. The provincial Conservative party, influenced by oil baron Carl Nickle, a federal Conservative MP from Calgary, among others, supported the government's plans to export gas, claiming that it was folly to deprive the province of revenues available for the taking in the spurious hope of long-term manufacturing development.[144] The issue, however, seemed to excite little interest outside of political circles. The funding of municipalities held more interest for voters.

The Liberal party seems to have been dominated by urban lawyers and other professionals who regarded the Social Credit regime as unduly cheap in its grants to municipalities.[145] As we have seen, the view that the government was doing too little to help the growing cities had support from business organizations. It also had the support of the trade unions, but it would seem that the Liberal message won greater acceptance among solid middle-class elements than among the working class.[146]

The Liberals, who emerged during the 1952 election as the major opposition party, put the government on the defensive regarding aid to municipalities in both the 1952 and 1955 elections. For example, J. Harper Prowse claimed during the 1952 election that the Manning administration was 'keeping their own balance sheet in order by throwing on the shoulders of your local government all of the major responsibilities.' He noted that while the province had retired its pre-war debts, municipal debt had almost tripled since the war, rising from $42 million in 1945 to $116 million in 1952. Nationally the increase over the same period was only 2 per cent.[147]

Municipal Affairs Minister Edgar Gerhart responded that such criticism ignored that Albertans paid less in combined provincial-municipal taxes than residents of either Saskatchewan or Manitoba, which had, respectively, CCF and Liberal provincial administrations. He also noted that the province was making loans available at low interest rates for self-liquidating projects such as sewer and water systems.[148]

But in 1955 the Liberals were back on the attack, noting that property taxes in Alberta averaged five dollars more per capita than property taxes in the other two

Prairie provinces.[149] Premier Manning replied weakly that Alberta citizens demanded higher municipal standards of service than other Canadians.[150]

It was only after the major Liberal breakthrough in 1955 that the government took serious steps to weaken the impact of the opposition's charges of government unfairness to municipalities. But that breakthrough seems to have been less the result of anger about particular Social Credit policies than shock at a series of scandals that emerged just before and during the election. The religious halo which Manning's religiosity placed over the government tarnished briefly, and significant numbers of voters were angry enough that they voted for other parties, mainly the Liberals.

In 1952, however, there had been no scandals. The Liberals, with little rural support, had no real chance of unseating the government. Their major aim in the election was to establish themselves, rather than the CCF, as the real alternative to the government. The CCF, whose membership continued to slide,[151] tried to moderate its image as much as it could, presenting the Saskatchewan government as a shining example of what a socialist government could do in Alberta. In practice, however, the CCF tended to emphasize the same issues as the Liberals, and in the conservative environment of the period it would appear that more Albertans trusted the Liberals not to push too far. The Liberals won 66,738 votes and three seats in 1952 while the CCF won only 41,929 votes and two seats. The Conservatives, despite few candidates and a small vote, won two urban seats. That left one seat for R.D. Ansley, the Manning-rejected Douglasite whose Leduc constituents remained loyal, and fifty-two seats for the government.[152] But the Liberal advance proved sufficient to give that party the edge with dissatisfied voters when a surprise election was held only three years later.

Premier Manning seemed stunned and unable to react as a variety of charges made by the opposition in 1954 and 1955 suggested abuse of the public trust by cabinet ministers and MLAS, past and present. The issues involved included the government's procurement policies regarding both land and materials, its tendering practices, and the treasury branch's alleged favouritism to MLAs in the granting of loans. The opposition demanded judicial inquiries into their various charges, but the government refused and called a snap election in June 1955, only three years after the previous general election.[153] The opposition parties all concentrated their fire on alleged government improprieties. The favourite target of attack seemed to be the large loans made by treasury branch to a cabinet minister, a party official, and two Social Credit MLAs who allegedly lacked the collateral which most other citizens would have required to get the loans.[154] Typical was J. Harper Prowse's imaginative juxtaposition of treasury branch with the British treasury: 'What do you suppose would be the reaction of the British people, and in fact, the whole democratic world, if tomorrow the British newspapers and the world press services carried reports stating that former Prime Minister Churchill, present Prime Minister Sir Anthony Eden, members of the British Cabinet and Conservative members of the House of Commons had been secretly borrowing money from the British treasury?'[155]

Another favourite charge was that the government was specifying a particular form of concrete in its building contracts because former cabinet minister Norman Tanner and his relatives held a substantial interest in Alberta Ytong, the company which manufactured this building material. Tanner had been minister of lands and mines (later mines and minerals) from 1937 to 1952, and in the three years after he left government had become president of Alberta Gas Trunk Line Company, president of an independent oil company, and director of Alberta Ytong as well as of a chartered bank. The financial success of this former minister caused Conservative leader W.J.C. Kirby to question: 'Are there still fifty [big shots]? Oh No! Their number has been increased to fifty-one.'[156] It was a cheap shot when one considers that the Social Credit government had long since abandoned talk of fifty big shots, but it reflected the opposition parties' desire to tarnish the Social Credit image of providing honest government.

Manning used the civil service to collect information on opposition members who had received treasury branch loans, grazing leases, oil leases, coal-mining leases, or any other contracts that indicated potential gains by way of the public purse.[157] Apparently he found little of interest, because Social Credit did not really respond in kind to opposition charges during the election. Instead, Manning, on the eve of the election, charged that his opponents had used slander and innuendo throughout a dirty campaign and stated that he was considering filing libel suits.[158]

The province's daily newspapers, except for the *Medicine Hat News*, played up opposition charges and most called for the government's defeat. During the years of the CCF challenge, the newspapers begrudgingly supported the Social Credit administration. Now that the socialist threat had proved chimerical, the antagonism of urban professionals found expression in the newspapers, with the *Calgary Herald*, in particular, reviving the vitriol that had marked its attitude to Social Credit in the Aberhart period. Social Credit, they said, was 'thinly disguised fascism.' It would seem that the men and women of humble origins who composed the Social Credit government were still regarded with some contempt by the urban establishment despite the conservatism of the adminis-tration.[159]

The opposition attacks had their effect. Social Credit's popular vote fell from 56 per cent in 1952 to 46 per cent in 1955. More serious from the government's point of view was that the party lost fifteen of its fifty-two seats, producing a twenty-four–person opposition to face the thirty-seven members on the government side. It was the first significant opposition since the 1940 election, and it consisted of fifteen Liberals, two CCFers, three Conservatives, one Independent Social Crediter, one Liberal-Conservative, one Coalition candidate, and one Independent.[160] The government had also to be concerned that the Tories and Liberals had managed to co-operate in many rural seats to ensure that their respective supporters gave their second choices to the other party.[161] Worst of all, they had to accept that the under-represented Edmonton and Calgary ridings, which produced all or most of the handful of opposition seats in 1944, 1948, and 1952, were no longer the only vulnerable ridings. Another sobering result of the election was that the tendency of the Liberals to soak up opposition votes, in evidence in 1952, had been reinforced. Under Prowse's leadership, the party had won 31 per cent of the vote as against 9 per cent for the Conservatives and a mere 8 per cent for the once-feisty CCF, whose leader, Elmer Roper, had been defeated in Edmonton despite the party's gains in east European wheat-belt ridings in east-central Alberta.[162]

Manning reacted with political astuteness to the voters' rebuff. He set up a royal commission to inquire into the specific allegations made by the opposition parties before and during the election. The commission was headed initially by Justice H.J. Macdonald of the Supreme Court of Alberta, who later resigned because of ill health. The commission's senior counsel, J.C. Mahaffy, who had been associated with the Independents opposing Social Credit in the forties, became the new chairman.[163] When the commission reported in July 1956, the government proclaimed itself as having been exonerated of all wrongdoing.[164]

This claim was technically correct: the commission found no hard evidence that anyone in the government or the civil service had lined his own pockets thanks to particular government deals. But its detailed comments on the allegations suggested slack management throughout the government. For example, land purchases were often made by means of informal negotiations between ministers or civil servants, on the one hand, and landowners, on the other, often without any independent appraisals having been made.[165] Thus it was hardly surprising that some might suspect that friends of the government might be getting a better deal in land arrangements than others. The commission called for all land purchases to be centralized in one department, under the direction of 'a competent and experienced person' who would, as a general rule, have independent appraisals conducted.[166] The opposition had suggested that Manning himself had been a beneficiary of the lax arrangements regarding land sales when the Mines and Minerals Department expropriated some of his land; but the commission flatly disagreed.[167]

The informality regarding land acquisitions was found to apply to some extent to the awarding of highway contracts. The commission rejected as unfounded the specific opposition allegations that certain individuals and firms had received benefits because of their government connections, but the commissioners called for an arm's-length system of awarding contracts in which ministerial interference (which had led to the opposition's suspicions) would be disallowed.[168] Similarly the commissioners called for arm's-length dealings between government purchasing officials and firms wishing to do business with the government. The commission, although it believed the officials who claimed they had given no special treatment to Alberta Ytong because of its connection with Norman Tanner, was disturbed that this firm had paid expenses for departmental representatives to view the use of its materials in several countries. It recommended that only the government should pay the costs of officials' visits outside the province.[169] Finally, the commission concluded there was no evidence that pressure had been placed on treasury branch officials to grant loans to MLAS with insufficient collateral. None the less, it noted, branch officials might feel under pressure to grant such loans even without direct pressure being applied. The treasury branches, it recommended, should have tougher, formal rules regarding the granting of loans.[170]

The informality of government operations at this time was obvious from the commission's report. Although the commission did not deal with the further issue of how the government went about hiring the officials who, along with the ministers, operated this informal system, the fact was that patronage and nepotism were rife throughout government operations. Aberhart, in 1940, indicated his unwillingness to hire government opponents even for such positions as labourers, stenographers, and truck drivers.[171] Little changed until the 1960s, when strict legislation, enacted in 1959, created a relatively well-defined selection procedure. The director of personnel, writing to the provincial treasurer in 1961, was blunt about the situation before 1959:

In the absence of proper standards and procedures for measuring ability, the weight of personal influence tended to dominate appointments and it frequently made itself felt, not only through the medium of the Ministers and MLAs, but also through departmental officials from Deputy Minister to those of much lower rank who knew how to pull the proper strings in order to help their friends and relatives who wanted to enter the provincial service. The fact of the matter was that, except in particular cases where proper qualifications and capability were clearly essential, there was little systematic or recognizable control over appointments, either by the Ministers or anyone else.[172]

The result, claimed the director of personnel, was a bloated civil service of dubious overall competence. He noted that Alberta's proportion of civil servants per capita was higher than in other Canadian provinces, but not because more services were being provided: 'There is every indication however that the relatively high figures for this province are attributable to the past poverty of our employee recruitment and selection efforts.'[173]

But the casual, nepotistic character of government operations had not been the target of the opposition in 1955. Opposition charges were clearly ones of corruption in specific instances of government operations, and the commission ruled that no acceptable evidence of these improprieties existed. The government moved relatively quickly to implement the commission's recommendations, and the opposition's best case against the government began to dissipate; the opposition itself would largely be dissipated in the 1959 provincial election.

The results of the 1955 election proved the benefits of a strong opposition in a parliamentary system. Premier Manning demonstrated a willingness to act on some of the opposition's long-standing complaints, particularly regarding aid to municipalities. The tightening up of government procurement and hiring policies would also not likely have occurred without the election of the large opposition group in 1955.

As earlier noted, the government continued rhetorically to suggest that municipalities must shoulder much of their own costs in areas where they provided services, and it refused, for example, to pay the full costs of relief despite the large federal grants for social assistance. But the government agreed to provide the municipalities with a third of the revenues it received from oil royalties. In 1957 it also partly yielded to municipal complaints about being forced into the public land market and established the Alberta Municipal Financing Corporation, 'a non-profit corporation to assist in municipal financing by purchase and sale of municipal securities at lowest possible cost, and to provide a convenient and accessible means to the people of the province of investing in the debentures and other securities of provincial municipalities.'[174] The AMFC served as a provincial banker for at least part of the municipalities' borrowing requirements, and the province expanded the corporation's usefulness to the municipalities during the 1957 session by allowing them to receive loans from it for local hospital requirements.[175] In 1960 the province legislated government guarantees on the borrowings and securities of the corporation.[176]

It was in the area of education, however, as we have seen, that Social Credit made its biggest financial commitments in the late fifties. The Social Credit League, worried about the long-term meaning of the 1955 election results, sponsored a poll in November and December 1956, which sounded Albertans' attitudes closely. The poll found that 53 per cent of those polled were prepared to vote Social Credit in a provincial election, a gain of 7 per cent for the government since the June 1955 election. Indeed, 76 per cent had a favourable opinion of the government; 52 per cent indicated Manning as their choice for premier, while surprisingly only 5 per cent picked Prowse and 1 per cent picked Roper (35 per cent expressed no preference).[177] It was only in the education area that some unease with government policy surfaced. The royal commission appointed months after the poll was conducted, and the government's commitment to spend massively to implement commission recommendations indicated government willingness to mollify criticisms in an area of vulnerability.

The 1956 poll results reflected the general satisfaction of Albertans during a time of prosperity. Asked to indicate 'two or three matters [which] are the most important to people of Alberta,' none mentioned unemployment or the cost of living, a gap that would have been unthinkable twenty or even ten years earlier. Even the development of natural resources received a mention from only 31 per cent of respondents, whereas education was mentioned by 73 per cent and medical services by 54 per cent. When individuals were asked to list purposes for which government revenues from oil and gas should be spent, 61 per cent included education, 54 per cent the highway system, and 45 per cent aid to municipalities. Only 13 per cent mentioned the citizens' dividend, despite the fact that the government had committed itself to implementing such a dividend.[178] Again such a result would have been unlikely in 1936 or 1946. It is no wonder that the province paid out citizens' dividends for only two years; obviously most people believed that resource money was better spent on government services than on pay-outs to individual citizens.

The government's recovered popularity was aided by the half-hearted character of the opposition attack in the legislature. Despite its size, the opposition appeared to develop few coherent themes. If the poll results are to be believed, the opposition might have had difficulty in doing so. The province's economy was dangerously dependent on oil and gas revenues and the energy industry was largely controlled by foreigners, but the Social Credit poll concluded that only 'a small minority' cared about foreign domination. 'Primarily voters want a speed-up in development of resources so the resulting revenues will be a means of tax relief and a source of funds for expanded government services.'[179] Some 27 per cent of Albertans qualified the province's handling of Alberta's oil and gas resources as good and 38 per cent qualified it as fairly good. Only 11 per cent said the government record was not too good, 3 per cent claimed it was poor, while 21 per cent had no opinion on the subject.[180]

J. Harper Prowse seemed to flag as Manning, learning lessons from the 1955 election, proceeded to incorporate most of the opposition's demands into legislation. Prowse had long been frustrated by the egregious interference of the federal Liberals in provincial affairs, and the growing unpopularity of the federal Liberals reflected on the provincial party. Dispirited, he resigned as party leader in 1958 to establish a legal career.[181] His replacement, J. Grant MacEwan, while a venerable Alberta institution in his own right, was a gentle man who could not clearly delineate how his party's positions overall or on specific issues differed from the government's.

The 1959 election gave Social Credit its biggest seat victory to date. Sixty-one of sixty-five seats went to the government, one each to the Liberals and Conservatives, one to a Coalition candidate, and the final seat to the old Douglasite R.D. Ansley. It was a distorted legislature since Social Credit had, in fact, received only 55 per cent of the votes with which it had taken 94 per cent of the seats.

For the Liberals, receiving fewer than half the votes they had received in 1955, the election was a rout. The Conservatives, benefiting from Albertans' positive assessment of the federal Conservative government elected in 1957 and re-elected in 1958, almost tripled their vote, although the first-past-the-post system converted their 24 per cent of the vote into only one seat. As for the CCF, it received a derisive 4 per cent of the vote and no seats. Indeed, it contested only thirty-two of sixty-five seats.[182] This party could find little favour now in a province where issues such as economic diversification, unemployment, public ownership, and foreign ownership had little resonance. The party retreated into concerns about foreign policy, which perhaps interested even fewer Albertans.[183] The 1959 result, more than any other, tended to make Alberta appear a one-party province, even if almost half of all Albertans were still unwilling to vote for the government party. It was, in any case, a shell of a party that stood at the base of the popular Manning government.

As we saw in chapters 3 and 4, the radicals in the Social Credit League gradually left the organization as it became clear that the government had little sympathy for their views regarding treatment of the unemployed or of united fronts of left-wing forces. Aberhart's disregard of convention resolutions and Manning's embrace of extreme anti-socialist views caused a great shake-up in the league. The Douglasites, meanwhile, having embraced wholeheartedly the new pro-capitalist line, found themselves more or less purged from the league in 1947 and 1948.

The departure of both the radicals and the Douglasites left few paid-up members in the league despite the government's electoral popularity. In 1950, only 3692 members renewed; in 1951, 3991; in 1954, 3520. Only in election years, as prospective candidates brought in personal supporters, did membership sales blossom; 17,773 members were registered in 1952 and 10,782 in 1959. But even these figures paled against those of the late thirties.[184] When one considers that membership in the league was an aid to those who sought work in the patronage-infested provincial civil service, the figures on membership are truly unimpressive.

None the less, Manning, while no more willing to be dictated to by a party organization than was his predecessor, did attempt to make the league constituency organizations more relevant. Changes in the League's constitution made in 1947 removed the provincial advisory board, which in conjunction with local constituency delegates chose party candidates under Aberhart. This system had given the party leader a great deal of latitude in choosing local candidates. After 1947, however, the constituency organizations would choose their own candidates, the same practice followed by other parties in the province at the time.[185]

Interestingly, the revised constitution also struck out a 'principle of association' section which, among other things, had committed the league to such principles as national non-contributory state health insurance, home-building loans 'at the cost of financing,' 'just prices including parity of prices to primary producers' and 'fair wages to workers.'[186] Manning, having embraced the capitalist system with a passion, did not want to include socialist-sounding rhetoric in the party's constitution. He may have also hoped to attract conservatives who had once shunned Social Credit.

The apathy of Albertans towards the party worried league members. One wrote Manning in 1947 to note that the study groups, once the core of the movement, had ceased to exist in Edmonton and that young people were simply not being recruited to the movement.[187] A resolution passed at the annual convention in 1951 noted that neither the groups nor the constituency associations were active in the rural areas. The result was that 'hardly any of our younger generation or the newcomers to the province have any understanding of the Social Credit proposals and their applicability to the better distribution of the nation's productive wealth.'[188] But the concern, while shared by party officials, led to little change. This was not a period of political activism in Alberta, and no party enjoyed a mass membership.

Still, the old radicalism had not been completely extinguished. The 1951 convention, for example, debated resolutions in favour of state medicine, an increase in provincial supplements to the old-age pension, state automobile insurance, state ownership of hydroelectric utilities, provincial subsidies to co-operative building associations, and the establishment by the province of old-age homes in every constituency. Significantly, none of these resolutions passed, and many failed even to come to a vote.[189]

The conventions had indeed become little more than gatherings of government cheer-leaders. Although some delegates always balked, the conventions were carefully stage-managed, with most key resolutions to be debated coming from constituencies represented by cabinet ministers. The cabinet and the party officials took pains that most of convention time was given over to either congratulating the government on programs already undertaken or extolling it to take initiatives that, in fact, it had already decided to take.[190]

The low membership and the general apathy, however, did not deprive the league of the ability to organize effectively for elections. As Owen Anderson notes, the party became 'highly electoral in orientation, in many cases holding only annual meetings when there was no electoral activity, as contrasted to the former frequent and regular meetings and activities.'[191] The party charged its small membership only one dollar per year as a membership fee,[192] but its pro-business bias allowed it to raise sufficient funds to employ two full-time organizers, sponsor regular broadcasts by the leaders, and advertise effectively at election time.[193] From 1956 on, it was also able to produce a party organ, called *The Busy Bee*.

But an electoral machine and a social crusade are not easily compatible, and Social Credit's protestations of being more than just another conservative party increasingly sounded hollow. As it happened, however, both the provincial and national leaders remained ardent monetary reformers at the same time that their views on most subjects other than monetary policy placed them well to the right of the mainstream of all other parties, including the Progressive Conservatives.

'Godless Materialism Condemned: Convention Speakers Urge Return to God as Necessary to Survival.' So ran a front-page headline in the *Canadian Social Crediter* in December 1950.[194] With the secular radicals and Douglasites out of the organization, religious elements who had been attracted to the Social Credit League because of its evangelical Christian leadership became more prominent in the league overall. The league's peculiar philosophies were wrapped in the gospels and made sacred.

Manning indeed was motivated by religious ideals. We noted in chapter 1 David Elliott's view that Aberhart, all the while claiming that his religious fundamentalism remained unchanged, had drifted in the thirties towards views that resembled the social gospel. Manning, in contrast, while perhaps appearing at the time as Aberhart's faithful acolyte, does not appear to have embraced social gospel views comfortably. Like many other fundamentalists, he viewed humans as essentially alone in a struggle to achieve eternal salvation and believed that a collectivist state belittled this struggle and made individuals more vulnerable to behaviour that might lead to eternal damnation. As one commentator explained: 'Socialism, to Manning, is a system which largely prevents the individual from attaining the state of grace and hence salvation, because it proposes an economic doctrine of state control of means of production, which de-emphasizes the individual struggle for salvation, and a social doctrine of giving to the individual societal benefits such as free medical care and a guaranteed income, which breeds idleness and hence allows the evil tendencies of the individual to come to the fore thereby causing a breakdown of his relationship with God.'[195]

Manning, in his public addresses outside of his weekly Bible-thumping 'Back to the Bible Hour' radio program, attempted to avoid religious language and to explain his goals in secular terms. Still, these speeches were as consistent with evangelical notions as politically feasible. The function of government, he wrote in *The Busy Bee* in December 1956, was: 'to administer the public affairs of the electorate in accordance with policies dictated by the people themselves through their elected representatives. It is not the function of government to invade the fields of individual and co-operative enterprise, to assume responsibilities which rightfully belong to the individual citizen or interfere with the rights of individuals except to insure the equal rights of others and the effective implementation of those policies which the people themselves have requested and approved through their elected representatives.'[196] The provision of social welfare was to respect this anti-collectivist bias and, in a sense, to ensure that the individual achieved salvation on his own. In secular (and sexist) terms, Manning put it thusly: 'A major objective of organized society should be to assist each citizen to obtain through his own enterprise sufficient financial resources to enable him to obtain for himself and his dependents an acceptable standard of social welfare without dependence on State welfare services. To the extent that this is impossible, society collectively must assume the cost of an acceptable standard of social services to bring such services within the financial range of each individual citizen.'[197]

But in the process, where did individualism end and state collectivism seem to take over? Manning argued that it was where the state imposed a monopoly on a service that the sinful philosophy of state collectivism scored a victory. He seemed rather unconcerned about the economic power of a private monopoly such as Calgary Power or of the oil cartel, whose cartelization was actually abetted by the policies of a government agency. But he rejected public monopolies even if his government did not take politically foolish risks such as the denationalization of the provincial telephone monopoly (a monopoly that applied everywhere except in Edmonton, which ran its own municipal phone company). When a letter writer in 1948 complained that the provincial cancer clinic, which provided free cancer treatment, was 'socialistic,' Manning replied:

'... under the system that we are endeavouring to operate in this Province these services do not eliminate similar services being provided by individual medical practitioners or institutions. In other words, under a Socialist state the ultimate end is a state monopoly over all business enterprises and social services whereas under a free economy such state services as provided operate side by side with similar services available to those deserving them from private practitioners or institutions.'[198]

As we note in the next chapter, this view would, in the sixties, cause a bitter conflict over medicare between the Alberta government and the federal government. Indeed the Alberta government, with its opposition to centralization dating from *The Case for Alberta*, was at odds on general principles with much of the drift of federal policy in the 1950s, although it was not until the sixties that Manning fashioned a thoroughgoing critique of federal policy in terms other than constitutional ones.

In the fifties, the provincial critique was simple: the federal government was taking far more from the province than it was giving back. Federal revenue collections in the province were said to have risen 252 per cent from 1948 to 1955, with only a marginal increase in the province's take from the federal-provincial tax rental agreement. Under this agreement, the provinces received back a negotiated percentage of federal income tax collections. Manning, aware that his provincial Liberal detractors blamed the province for every rise in municipal property tax, liked to turn the argument around by blasting the federal Liberal government for taking money out of the province which, he claimed, could be used to help the municipalities.[199] At the same time, as we have seen, ministers attacked the municipal authorities as loose spenders.

The voice of the Alberta government in Ottawa was, of course, the federal Social Credit caucus, which, before it was wiped out in 1958, consisted mainly of Alberta representatives with a few British Columbians. British Columbia had elected a Social Credit administration in 1952 after its governing Liberal-Conservative coalition had fallen apart; the example of the successful Manning administration, not Social Credit monetary policies, attracted conservative-minded British Columbians, but they proved less willing than their Alberta counterparts to elect Social Crediters federally as well as provincially.[200]

Solon Low and his caucus continued to act as the fearless voices against the merciless conspiracy, from which, at Manning's behest, they had exonerated the Jews. Their journal, the *Canadian Social Crediter*, as noted earlier, attacked marketing boards and trade unions and any other manifestation of co-operative (always called 'collectivist' or 'dictatorial' in their lexicon) action by ordinary citizens. The CCF, noted this worthy journal in 1955, was 'Communism ... in Short Pants.' 'Is there any difference,' asked the editor, 'between the CCF and the

Labour Progressive Party (Communist)?' His answer: 'Only in the mechanics of organization. One does not have to have a Communist membership card to follow the Communist line.'[201] The cause of this outburst was the unwillingness of half of the CCF caucus to support the rearming of West Germany and its entry into NATO. Communists opposed West German rearmament, and half the CCF caucus did as well; therefore ... Such logic emanated continually from the federal caucus and its party organ.

According to John Barr, Manning, 'his rhetoric notwithstanding ... went along with the general trend to big government; in fact, he owed an important part of his success as a politician to the fact that he knew when to yield to it, when to resist it, and when to seem to resist it.'[202] Although this observation has some surface truth, it seems a bit vacuous to dismiss Manning's administration as simply another example of 'big government' and to find no connection between the rhetoric and the reality. In fact, the Manning regime, true to its word, followed a pay-as-you-go policy and resisted calls for government regulation of the oil and gas industry (other than the regulations which the industry wanted itself), for marketing boards, for rent controls, for government housing construction programs, for subsidies to new industries, for free hospitalization and medical care, for public power, and for complete provincial responsibility for relief. The government largely limited itself to the provision of educational services, the building of highways, and the provision of social services to those deemed to be in need. Its spending habits were so conservative that many elements of the business community believed it did too little to aid municipalities with education costs and the costs of providing the infrastructure for expanding populations. In the late fifties, it took steps to obviate such criticism, although it continued to denounce the lack of a pay-as-you-go policy on the part of the municipalities.

Of course, with revenues so flush, the Alberta government could build up reserves and yet spend so much money in the areas where it chose to spend as to surpass expenditures per capita in education, social services, and highway-building in all other provinces. But this spending seems less proof of 'big government' than of 'rich government.' In the 1960s, as we see in chapter 6, Premier Manning began to present Alberta's approach as an alternative to that of the federal government and of most other provinces.

In the meantime, whatever Canadians in other provinces thought of Social Credit, the Manning government both reflected and influenced changing public opinion in Alberta about the role of government. The half-life decline of left-wing voting in each election after 1944 coincided with the growth of prosperity in the province and declining fears of unemployment and price gouging, fears which once had rallied farmers and workers to parties identified with opposition to corporations. The decline of the small farmers and the disappearance of unemployed organizations and the coal miners removed the major radical players from the economic and political arena. The oil industry workers, white collar and blue collar, and the capital-intensive farm owners joined with the business groups in applauding the Manning message about the respective roles of business and government: in the 1950s, the system seemed to be working. Presumably most Albertans did not share the Social Credit leaders' views about conspiracies and few seemed anxious to participate actively in the Social Credit League. But in the Cold War environment of the period, the general lines of Manning's ideas were well received and a right-wing political culture replaced the left-wing, or at least rebellious, political culture of the pre-war period. There was still distrust of Ottawa, not because it gave the province too little at a time of need, as people complained in the thirties, but because it took revenues away and thus limited the oil companies and Manning from doing their unfettered best to make the province even richer. By the end of another decade, however, while distrust of Ottawa remained unchanged, disillusionment with Social Credit began to creep in.

6   Defending Jerusalem
and Spreading the Gospel:
The Late Manning Period

The very heart of true Christianity is that an individual who has been made a new
creature by a miraculous spiritual new birth reflects that spiritual experience in
everything he thinks and says and does.

There is no way in which a truly born-again Christian can divorce his own nature from
any phase of his activities from that time on nor would he ever desire to do so. It has
always been my belief that there is great need for Christian men and women in public
life for, after all, if we are not going to have our public affairs guarded by those who
appreciate and know the importance of spiritual matters, how can we expect other than
more materialism and more godlessness to develop in our land. In my opinion, it is
completely contrary to the Scriptures that Christians, who are intended to be the salt of
the earth should avoid the field of public life where the influence of their Christian
experience is so desperately needed.[1]

This viewpoint, expressed by Manning in 1964, seems to confirm the
observation made in the previous chapter that Manning's political views cannot
be divorced from his religious views. Manning, after all, throughout his
premiership and for years afterwards, hosted radio's 'Canada's National Back to
the Bible Hour,' which featured hard-line evangelical views. The show included
taped sermons from other evangelical leaders across North America,[2] and among
his friends Manning counted Billy Graham, the famed evangelical showman.
Indeed Manning led a drive to have Graham do a cross-Canada Crusade for
Christ tour as a Canadian Centennial project. As he wrote Graham in December
1965, after having formed a national invitational committee: 'We believe there is
in Canada today, as we approach the end of our first century, a unique set of
circumstances which makes this the opportune time for an all-out effort to bring
about a genuine national spiritual awakening. It is our earnest hope and fervent

prayer that God will lead you and your assistants to spearhead such a national effort for which we believe the need is great and the time ripe.'[3]

Manning was thus actively involved in bringing religious ideas into the secular arena of an event such as the Centennial. Although he maintained, as a political figure, friendly relations with churchmen of varying denominations, he shared the evangelical view that the mainstream churches had gone soft on the Good Books. He wrote one American fan: 'There is no doubt whatever in my mind as to the absolute infallibility of Holy Writ and the responsibility of every born again believer to contend earnestly for the faith once delivered unto the saints. Radio affords an opportunity of reaching many with the pure, unadulterated Gospel of grace, who otherwise are not being reached from our present day pulpit.'[4]

Manning, as we saw in chapter 5, also preached a secular gospel – a gospel of individualism – which to him related closely to the Gospels themselves. This gospel was, in his mind, challenged by the pernicious collectivist doctrines, whose proponents had formed a diabolical conspiracy to promote unrest in order to forward their views. By the sixties, Manning was convinced that the declared socialists were no longer the only enemy of individualism. Just as the mainstream churches had gone soft and fallen almost into the camp of the unbelievers, so the old-line political parties had let down their guard and dangerously embraced the socialist philosophy, often without considering the implications of actions taken for reasons of political expediency. Increasingly, Manning felt the need to draw a line between Alberta's views on the role of government and the views expressed by Liberals and Conservatives, both federally and provincially. In the present chapter, I look at how Manning attempted to develop a 'social conservative' style of governance for Alberta and to spread the philosophy of the Alberta government beyond provincial borders. The chapter begins with an examination of the province's social service set-up and the clash between the values it expressed and the values implied in federal programs of the sixties.

Alberta in the 1950s, as noted in the previous chapter, was outspending other Canadian provinces in the areas of education and social services. In the 1960s, Social Credit continued to expand these services significantly. Education costs, which had accounted for 15.1 per cent of government expenditure in 1956, accounted for 20.4 per cent in 1966 and then peaked at 33.4 per cent in 1971, the last year of Social Credit power. Health and welfare expenditures climbed from 16.2 per cent of the provincial budget in 1956 to 26.5 per cent in 1966 and 28.5 per cent in 1971. Some 27 per cent of all new jobs created in Alberta from 1961 to 1971 were in the area of non-commercial services such as hospitals, educational institutions, welfare organizations, religious organizations, and private households.[5]

Economist Ed Shaffer, commenting on this impressive growth of the government sector, noted:

The Social Credit government could have used the funds [from royalties] to lessen income inequalities and to reduce poverty. But this was not done because such a redistribution would undermine the incentives of the market system – income inequality is essential for the survival and the efficient operation of capitalism. Therefore they decided to spend the funds on social services in such a way as to minimize the redistributional effects.

The Socreds greatly expanded the health care system, providing free medical services to all segments of the population. This expansion unquestionably benefited the working class, the farmers and the poor much more than the upper class. It represented a limited redistribution of income with a minimum impact on incentives. The Socreds also expanded post-secondary educational facilities. The chief beneficiaries of this policy were the middle and upper classes.[6]

This summary may sound like an unkind Marxist assessment of the Social Credit record, but it is quite consistent with the government's own assessment of its approach. In its blistering 1967 brief to the federal government regarding the *Carter Royal Commission Report on Taxation*, the Manning government rejected notions of direct government intervention to achieve redistribution of income and stressed the importance of individual incentives, even relating the educational system to Manning's 'levelling-up' and 'trickling-down' theories of wealth creation and the attack on poverty. Echoing many business briefs on the Carter report,[7] the Alberta government said: 'We agree with the Commission's suggestion that society is committed to improving the well-being of Canadians having the least economic power. However we feel this objective can best be achieved by attempting to maximize economic growth. The Commission's approach, which would penalize Canadians for trying to improve their lot, is inconsistent with the education and training policies of various levels of government.'[8] Later in the brief, citing the Alberta government's *White Paper on Human Resource Development*, prepared earlier that year, Manning proclaimed: 'While human resources development demands top priority, the cold hard fact remains that the amount of materials and finances which can be committed to this task are strictly proportional to the level of physical resource development. It is totally unrealistic to be concerned with social development and at the same time to be unconcerned about economic development. It is unrealistic to make demands relative to human resources development without giving consideration to ways and means of stimulating the increases in physical resources development required to make humanitarian proposals physically possible and economically feasible.'[9]

At the provincial as well as the federal level, such an ideology dictated, in Manning's view, a rather limited intervention of government into the free market-place (although, as we have seen, the government's oil 'conservation' policy and the defence of the Calgary Power monopoly suggested that the market-place was somewhat riddled with monopolistic and oligopolistic practices). And to ensure that there were adequate deterrents to runaway costs that might result in tax increases, which would dampen incentives to earn large incomes, this ideology also dictated a great deal of care in the establishment of social welfare and health programs.

In the health area, that meant medical premiums and hospital deterrent fees. In the fifties, the hospital fees had been a dollar a day plus full payment of hospital services regarded as 'extra' by the province. In the sixties, the fee climbed to two dollars a day for active patients and a dollar fifty per day for chronic patients. According to Health Minister J. Donovan Ross, the deterrent fee was a 'co-insurance' payment, 'a partial payment of the total operating costs for insured benefits that through time and custom has been a desirable means of patient participation towards the operational costs of hospitals.'[10] The advantages of co-insurance, according to Premier Manning, were: 'First, it leaves with the individual obtaining the service at least some measure of personal financial responsibility and, secondly, such a fee minimizes patients staying in a hospital longer than necessary.'[11]

Similarly, medical premiums required that patients place upfront, each month, monies that ensured them specified medical services. This policy was seen as superior to an across-the-board medicare program financed from general revenues and thus supposedly disguising costs to Canadians and contributing to over-use of the medical services available. The Alberta medical scheme, interestingly, was implemented in Alberta in 1963, shortly after Saskatchewan's CCF-NDP government legislated a universal government insurance program that precipitated a doctors' strike in 1962. The Alberta scheme, by contrast, was voluntary and involved little more than the province's establishing an insurance plan via private insurers in Alberta who were willing to accept the maximum premium fixed by the government in consultation with the College of Physicians and Surgeons. The college, which previously had organized a similar scheme under its own aegis, endorsed the government plan, which presumably, the college hoped, would fend off advocates of the Saskatchewan scheme, under which the government was the sole insurer as well as the arbiter of doctors' fees.[12]

To counter criticisms that the Alberta Medical Insurance Plan would be available only to those with the means to pay premiums, the government announced that it would pay provincial subsidies on a sliding scale to citizens with taxable incomes below five hundred dollars.[13] This plan was indeed one of 'limited redistribution.'

The means test, added to a sliding scale for degrees of poverty, was also applied to provincial welfare. The amended Public Welfare Act of 1960 merged mothers' allowances, widows' pensions, disabled persons' pensions, and supplementary allowances for pensioners into one means-tested program. The municipalities would no longer be expected to pay any portion of the above programs. The legislation proclaimed as its purpose to ensure 'that no resident of Alberta lacks such things, goods and services as are essential to his health and well-being, including food, clothing, shelter and essential surgical, medical, optical, dental and other remedial treatment, care and attention.'[14] From the government's viewpoint, the groups to be aided were the unemployed unemployables – those who, because of age or physical or mental health, were unlikely to find work if they sought it – and mothers with custody of dependent children.[15] Once again, in its determination of recipients of social allowances, the government maintained the notion that incentives to work should not be interfered with.

In practice, all of the desperately poor were not cared for by the province, despite the stated aim of the 1960 Welfare Act amendments. For starters, under the Mothers' Allowance Act, women living common-law were denied aid when they ended up looking after their children on their own. Despite having been made aware that this practice caused cases of hardship,[16] the Manning government, governed by the moral code of the conservative-minded, did not change the rules when the Mothers' Allowance Act provisions became part of the Public Welfare Act. In one case, a woman with four children in her care was denied temporary relief while her common-law husband had an operation because, in the opinion of the director of the Public Assistance branch, the parents 'were contributing to delinquency of these children in that they were living together illegally.'[17]

Not only those living in sin were left high and dry. A woman whose legal husband had died after a thirteen-month stay in hospital wrote Manning that she was 'left with nothing but the clothes on my back and doctor and hospital bills.' The hospital bill was $417, a whopping sum for a woman whose job as a hospital ward aide grossed her only $158 a month in 1963. Forty-six years old and under doctor's care herself, she asked Manning in desperation if the government could not help her in some way. He answered her letter by suggesting she contact the Canadian Cancer Society to see if they could help her.[18] There were many others who, like this woman, found that 'co-insurance' was beyond their means when tragedy struck.[19]

Other people complained equally bitterly that circumstances made it impossible for them to pay their bills. For example, an old-age pensioner in Black

Diamond wrote Manning that she had no water supply in her home. She had had a well, but the municipality 'drained it dry' when it built a waterworks. On her seventy-dollar-a-month income she could not afford to install water and sewer services in her one-room shack. Yet, ironically, she was none the less required to pay the municipal water tax.[20] Manning's reply indicated a certain myopia about the position of those left behind in oil-rich Alberta:

There is no doubt the modernization of our towns in Alberta is causing a problem to some of our people who are on fixed incomes, such as old-age pensioners who find it difficult to afford the necessary improvements to their homes ...

The only suggestion I can make is that possibly you might wish to approach your Treasury Branch or Bank with a view to discussing the possibility of a loan for the improvements required to your home ... I would also point out that your municipality, by installing water and sewer services, has greatly enhanced the sale value of property in the entire town which is even reflected in those properties, such as your own, not presently connected to the water services.[21]

One group of Albertans whose property values were not increasing very much were the native people of isolated communities. Apart from a small number of bands lucky enough to have oil underfoot in commercial quantities, Alberta's native people were left untouched by the province's post-war prosperity. Indeed, as late as the end of 1966, many poor, isolated settlements had not yet been placed within the ambit of the welfare department despite the assurances of the 1960 legislation that all Albertans in need would be cared for.[22]

The Manning government, in its latter years, did, to its credit, decide that something must be done to lift native people out of their poverty. It is, however, misleading, if not nonsensical, to imply, as does John J. Barr, that the Social Credit government was responsible for 'the quiet development of nothing less than a social revolution among Alberta's native peoples.' For Barr, James Whitford, the head of the modest community development program launched by the government in 1964, is a great liberating hero: 'Right from the start, and somewhat deliberately, Whitford and his men were a thorn in the side of a good part of the Alberta establishment. They antagonized Indian Affairs officials, churchmen, white merchants, provincial civil servants, and often the Indians themselves. They were cast in the role of "change agents" and they threw themselves against barriers of ignorance, apathy and bureaucratic inertia with great dedication. Their objective was nothing less than the destruction of the legal and administrative relationships and racial attitudes perpetuating native dependency – the liberation of both white and native.'[23]

In fact, the objective of 'Whitford and his men' was 'nothing less' than the integration of native people into the Euro-Canadian mainstream, and some of the antagonism they incited resulted from their contempt for native culture and values which, in their opinion, were the cause of native poverty rather than strengths that might point the way to liberation. Indeed, in their emphasis on native people as individuals requiring economic liberation, they shared Manning's world-view, in which there were only individuals facing their Maker and collectivities were incidental. The first community development officer hired, Terry Garvin, a former RCMP officer who worked in the Fort McMurray area, was proud of the assimilationist attitude in the program. In an article he co-authored for a magazine in December 1966, he spoke proudly of how he had rid the Fort McKay band of an unpopular chief by demonstrating that the man had been fired by his corporate employer, Bechtel, for bootlegging. At the meeting where the chief was exposed, the people were asked: 'Was this the kind of leader they wanted? How could he talk to them about good work habits?'[24]

Garvin's boss, James Whitford, shared these assimilationist views. In July 1966 the Alberta government had been shocked by a demonstration at the legislature of 56 Indians and Métis from the remote settlement of Wabasca, population 1400, situated 278 miles northeast of Edmonton and 90 miles northeast of Slave Lake. The people of this community, which was about evenly split between Treaty Indians and Métis, had formed a timber co-operative in 1965 'in the hope of logging and milling a million or more feet of timber so as to convince Forestry officials to give them a special reserve of land for timber milling and logging.'[25] This bid for economic independence, however, failed to prevent the Forestry officials from granting the land to other companies, with Federated Co-op receiving the lion's share of the land reserves. Angrily, some local people chose to demonstrate in Edmonton to draw attention to what they considered to be unjust treatment. A community development officer had been posted in Wabasca since 1 November 1965, and naturally some government people worried that their own employees might be instigating the locals to revolt. But Whitford made it plain that he had not supported the demonstration tactic; in fact, he disagreed with the native people's cause in this instance. The government had offered to train local native people to operate and service the heavy equipment involved in harvesting local timber and to ensure that they received many of the jobs that the logging would create. But it had rejected their insistence on local control over the resources because the government position was 'that most people in Canada are in the same position; hardly anyone outside of farmers own the resources which they work to obtain their livelihood.'[26] Whitford sided with the government, claiming that 'the weakness of the Wabasca position lies in believing that they must control the natural resources which they are harvesting in order to be truly independent and free citizens.' Better communication by the government of its position was seen to be the solution.[27] Clearly there was little understanding and less support from Whitford for collectivist views that flowed from historical traditions. If Albertans as a whole were prepared to accept outside control of their natural resources, why did the native people get so hung up on the control issue?

Large pockets of poverty continued to dot the map of Alberta, even within the two major cities. The Manning government, in its latter years, proved willing at least to research the causes of this poverty,[28] but as its brief regarding the Carter Commission and its reaction to the Wabasca incident, respectively, indicated, its notion was that solutions lay in allowing the private sector to expand the overall economy and in using the public sector to assimilate individuals to the values and skills necessary to succeed in a market-place – based economy. In the view of the Alberta government, however, federal governments of the post-war period, both Liberal and Conservative, did not share its perspectives on wealth creation and distribution.

In the thirties, antagonism between Alberta and the federal government had developed because the latter disallowed some of the Social Credit administration's radical proposals. The result had been demands, made in *The Case for Alberta*, for a strengthening of provincial powers relative to federal power. By the late fifties, while the Alberta government still battled centralization of power, its argumentation had changed: in its view the federal government had now become the dangerous experimenter. The range of irritants in federal-provincial relations was broad and, on the surface, may simply seem to be the result of long-standing regional grievances. But while the regional factor cannot be discounted, the ideological factor should be sharply in focus. After all, neither the Saskatchewan nor Manitoba governments of this period were particularly out of harmony with federal thinking (at least while the CCF-NDP remained in power in Saskatchewan). The Alberta Social Credit goverment, unlike the Lesage Liberal government in Quebec from 1960 to 1966, was not so much interested in building up the power of the provincial state relative to the federal state apparatus as it was in downgrading in general the role of government in society.

Some of the province's complaints did seem to stem from the self-interested perspectives of a wealthy province. For example, Manning had attempted without success to convince both Liberal and Conservative federal governments that natural resource revenues ought not to be counted alongside revenues from taxation in the calculation of equalization grants. Alberta, as the highest-revenue receiver, was excluded from such grants, but as Manning continually pointed out, if oil royalties were regarded separately from taxation revenues, the province's net revenues would be below the Canadian average and the province would receive equalization grants. Manning could not convince the federal administrations with which he dealt that, because the oil would eventually be gone, Alberta was being penalized in having these temporary revenues used to justify a larger federal take in taxes from the province than Alberta received back in federal spending.[29]

Less self-interested and more ideological was Alberta's campaign against taxation of privately owned public utilities while Crown-owned utilities went free of federal tax. After Quebec's nationalization of the remaining privately owned utilities in that province in 1962, Alberta was 'one of the few, if not the only province, in which the greater part of electric power is generated by private power companies.' Manning, having failed to convince the Diefenbaker government to exempt the private utility companies from corporate income tax, campaigned with the Liberals to achieve the same end. Finally in 1965, at a federal-provincial conference, Finance Minister Walter Gordon announced that his government would give in.[30]

Manning's campaign on this issue was more than just a defence of Calgary Power, the company with the near-monopoly over electrical power in Alberta (it excluded Edmonton and a few other municipalities). It was an example of his total opposition to government ownership of industry. His hard line on this issue was in evidence in a speech given to the annual convention of the (American) Northwest Electric Light and Power Association in September 1962: 'My contention is that it is foreign to the democratic government purpose and responsibility to be in the physical ownership and operation of industry of any kind. I quite appreciate that there is a line drawn by many between public utilities with their peculiar characteristics inherent in them and industry generally. But I submit if we are going to accept the premise that it is a responsibility of democratic government in free enterprise society to own and operate business, then where are we going to draw the line?'[31]

While Manning received satisfaction on the power company issue, he received no satisfaction at all in his ideological battles with the federal government over medical care. When the federal hospitalization program came into effect in 1958, provinces had their grants reduced if they charged hospital fees, since the purpose of the program was to guarantee hospital care for all. The Alberta government rejected the argument that hospital charges were a penalty against the sick and continued to charge its 'co-insurance' fee, arguing curiously that such fees were not qualitatively different from across-the-board hospital premiums charged to every household in other provinces.[32] But the change from a Conservative to a Liberal administration in Ottawa brought no change in attitude on this issue and the Alberta government refused to back down, claiming that Ottawa's approach 'discriminates against a system designed to minimize the abuse of hospital services and reduce the aggregate cost to the two levels of government.'[33]

The Alberta government regarded the federal government's increasing involvement in the medical field warily. When Judy LaMarsh, federal minister of national health and welfare, suggested a federal-provincial conference on mental retardation, Alberta Health Minister Dr J. Donovan Ross objected that this was an area solely of provincial responsibility. He added: 'I am becoming increasingly concerned with the intrusion into the provincial fields of responsibility by the federal government ... No doubt my sentiments may not be shared by other provinces, who too often are concerned with the possibilities of getting additional financial assistance from the Federal Treasury, rather than following out the principles contained in our major Dominion statute.'[34]

The report of the Conservative-appointed Royal Commission on Medical Care in 1965 and the Liberal government's favourable response to the recommendations made by Mr Justice Emmett Hall and his colleagues favouring a national universal health insurance program unsurprisingly provoked anger in Edmonton. While eventually several premiers would balk at the detailed medicare plan worked out by the federal government, Alberta stood alone in opposing a medicare scheme altogether. At the federal-provincial conference of first ministers in July 1965, Manning's ideological opposition to a medicare scheme was elaborated. According to the minutes of that meeting:

Mr. Manning stated that in his view the principles of universal compulsory application are unsound in a free society. He maintained that the individual should have the right to decide the manner in which he received medical care and he considered compulsory universal application as a violation of this principle. People would be forced to do things in a certain way by the state, and for this reason Alberta could not agree with the compulsory principle.

Mr. Manning also took issue with the suggestion that the state should pay the full costs of medical care; this was both fundamentally unsound and unnecessary. He believed that society collectively should be responsible for bringing the costs within the reach of the individual but the state's responsibility should be limited to this ...

With regard to the suggested elimination of the commercial and private medical insurance plans now in operation, Mr. Manning expressed the view that these have been satisfactory to their policy holders and it would be unwise to eliminate them from medical insurance since this would mean a further interjection of government into private business.[35]

Manning was no longer content simply to attempt to convince the federal authorities of his way of thinking or to leave national campaigning on the issue in the hands of the much-factionalized, ineffectual national Social Credit movement. He made himself available to the national media as a critic of the proposed medicare scheme and the philosophy which, to him, it exemplified. He justified this national campaign by a provincial premier on the grounds that socialism was being foisted on an unsuspecting public and those in the know had a duty to speak out. As he wrote an Ontario radio station manager: 'I appreciated receiving your recent letter regarding our efforts to help the people of this nation realize that they are being led, step by step, into a complete welfare state. I am convinced there is a large section of the Canadian people who are completely opposed to this latest move towards state regimentation and many more who would be equally as opposed if they were aware of the implications of such a program and what it ultimately will mean to them, as taxpayers. To get factual information to the public along this line is one of the most urgent and important of our present national needs. I certainly intend to do everything I can to help meet it.'[36]

As the language of the Alberta government's opposition to federal health policy indicated, the Manning administration regarded federal attitudes overall to be unhealthily socialistic and those of other provinces to be submissive and opportunistic. The tendency to put federal dollars into programs for economic development of depressed regions – beginning with the Diefenbaker government but accelerating under the Liberals – also irked Alberta. Manning had rejected a proposal by Manitoba Conservative Premier Duff Roblin at the provincial premiers' conference in 1962 that a national body be formed 'to analyze the provinces' problems of growth and development,' and 'to advise directions that would improve economic growth.' While Saskatchewan's CCF government responded positively to such a notion and even the Social Credit premier of British Columbia, W.A.C. Bennett, expressed interest, Manning despaired of finding economic approaches that could satisfy all provinces and scuttled the proposal.[37] He was, in particular, unhappy with the apparent willingness of the other provinces to countenance federal regional development proposals. Although the federal government included the Peace River area of Alberta as one of the underdeveloped areas eligible for special assistance to attract industry, Manning alone among the provincial premiers opposed the principle of the Area Development Program, started by the Liberals in 1963.[38] Having opposed subsidies to industry to attract investors to Alberta, Manning was reviled by programs in which the federal government intervened in the market-place to provide incentives to firms to establish in certain places. As he wrote Lester Pearson in June 1965: 'Our chief concern with this program lies in the fact that it is a form of subsidization to a portion of private industry which is in direct conflict with private enterprise ... the government now proposes to introduce legislation to provide outright grants to manufacturing and processing enterprises establishing or expanding in designated areas. This is not in keeping with the free enterprise concept and could well be in direct conflict with economic feasibility so important if Canada is to develop a solid competitive position in world markets.'[39]

In general, Manning's views on economic and social issues corresponded to those expressed by the conservative spokespersons of Canadian big business, particularly the oil company magnates, whom he had befriended over the years. For example, in a letter to Imperial Oil president W.O. Twaits in 1965, he noted his agreement with the oil executive's views on the unfairness in the application of various federal taxation policies.[40] Manning's most clear statement in this regard was the earlier-quoted statement to the federal government in opposition to the Carter Commission report. Unsurprisingly, since his political philosophy clashed so completely with that of the commission majority, Manning found little to commend in that report and in the apparent new interest on the part of the federal government to promote secondary industry at the expense of primary industry and to promote domestic investment over foreign investment. Regarding secondary industry, which would be promoted by reducing the inflated depletion allowances that limited taxation on the resource industry, Manning was mainly concerned with the impact on his province. Noting the commission's claim that investment lost to the resource sector would be made up by investment in manufacturing, the Alberta premier said bluntly: 'It is impossible to visualize new businesses locating in Alberta with total annual investments anywhere near $750,000,000, the current level of annual cash expenditures for oil and gas exploration and development.'[41]

Manning rejected attempts to limit foreign ownership and to use the tax system to discourage Canadian investments abroad rather than at home as unwarranted market-place interventions. But the likely impact on Alberta was a key consideration. He pointed out 'Alberta's heavy reliance on the continual inflow of foreign capital' and did not accept seriously notions that the energy industry could find sufficient domestic sources of capital.[42]

Finally, Manning rejected the capital gains tax proposed by the Carter Commission in line with the commission's overall philosophy that all forms of income should be treated equally for taxation purposes.[43] He complained that such a tax would hurt both Alberta's oilmen and farmers and that 'it would seem imprudent to introduce such a tax in Canada, a relatively young country which is still in a "period of emergence" and which is short of investment capital.'[44]

Manning's opposition to federal economic and social policy did not end the list of differences between Edmonton and Ottawa. The Alberta government was also opposed to federal cultural policies, particularly with regard to Liberal efforts to strengthen the presence of francophones and the French language in the federal civil service and government operations across Canada. Before the federal Royal Commission on Bilingualism and Biculturalism was officially established in 1963, Prime Minister Pearson, only recently elected, sent a draft of the terms of reference to the provincial premiers. Manning, who as we have seen did not pussyfoot about his views, made his opposition to government aims crystal clear. Just as in his provincial policy towards native people, there was little room for the recognition of collectivities, so he had no sympathy for French-Canadian claims to a distinct culture within the Canadian mosaic which required government recognition and support if it was to flourish. He answered Pearson:

... in the matter of biculturalism, if the objective is to encourage citizens of all racial and ethnic origins to make their maximum contribution to the development of one overall Canadian culture embracing the best of all, we feel this would meet with widespread endorsation and support.

If, on the other hand, the objective is to give some form of official recognition to a dual English and French culture, we suggest that this is unrealistic and impracticable and we doubt it would meet with any widespread public acceptance ...

If the purpose is to extend recognition of French as an official language in areas and spheres beyond those in which it was guaranteed official status at the time of Confederation, we feel that it would not meet with general public acceptance and the consequences, in our opinion, would impair rather than strengthen Canadian unity.[45]

Although this forthright response earned Manning kudos at home, it caused some 'violent reactions' from the Quebec federal caucus of Social Credit,[46] which after the 1962 and 1963 federal elections contained the lion's share of Social Credit members. The crack between the western and Quebec federal Social Credit MPs, already deep, became a chasm. But Manning remained unrepentant. While promising that Alberta would expand offerings of education in the French language for the 'cultural enrichment' of Canadian society, he opened his statement to the federal-provincial conference on constitutional matters in 1968 by opposing constitutional entrenchment of language rights as recommended in the report, by then tabled, of the Royal Commission on Bilingualism and Biculturalism. He feared a 'constitutional Munich' if language rights were entrenched to appease the government of Quebec; where would the limits to special arrangements for Quebec end?[47]

While the issues of Quebec and the French language were the major causes of Alberta government alienation from Ottawa on cultural issues, the CBC, long hated by Social Credit, also remained a sore spot. The Alberta government's opposition to public ownership extended to media, and indeed Manning attempted in 1950 to sell off CKUA, the public radio station it had inherited from the UFA. But, as he admitted to a letter writer, 'the public protested strongly, indicating the appreciation of the noncommercial service to listeners by CKUA.'[48] None the less, the government saw no reason to stand aside from CKUA's programming decisions, including decisions about how the station should go about covering elections.[49]

Because it interfered with CKUA, the Manning government could not understand the greater, if not exactly total, reluctance of federal governments to intervene in CBC programming. As indicated in the previous chapter, Alberta believed the CBC 'flouted' rulings of the Alberta Board of Censors by showing movies such as *The Blackboard Jungle* and *The Wild One*, which the board had banned for showings in Alberta. The Alberta government was incensed that the federal government refused to intervene to clear Alberta's airwaves of these movies of dubious moral value.

There was thus little upon which Edmonton and Ottawa were in agreement in the 1960s. An interesting exception was the Canada Pension Plan introduced in 1965. On the surface this plan had the same features as the medicare proposal: it was universal and compulsory rather than means-tested for the needy only. But Manning, while leery about certain details of the plan, did not oppose it in principle because, he noted, many workers were not in any pension program and lack of pension portability between employers often meant that workers who changed jobs lost pension rights.[50] On the latter point, Manning shared the view of some conservative businessmen who opposed redistributive proposals in general but favoured the Canada Pension Plan for business-related reasons. As Manning explained to the premiers' conference in 1962:

Another factor disturbing all of us today, with the general high cost levels which prevail in the country is the pressure of unions in industry to retain men who are no longer required because of technological changes, for example on the railways.

If they are going to lose pension rights after spending ten or fifteen years in one industry, and then transferred to another, then we are going to have to contend with this union pressure to keep them in their original jobs. If we can have portability of pensions it will remove that kind of pressure to retain people in their jobs when technological changes have made their services unnecessary. Every man kept in that position is raising the cost of some service or commodity to the country as a whole.[51]

Although the Canada Pension Plan provided only a basic pension to Canadians rather than portability of private pensions, it could at least be seen as providing Canadians with a minimum protection for their old age and thus justifying to a degree labour-saving initiatives by employers.

The inconsistency evident in the pensions issue aside, Manning and Social

Credit generally did not stray from a principled, right-wing approach that cannot be reduced to regionalism cloaked in higher principles. Indeed, the Social Credit party took the surprising step of opposing wheat sales to Communist countries in 1962 at a time when grain farmers benefited enormously from sales to the Soviet Union and China. National leader Robert Thompson claimed that 'as a Christian' he could not support wheat sales to governments 'dedicated to the destruction of all we hold dear in the democratic way of life.'[52] Manning, the long-time fighter of socialism in all its guises, maintained with Thompson that the wheat did not reach ordinary citizens of Communist countries 'but rather the Red Army, whose avowed intention is the destruction of our democratic way of life.'[53]

On the whole, then, the prescriptions of the Alberta government and those of federal governments, both Conservative and Liberal, were at cross-purposes. Somewhat anticipating the neo-conservatives of the eighties, Ernest Manning's Social Credit regime, despite its radical roots, had become a critic of a post-war political consensus that maintained the private enterprise system but attempted to modify its rules by making the government a major economic player. In practice, this consensus, while it produced impressive social programs, achieved little redistribution of wealth among individuals and regions. And although it at least checked the tendency of the uncontrolled capitalist system to allocate even larger shares of the overall pie to the wealthy as the pie got bigger, in the opinion of Manning and others who thought like him the new government interventionism had the effect of preventing the pie from growing faster, and thus was self-defeating. We look now at how Manning attempted to put his ideology in practice on the home front and at the same time campaigned for a new national political alignment that would clearly pit conservatives against welfare-minded reformists.

Social Credit's social expenditures, rather than its right-wing ideology, no doubt explained the government's popularity in the post-war period. But, as we have seen with regard to health and welfare programs, the government's programs were more or less consistent with what it advocated on a federal level. Universality was eschewed in favour of the means test. The government was also largely true to its rhetoric against government subsidies to attract new businesses. Indeed, while other provinces established costly and ultimately self-defeating programs to use government money to lure private companies into their precincts,[54] Alberta steadfastly opposed such subsidies. Because of the prosperity of the energy sector, Alberta seemed less desperate about its future than provinces such as Manitoba, Saskatchewan, the Maritimes, and Quebec, all of whom lavished taxpayers' dollars on 'free' enterprisers looking for free rides. The Alberta government could take the high road, noting that its low corporate taxes should be enough of an incentive for industry to locate in the province. The minister of industry and development could, under these circumstances, write Alberta industrialists who supported Alberta's copying of incentives in place in Manitoba and Saskatchewan: 'basically the problem is whether public funds should be used to directly assist this or any company in similar conditions. At the moment the Government does not find that this is advisable. It is felt that any such subsidization will, in the long run, not be beneficial either to the company itself or to the community where it is operating.'[55]

But the Alberta government did violate its own free-enterprise ideology in several respects. For one, it gave a 2 per cent advantage to Alberta firms bidding for government contracts, arguing that in doing so it was merely compensating Alberta contractors for the discrimination they faced in turn in bidding for other provinces' government contracts.[56] For another, it provided all the capital to Canadian National to build a rail line to connect mineral-rich areas in the northwestern portion of the province with the Pacific Ocean. Although such a step was consistent with the activities of some of the federal regional development programs, none of which received Alberta's approval, Manning distinguished it from what he considered the general thrust of programs by the federal government and other provinces to promote industrial growth. It was an expenditure for infrastructure that would benefit all industry in an area, 'not inducement in which we are giving special concessions to a certain industry to locate in a particular area.'[57]

Manning claimed that 'large scale mineral development' in northern Alberta would be the ticket to later industrial development, and the Northern Development Council was established in 1965 to oversee the building of roads and airstrips to make the mineral exploitation of the region more attractive. No more was necessary, argued Manning, because a 'proper atmosphere for investment capital and for enterprise to do its work and to get its reward' was the best program for promoting economic development without regard to region.[58]

Perhaps the only damper on investors to occur in the later Social Credit years was a sop in 1964 to the party's earlier radical days. In 1939 the Aberhart government, in its attempts to protect citizens from financiers, passed the Judicature Act, which banned the so-called 'deficiency judgments' that forced foreclosed homeowners or farmers to pay the difference if the financier, on resale of the property, could not recoup the value of the earlier mortgage. The effect of the act was to allow a home-buyer or debt-ridden farmer to walk away from a property and start all over again rather than having the millstone of old debts around his or her neck. But in 1964 a judge of the Supreme Court of Alberta ruled legal a contract in which a mortgagee contracted himself out of the provisions of the legislation. The Alberta government, recognizing that many if not all mortgage-lenders would take advantage of such a loophole in legislation, passed an amendment later that year that made illegal any waiver of protections in the legislation.[59]

The Judicature Act aside, the Manning government was ideologically far to the right of the Canadian consensus in the sixties. Manning's battles with the federal government and other provinces over fundamental issues caused him to see himself more and more as a key player in a crusade to preserve basic values that were being eroded. In 1967 he presented 'A White Paper on Human Resources Development' to the Alberta legislature in an attempt to set down clearly the values that underlay the actions of his government and to provide a blueprint for actions by a government that was committed, from its viewpoint, to demonstrating compassion without interfering with the rights of individuals, including corporate entities.

John Barr notes the influence of Manning's twenty-five-year-old son, Preston Manning, a systems-analysis devotee, and several friends of the younger Manning in the preparation of the document.[60] Perhaps indeed Preston, a graduate in physics and economics who had produced a long study on the applicability of general systems theory to socio-economic development models, was responsible for the turgid, technocratic, secular language which seemed so out of place in a document prepared by the deeply religious and generally lucid Alberta premier. But beneath the bafflegab of certain pretentious schools of social science, the ideas of the white paper were vintage Manning. They provided the dry run for his book later that year, which applied the white paper's perspectives to the federal scene. So, for example, Manning's anti-collectivist orientation was now inelegantly phrased to be a commitment to integrating physical and 'human resource' development: 'to facilitate the harnessing of an economy based on the principles of freedom of economic activity and private ownership, to the task of achieving objectives stemming from humanitarian values and a social concern based on the concept that the individual human being is the supremely important unit of consideration.'[61]

Several graphs accompanied this puffery. And while the government largely restated its commitment to the values it had been proclaiming for years – including opposition to universal social programs and to subsidies for particular industries – it now promised confusingly to 'utilize the systems approach' in studying social problems. This approach, it claimed, meant 'the study of social problems and the analysis of government policies in their relation to the total socio-economic system, rather than on a limited departmentalized basis.'[62] More controversially, human social problems were to be seen as akin to problems involving the physical world. The government wanted to 'apply new and advanced methods and techniques, initially conceived for industrial applications, to the analysis of social problems and the formulation of programs for human resources development.'[63]

The major outcome of this commitment to a brave new world in which conservative values of free enterprise and individual initiative would none the less be sacrosanct was the Alberta government's large financial commitment to broad-based research. A Human Resources Research Council was to be established and mandated in its first year to produce two comprehensive studies 'designed to achieve a standard of excellence in the fields of mental health and penology.' Alberta's universities would be aided in increasing 'the supply of competent researchers in the physical and social sciences.' But above all, the government, true to its values, committed itself to contracting out government research, wherever possible, to private contractors.[64]

A 'Manpower for Human Resources Development' program would set aside $175 million for capital development projects of the three universities (including the new University of Lethbridge) and begin planning of a fourth university (Athabasca University) to ensure facilities for 'projected future demands for highly trained professional personnel.' New medical sciences centres were also planned as a way of attracting quality medical researchers and teachers to the province. The community development program, which applied social science research to the problem of underdeveloped communities, was greatly expanded, as was agricultural research. Although no new research program was undertaken to examine poverty, a program had been established the previous year in conjunction with the federal government to study seven representative areas, including poor areas in the two major cities, where 'social and economic deprivation' were judged to exist.[65]

In the area of industrial development the government offered little that was new. It still welcomed foreign investment and opposed direct subsidies, but it intended to have the treasury branches make borrowing easier for small businessmen and farmers, to build more resource railways, and to aim an 'Investment in Alberta' publicity campaign at middle- and high-income Albertans. Perhaps most promising, if also most questionable, was a plan to rebate federal estate taxes paid to the province. The federal government had decided only recently to rebate all estate taxes collected to the provinces from which they had been paid, and Alberta's decision temporarily gave it an edge over other provinces in attracting rich people (although within a decade all other provinces had followed suit).[66]

Manning also proposed work to develop two new indexes for social application. One, which showed his continuing contempt for the unions, was a 'productivity index' that would govern wage increases in Canada and replace the cost-of-living index. The other was a 'functionality index' that would allow the province to do 'scientific evaluation' of such institutions as schools, hospitals, and government departments.[67]

All in all, the white paper, which took a hundred pages to outline the government's philosophy and planned legislative initiatives, demonstrated the latitude available to a right-wing government in a wealthy province. It could avoid openly redistributive programs, all the while spending enough money to generate employment and meet various needs of various groups. But the paper also demonstrated how deadly in earnest Social Credit was as an ideological outfit. Manning was not content to outline programs; to him, the philosophy that underlay decisions about proper approaches to solving problems was as important as the programs themselves. None the less, the white paper finished with a naïve assessment of its contents that also seemed to underscore why many people felt that Social Credit, even shorn of its extremists in 1947, was not committed to the parliamentary system as it operated in all western democracies; that is, on the basis of political parties. Wrote Manning:

This paper is non-partisan ... If the time and energy, presently spent in political manoeuvering for partisan advantage, were instead channelled into a supreme constructive effort to solve the problems and meet the challenges confronting our nation, Canadians would not only be happier but infinitely further ahead. In such a context, the role of the party in power is not to govern for party's sake, but rather to solve problems and give leadership in meeting challenges on the people's behalf. Likewise, the role of those designated as Her Majesty's Loyal Opposition is not to oppose the government simply for the sake of opposing, but rather to aid in the solving of problems by keeping vigilant watch for error and by presenting alternate proposals which will lead to more effective solutions and better legislation.[68]

But while such non-partisan pragmatism was Manning's prescription for Alberta, it wasn't really his solution for the rest of the country. The creeping socialism that he believed was infesting the old-line parties and constantly causing squabbles between Ottawa and Edmonton could be resolved only by a new political alignment in which conservatives, theretofore divided by increasingly meaningless partisan associations, would be united to fight socialists and liberals. The white paper outlined the political approaches that modern conservatives with old-fashioned values could embrace. Now, however, what was necessary was the formation of a national political movement capable of carrying these ideas to the nation's capital.

Manning had, for some time, despaired of Social Credit's chances of ever forming a federal government. But he believed that many Canadians who voted

Liberal or Conservative shared his view that federal government spending was uncontrolled and too intrusive into the operations of business and the lives of individuals. Obviously, however, outside Alberta and to a lesser extent British Columbia, such Canadians had not chosen to support Social Credit, whether because they regarded its monetary policies as cranky or simply because they assumed that party was not a credible contender to form a government. The federal election of 1962 brought a breakthrough for Social Credit in Quebec when twenty-six seats were won by the Créditistes, thanks to the popular image of the party's Quebec leader, Réal Caouette.[69] But with only four seats won by Social Credit in the west, the Social Credit caucus became a battleground between national leader Robert Thompson and Caouette. In the federal election in 1963, the Créditistes dropped from twenty-six to twenty Quebec seats with the westerners doing no better than retaining their four seats. The bickering between the westerners and the Québécois continued.

Caouette and a faction of the Quebec MPs were hard-line Douglasites of the type that Manning had earlier pushed out of the Alberta party. They reviled Manning as a conservative in Social Credit clothing, which was probably not far off the mark. There was also, as noted earlier, great resentment at Manning's hard-line stance against bilingualism and biculturalism. A further offence to Quebec nationalist feeling was Manning's support for Thompson as national leader in a contest against Caouette on the grounds that a French-speaking Catholic leader would harm the party's chances in western Canada.[70]

Even before Caouette and his majority faction of the Quebec caucus bolted the national Social Credit party in September 1963, Manning had begun to muse publicly on the need for political realignment in Canada. In early 1963 he told Charles Lynch of Southam News that he believed Canada was going through a 'transition period,' out of which a two-party system would emerge. One of these two parties would be a conservative party which would, however, have to address the monetary question because high levels of taxation and increased public debt were 'driving people into socialism.' None the less, he stressed that the new party would not be 'primarily' a social credit party. Social Credit, he said, was a 'philosophy first and a party second.'[71]

By the time of the 1964 Social Credit provincial convention in November 1964, the Quebec split had occurred. The Ralliement des Créditistes, the Quebec wing of the party, after a show-down between the Social Credit Association National Council and Caouette, disavowed the national council and voted to establish a new nation-wide Social Credit organization. Six of the twenty Quebec MPs, in turn, rejected Caouette's action and remained loyal to Thompson and the existing national organization.[72] This left parliament with two hostile Social Credit factions, one of fourteen MPs led by Caouette, the other of ten MPs led by

Thompson. The Thompson group further shrank in 1964 when two Quebec MPs defected to the Conservatives.[73]

Manning told the Social Credit convention in 1964 that the extremists who claimed to represent Social Credit views in eastern Canada had destroyed the party's chances of a national take-off. Instead, the Alberta party should now seek 'a realigning of political strength on the basis of conviction, instead of on the basis of partisanship and expediency.'[74]

The convention passed this resolution, which reflected Manning's thinking on the political challenges of the day:

Whereas there is strong evidence of Socialism creeping into our governments today, and

Whereas we believe much of this is caused by the insecure position of our people and the inability of our Federal Government to cope with the economic problems which face us, and

Whereas if nothing is done to maintain our Free Enterprise Way of life and individual and personal freedom we will lose these precious bulwarks of society by default to Socialism or even Communism, and

Whereas we firmly believe that the basic principles which formed the basis of our Social Credit Movement, if applied, would solve this problem, and we further feel that because of circumstances and misunderstanding there are many who will not join with us in our efforts as a movement to maintain the Free Enterprise Way of Life:

Therefore be it resolved that we instruct our Provincial and National Social Credit organizations to encourage the realignment of all those who believe in the Free Enterprise Way of Life to band together in a program with as many points in which there can be general agreement, and to join a common effort to preserve the Free Enterprise Way of Life.[75]

But while Manning's speech and the resolution seemed to point to an effort to start a new party, Manning resisted that interpretation of his efforts. He insisted that the time was not propitious for the formation of a new party but it was time 'to encourage the realignment of political thinking in order that the Canadian people may have a clear-cut alternative in the exercise of their freedom.'[76] In other words, his crusade was one of ideas. Above all, as with his Billy Graham tour, he wanted to change people's thinking.

On the ground, however, Manning was also concerned lest the real free-enterprise supporters divide their efforts in elections and, by splitting their votes, elect NDPers or left-leaning Liberals. In many rural constituencies in Alberta there was tacit support by Social Credit riding leaders for federal Conservative candidates.[77] Manning hoped in vain to have such support reciprocated in provincial elections. When the NDP won its first Alberta seat in 1966, in a provincial by-election in Pincher Creek–Crow's Nest Pass, Manning wrote a disquieted Conservative MP, Eldon Wooliams: 'Our government candidate lost by less than 140 votes, or to put it another way, the NDP has gained a foothold in the Legislature of Alberta because the free enterprise vote was divided between the Conservative candidate and that of the government party. Isn't this a situation that we should try and avoid if possible?'[78]

The situation was not avoided. Indeed, in the 1967 provincial election, the Conservatives proved to be Social Credit's major contender in most seats. Perhaps then it is not entirely unfair to suggest that Manning's book, *Political Realignment: A Challenge to Thoughtful Canadians*, which appeared later that year, was in part a call for the Conservatives to butt out of Alberta provincial politics in exchange for a Social Credit folding of the tents federally in the province. But given Manning's repeated calls for political realignment from 1963 onwards and his principled arguments with the federal government throughout the sixties, it would be incorrect to dismiss the book in these terms. It appeared, in any case, too soon after the election to have been mainly inspired by electoral considerations. Indeed Manning now sought to carry the political principles embodied in his government to the national scene, and he had a reasonably clear idea about the vehicle for this task.

Alfred Hooke notes in his rambling autobiography that Manning was indeed at work on the book before the election, but that he was hardly alone in his project:

On at least two occasions Mr. Manning told me in his office that he had been approached by several very influential and wealthy Canadians and that they wanted him to head up a party of the right with a view to preventing the onslaught of socialism these men could see developing in Canada. They apparently had indicated to him that money was no object and they were prepared to spend any amount necessary to stop the socialistic tide ...

Mr. Manning indicated to me also that he was working on a book which he hoped to publish in the not too distant future, in which he would endeavour to outline the views these men represented and recommendations he would make in keeping with their views.[79]

Hooke, although as anti-socialist as Manning, was aghast that among the backers of this new political project which interested Manning greatly were financiers – apostles of financial orthodoxy. The *Calgary Herald* later noted that Manning had aid in the production of both his white paper and his book from the National Public Affairs Research Foundation, an organization that has evolved today into the National Citizens' Coalition. Its president was R.A. Brown, Jr, president of

Home Oil, and its board of directors included Cyrus McLean, chairman of B.C. Telephones, and Renault St Laurent, wealthy lawyer and son of former prime minister Louis St Laurent.[80]

Political Realignment was a blend of Manning's clear ideological thinking expressed in lucid language and his newly acquired technocratic ideas (or at least language), which made his white paper dreary reading. In clear language he noted that 'the distinctions between the Liberal and Conservative Parties are rapidly being reduced to the superficial distinctions of party image, party labels and party personalities.' But in murkier language borrowed from the white paper he extolled the systems approach for determining government policies.[81]

Manning labelled his philosophy of governance 'social conservatism,' its aim to 'harness the energies of a free enterprise-private economic sector to the task of attaining many of the social goals which humanitarian socialists have long advocated.'[82] In his view, the national social credit party embodied social conservative goals, but eastern extremists within the Social Credit movement as well as a caricature of Social Credit in the media as the party of 'funny money' rendered the party incapable of attracting broad support. He therefore advocated that 'in the national field, the Social Credit Party can make its maximum contribution to the furthering of its own ideals and principles, and more importantly to the well-being of the country as a whole, by doing everything within its power to encourage and assist in bringing about an effective reorganization of the Progressive Conservative Party of Canada. Social Credit supporters, however, must insist that reorganization occur on a basis which will enable them, without sacrificing their convictions, to join with and support such a reconstructed political movement.'[83]

The provincial convention of Social Credit later that year, however, balked at any integration of its own organization with the Conservatives. The convention endorsed 'in general principle the concept of the social conservative position' outlined in Manning's book but resolved only to work to make these principles the operative ones in Canadian political life without making any mention of the Conservatives.[84]

None the less, Social Credit as a national movement was already rapidly disintegrating. Réal Caouette's Créditistes represented an enclave of rural Quebec and held no interest to English Canadians outside of a far-right fringe. As for Robert Thompson, the national leader of the national Social Credit party, the hopelessness of his task led to a defection to the Conservatives in 1967. Like Manning, Thompson had for several years been calling openly for political realignment to unite conservatives and had critiqued the Conservative party from the right, claiming that it was not vigilant enough in its protection of individualism. By 1967 he believed, however, that such criticisms were better made inside that party than on the outside from a rump party with little national profile. Bud Olson, meanwhile, the other Alberta Social Credit MP, never a monetary social crediter in any case, surprised Canadians by throwing in his lot with the governing Liberals rather than the Conservatives.[85] These two defections ended for good chances of future Social Credit federal representation from Alberta.

Having made his pitch for Canadian politics to be more ideology-based than image-based, Manning, despite his wealthy sponsors, did little more to attempt to shake up national politics. He had perhaps unwittingly eroded support for his party provincially by implying that the Progressive Conservative party be the real focus for conservatives' attention, although that was hardly his intent. As we have seen, he did not consider the Progressive Conservative party of the fifties and sixties to be truly conservative, and his real goal was to sharpen ideological debate in Canada rather than sink his party into an unreconstructed national Progressive Conservative party. None the less, he had managed in 1967 to produce both a provincial white paper and a nationally distributed book with remedies for Albertan and Canadian economic and political maladies that had scarcely a word in them about monetary policy. Whatever Alberta Social Credit represented in the late sixties, it was no longer a monetary-reform outfit. Preservation of the 'Free-Enterprise Way of Life,' rather than creation of a national dividend, had become the central concern of the Alberta government. But although in a general way most Albertans seemed to favour the free-enterprise system, as the sixties wore on there was increasing criticism of the Social Credit regime's brand of free enterprise.

Most criticism of the government came from the cities. As Thomas Flanagan notes, there had always been a 10 to 14 per cent differential between Social Credit support in its 'heartland' – south of Edmonton and east of the Rockies – and its support in the two big cities. In 1955, for example, while the party's province-wide vote was about 46 per cent of the total, it earned 52 per cent of the heartland vote and only 40 per cent of the Edmonton-Calgary vote. By 1959 its urban vote had climbed to an impressive 51 per cent which was still well under the 62 per cent heartland vote and the province-wide total of 56 per cent.[86] In the sixties, as in the fifties, opposition came from the labour movement as well as from municipal authorities.

The labour movement attitude to the government, divided in the early fifties, had become one of unified opposition by the end of that decade. The Labor Act amendments of 1960, which ignored labour complaints about company unionism and placed more impediments in the way of organizing workers and making strikes effective, proved to be a final straw. In common with the labour movement across the country, the Alberta Federation of Labour leadership worked to create the New Democratic Party.[87] It put more effort into the political sphere than did the labour movement in several other provinces, if only because the legislative climate cramped its ability to do its basic job.

The AFL had not been happy with the principled left-wing radicalism of the CCF in the fifties, believing that its utopian leftism was unattractive to Albertans as an alternative to a right-wing but high-spending government. Its leaders wanted a more moderate social-democratic alternative that would oppose the private-enterprise ideology of Social Credit without calling for the nationalization of anything that breathed or moved. Most of all, they wanted to elect a government that would ban company unions, guarantee union security, increase minimum wages, decrease maximum hours, and rigidly enforce statutes designed to guarantee worker safety. They worked to make the New Democratic Party in Alberta a moderate leftist party and to isolate the radical CCFers within the new outfit.[88] In 1962 Neil Reimer, the Alberta leader of the Oil, Chemical and Atomic Workers, a union frustrated in its organizing efforts by the government's leaning to company unions, became the provincial NDP's first president and the next year its first leader. Reimer was a strong advocate of the more cautious line for Alberta socialism, and despite his gruff labour-boss style, which turned off many voters, he managed to cause Manning much concern if only because NDP criticism of the government was so thoroughgoing and detailed.[89]

Manning, however, did not give in to labour pressure to change the Labour Act. He merely listened politely as labour leaders explained in 1962 that the 1960 amendments had resulted in manual workers' and low-level supervisors' being denied the right to unionize, thanks to employers' designating them as managers, as allowed in the 1960 changes, and receiving Board of Industrial Relations' acquiescence. Groups such as nurses, lab technicians, and X-ray technicians, who had considered unionization, were shocked to learn that the law deprived them of this right.[90] Manning also showed insensitivity to labour and the cities more generally in appointing in 1964 a committee composed primarily of rural members to review workmen's compensation.[91]

Manning did, at the very end of his term, give the Civil Servants Association (later renamed Alberta Union of Public Employees) the right, which Saskatchewan workers had enjoyed since 1945, to engage in collective bargaining. The civil service, riddled with patronage appointments,[92] had been pliant and did not strongly press the demand for unionization, despite its membership in a national organization of civil servants dedicated to achieving full bargaining rights for public servants.[93] The rewritten Public Service Act made the CSA the sole bargaining agent for the government, but its bargaining rights were limited. The minister of labour had final authority regarding what issues were negotiable, and if disagreements between the negotiating parties could not be resolved by mediation there would be no compulsory arbitration. Instead, the cabinet alone would impose settlement on issues in contention. Strikes were not expressly forbidden, but, given the cabinet's ultimate powers to impose a settlement, they were understood to be forbidden.[94]

Although the government proved closed-minded to labour calls for greater union rights, it did bend, in part, to labour calls for legislation to prevent discrimination in the workplace against women and minorities. Such concerns were new to the Alberta labour movement, which had been sexist for most of its history and, as we have seen, with reference to Hutterites and the Japanese, racist. The Human Rights Act of 1966 prohibited discrimination in the workplace on the basis of race, religion, colour, ancestry, or place of origin. An administrator appointed under the act would attempt to resolve disputes but, if he or she could not, would set up a board of inquiry with the mandate to determine if someone accused of a racist practice should be prosecuted in court.[95]

A Women's Cultural and Information Bureau Act, passed the same year, established a branch of the public service to treat employment, legal, cultural, and social problems facing women. Its mandate, however, was limited to research and propaganda as opposed to affirmative action or the right to bring cases of apparent discrimination to court.[96] The government itself, however, maintained a policy against hiring spouses of people with government jobs (under the heading 'employment of married women within the Government Service').[97] It had, indeed, before 1966 done nothing to create opportunities for employment of women, and while its leaders rarely talked about the issue of married women working, its opposition to day-care financing suggested reluctance in this area.

But if the government had not spent money on day care, it spent bundles on the schools, only to find that the urban school-boards were still dissatisfied. In 1961 the government had established a foundation plan to finance school divisions on the basis of 'equalized assessments,' which meant apportioning grants to schools on the basis of a uniform mill rate across the province. Local boards could then assess local taxpayers for a supplementary assessment if the fixed mill rate plus the government grant left them with a shortfall. The government regarded the foundation plan as superior to cost-sharing, which favoured wealthier municipalities.[98]

The urban school divisions, although the big losers, could not openly oppose a scheme to equalize educational opportunities for rural Albertans. Instead they retreated to a familiar theme from the fifties: the provincial government was placing too much of the burden for public expenditures on the municipal property tax. Calgary Public School Board chairman Glenn Holmes, in a brief to the province in 1965, made the argument succinctly: 'While we have no quarrel with the theory of equalized educational opportunity, and indeed support it, the problem is that the home owners of Alberta are bearing an undue share of the burden of equalization. A larger portion of equalization should be paid for out of the general revenue of the Province. It must be pointed out most emphatically that payments from the Foundation Plan do not supply the funds necessary for an urban area to provide an adequate educational service. Supplementary requisites are a fact of life in all urban and in most rural areas of Alberta.'[99] Holmes went on to argue that an urban centre required 'more administrative and supervisory personnel' than did rural centres. He also noted that the urban schools, unlike rural schools, often provided good libraries, guidance counselling, and extra educational options, all of which were not considered in the granting of foundation plan money. In short, the public schools officials in the cities thought the province was attempting to reduce their services to the unimpressive levels of rural schools.

Months before the 1967 provincial election, urban anger at the government's rural bias also emerged over a rural-dominated legislative committee's report calling for one omnibus Municipal Act to replace the four major pieces of municipal legislation. The City Act would be sunk together with the Town and Village Act, the Municipal District Act, and the Controverted Municipal Elections Act. The government foolishly drew up a bill that followed the committee's recommendations, only to be forced to withdraw it after the city councils in Edmonton and Calgary angrily denounced their inclusion under legislation that made them subject to the same close provincial scrutiny to which backwoods councils had always been subject. The Edmonton submission interestingly was presented by the council's legislative committee, chaired by future provincial Conservative cabinet minister Neil Crawford, with Lou Hyndman – former Alberta Conservative party president and another future Tory minister – acting as the committee's special counsel. The Calgary council, which denounced the government proposals in strong language, included future Conservative minister Roy Farran and future Tory MLA John Kushner.[100]

Complaints of the government's insensitivity to the cities and to municipalities generally as well as the traditional attacks on Social Credit give-aways of provincial resources to large, foreign interests had cut little ice in the provincial election of 1963 in which Social Credit repeated its success of 1959, actually reducing the opposition from four to three seats. With 56 per cent of the vote, the Social Credit Party won 95 per cent of the seats (sixty of sixty-three), even ridding itself of the Independent Social Crediter, R.D. Ansley in Leduc. It faced only two Liberals and one Coalition candidate in the opposition benches.[101] But the aging of the government, the whiff of scandal, and the emergence of an attractive Conservative leader made the 1967 election a different story.

By-elections in 1965 and 1966 demonstrated a weakening of Social Credit support. In March 1965 the Liberals carried Edson with the NDP coming a close second. In October 1966 it was the NDP's turn, although this time Social Credit was within 140 votes of victory.[102]

Garth Turcott, the Pincher Creek lawyer who won for the NDP, quickly established a name for himself as a muck-raker who accused a cabinet minister, Alfred Hooke, and a former provincial treasurer, E.W. Hinman, of improprieties. Hinman had been fired from cabinet in 1964 because his business affairs could be seen as in conflict with his cabinet duties. According to Larry Pratt, Turcott was reluctant to assume the role of scandal-monger but was pressed into service by NDP leader Neil Reimer, who believed that the Social Credit regime must be exposed as a hypocritical outfit hiding behind religion to disguise its anti-democratic and sometimes outrightly corrupt behaviour.[103] Less than a month before the provincial election writ was issued in late April 1967, Turcott formally charged in the legislative assembly on 3 April that Hooke and Hinman had 'used or attempted to use' their office for personal gain and, in Hooke's case, also for the gain of friends and business associates.[104] While the election was in full swing, Manning, who had castigated Turcott as irresponsible and forced a legislative vote of censure against him, appointed a one-man royal commission to investigate his charges. The commissioner was the Honourable Mr Justice W.J.C. Kirby, a one-time Alberta Conservative leader who, as noted in chapter 5, had been one of the leaders in the attempt to demonstrate Social Credit corruption during the 1955 election. Justice Kirby did not report until October 1968, at which time he rendered his view that Turcott's charges were unfounded. He did, however, as we note later, suggest that both Hinman and Hooke were naïve about the position of a cabinet minister and did not always take care to preserve the appearance as well as the reality of a separation of their government duties and their business interests.

The Turcott charges, however, underlined, in the same way as the 1955 charges had, that Social Credit ministers, despite their religious, squeaky-clean image, had not exactly taken vows of poverty. Although few could be sure that the extensive land and financial deals detailed by the NDP amounted to corruption, many could suspect that cabinet ministers were spending much of their time minding their own profit-making interests rather than the interests of the government store.

A recent article suggests that in the 1967 election the NDP concentrated single-mindedly on the issue of corruption to the near-exclusion of other issues.[105] Perhaps this was true of NDP leaders' emphasis in public speeches, but it was not true of their public advertising, which tore apart the government record in a variety of areas and suggested NDP alternatives.[106] Social Credit, in any case, seemed obsessed with refuting a variety of charges emanating from the NDP and with eviscerating the party whose leaders and sole MLA had impugned the government's reputation.

Indeed there is strong evidence in the premier's papers that the Social Credit organization, with the full knowledge of the premier, had a mole in the NDP organization. Within a week of the campaign opening, Manning had in hand a memorandum that listed a three-week plan of NDP advertisements for the election. Eight days after the campaign opened, Social Credit had available for the printers a pamphlet entitled *Truth versus Misrepresentation*, which gingerly disputed every charge that the NDP had planned to make during the election.[107] Manning continued, throughout the election, to act as if the NDP were the chief threat. No doubt the ideological gap between his party and the 'socialists' (who were certainly not presenting themselves as very far to the left) made them an attractive opponent to a right-wing ideologue like Manning, who defended the 'Free-Enterprise Way of Life.'

Just days before the election, for example, Manning, in an election speech, made continuous reference to the NDP and the 'socialists' and their claims regarding alleged give-aways by the province to the energy companies. The NDP had promised to raise oil royalties to rates comparable to those levied in Texas and Oklahoma and to develop the tar sands in northern Alberta under Crown ownership.[108] Oil revenues under the NDP, the party promised, would pay for increased social services while still allowing a tax cut. But Manning pooh-poohed such suggestions. Ignoring the clear evidence that American oil-producing states charged oil companies far more per barrel than Alberta did, Manning stated flatly: 'And then of course you have the socialists telling you that they would get it out of the oil industry. I have already pointed out to you that we are now collecting from the development of our oil and gas resources, the highest returns to the public of any oil-producing area in the world.'[109] Altogether, he said, $2.25 billion had flowed into government coffers since 1947. As for the oil sands, NDP charges that a monopoly had been granted to Great Canadian Oil Company in return for twenty-five cents per acre were rejected. Although GCO had the largest lease of oil sands lands, argued Manning, most of the tar sands remained unleased and there were twenty-nine other companies with leases. Above all, however, Manning, who was not willing to attack the oil companies or to deny that his free-enterprise government gave these companies a wide berth when policies affecting them were made,[110] emphasized his well-worn line that continued energy development in Alberta was not a given. Production and transportation costs in the province were relatively high, and so what Alberta must continue to provide was 'a stable political climate in which investors are not afraid to take the gamble involved in such development, which they are afraid of if there is any threat of socialistic intervention.'[111]

The Social Credit pamphlet *Truth versus Misrepresentation* also wrote off

NDP complaints that property taxes still paid most of the cost of education and that power rates were too high and could be lowered through public power.[112]

Ironically, however, during the election Manning had virtually nothing to say about the Alberta Progressive Conservative party. Yet it was this party, rather than the NDP, which proved to be the major alternative to Social Credit to many voters. Larry Pratt suggests that the NDPers succeeded in weakening the public image of the government but in so doing provided their party with so bloody-minded an image that voters were not well-disposed to regard the NDP as a palatable alternative.[113] Whether for this reason or because voters wanted the continuation of conservative policies but under new, clean leadership, the Conservatives under Peter Lougheed won 26 per cent of the vote and six seats, five of them urban. Six of sixty-five seats may have seemed a poor harvest for one-quarter of the votes, but only a fraction smaller percentage vote had won the CCF merely two seats in 1944 and the Conservatives just one seat in 1959. Social Credit won less than 45 per cent of the vote and only 39 per cent of the combined Edmonton-Calgary vote but carried fifty-five seats or 85 per cent of all seats. The hapless NDP, meanwhile, continued to demonstrate the unkindness of the first-past-the-post system to Alberta socialists by receiving no seats for its 16 per cent of the vote.[114] The Liberals, by contrast, with 11 per cent of the vote, held Edson and won two other seats after a campaign in which they presented themselves as a moderately left-of-centre alternative.[115]

The Conservative party revival, which caught the other parties by surprise, had begun with the election of wealthy lawyer-businessman Peter Lougheed to the party leadership in 1965. At the time, the provincial party was moribund. But Lougheed, the thirty-seven-year-old grandson of former Alberta senator and millionaire Sir James Lougheed, was personally ambitious and doggedly determined to unseat Social Credit.[116] The Conservatives, according to Larry Pratt and John Richards, represented an arriviste upper middle class in the cities who resented Social Credit's passive rentier attitude to the oil industry and lack of interest in diversifying the provincial economy. While they shared such attitudes with socialists and trade union leaders, they were uninterested in greater social justice; instead they wished to strengthen the power of their own class against that of the foreign oil interests, which seemed to call the shots in Alberta while leaving Albertans in the traditional position reserved for hinterland residents – as hewers of wood and drawers of water. Among those identified in the seventies as sharing Lougheed's perspective were representatives of such Alberta-based firms as Mannix, Nova, ATCO, and the Alberta Energy Company as well as some 'dynamic' oil-related businesses headquartered in Calgary. Professionals such as corporate lawyers, engineers, geologists, and financial consultants are also seen as part of this group concerned with diversification of the province's economic base.[117]

While Lougheed and a few other Conservative leaders perhaps thought in such sophisticated terms, most Conservatives of this period thought in the traditional terms of Social Credit's urban non-socialist opposition: the government was too rural-oriented, too dogmatic in its conservatism, and too smug because of its long years in office. The 1966 Progressive Conservative convention approved a set of 'Guideposts' that demonstrated the fuzziness in thinking of a party whose basic values were not profoundly different from those of Social Credit. Individualism and free enterprise were extolled, but the party implicitly aligned itself with NDP and Liberal criticism of Socred energy policy when it added that private enterprise notwithstanding, there must be 'adequate returns to our citizens for the fortunate location of these resources within our boundaries.'[118]

Some federal Progressive Conservative MPs feared that Lougheed's desire to provide more than token opposition to Manning would intervene with their cosy arrangements with provincial Social Crediters. They resisted Lougheed's attempts to copy the NDP model and build strong constituency-level organizations. Most party contributors, meanwhile, specified that their donations were for the federal wing, thus reflecting a general view that Social Credit was the real provincial wing of the federal Conservative party, albeit a wing more conservative than the federal organization itself.[119] None the less, Lougheed was able to organize about twenty-five working constituency organizations and concentrated his party's efforts in these ridings in a successful attempt to establish a significant Tory legislative presence. Lougheed then proved himself a skilful orator and an attractive television personality in an election-eve leaders' debate in which Manning had, perhaps unwisely, agreed to participate. Lougheed was not more impressive a speaker than Manning, but his ability to show well against the veteran premier certainly aided his party's electoral chances.[120]

Manning was surprised by the election results, which saw his party fall from 56 to under 45 per cent of the vote, compared with 1963, and drop seven seats. The government's record and its 'White Paper on Human Resources,' promising a dynamic, free-enterprise, technocratic future, had seemed foolproof election material. Yet the government now faced the largest opposition since the 1955 election, and worse, the leader of the opposition, unlike Harper Prowse in 1955, already a political war-horse, was an attractive new face on the Alberta political scene. What had gone wrong? Manning asked each of his ministers to write his assessment of the campaign, and the responses indicate an ill-disguised belief among many of them that Social Credit's problems were long-term. Industry Minister Russ Patrick noted that the government's longevity made it vulnerable to criticisms, whether founded or unfounded. Many voters, he claimed, simply accepted at face value the opposition party's view that the government was arrogant. But 'the youthful and favourable "Kennedy" type *image* which Lougheed projected well, was the main reason for the Conservative impact which reduced the Social Credit percentage of total vote.'[121]

Dr J. Donovan Ross, the minister of health, suggested that the Socreds might have erred in writing off the Conservatives as a clone of their own party about whom little need be said: 'Certainly the substantial gain of votes of Mr. Boddy, the Conservative member in my Constituency, suggests that the people felt that since we were suggesting that the Conservatives were not too different from ourselves that if they wanted to put in an opposition vote to smarten up the Social Credit party, then their safest way of doing it was to vote Conservative.'[122] Social Credit rural ministers noted that there were more and more rural voters who felt the need for more opposition. Either, as Lands and Forests Minister Henry Ruste suggested, there was anger because their area had no manufacturing industries to employ children leaving farms,[123] or, as Minister without Portfolio A.O. Fimrite noted, the distribution of such government institutions as hospitals did not favour constituencies equally.[124]

Interestingly, few ministers wished to raise the obvious question of the Hooke-Hinman allegations as an election issue. Hooke himself, by now a hidebound right-winger, attributed his own loss of votes in his Rocky Mountain House constituency (which he nevertheless carried with a large plurality) to constituent anger about the maze of government regulations in a variety of areas and the arrogance of civil servants whose attitude people blamed on the government that hired them.[125]

A.O. Fimrite, the Spirit River member, admitted that the NDP allegations did have an impact because some people believed that where there was smoke, there was fire. Considering that his constituency would never again return a Social Crediter, he was no doubt correct in his sober assessment that 'the strongest asset in my constituency to ensure the Government's return was the fact that you, the Premier, were still at the helm of the ship.'[126]

But Manning remained at the helm for only another year and a half. During that period the government, despite its ambitious pre-election white paper, appeared asleep at the switch while the Tories under Lougheed were feisty. The Conservatives, representing Edmonton and Calgary seats, championed urban causes and more generally took up the cudgels for the municipalities, much as Prowse had tried to do in the 1950s.

The government attempted in 1968 to reduce urban criticism of provincial education spending by increasing its grant to local school-boards sufficiently to prevent municipal contributions from exceeding one-third of the total fund.[127] But in a motion of non-confidence just days afterward, Lougheed identified his party with critics who claimed that the province overburdened property taxpayers in order to create a mythology of low provincial taxes. The government, he said, 'failed to establish budgetary policies to relieve the property taxpayer of an unfair and inequitable burden for the rising costs of education and to provide adequate sources of permanent revenues to assure municipal financial stability to meet changing Alberta needs.'[128]

Lougheed's Tories were also in touch with new public issues such as the need for expanded day-care facilities for the growing number of working mothers. The Social Credit government had been reluctant to provide public monies for day care and balked before a Conservative motion in February 1968 calling for a greater commitment on its part to act.[129] After debate, however, the government, not wishing to appear entirely closed-minded to the new pressures for a government service, amended the Conservative motion to read: 'in cooperation with municipalities, organizations or private individuals as circumstances require and finances permit.' This pledge was weak enough to establish the point that the Conservatives were a better bet for voters interested in having the government's commitment to day care broadened.[130]

The liberal, welfarist ideas which Manning deplored and against which he hoped to create a new 'social conservative' political formation had taken hold of many Albertans, particularly in the cities. The Social Credit government was becoming increasingly unrepresentative of the aspirations of Alberta voters. Meanwhile, the pliant Social Credit League, which would be called upon in late 1968 to choose a successor to Manning, equally appeared more and more an anachronism.

While Manning had become the darling of big capitalists, particularly in the energy industry, his party had not lost its initial plebeian make-up. Its candidates in later years were successful small and medium businessmen and a sprinkling of professionals[131] rather than the schoolteachers and Depression-ravaged small enterprisers of 1935. But just as the candidates of 1935, chosen only after Aberhart's blessing was received, were a cut better off than the party members as a whole, candidates in the sixties were unrepresentative of the party.

An in-depth study of the composition and attitudes of Alberta Social Credit members was conducted as a University of Alberta PhD thesis by Owen Anderson in the late sixties. Anderson was no ordinary PhD student. He was executive assistant to Premier Harry Strom, and his polling of party members was done with the active support of party president Orvis Kennedy. Kennedy, an MP from 1938 to 1940, was the party's veteran organizer and had served in an executive capacity in the party almost from its origins. Like many other party stalwarts, he found the 1967 election results portentous and so was happy to co-operate with the research efforts of a partisan which might yield clues about the party's weaknesses and those strengths on which it could build. Kennedy gave Anderson access to party membership lists and sent a personal letter to members who received Anderson's questionnaire, indicating the party's support for the research.[132]

Anderson sent out 2100 questionnaires to a random 10 per cent of those listed on the party rolls for 1967–8. Although 1967 was an election year and memberships could be expected to be inflated by people joining the party purely to be part of a candidate-selection meeting,[133] the party lists also included people whose memberships had lapsed as well as people who had bought three- or four-year memberships only to become inactive. The post office returned many letters, indicating that some people who had moved had not felt the need to let the party office know their new address.[134] None the less, Anderson received an impressive 715 responses,[135] mainly from people who were quite active in the party, and his results therefore probably did reflect the thinking of party activists as a whole if not of the entire paper membership. Anderson also conducted a survey of 500 Edmontonians and Calgarians against whose attitudes the Social Credit membership's attitudes on some issues were compared.

In the area of income, Anderson found, the Social Credit membership was broadly representative of Albertans as a whole, although the rich were over-represented: only one Albertan family in one hundred had an annual income above fifteen thousand dollars, while 5.73 per cent of Social Credit members had such a family income. As for the middle-income levels, 9 per cent of Albertans earned between ten and fifteen thousand dollars per annum, and 13.01 per cent of Social Credit members were in this bracket. Astonishingly, 17.06 per cent of Anderson's respondents earned less than three thousand dollars per year, an income which qualified them as poor; 20 per cent of the Alberta population were similarly poor. The modest-income group earning between three and five thousand dollars annually accounted for 30 per cent of the population and for 23 per cent of Social Credit membership.[136]

In other respects, however, the Social Credit members were unrepresentative indeed and largely fit the growing public image of Social Crediters as aging, rural, church-going conservatives. While half of Albertans lived in Calgary and Edmonton in 1966, only 18 per cent of party members were from the big cities. As noted earlier, the trend away from urban memberships had been visible since the early forties. The small towns, villages, and farms of Alberta accounted for 74 per cent of party members but for only 44 per cent of the population; 5 per cent of members and 6 per cent of the population were found in the small cities.[137]

The age gap between members and the population of Alberta over fifteen as a whole was striking. Fully 53 per cent of the members were over fifty against 30 per cent of the overall population; while the baby boomers between fifteen and twenty-nine made up 32 per cent of the over-fifteen group, only 7.83 per cent of party members were in this age group.[138] Indeed, Socred candidates, if richer than the party membership on average, were no younger: the average age of candidates in 1967 was fifty-one.[139]

While the party was not exclusively composed of fundamentalist Protestants, as some of its critics believed, these groups were unsurprisingly over-represented while Roman Catholics, who made up 25 per cent of Alberta's population, provided fewer than 10 per cent of Social Credit's members. Anglicans, United Church members, and non-Christians were also under-represented. More striking than all this was religious observance. While more than half of the five hundred people randomly surveyed by Anderson in Calgary and Edmonton never attended church, only 1 per cent of Social Credit's members never attended. Indeed, fully half went to church at least once a week.[140]

Anderson's information on occupations of the members surveyed did not make for easy comparisons with the general population. Half of those who responded were either farmers or housewives, and the housewives were not asked the occupations of their husbands. None the less, farmers would appear to have been over-represented while unskilled workers had little representation. Professionals were reasonably well-represented as were white-collar workers, but these broad categories were not broken down further.[141]

The attitudes of the members reflected broad agreement with the government's views, hardly surprising when one considers Manning's dominance in both the government and party; presumably, most people who were not 'social conservatives' stayed away from this party. But the Calgary-Edmonton group interviewed by Anderson was less conservative. For example, 84 per cent of this latter group favoured more government support to higher education while only 49 per cent of party members favoured such support; and 47 per cent of the urban group regarded student protests favourably while only 10 per cent of Social Crediters were well-disposed to such protests. A clear majority of the urbanites supported legalized abortion and easier divorce; Social Crediters were largely opposed. While 42 per cent of the general public wanted the death penalty abolished, only 18 per cent of Social Credit members were abolitionist. Anderson observed that younger members of Social Credit were generally more liberal on most issues; but younger Social Crediters were a small group in a party whose recruiting efforts among the young, despite the creation of a Youth Ministry by the government in 1966, had largely failed.[142]

Significantly, among Anderson's sampling of the province's Social Credit members, 25 per cent claimed that they generally voted Conservative federally. Although 61 per cent indicated that they generally voted Social Credit, six out of ten members voting for their own party federally is hardly impressive. Negligible numbers voted Liberal or NDP, and almost one in ten appears to have had no clear allegiance federally. The high Conservative vote suggests that many would not have been displeased with Manning's suggestion that open Social Credit involvement with the federal Conservatives should be considered.[143]

Social Credit in the sixties thus presented an interesting phenomenon: a party largely composed of average- and lower-income Albertans who elected a government composed of upper-middle-income earners who, in turn, extolled big business interests and espoused a levelling-up theory of distribution of wealth. Ernest Manning's tying together of individualist religious views with economic individualism and his apparent lack of concern that the major 'economic individuals' to be defended were corporate rather than made of flesh gave the party a reasonably coherent philosophy. Increasingly, the critique of the money-lenders, the only remaining radical feature of the party in the fifties, became so hollow that Manning rarely voiced it while the new cabinet ministers of the sixties, although hardly young, seemed barely aware of and less interested in Douglasite monetary theories. The government concentrated its energies on attracting new investment capital and attacking federal spending and taxing programs, which they believed could only impede new investment and, therefore, growth.

Alberta seemed a rarefied environment for the experiment with 'social conservatism' that Manning and his ministers claimed to be performing. Oil and gas exploitation yielded large revenues even with low royalties, and the government could confidently spend lavishly on education, roads, and certain social services without resorting to universal social programs or to openly redistributive measures. But, as we have seen, while this social conservatism satisfied a majority of Albertans and even drew a respectable representation of poorer, religious rural dwellers into the Social Credit League as members, it did not work for everybody. The fact that the government was studying poverty as a problem indicates how far it had to go in removing it; indeed, with 20 per cent of families below the poverty line, Alberta had as many poor on average as Canada as a whole, despite the province's superior wealth per capita. Clearly the province's anti-labour legislation, its laissez-faire attitude to industrial development, and its neglect followed by its manipulation of native people had created an economically stratified society even if class tensions remained relatively submerged. Albertans, however, had been conditioned, it would seem, to fear the effects of too great a change with the result that the Conservatives had emerged as the major opposition party. The next chapter outlines Social Credit's efforts to stave off the Conservative challenge before the provincial election of 1971 and looks at the party's gradual falling apart as it struggled to maintain a political space for itself after its 1971 defeat.

7   The Road to Disintegration

In September 1968 Ernest C. Manning announced that he was retiring from the premiership of Alberta after more than a quarter-century in the post. A leadership convention two months later, the first in the Social Credit League's history, chose Municipal Affairs Minister Harry Strom as Manning's replacement. Strom ran the province for only two and a half years before facing his first election as premier. In that election, the resurgent Progressive Conservatives carried two-thirds of the seats and ended thirty-six years of Social Credit rule. Used to the spoils of power, Social Credit proved an inept opposition party. Its attempts to find ideological ground not covered by the Conservatives gave the party a sharply reactionary image and, for those leery of the aura of wealth and slickness about the new governing party, reduced its ability to provide a reasonable alternative. Ultimately the party's ranks thinned to the point where other right-wing parties, particularly a western separatist party, moved in on Social Credit's much-reduced stock of voters. Finally, deprived of both members and voters, it was taken over by right-wing extremists of the type Manning had purged in the late forties. By the mid-eighties, no one of importance connected with the Social Credit government and party of the Manning and Strom periods remained in Alberta's Social Credit League; it had become the exclusive property of bigots and kooks. In this chapter, I trace the party's fall in the post-Manning period and question whether the slide that seemed to begin once the venerable premier left could not have been reversed at various points.

Shortly after the resignation of Manning came the report of the Kirby Commission into alleged influence-peddling by Hinman and Hooke. Like the 1956 commission on ministers' activities, this commission found no evidence that a government minister had clearly abused his high office. But, like the 1956 report, the 1968 commission raised questions about the internal operations of the Social Credit government. The Mahaffy report had suggested a pattern of informality in government contract-granting and purchasing that would have been unacceptable in any large, private corporation. Such informality, coupled with the fact that the government was riddled with poor appointments based on patronage and nepotism, suggests that the public image of Social Credit as providing a 'businesslike' if unimaginative administration of the province's affairs was somewhat mythological.

The Kirby report raised doubts about the public-mindedness of the two cabinet ministers it investigated, even if it concluded that neither had used his position to pressure government agencies or private individuals to make certain decisions that resulted in a personal benefit. But the John J. Barr intepretation, which accorded with the Social Credit interpretation of the time, that Kirby merely 'chided' their 'lack of discretion in some of their business dealings'[1] is an understatement indeed. Kirby outlined a variety of their dealings, which on the surface could appear as conflicts of interest with their ministerial duties. Lord Asquith, the British prime minister from 1908 to 1916, he noted, had said that ministers must not enter transactions 'whereby their private pecuniary interest might, even conceivably, come into conflict with their public duty.'[2] By these standards, Hooke and Hinman came off badly.

Hooke was involved in a variety of land deals while he was minister of municipal affairs. There was no evidence, for example, that he used his office to press for the development of Sherwood Park, a bedroom community near Edmonton where he owned land and made a profit of $64,000 from its sale once the government approved suburban development.[3] 'However, Mr. Hooke's involvement in this development could, and indeed did, give rise to the suspicion that he was using his office for the personal gain of himself and his associate Campbell. In so exposing himself to such suspicion his conduct in my view was imprudent in the sense of the observation made by Prime Minister Asquith quoted earlier in this Report.'[4] Similarly, Hooke was judged harshly by Kirby for getting personally involved, as co-owner of a house-building firm, in a damage claim against the City of Edmonton for failing to renew a certain lease at the same time that Edmonton was appearing before the Local Authorities Board trying to annex industrial areas adjacent to the city. Wrote Kirby: 'In my view, it was imprudent for Mr. Hooke, in view of his position as Minister of Municipal Affairs to have become personally involved to the extent that he did in a dispute between a company in which he had a substantial financial interest and a municipal corporation, and thereby create apprehension on the part of the City Commissioners, particularly Hamilton, even though it was unfounded.'[5]

Edgar Hinman's amassing of a private fortune during ten years in the cabinet also drew barbs from Kirby. Regarding Hinman's association with wealthy Edmonton businessman Jacob Superstein, Kirby wrote:

Superstein assumed he was deriving substantial benefits from his association with the Provincial Treasurer. This assumption demonstrates how imprudent it was of Mr. Hinman to have placed himself under obligation to Superstein by accepting the loan to B and R Service, and the personal loan to himself, and to have become involved to the extent that he did in Superstein's business affairs ... By this imprudence he rendered himself open to the same assumption by anyone aware of this relationship, notwithstanding, as pointed out by Davey, Superintendent of Treasury Branches, that the granting of credit by Treasury Branch is not subject to any control either by the Provincial Treasurer or by the Treasury Board, of which Hinman was Chairman, and that he did not in fact in any way intervene with respect to this interim financing.[6]

It might be unkind to question whether a minister need 'intervene' to get what he wished from a civil service rife with patronage and nepotism in which the interests and desires of the minister would be likely commonly known. In any case, however, Kirby was clear that neither Hinman nor Hooke could, by the laws of evidence – one is innocent until proven guilty – be labelled guilty of Turcott's explicit charge that the ministers had set out to use their offices to gain benefits.

But just as the wealth of Norman Tanner had surprised many Albertans who regarded their government as being composed of plain folk like themselves, the report on Hinman and Hooke illustrated again that Social Credit ministers, during or after their stay in government, appeared miraculously to prosper. The point was particularly emphasized when, within months of leaving government, Manning had become a director of the Canadian Imperial Bank of Commerce, Stelco, Pacific Western Airlines, Manufacturers Life, Melton's Real Estate, Alberta Gas Trunk, McIntyre Porcupine, and Underwood and McLellan.[7] The bank directorship particularly shocked old Social Crediters like Hooke,[8] just as Tanner's appointment to the board of the Dominion Bank of Canada shortly after leaving the cabinet in the fifties had raised questions about the sincerity of Social Credit ministers' thunderbolts against financial orthodoxy. Such events weakened remaining pretensions that Social Credit was qualitatively different from other conservative administrations: more high-minded, and governed by God rather than by Mammon. Increasingly its halo tarnished, and Social Credit and its leaders had to bear comparison with the Progressive Conservatives and their image-conscious leader, Peter Lougheed. Harry Strom, Manning's successor, and his handlers understood the challenge before them, but the ideological restraints of 'social conservatism' set by Manning made their task difficult.

For twenty-five years Alberta Social Credit and Ernest C. Manning had been synonymous. He had established early in his premiership that his ideas must prevail in cabinet and caucus, and his purge of extreme rightists and of Arthur Wray, who clung to the fuzzy radicalism of the Aberhart period, showed his resoluteness. Despite his serious manner and his social reserve, Manning, thanks to Aberhart and the Bible Institute, had developed a sense of theatricality that became an important asset in establishing his presence among Albertans. In Manning, it was felt, one could trust implicitly that the province was in clean hands. The business community in particular came to admire his philosophical individualism, particularly since it caused him to accept their opposition to government programs whose specific aim was to redistribute wealth.

Although many of Manning's ministers through the years were competent in their portfolios, none other perhaps than the colourful Alfred J. Hooke developed much of a public profile. Day-to-day administration might be in their hands but policy development, such as it was, always seemed to be Manning's province. In any case, the Social Credit–sponsored radio and television programs to propagandize government achievements made little use of ministers other than Manning when new policies were introduced.

In the last years of Manning's regime, he appeared to consult not with his cabinet colleagues but with his friends from big business, who were hoping to woo him to the national scene, with his son, Preston, and with Preston's young, educated, technocratic right-wing friends.[9] But Manning groomed no heir apparent either from the cabinet or from his latter-day consultants and there were no ministers in his government who appeared obvious contenders for his job and adequate opponents to the upstart Conservative leader.

Ultimately, Preston Manning and his friends proved to be kingmakers. Having won the senior Manning to their view that modern business and scientific ideas could be applied to find conservative solutions to social problems, they sought a successor for the premier who was similarly receptive. There was no obvious candidate among the fuddy-duddy old men of the Manning cabinet. Robert Clark, the minister of youth, might be a possibility but he was still in his twenties and unlikely to be acceptable to older party members. In the end, they settled on Harry Strom, who had become municipal affairs minister earlier that year and previously had served as agriculture minister. A wealthy farmer from southern Alberta, Strom was the type of successful, religious, rural family man likely to appeal to older party members. His appeal to the young Turks of the party was that he was open to new ideas.

The year before, for example, Strom had demonstrated his receptivity to the idea of 'preventive welfare,' a notion that the 'systems approach' group favoured. As chairman of the new Human Resources Development Authority, a major product of the Manning White Paper on Human Resources, Strom locked horns with crusty Alfred Hooke, who regarded the new technocrats, with some justification, as half-baked flakes. Hooke had only recently become minister of public welfare and he raised serious objections to the fuzziness of the Preventive Social Service Act of 1966. This act, which had been encouraged for several years by department officials,[10] set aside funds to be granted to municipal programs designed to get – and to keep – people off the welfare rolls.[11] Its parameters were so poorly defined that, in Hooke's view, municipalities were rushing to create vague programs so that they could receive government funds and reduce their own welfare costs. While Hooke attempted to convince Manning that no further grants be approved, so as to allow a balanced budget for 1968,[12] the Human Resources Development Authority moved to reduce Hooke's authority to delay approval of preventive social service programs.[13] Although Strom's officials may have played a greater role here than Strom himself, within government circles Strom became clearly associated with the side of the experimenters, not the traditionalists.

Strom promised little during his leadership campaign except to initiate a 'Head Start' program for the children of the poor, modelled after the largely futile 'Great Society' program the United States designed to equalize educational opportunities for ghetto children in that country, and to launch a major study of educational programs necessary to carry Alberta into the twenty-first century.[14] The stress on education and training fit in well with the ideas of the 'social conservative' systems-approach group who believed that conservatives must raise such issues as poverty, which theretofore had become the property of liberals and socialists by default. But while leftists might call for collectivist solutions such as government job creation and wealth redistribution, the social conservatives called for better educational opportunities and other community opportunities directed at individuals who might then be expected to pull themselves out of poverty.[15]

Preston Manning's involvement in the Strom campaign made it appear, probably correctly, that Premier Manning, nominally neutral, favoured Strom as his successor over Raymond Reierson and Gordon Taylor, the other strong contenders and men who might be regarded as old-fashioned conservatives, little interested in the mumbo-jumbo of the white paper.[16] Strom indeed won, but a fifty-five-year-old farmer from southern Alberta would have a difficult row to hoe to convince the increasingly alienated urbanites of the province that he represented the political change that Albertans increasingly seemed to want.

The young Turks, as they had hoped, came to play a significant role in the evolution of policy during the brief Strom period. Among their number were talented individuals such as Owen Anderson, executive assistant to Strom for a period and later co-ordinator of federal-provincial research and policy development; John Barr, executive assistant to the minister of education; and Don Hamilton, Strom's executive assistant at the time of the 1971 election. Anderson was only twenty-three when Strom became premier but had already played a role in the determination of the contents of Manning's White Paper on Human Resources. He was also, as noted in chapter 6, responsible for producing a thesis that provided the first detailed profile of the Social Credit League membership and its views. Barr was twenty-five and had a background in journalism, while Hamilton, who entered the lists as a Social Credit candidate against Don Getty in Whitemud in 1971, was a United Church minister 'who made a modest success of business before turning to politics.'[17]

These three, according to David G. Wood, 'were responsible for the Task Force on Urbanization and the Future; for the creation of the Intergovernmental Affairs office; for early childhood programs; for a province-wide magazine, "Land for Living."'[18]

None of these young men nor Strom himself had anything to say about monetary policy. They were social conservatives rather than social crediters and they supported an activist government whose aim was to promote individual opportunity and, in so doing, minimize the socialist threat. They did not always speak respectfully of the Social Credit party as it had operated in the preceding decades or of the party faithful from that period who remained active and demonstrated hostility to proponents of change. Just months before the 1971 election, for example, Hamilton provided this irreverent overview of party history in *Insight*, the glossy party organ which in the Strom period replaced the black-and-white little magazine, *The Busy Bee*, that served as party house organ from 1956 to 1968.

My analysis is that Social Credit started as a movement of the people – almost a revolutionary movement which began really on the left in many ways, but had the characteristics of the Western Canadian – independence, individual responsibility and that sort of thing.

Beginning about the end of the 1940s, it went progressively to the right, and in the 1950's was very much a right wing kind of party. I think partly due to the influence of Preston Manning on his father's thinking, the party veered back to the left in such things as the White Paper on Human Resources and the concepts contained in it.

Now I see it in the centre with some good social legislation and a feeling they want to stay on the right instead of the left. But there is a tension in the party created by some of the younger, newer thinkers who have come in and are pressing the social legislation and the old-line thinkers who came into the party in the late 1940s and see it as it was then.[19]

Someone who could find leftism, however vague, in Manning's white paper would be confusing technique with ideology since Manning expressed no important change of view in this document, except to claim that a 'systems approach' would help to rationalize programs and better serve the 'social conservative' ends he had espoused throughout his premiership. His comments on the Carter Commission later that year and his government's rebate of 100 per cent of estate taxes to everyone including the very rich demonstrated his continued opposition to wealth redistribution and 'regimentation' of industry. But to the young Social Crediters, mesmerized by technique, the battle with the Social Credit old-timers to achieve a 'scientific' right-wing approach to problems rather than rely on seat-of-the-pants solutions was a crucial one. It was also coincidentally a battle to change the Social Credit image in the public mind and to convince voters that the old Social Credit government was renewing itself and that there was no need to turn to Peter Lougheed's untried Conservatives.

The new approach produced a major governmental reorganization in 1971, with health and social development combined, a hospital services commission established, and a department of the environment with its own minister launched. Alberta was indeed the first province to establish a ministry of the environment. Earlier, as noted, intergovernmental affairs was established as a ministry. All in all, the government had been rearranged so that questions susceptible to the systems approach had been separated out and placed under a single authority.[20]

Reorganization of government departments, however, while it may lay the basis for better planning of programs, has little immediate impact on voters. Responding to the public's desire for ever-increasing educational opportunities and to increasingly fashionable 'human capital' views, whose currency among conservatives was obvious in the evidence before the Royal Commission on Education in the fifties as well as in Manning's white paper, the government vastly expanded education spending at every level. From 15.1 per cent of provincial expenditures as a percentage of receipts in 1956, education had climbed to 20.4 per cent in 1966, and then over the next five years soared to 33.4 per cent of the total budget.[21] Interestingly, while a 13 per cent surplus of receipts over expenditures had been recorded in 1966, huge increases in educational spending over the next five years wiped it out. The government posted small deficits in 1970 and 1971 and drew on surpluses of earlier years to the hypocritical shock of the Tories, for whom government expenditures on education were never high enough.[22]

Despite their willingness to fund ambitious building programs by the universities, colleges, and technical schools as well as to provide more money for the schools, the Strom government would not accept the long-standing position of all opposition parties that the government should place an upper limit on property taxes resulting from education costs. Nor would it take over the municipal portion of welfare costs. In these areas, the 'social conservative' (that is, Manning) view, that local governments and/or individuals must bear a share of costs for services delivered on their behalf as a deterrent to unwise spending, remained intact.[23]

Similarly intact was the Alberta government's opposition to federal programs which Manning had attacked. Bilingualism and biculturalism, tax reform, medicare, and regional development programs were subjects of hostile attack. Interestingly, however, while Manning had attempted to present his opposition to federal programs mainly in ideological terms, the Strom team preferred to emphasize regional concerns. Obviously, Manning's positions were formed in part by his perceptions of provincial interests, but unlike Harry Strom he seemed to feel little need to invoke provincial pride. He rarely spoke of regional interests because he was well aware that on most issues of federal-provincial relations the four western provinces and/or the three Prairie provinces were not in agreement. But the young men behind Strom, aware of the power of Quebec's appeal as a separate culture and region requiring special treatment from the federal government, wished to cast western Canada in the same light.

A book of essays edited by Barr and Anderson in 1971 exemplified the new approach. Its title *The Unfinished Revolt: Some Views on Western Independence* shamefully exploited the emergence of separatism as a major issue in Canada after the Parti Québécois took 24 per cent of the votes in a provincial election in 1970. There was no western independence movement in 1971, but Barr and Anderson none the less correctly noted that such old western grievances as freight rates and tariffs still caused disgruntlement among westerners. They threw the new federal programs of the fifties and sixties into the same bag as the traditional western grievances, labelling them as eastern-inspired and a burden on western Canada.

For example, Barr in his article 'Beyond Bitterness' attacked proposed federal tax reforms in regional terms. Finance Minister Edgar Benson had offered a watered-down version of the Carter reforms in a white paper presented to parliament in November 1969, and business pressure from all regions of the country eventually forced a further weakening of the reforms before an emasculated set of tax reforms reached parliament in 1971. None the less, Barr, ignoring the national character of conservative resistance to tax reform, including measures designed to favour domestic investors over foreign investors, commented: 'The thought that Mr. Benson was prepared to sabotage United States investment in Western Canada as a part of a federal tax-reform scenario outraged Westerners, not because they love Americans but because they know what the alternative to American investment is for *them*: a return to economic stagnation.'[24]

What had been for Manning a national imperative – the need for American investment – became for the new Social Credit team merely a regional question. Similarly, while Manning had argued against official encouragement of bilingualism and biculturalism by proclaiming that the whole nation should be left alone to produce a single culture (the standard 'melting pot' argument), the Strom group were more inclined to view the language issue from a regional perspective. Wrote Barr: '... the creation of a French language television station in Edmonton – where fewer than six percent of the viewers list French as their mother tongue but almost eight per cent of the viewers list German and eight per cent Ukrainian as their mother tongue – says some interesting things about the determination of the federal government to push a bilingual policy on all parts of the country, regardless of local needs or circumstances.'[25]

The rejection of bilingualism did not prevent these champions of western Canada from invoking Louis Riel, whose efforts had brought official bilingualism to the west, as a spiritual forbear. Although the Social Credit government had done little more for the descendants of Riel's Métis than to place some of their number in bleak colonies that received little provincial funding, Owen Anderson chose to regard the French-speaking Métis leader as an integral part of a tradition of western dissent to which Social Credit was also heir. That the federal government suppression of the 1885 rebellion had largely cleared the way for European settlers to inhabit Indian and Métis lands did not appear to becloud the argument that the west, like Quebec, had a history of resistance to Ottawa's rule.[26]

Anderson, the major figure in Alberta's new federal-provincial relations bureaucracy, seemed, like Barr, to slip invariably into Quebec-bashing in his comments on federal policy towards Alberta. In this respect he probably fairly reflected the feelings of many westerners, who, however unfairly, regarded the federal government as overly solicitous of the views of Quebec voters. For example, Anderson claimed that Ottawa had erected barriers to the entry of western oil into eastern markets which, at the time, were mainly served by oil imported from Venezuela. He charged that the federal government refused to discourage imports at a time when only half of the country's oil needs were provided internally because Quebec voters would react bitterly to having to pay one or two cents more per gallon of gasoline.[27]

In general, Anderson and Barr argued for a less interventionist federal government as the solution to most problems and in this sense were not far off the Manning position. Interestingly, however, these new-wave Alberta conservatives seemed not to share Manning's concern over salacious and subversive movies. While Manning had asked the federal government to keep such offerings off the airwaves in God's province, Anderson denounced the 'cultural censorship' implied in the policy of the new Canadian Radio-television and Telecommunications Commission's limiting of American offerings on the Canadian networks.[28]

Premier Strom, influenced by his young advisers, proposed that much of Ottawa's alleged interference in areas of provincial jurisdiction and its resultant need for more tax dollars could be jettisoned in favour of a federally financed guaranteed national income plan.[29] Talk of such a plan was widespread at the time, although not all of its proponents by any means saw it as an actual replacement of but rather as a supplement to existing federal programs whose total impact on the distribution of wealth in Canada had, incidentally, been marginal. Barr expressed the conservative vision of a guaranteed income plan. It would: 'replace the present ineffective patchwork-quilt of regional incentives and regional development programs. The plan would create a modest level of guaranteed income, sufficient to enable one to live at a spartan but healthy level. Beyond that the problem of "regional inequality" would be left to the working of the free market and stepped-up programs of manpower retraining and mobility grants by the federal government.'[30]

The guaranteed income plan along with a call for an elected Senate with equal representation from all regions provided Barr's main prescriptions for dealing with alleged regional inequalities. The elected Senate idea would be a recurring one among Albertans claiming that central Canada exerted overwhelming pressure within the existing federal system.[31]

The 'social conservative' philosophy joining traditional conservatism to scientific management with a bit of old-fashioned regional dissension tossed in for good measure failed to provide the Strom government with the image of dynamism that its younger civil servants tried to create. An ecology corps was created 'to give unemployed students an income and a role to play in environmental protection,' and at the last minute a Department of the Environment with regulatory powers was established.[32] Employees of Alberta Government Telephones were given access to the Alberta Labour Act, removing the Manning tradition of treating Crown corporation employees as civil servants to be denied full bargaining powers (such as they were under the Alberta Labour Act).[33] Royal commissions on the future of the cities and on post-secondary education were established.[34] But none of this seemed to remove the impression that the new Social Credit team was merely borrowing ideas from the Lougheed legislative group. Strom himself, as John Barr notes, appeared remote and dour on television despite being warm-hearted in person.[35] Lougheed and some of his desk-mates, meanwhile, seemed to be masters of the medium.

The Conservatives began to gather momentum before Strom had an opportunity to present a legislative program. In February 1969, just two months after Strom became leader, Bill Yurko, an Edmonton engineer, carried Manning's Edmonton seat in a by-election. Later that year when Liberal Bill Switzer died, the Conservatives carried his Calgary seat. When the remaining Liberal in the legislature subsequently defected to the Tories, followed in a few months by the Independent member for Banff-Cochrane, the crystallization of the Conservatives as *the* non-socialist opposition to Social Credit was complete.[36] The provincial Liberal party, damaged by the renewed unpopularity of its federal wing, lapsed into a two-decade coma.

The Conservatives presented themselves as a party of openness and of fresh ideas. In the 1969 session, for example, their calls for open government included pleas for greater independence of constituency MLAs from party discipline, the opening of legislative committees to the public, and the opening of the legislature to radio and television coverage.[37] The largely urban Tories also demonstrated their sympathy with urbanites' frustrations over Social Credit priorities by calling for provincial financing for urban transportation. The newly elected Bill Yurko noted that urban residents were increasingly dependent on 'automobile and high speed transportation systems' for work and recreational purposes and that the attraction of industry was dependent as well upon good transportation facilities. He called for the establishment of a commission with representation from the province's nine urban areas to: '(1) Study in detail the future of existing new satellite cities and towns and traffic patterns in and around said areas of Alberta and evolve blueprint for the year 2000. (2) Study and make specific recommendations respecting long range financing of urban transportation systems.'[38]

The establishment a year and a half later of the even more wide-ranging Task Force on Urbanization and the Future indicated the government's understanding that it was increasingly perceived as out of sympathy with the needs of non-rural residents. But while an opposition calling for a commission of investigation may receive public support for being innovative, a government which follows such advice and does no more – particularly a government perceived as old and creaking in the seams – simply appears vacillating. And the task force was established too close to the 1971 election to report, never mind have its recommendations implemented.

In the 1970 legislative session, the Conservatives stole the spotlight with twenty-one bills designed to present themselves as an alternative to the cautious Social Credit regime. More important, the Conservatives were busily engaged in organizing strong constituency organizations and developing a campaign for the next provincial election which revolved around Lougheed as a leader. Lougheed had himself determined such an approach even before Manning's retirement, stressing in a July 1968 document that a leader 'along the Trudeau style' and using 'the Kennedy approach of a set speech with some improvisation' would provide the most effective campaign. The replacement of the respected Manning with a lesser-known figure made this approach even more promising.[39]

Lougheed did not wait for the election to make himself known personally to Albertans. He travelled the province, in each area meeting local officials and leaders of business, farm, and labour organizations. His burgeoning party held policy conferences and, in general, did all that was possible to establish itself as a competent alternative to the old Socred administration.[40] Short on policy specifics, the Conservatives none the less appeared open to what the people had to say – a convenient position open only to opposition parties, from whom endless willingness to listen cannot be read as an excuse for inaction.

Strom and his associates attempted to respond in kind to the Conservative image-building thrust. Edmonton lawyer Bill Johnson became league president in 1969, replacing the redoubtable Orvis Kennedy. The next year, Johnson and his executive announced a 'new look' for the league's annual convention. The party would have a new logo, featuring a stylized 'S' above with a 'C' below, all in fluorescent green. Cabinet ministers would face newscasters from 'hot benches' to account for the government's performance. Up to six additional delegateships per constituency were reserved for the minuscule group of party members between the ages of eighteen and twenty-five to disguise the fact that, as indicated in chapter 6, party members on average were over fifty years old.[41] Attempts were made, meanwhile, to revive dormant constituency organizations, and the party claimed more than 30,000 members at the time of the 1971 election.[42] This figure, if accurate, was an increase of about a third since 1967 and indicated that in rural constituencies at least candidates for a Social Credit nomination still thought it worthwhile to beat the bush to sign up their supporters as party members.

The major cities, however, according to the 'rates and information' pamphlet for *Insight*, the party publication, remained barren terrain for Social Credit recruitment. Only 19.3 per cent of copies of *Insight*, sent to all members, were mailed to addresses in Edmonton and Calgary, where more than half the population lived. While 10.8 per cent of copies went to 'intermediate urban centers' (an undefined category), 35.7 per cent went to rural areas and 34.2 per cent to small towns and villages.[43] The Social Credit geographical profile of membership reflected the Alberta of 1935 rather than of 1971.

None the less, the electoral map still gave over-representation to the rural population, although the under-representation of the cities had been alleviated somewhat by the Strom administration. Ten seats were added in an electoral redistribution before the 1971 election, seven of them in the two large centres. It was in the cities, it was generally conceded, that further Tory gains were inevitable. But the countryside, many felt before the election, would remain loyal to Social Credit, which had bequeathed upon them endless miles of highways and large grants to schools whose trustees appeared far more grateful for the bounty than did their still-complaining urban counterparts.

Differences between the two major parties were not easy to discern. The Tories, as indicated previously, called for greater provincial spending to alleviate municipal spending on education and transportation, at the same time denouncing the tiny deficits of the last two years of Social Credit rule. While the Conservatives generally appeared more interventionist in their orientation than Social Credit, one of their bills in 1971 called upon the government to consider handing over unspecified Crown corporations and operations to private enterprise. And while Highways Minister Gordon Taylor, speaking for the government against the motion, said 'the interests of the people of Alberta have to come first,' four government MLAs joined in supporting the Tory motion. Two of the dissidents, Alfred Hooke, representing Rocky Mountain House, and John Landeryou, from Lethbridge, had been among the first crop of Aberhart members in 1935.[44] Hooke indeed, excluded from cabinet after Strom's accession to power, often seemed to be a member of the opposition rather than the government, and Strom's inability either to convince him to tone down his public criticisms or to sit as an independent created dissension within the party and caucus. Ironically, Hooke's independent stance and his ability to carry with him a small group of government backbenchers on some issues refuted the Lougheed charge that Social Credit, at least in the Strom years, stifled its backbenchers. But the bitterness of the Hooke attack and the premier's bafflement before it did not likely aid the government's cause.[45]

During the election, the two major parties made similar promises. Social Credit promised one thousand dollar cash grants for home purchasers, while the Tories promised to double the provincial housing budget. Both parties promised urban transportation funds and various subsidies for pensioners. The Tories, however, went somewhat further than the government in some of their spending and tax-concession promises. They would eliminate, they said, the portion of property tax then used to pay for basic education programs and would provide property tax credits to homeowners and renters.[46]

In the end, however, specific promises doubtless played less of a role than the issue of whether, after thirty-six years of government by the same party, Alberta did not need a change. 'Alberta deserves a fresh start and the Lougheed Team can provide it' was the Conservative theme for 1971.[47] Lougheed had been briefly, in the 1950s, a quarterback for the Edmonton Eskimos; the emphasis on him as a vigorous man in the prime of life and a successful team player in sports, business, and law appealed to many voters to whom Social Credit, with Manning gone, appeared a tired old machine with its engine removed. As Allan Hustak writes in his favourable biography of Peter Lougheed: 'Thirty-six years of "God's government" had come to an end. It was an awesome victory for Lougheed but in terms of Alberta's history it was a triumph of style rather than of substance – the secular equivalent of a revival meeting – a new minister had been selected to do a better job than the old one but the faith remained the same. There was no substantive change in political philosophy.'[48]

The 'awesome victory for Lougheed' bore no resemblance to the election of 1935 that had brought Social Credit to power. Although Albertans have been painted exaggeratedly as followers of Pied Pipers who leap together from one party to another, leaving their former political home in shambles, Social Credit suffered no resounding defeat in 1971. The Progressive Conservatives carried forty-nine seats to twenty-five for Social Credit and one for the NDP. With a third of the legislative seats, an opposition party could hardly be said to be on the way to extinction.

The popular vote indeed demonstrated once again how easily the first-past-the-post system of voting distorted the intentions of Alberta voters. With 46.4 per cent of the total vote the Conservatives had won almost two-thirds of the legislative seats. Social Credit, with 41 per cent of the vote, had lost only 3.5 per cent of its vote in 1967; indeed, with a larger electoral turn-out in 1971, the absolute number voting Social Credit in 1971 was marginally higher than in 1967.[49]

The major difference between 1971 and 1967, indeed between 1971 and every election since 1940, was that Social Credit faced a fairly united opposition. Lougheed, by turning the provincial Conservative party into a personal vehicle, de-emphasized the connection of this party with the federal Conservatives who had dumped John Diefenbaker in 1967, making it a comfortable political home both for traditional western Conservatives as well as for federal Liberals whose provincial party had collapsed before their eyes. The New Democratic Party, led since 1968 by young schoolteacher and party organizer Grant Notley, had sunk all its capital in the ultimately failed attempt to pursue Hooke and Hinman before Justice Kirby. Its political purse empty, the party concentrated on a small number of seats and managed barely to elect Notley in the Spirit River–Fairview seat in the Peace River district. But its overall vote had fallen from 16 to 11 per cent between 1967 and 1971.[50]

Social Credit, thus, need not have felt in 1971 that Albertans had massively rejected the party. There were, however, ominous portents. The party had managed to carry fourteen of twenty seats in the two big cities in 1967 with only

39 per cent of the vote, thanks to large numbers of three- and four-way contests in which the split of opposition party votes allowed Social Crediters to win with modest pluralities. In 1971, its vote shaved by another five per cent in the metropolitan ridings, Social Credit carried only three of twenty-seven seats in the big cities, all three in Calgary. Indeed, outside Edmonton and Calgary, the Conservatives overtook Social Credit in only twenty-five of forty-seven seats (excluding the NDP-won seat) and were slightly behind the Strom forces in popular vote. So any rebuilding of Social Credit either would have to seek to restore party popularity in the cities or would have to reject the urban voters altogether and attempt to build upon rural resentments against the metropolis to firm up a still-mighty sentiment in favour of 'God's government.'

First, however, Social Credit had to come to terms with being in opposition. Never before had this party been in opposition. It had nary a provincial member before the electoral sweep of 1935 and then for thirty-six years – going through several guises – never lost its position as the party of government. Its initial radical and monetary-panacea phases having passed before the death of Aberhart, the party had gradually become the lap-dog of Premier Manning, whose combination of evangelical religion, anti-socialist rhetoric, courting of the oil companies, and lavish spending on schools and education eventually bore the label of 'social conservatism.' Under Strom the ideological content of the '*social* conservatism' had not been made clear, and it now became necessary for the Social Credit opposition caucus and the Social Credit League as a whole to determine whether they had any fundamental differences with the Conservatives. Lougheed's caginess between 1967 and 1971, sometimes attacking the government from the right, sometimes from the left, made it difficult for the league to plan strategy before the new government showed its hand.

In their controversial account of the economic strategies undertaken by Saskatchewan and Alberta in the 1970s to free themselves from over-reliance on resource extraction for economic survival, Larry Pratt and John Richards attempt a social portrait of the Lougheed Conservatives. For these authors, Lougheed's 'interventionist provincial government' served as an instrument to 'nurture the development and defend the interests of an ascendant regional bourgeoisie.'[51] During the seventies, they argue, this bourgeoisie, via the Conservative government, attempted to increase revenue from the province's energy resources in order to finance policies that would encourage economic diversification in Alberta, with an emphasis on secondary manufacturing. Among the members of this arriviste bourgeoisie these authors count Alberta-based energy and construction giants such as Mannix-Loram, Nova, ATCO, and the Alberta Energy Company. More generally, within the ranks of those tired of the 'passive rentier' approach of Social Credit were the professional groups who benefited from the growth of the Alberta economy – including corporate lawyers, engineers, geologists, and financial consultants – and feared that failure to diversify would result in stagnation of that economy as resources were depleted.[52]

Richards and Pratt were guardedly optimistic in 1979, when world oil prices were at record highs, that the strategy of the Alberta Tories might work. Many commentators at the time were sceptical, but, with the drop in oil prices and oil demand that began in 1982, hopes of diversification dimmed and questions were raised over whether the Tories had not frittered away monies that might have aided in diversification.[53] Pratt himself had noted in an earlier book that the Alberta government, in its eagerness to support development of the Athabasca tar sands, poured in millions of dollars in infrastructural, training, and financing costs without ensuring that the multinational companies involved provide opportunities for Alberta-based firms to develop and profit from technologies required to service the giant projects.[54]

It would seem, in fact, that the oil boom, which Conservative rhetoric treated as the opportunity to fund diversification of the Alberta economy, proved to be its opposite. Private investment in the province was largely attracted to the energy sector and to a booming real estate market, while government funds, as Pratt's earlier book indicated, were also largely directed towards the needs of the energy sector.

None the less, the success or failure of the rhetorical Lougheed strategy for the Alberta economy, as it emerged gradually after the election of the Conservatives in 1971, does not disprove the Richards-Pratt analysis of who the new political rulers of Alberta were. Indeed, as is often the case with regional bourgeoisies hoping to gain greater influence within their colonial-dominated economies, the ideological commitment to the existing economic system – which in Canadian terms means state subsidies for major business ventures as much as it means any supposed free operation of the market-place – limits the degree to which new policies designed to strengthen local capitalists are pursued. In Alberta's case, although the Tories did skirmish with the multinational oil companies over royalties, the main target of attack was the federal government, which, especially after the spectacular rise of oil prices in late 1973 after the Yom Kippur Middle East war, was seen as trying to muscle in on Alberta's resources by attempting to increase its own revenues and to control prices charged Canadian consumers of Alberta energy.

The Conservatives' ability to rally rich and middle-class Albertans behind their banner and to drape their party in the provincial flag as champions of western interest against the hated 'east' (central Canada) left Social Credit in a precarious position. The Manning Socreds, as we have seen, were largely a party of farmers, small-business people, and lower-middle-class rural residents. Although the big oil companies were happy to finance the party's electoral needs, their executives played no conspicuous role in either the government or the party. The unlikely marriage between the major benefactors of the Alberta boom and the more modest party membership was performed by Manning with his religiously based opposition to all forms of socialism and advanced liberalism. Many members of the upper middle class of professionals and executives had supported Manning with their votes, grateful for the low taxes his regime levied upon them, but few joined his party, which, because of its origins, appeared too plebeian. Many, as the Social Credit poll in 1956 revealed, supported free-enterprise opposition parties, which they regarded presumably as less ideology-bound than the Manning party. The latter-day Manning attempt to renovate his party's dogmatic laissez-faire image with a new technocratic language and an emphasis on social engineering had won only a coterie of middle-class converts to the aging government party, especially since the Lougheed Conservatives provided an alternative political home for the 'arriviste bourgeoisie' with a chance of unseating Aberhart's successors. Even in 1971, despite nominating thirty-seven new candidates for the seventy-five Alberta seats, 'a break-down of candidates' occupations shows the continued domination of small businessmen, teachers and agriculturists in the Socred election team.'[55] While some of the 'small businessmen' were indeed big fish within the areas in which they lived, they were generally men who had made their money in the service sector and were indirectly dependent upon the health of the resources sector for their prosperity.[56] Lougheed's candidates included eleven lawyers, but Social Credit had only two lawyers on its slate. None the less, the relatively modest circumstances of the 1971 Social Credit candidates should not be overstated. The party had gone out of its way to attract a broader base of candidates, and it did nominate several professionals and substantial business-men, none of whom, however, won their seats.

Once the election was over, Social Credit's ability to keep even its small group of well-educated and / or rich members declined. It no longer offered the spoils of power, and its remaining activists were not the younger opportunists recruited by Strom's young men but the older, dogmatic members of the Manning period who embodied the classic 'petit bourgeois' values of thrift and self-reliance and appeared unconcerned that the 'social conservative' philosophy of their long-time leader had allowed the Alberta economy to become overly dependent upon resource extraction, foreign-controlled, and riddled with glaring inequalities. The interventionist state, after all, like the banks and the labour movement, was part of the insidious conspiracy aimed at enslaving ordinary people like themselves.

Harry Strom was not particularly representative of their thinking. Although he was a religious, well-to-do rancher of conservative bent, he was not the ideologue that Manning was and he seemed to lack any clear vision for his party. As leader of the opposition, he found little in the new government's actions to which he could take strong objection.[57] He did not protest when the Lougheed government, shortly after it assumed office, announced its intention to increase petroleum royalties. Although he warned that such action could limit new investment in the energy sector,[58] neither he nor his colleagues could find much enthusiasm for a defence of companies whose large profits would be touched rather slightly by the new government's gesture. In December 1972 Strom resigned as leader so that the party might attempt to find a younger leader who might develop a profile over the next few years as a dynamic alternative to Lougheed.

Strom's mantle was supposed to fall on Robert Clark, a successful farmer in his early thirties who represented Olds-Didsbury and had served as minister of youth under Manning and minister of education under Strom. Clark had chaired Strom's leadership campaign in 1968, and like Strom he was a flexible right-winger who would have preserved Social Credit more as an alternative administration than as an alternative vision to the Progressive Conservatives. Enjoying caucus support and the support of the younger Social Crediters, Clark was expected to win the well-attended convention in February 1973, which chose the party's new leader.

The dictates of political realism almost allowed predictions of Clark's win to come true. A youngish, non-dogmatic, articulate, experienced former cabinet minister who held a fairly safe legislative seat could present Social Credit as a voice of the future rather than of days of past glory. But a party majority, unhappy with the timid attack of Strom and company on the new government, wanted a leader who would represent more forcefully a traditional Manning vision for Alberta as an alternative to the interventionism of the slick lawyers and businessmen who then held the levers of political power. For some, Gordon Taylor, the veteran highways minister of the Manning period and member for Drumheller since 1940, served the purpose. But most, despite being aged themselves, recognized that a leader in his sixties would be a liability.

And so it was that the convention in February 1973 turned to a political unknown: Werner Schmidt, a forty-one-year-old educational administrator whose religiosity and reactionary views endeared him to the Manning generation of Social Crediters. Schmidt had been raised on his family's farm near Coledale in the far south of the province, where Social Credit support was particularly high in the party's years in office, and had been employed in the sugar-beet fields and as a trucker while working towards his two university degrees. From 1966 to

1969 he had served as executive director of the Alberta School Trustees Association. In 1971 he ran unsuccessfully as a Social Credit candidate in the provincial seat of Edmonton-Belmont and was soundly defeated by a Conservative in that party's sweep of the capital city.[59]

Schmidt won a second-ballot victory over Clark of 814 to 775 votes[60] and proceeded over the next two years to provide Albertans with an alternative vision for the province's economic development to that represented by Lougheed. For example, the new government created the Alberta Energy Company as a vehicle for increasing participation by Alberta investors in all facets of petroleum development. The corporation was to be partly under public ownership and partly controlled by private shareholders. It followed, in fact, a model set by Manning when Alberta Gas Trunk Line Company was established in 1954 with a monopoly over gas-gathering within Alberta. Although common stock shares in AGTL were issued, voting shares and membership on the company board were divided equally among four groups: gas producers, gas exporters, Alberta's gas utilities, and the Alberta government.

For Werner Schmidt, however, the Alberta Energy Company, rather than being a logical extension of past Social Credit policy, was a massive government entry into areas where 'private enterprise has managed heretofore.' He claimed to see no government role in 'the pipeline business, the electrical power business, the gas exploration and development business, and the tar sands oil extraction business,' all areas in which the Alberta Energy Company would have some involvement.[61] In contradistinction to Conservative interventionism to favour Alberta-based capitalists, Schmidt counselled 'a minimum of government.'[62] But his zealous opposition to all involvement of government in the economy outside of the social services and education areas proved no asset to his party. Instead of concentrating on who was mainly benefiting from Conservative expenditures in the economic development area, as Clark might have done, Schmidt limited himself to a blanket ideological attack on the government with little comment about the specifics of its programs.

The Social Credit platform in 1975 reflected Schmidt's lack of political realism, if also his courage of political convictions. Not only should resources be developed solely by private enterprise but, he believed, even farmers must stop relying on government for subsidies: 'Our agricultural economy will operate most efficiently when it "stands on its own." Government should assist only in research, technical advice, marketing assistance to farmers and farmer organizations, and meeting emergencies and catastrophies.'[63] Even Ernest Manning, for all his devotion to the justice inherent in the operations of the market-place, had not been willing to attack assistance to farmers, especially since most of it came from the federal government. Schmidt was indeed rather more consistent than

Manning, who as we have seen was happy to implement government regulations when the oil industry required them and to protect the Calgary Power hydroelectric monopoly. Schmidt simply wanted the government to absent itself from the operation of the economy altogether.

Schmidt's a priorism neither held his party together nor attracted much support from Albertans. In June 1973, four months after becoming party leader, Schmidt ran in a by-election in the riding of Calgary Foothills and was badly trounced by the Conservative candidate. In September, Social Credit house leader James Henderson left the party to sit as an Independent and caucus chose Bob Clark, Schmidt's rival for the leadership, as his replacement.[64] Party membership, which had stood at 30,000 for the election year of 1971, reached only 6000 before the 1975 election, reflecting the disinterest in Social Credit nominations outside of ridings already held by the party.[65]

Lougheed called the election for March 1975, promising an all-out defence of Alberta interests in dealing with the federal government regarding the energy sector and announcing the establishment of a trust fund, to be called the Alberta Heritage Investments and Savings Fund, in which a portion of oil royalties annually would be banked to make room for investments by the province in economic development and diversification.[66] Against the image of a forward-looking, province-protecting white knight projected by Lougheed, the earnest-looking Schmidt appeared a dinosaur clinging to a political viewpoint that, while having some support in generalities among rural residents, had little support in the details.

Social Credit incumbents tended to run local-oriented campaigns in which little was said directly either of Lougheed or of Schmidt. They appealed to their constituents to remember the services they had performed for them as local representatives and played upon feelings among many rural people that Lougheed and company were city slickers who did not concern themselves as much with rural issues as did the incumbent Social Crediters.

This strategy worked for only five of the seventeen incumbents who chose to run, of whom one, the veteran Gordon Taylor, ran as an Independent Social Crediter. No previously unelected Social Crediter came even close to taking a seat,[67] and Schmidt lost in Taber by almost two to one to a Conservative. The once-mighty party of Aberhart and Manning suffered a humiliating defeat, dropping from 41 per cent of the vote in 1971 to only 18 per cent in 1975. The party that had lost urban Alberta in 1971 after becoming too identified as a rural party had now also lost most of its rural strongholds, having failed to develop a politics that could express rural reservations with Lougheed without having to promise to leave farmers almost totally without government aid.

The Progressive Conservatives carried sixty-nine of Alberta's seventy-five ridings with 63 per cent of the vote in 1975, a better performance in the popular vote than even Social Credit had ever achieved. Social Credit had four seats, while Grant Notley of the NDP and Gordon Taylor held the remaining two seats. A new political dynasty had been established, and the future for Social Credit looked bleak. The province was wealthier than ever, and while Tory policies, much as Social Credit policies, favoured the better-off, there was enough money to go around to keep most voters happy.

The hapless Schmidt resigned as party leader shortly after the election. He had been a disaster looking for a place to happen and he left behind a practically non-existent provincial organization: short of members, finances, and self-confidence. The party now turned to Bob Clark, who had been re-elected handily in Olds-Didsbury and had not entirely given up on the party's chances to outlive the Schmidt fiasco and to offer a viable, right-wing alternative to the Lougheed forces. Clark did not reject Schmidt's position against government involvement in productive enterprises, and he promised that a Social Credit government would sell government shares in the Alberta Energy Company, in the Syncrude tar sands plant near Fort McMurray, and in Pacific Western Airlines, all of which had been acquired in the Lougheed years.[68]

But Clark did not limit himself to listing things government should not do. While he attacked 'big government, big business and big labour' as being in cahoots in Alberta, it was not his view that small business people and farmers, the backbone of what was left of his party, needed no government help.

Indeed, the party now 'promised a comprehensive program of support of small business,' including start-up capital grants and low-interest loans. It also proposed 'renewed emphasis on people programs, especially on innovative programs in the health and education fields,'[69] echoing complaints from the NDP and myriad pressure groups that the purse-strings of the provincial treasury were held rather close where social spending was concerned. The Manning and Strom governments, because they had spent little on economic development, had poured large chunks of their revenues into 'people programs,' and the declining portion of provincial expenditures going to education and social services was cited as a turning away from humane priorities. Social Credit in 1979 promised to extend Alberta Health Care Insurance Plan coverage to include dental care for children under twelve and to expand dramatically educational services to the handicapped and home-care services to the old and the ill.[70]

But Social Credit's most attractive vote-getting promise in 1979 was the elimination of provincial income tax on the first $16,000 of taxable income. Such a move would have exempted three-quarters of Alberta taxpayers from provincial income tax and cut everyone else's taxes as well. Revenue for this measure, it was claimed, was easily available from the then-large provincial budget surplus.[71] Ironically, except in its last few years of office, Social Credit had regarded budgets without current-account surpluses as anathema, leading the province back to the humiliating dependence on bankers that had plagued Alberta governments before 1945.

Social Credit faced mighty difficulties in selling the Clark package as an alternative to Lougheed's triumphalism. The party's losing image had lost it financial support from business and electoral worker support from former members. Above all, the party had to contend with Peter Lougheed, who had convinced large numbers of Albertans of all social classes that his alleged program to develop and diversify the economy was for the benefit of all. More to the point, perhaps, his continual battles with the federal government provided him with a well-cultivated image as champion of the exploited Alberta people against the hated 'East.' Ignoring the fact that no provincial party had opposed his government's positions in federal-provincial relations, Lougheed in 1979, as in 1975, tried to turn the election into a plebiscite in which Albertans were asked to elect only Conservative MLAS so that the government could claim that it spoke for all Albertans when it negotiated with the federal government.

Whether or not the plebiscitary logic of the government captured the public imagination, discontent with the Conservatives was still too meagre for Social Credit to stage a come-back. The four sitting MLAS were re-elected, but they were not joined by new desk-mates. The party's popular vote had increased marginally from 18 to 20 per cent,[72] but there was no indication that any revival was in sight. Indeed, 1979 would prove to be the last year in which Social Credit contested an Alberta election as a serious political outfit. The rise of separatist sentiment in the province over the next several years, provoked in part by Lougheed's demagoguery, provided a new outlet for right-wing sentiment and left Social Credit without a constituency.

Western separatist movements, fuelled by redneck hatred of Pierre Trudeau, bilingualism and biculturalism, the metric system, and high taxes, came and went in the seventies in western Canada, usually finding their greatest strength in central Alberta. But it took the October 1980 budget of the Trudeau government to bring respectable elements into the movement and to give it a serious audience in the province. The federal government, fulfilling promises made in the February 1980 election that had overturned the short-lived Joe Clark Conservative minority government, introduced a so-called National Energy Policy. This policy, which envisaged a transfer of a large share of petroleum assets from American multinationals to Canadian investors, also increased the federal government's share of revenues from oil production. All aspects of the policy were denounced by Peter Lougheed, who promptly announced a cut-back in the flow of oil and gas to central Canada until the budget policies were withdrawn.

Some sections of the petroleum industry went further and called for outright separation of the west from Canada in order to protect industry profits and American investors. Carl Nickle, millionaire oilman and former Conservative MP, led this group. He allied himself with West-Fed, a separatist group led by wealthy and cranky implements-dealer Elmer Knutson. Knutson was rabidly anti-Quebec and patented a curious constitutional theory that the 1931 Statute of Westminster had given sovereignty to the Canadian provinces, thus removing the federal government's right, without specific authorization by provinces, to make rules within their territories. 'Oil-well-servicing businessmen, consultants and drilling contractors' were attracted to the new separatist groups, which also included a party called Western Canada Concept, the creature of British Columbian Doug Christie, a right-wing Victoria lawyer. But the hard-core supporters 'were rural residents, small businessmen, and farmers throughout the West.'[73]

The attraction of separatism for right-wing elements of their natural constituency bode ill for Social Credit, which had been heir to a regional protest with which it had consciously identified in the Strom years, though rather less so in the Manning years. The party leaders, however, remained federalist and seemed generally to take a 'me too' stance on issues of federal-provincial relations raised by Lougheed.

February 1982 marked a watershed both for Social Credit and for the separatists. Bob Clark had resigned as party leader in 1981 and a convention in late 1981 had chosen Rod Sykes, former mayor of Calgary and lifelong Liberal, as his successor. When Clark subsequently resigned his Olds-Didsbury seat to become a private consultant, a by-election was called by Lougheed for February 1982. It was during this by-election that Gordon Kesler, oil company scout and rodeo rider, created a political upset by carrying a seat for the Western Canada Concept. Kesler, taking advantage of his constituents' paranoia about Trudeau's intentions regarding constitutional revision (failure to include a property-rights guarantee was regarded as proof of imminent Communist take-over), appealed for voters to send both Edmonton and Ottawa a message of anger. A vote for the status quo, which in Olds-Didsbury was Social Credit, would not be noticed; a vote for a separatist would not be missed.[74]

Social Credit's failure to hold one of its remaining strongholds precipitated a coming apart at what were, by then, rather loose seams. Sykes found a pretext to resign; Fred Mandeville, one of the remaining three MLAs, announced that he would not be a candidate in the next provincial election; and Ray Speaker and Walter Buck, the other Socred MLAs, announced that they would run as

Independents. The Social Credit party's career, even as a minor political force, was over.[75]

Social Credit ran only a handful of candidates in the provincial election of 1982 and received less than 1 per cent of the total vote.[76] The party might have been allowed a decent burial except that its corpse proved a convenient vehicle for a small core of Douglasite monetary fundamentalists and a vicious group of Nazi apologists and hate-mongers who felt comfortable with Douglas's racial views.

In December 1982, Jim Keegstra, mayor of Eckville, was fired from his teaching job by the Lacombe County school-board for his rabid anti-Semitic teachings in his high school social studies classes. His firing was widely publicized and he was subsequently prosecuted and convicted for violations of federal hate laws. Shortly after his firing, Keegstra was elected second vice-president for Alberta of the national Social Credit party. The national party leader, J. Martin Hattersley, an Edmonton lawyer who was committed to Douglasite monetary views but rejected Douglas's racism, attempted to fire Keegstra from his new position. He cancelled the party memberships of Keegstra and two party officials who were openly supporting Keegstra and his teachings that Jews were taking over the world by stealth in a bid to eradicate Christianity and capitalism and that, along the way, they had invented the Holocaust out of whole cloth to win sympathy for themselves. But in the end, Hattersley lost. 'At a special executive meeting the dismissals and cancellations were overturned and Hattersley himself was forced to leave the party. Keegstra once again became vice president. There is not much left of the federal Social Credit Party in Canada or in Alberta today, but what there is seems to be as anti-Semitic as Douglas Social Credit ever was.'[77]

Thus, the post-Manning period began with Social Credit charting a moderate right-wing route having little to do with the monetary radicalism of its founders, the social radicalism of its thirties urban activists, or the bigotry of some of its activists and elected representatives of the forties. It ended fifteen years later with the party moribund and its corpse invaded by racist body-snatchers. Their racist venom, reminiscent of Douglas's bigoted views, should not, however, obscure the fact that Social Credit, in office, whatever the conspiratorial views of its leaders, had been authoritarian and right-wing but never fascist and genocidal. It was only the departure of the respected party leaders and most of the members that left the party shell available to kooks and fascists. It is indeed unfortunate for democracy in Alberta that Bob Clark narrowly failed to gain his party's leadership in 1973 and to keep the party alive as a moderate right-wing alternative for those who felt excluded from Lougheed's Conservative clique of better-educated business and professional people but disdained the left-wing alternative offered by the NDP. But the fear and distrust of government involvement in the economy and of the welfare state engendered by Ernest Manning attracted members who, in many cases, were even more consistent in holding these views than the practical Manning deemed feasible in political life. The result was that Social Credit, for a period, failed to articulate the real wishes of its constituency – to kick welfare recipients in the rear but also to provide extensive subsidies for virtuous farmers and small businessmen. Unhappily, by the time it again expressed its more traditional views, the party had fallen too far into disrepair to be taken seriously by many people.

8   Social Credit and the
Debate about 'Populism'

Thus far, I have dealt with Social Credit as largely an Alberta phenomenon. But how unique to Alberta was a political movement of this kind? This chapter explores two topics related to Social Credit which have sparked lively debate. The first is the extent to which Social Credit can best be understood as a 'populist' movement and thereby related to a variety of other political movements in Canadian history as well as the history of a number of other countries. The second topic concerns the extent of similarity between Alberta Social Credit, at various phases of its existence, and the other major 'populist' party formed in the 1930s, the Co-operative Commonwealth Federation. It is in the light of these two discussions that our final concluding notes in chapter 9 are written.

'Does the anger of Middle Western farmers against urban lawyers, the droolings of Tolstoy over muzhiks, the rationalizations of East European resentment against alien traders, and the slogans in terms of which rulers of new nations legitimate themselves and subvert liberal institutions – do all these have a common intellectual source, and are they parts of one phenomenon?'[1] This question, which opened a book on populism in 1969, has by no means a simple answer. The immense differences in experience among the groups mentioned above would suggest a negative response. None the less, scholars have identified similarities in their political behaviour, which are usually described by the term 'populism.' The term is by no means an unproblematic one, since, depending upon the author, it can refer to a particular political style, a particular method of political organization, an organization of particular social groups, a particular political program, or some combination of these elements.

One useful, if rather broad, definition of populism has it include all political movements which mobilize support with appeals that cross class and ethnic lines and invoke the need for popular control over 'a network of concentrated political and / or economic institutions allegedly wielding unwarranted power.'[2] Move-ments of this type share a political rhetoric or style but not a common ideology; there are right and left variants of populism. In the former variant, the enemies of the common people tend to be identified as the banks, the Jews, and bureaucratic government; the underlying economic system is itself subjected to only superficial criticism, and a small group of conspiring, grasping individuals are seen as perverting the otherwise smooth operations of the capitalist system. The left-wing variant of populism, although also regarding the fundamental cleavages in society in such vague terms as 'the people' versus 'the interests,' tends to regard large-scale capitalist industrial organization of the economy as the central problem. While the right-wing populist calls mainly for the exposure and humbling of the conspirators, the left-winger proposes fairly widespread state intervention to achieve fairness.

Ernesto Laclau, for example, notes that both the Fascist party under Mussolini and the contemporary Communist party of Italy (PCI) are organizations that have populist elements.[3] For Laclau, the PCI, despite its commitment to Marxism-Leninism with its emphasis on conflicts of social classes, appeals for support not by presenting itself as the representative of a single class but as a representative of the 'people' against the 'power bloc.' Laclau observes that theorists who conceptualize populism in terms of a particular ideology or as the expression of a particular social class miss the similarity in the style of appeal of diverse 'populist' parties.

Laclau rejects the 'class reductionism' of certain other Marxist writers, such as Nicos Poulantzas, who view political parties as the expression in the political sphere of the interests of determinate social classes within the mode of production.[4] Such a view, Laclau notes, wrongly assumes that the character of the conflicts found in the economic sphere is reproduced in the political sphere. Where it becomes the organizing principle of politically inclined workers, he argues, the results are disastrous. Of the workers' movement in Germany, for example, Laclau writes:

Class reductionism, then, was closely linked to the class practices of the workers' movement before the First World War. In the immediate post-war period it had still not been overcome: the workers' movement remained dominated by a narrow class perspective, and it lacked any hegemonic will in relation to the exploited classes as a whole. For the reformist faction the question was one of reconstructing the machinery of the bourgeois state as soon as possible, to re-establish the conditions of negotiation which had enabled the working class to obtain increasing benefits. For the revolu-tionary faction the aim was to carry out a proletarian revolution and install a soviet regime. But in both cases, exclusively class policies were pursued, which totally ignored the problem of popular-democratic struggles ... The failure of the various class attempts – revolutionary or reformist – to overcome the crisis led to the demoralization and demobilization of the working class; the lack of articulation of popular interpellations with socialist discourse left this flank increasingly exposed to the ideological influence of fascism.[5]

Shorn of jargon, Laclau's message is that a political party which narrowly attempts to represent the interests of one social class will fail to appeal to other social groups. Its resultant failure to achieve political power will ultimately alienate even those whose interests it initially sought to exclusively reflect. In Laclau's view, then, the populist style, which sophisticates regard as demagogy, should not be shrugged off. Just as right-wing populists have attempted to pass off their bigoted, conspiratorial views as expressions of popular will, so too left-wing forces can only seek to speak for the majority if they pick up upon widespread popular concerns and articulate solutions to them in language that appeals at some level to all groups other than the ruling class. 'The struggle of the working class for its hegemony is an effort to achieve the maximum possible fusion between popular-democratic ideology and socialist ideology. In this sense a "socialist populism" is not the most backward form of working class ideology but the most advanced – the moment when the working class has succeeded in condensing the ensemble of democratic ideology in a determinate social formation within its own ideology.'[6]

In this light, populism understood as a political style that emphasizes broad popular cleavages with the power bloc can be viewed as a useful tactic that might achieve some good in the right hands. Thus, from Laclau's vantage-point the Italian Communists, while allegedly imitating some of the rhetorical style of the Italian Fascists, have managed to make socialism an attractive alternative to at least portions of all exploited groups in Italian society rather than simply to the blue-collar workers to whom traditional Marxist-Leninist parties once seemed to limit their appeal.

Laclau's view that individuals are more susceptible to rhetorical 'populist' appeals that make use of national, traditional symbolism than to open class-based appeals has some currency in the literature on Latin American 'populism.' Steve Stein, for example, writing about Peru, notes that the weakness of class-based organizations in Latin America has allowed a variety of political organizations with radical rhetoric and conservative practices to win broad-based electoral support. For Stein, 'populists' refers to electoral coalitions that cross class lines, have a charismatic leader at the helm, espouse an ideology that emphasizes corporatist ideals, and reject class conflict or 'a major reordering of society.' Such organizations are usually urban-based and have middle- and even upper-class sectors as leaders, with workers providing the electoral base. In such parties, claims Stein, who concentrates on APRA in Peru, workers accept 'patently dependent relationships with their leaders' and are 'essentially passive with regard to the administration of political power.'[7] Peronism in Argentina and parallel movements in Brazil and other Latin American countries are often described in the literature as sharing the above characteristics with APRA.[8]

While Laclau's observations help to explain the popularity of certain Latin American political formations, they have been criticized by some Marxists because of their essential pluralism. Nicos Mouzelis, for example, believes – although his criticisms are regarded by many as exaggerated – that Laclau overstates the role of parties as political brokers among social groups. Over-concentration on superficial similarities in rhetoric, he notes, ignores that each party is characterized by a specific form of organization, a specific relationship with social classes, and a specific ideology.[9]

Populism for Mouzelis is only useful as a term to describe parties that have a plebiscitary character. These are parties – and the early Social Credit movement would arguably fit this bill – in which charismatic leaders make a direct appeal to the rank-and-file. The middle levels of the party are largely unimportant in formulating policy directions. The day-to-day practice of such parties, unlike fascist parties, which ultimately rely on coercion to achieve assent, is dependent upon this relationship of leaders and led. This relationship, while authoritarian and even sometimes mindless, does depend upon consent of the governed.[10] To Mouzelis, Laclau's ability to demonstrate rhetorical similarities among parties is less significant than 'what complex articulations exist between the party's official ideology, long-term policies and day-to-day organizational practice.'[11] He regards Laclau's answer to Poulantzas's class reductionism as extreme: a political party organized initially to represent the aspirations of one class, such as the working class, is seen as having the ability to win over all popular social classes by cleverly tying its aims to popular-democratic rhetoric. Or, as Mouzelis puts the matter, Laclau is guilty of 'the portrayal of ideological themes as highly malleable and free-floating classes being capable of articulating and disarticulating ideological interpretations at will.'[12] In fact, Laclau does recognize that there are limits to the malleability of ideological themes. What he questions, no doubt correctly, are the views of those like Poulantzas who believe that ideological themes have rather restricted flexibility.

Mouzelis's characterization of populism, while restricting the application of the term more than Laclau's characterization, does none the less suggest links between certain urban-based phenomena in the Third World, such as the Latin American parties mentioned above, and rural-based parties with a plebiscitary character. Other observers, however, apply the term populism strictly to agrarian parties within regions dominated – both numerically and in terms of economic weight – by small-holding farmers. John Conway serves as an example of this group.

Conway takes a position midway between Laclau and Poulantzas within the Marxist framework regarding the relationship of social classes and parties. He subscribes to Poulantzas's view that a political party is, at bottom, the expression of the interests of a particular social class, but he observes that this limitation does not prevent a party from attempting genuinely to satisfy interests of other social classes that do not conflict with the interests of its primary clientele. Following V.I. Lenin, Conway defines populism as 'the characteristic political response of the agrarian petit-bourgeoisie (and other small producers) to the consequences of capitalist modernization for them as a class. Indeed Populism is viewed as a protest against capitalism and a proposed developmental alternative presented from the point-of-view of the agrarian petit-bourgeoisie, a point-of-view rooted firmly in their material position, as a class, in the structure of developing capitalism.'[13]

But are the phenomena that define a 'characteristic political response of the agrarian petit-bourgeoisie' relatively similar from place to place and over time? Conway implies that they are and indeed chastises the two schools of writing on American populism for failing to see that each populist movement, in its efforts both to gain broad support and to defend the economic interests of small farmers and small businessmen threatened by capitalist industrialization, has a progressive as well as a reactionary face. Such a recognition of the two-sided character of populism, he claims, has characterized the works of Russian theorists, including Lenin, who have analysed the operations of pre-Revolution populist movements in their country.

Writes Conway:

Unwilling to recognize the roots of Populism in the interests of a concrete social class, the agrarian petit-bourgeoisie, both the revisionists and the counterrevisionists fall into the trap of partisanship. One side, like Hofstadter, et al., sees Populism cynically – as the reactionary and blind response of rural small holders to the threat of modernization. The other side, like Hicks and Pollack, ignores this very real thrust and sees only the progressive aspects of the movement. In Russian scholarship there is a clearer and somewhat more balanced perspective on populism – it is the response of a threatened class, but its totality cannot merely be understood in crass and vulgar class-interest terms. Populism was also a conscientious effort by a class not only to save itself materially, but to build a better society.[14]

In practice, it would seem that, as the terms 'left populism' and 'right populism' imply, farmers' movements have reflected quite divergent ideologies. It is simply false to imply as Conway does that each of the movements of the independent petite bourgeoisie of the countryside has, in near-equal dose, progressive and reactionary characteristics, except in the obvious sense that most political movements, regardless of their class composition, have such character-istics. Such reasoning can easily lead one to obscure the differences between movements dominated by small farmers as different in ideology and legislative achievement as, on the one hand, the socialist-leaning Farmer-Labor party of the inter-war period in Minnesota[15] and, on the other, the racist Populist party of the southern states in the late nineteenth century.[16] While social class is a powerful determinant of ideology and political allegiance, there is no simple equation that can be set up between a social class and political behaviour. As Laclau notes, individuals and even classes respond only indirectly to their objective material position in forming political allegiances; their understanding of their interests is mediated by popular traditions, which vary between countries and regions. And, as Conway indicates, social groups wish to believe that their own interests (or what they perceive as their interests) are the interests of all and wish to establish social programs supposedly designed to better society as a whole. This thinking leaves a vast scope of possible programmatic initiatives and cross-class alliances open to any group interested in achieving political power. Overall differences in political milieu can make the difference. In the case of the Farmer-Labor party in Minnesota, for example, while farmers dominated, the influence of labour-based socialist ideology originating in Minneapolis played a big role in the movement's overall direction. A similar example is presented by North Dakota's Non-Partisan League. By contrast no such influence was available to shape the views of the populists of the deep south.[17]

None the less, in the Canadian case, the literature on populism that concentrates on social class has tended, in recent years, to wish to demonstrate that the gap between the CCF and Social Credit, once regarded as a gulf, is greatly exaggerated. Because Social Credit is regarded as having been a right-wing movement, this literature has had a tendency to attack long-held, well-documented views that the CCF was fairly far to the left in Canadian terms.

The literature before the seventies on the CCF and Social Credit suggested that these two parties formed part of two rather different reactions by rural groups to increased vulnerability within the market-place. While both groups were referred to as populist, the term was of no obvious help in explaining the opposed programs of these two organizations. Seymour Martin Lipset placed the CCF within a North American framework of agrarian organizations whose demands are 'in many respects more socialistic than the nationalization policies of some explicitly socialist parties.'[18] But Social Credit, outside of Mallory's account (as noted in chapter 1), was seen as a right-wing party attempting to save hapless and hopeless small businessmen and farmers from both bankers and socialists.

In the 1970s, a new interest in Marxist class analysis provoked a re-examination of the two movements which for many years had been regarded as the poles of respectable Canadian politics and concluded that they were not as dissimilar as once proclaimed. R.T. Naylor, in a short, strident piece in 1972, notes that the social class base of the CCF and Social Credit movements was the same. Making the assumption that a determinate social class subscribes to but one ideology and that political parties based on the same social class therefore reflect the ideology of that class, Naylor says pointedly:

The CCF was not an agrarian socialist movement ... The farm adherence to the CCF in Saskatchewan was opportunistic; it followed Fabian leadership not because it was Fabian but because policies were proposed which appealed to the objective class position of the farmers. As to the contradiction between Social Credit and CCF emerging from identical conditions, it ceases to exist once these movements are viewed in terms of objective class standards rather than subjective standards of the leaders. The two movements are indistinguishable. For the farm constituency, the policy proposals of both groups were identical.[19]

Other scholars, while being more respectful to these two movements than Naylor, have largely supported his conclusion that these two movements were similar (but without going so far as to agree that they were 'indistinguishable'). Peter Sinclair, for example, writes: 'The emergence of Social Credit and the Cooperative Commonwealth Federation (CCF) from similar social conditions in Alberta and Saskatchewan is best explained by stressing how the popular elements in each were consistent with the petit bourgeois character of the most numerous class in each province.'[20] In a study of the CCF's rise to power in Saskatchewan, Sinclair suggests that the CCF in Saskatchewan began to shed its socialist origins almost from the start; when it won office in 1944 it was, in his view, a moderate reform party.[21] While John Bennett and Cynthia Krueger argue that the CCF retained many of its ideological principles until the election of 1944, they accept Sinclair's view that the party in office could not be viewed as following a socialist program.[22]

But it is John Conway who makes the most detailed attempt to demonstrate the resemblance between the CCF and Social Credit in terms of their initial rhetoric and their records in office. In his PhD thesis, he examines at length the farm-related legislation of the governments of Saskatchewan and Alberta to prove that both governments were the representatives of the interests of the 'petite-bourgeoisie' of independent commodity producers and that both were solicitous of that class's point of view.[23] Elsewhere, Conway observes that the two parties initially offered somewhat varying remedies for the Depression to the agrarian petite-bourgeoisie.[24] In office, however, their programs were similar and both passed some legislation favouring the urban working class in order to broaden the base of government support beyond the farming community. Both parties, 'despite their differences in rhetoric ... pursued the notion that a basic social security must be the right of all citizens, including the means for subsistence with dignity for those in genuine need.'[25] Indeed, Conway suggests that the Saskatchewan CCF was unhappy that the national party made common cause with labour to form the New Democratic Party in 1961. The Saskatche-waners 'reluctantly made the transition from being a party of the agrarian petit-bourgeoisie to being a social democratic party with its main constituency, nationally at least, among the Canadian working class.'[26]

Conway is aware, of course, that the Alberta Social Credit party, after the early forties, in the face of a CCF opposition, 'degenerated rapidly, in its rhetoric at least, to a party of the right.' But he sees no great significance in the rather opposed trajectories which the two 'populist' parties followed: the one party's move to the right, it is suggested, is mainly rhetorical; the other's move to the left is reluctant. On the whole, Conway's presentation of the history of the two parties is designed to demonstrate that each, in common with all populist parties, displayed both progressive and reactionary tendencies.

Unfortunately the Naylor-Sinclair-Conway thesis simply does not accord with the facts. Naylor's argument is particularly specious. He believes that the mere labelling of a party as 'petit bourgeois' tells the whole story. The petite bourgeoisie, and presumably all other social classes, are assumed not only to have 'objective' interests but subjectively to know what they are and to act upon them in concert. This is a suspicious view of political behaviour, rather in keeping with the vulgar Marxism of Poulantzas on this question.

Sinclair and Conway are, of course, on stronger ground in demonstrating that the CCF moderated its course as it headed towards power. But a similar argument has been made for most labour-based social-democratic parties as they near office and later assume political power.[27] None of the revisionist scholars of the Saskatchewan CCF compares its performance with that of social-democratic parties elsewhere, but there is little in their writings or that of the 'agrarian socialist' school to suggest that the comparison would be unfavourable. The revisionists, on the one hand, are too quick to attribute CCF backtracking from socialist principles to the class position of farmers and rather unwilling to explore other factors that have led social democrats everywhere to follow a similar scenario. On the other hand, the revisionists, while ably observing the limitations of the CCF in office in Saskatchewan, give rather short shrift to its achievements. Lipset emphasized those achievements. Conway's suggestion that the opponents of the CCF fusion with labour were clinging to 'petit-bourgeois' ideology in opposing the alliance is open to challenge; most opponents of the alliance regarded Canada's labour leaders as too conservative to be in a socialist outfit and were convinced not that the NDP would be too radical but that it would not be sufficiently radical.[28] The revisionist account of Alberta Social Credit, meanwhile, is misleading on most every count. In the first instance, as noted in chapter 2, the initial Social Credit League was not the product of agrarian petit-bourgeois revolt; it enjoyed a solid core of both working-class and middle-class urban political activists before it swept the countryside, and indeed it was the urban converts who fanned out to every small community in the province to do the sweeping. As noted further in chapter 3, during its first term in office Social Credit included thousands of working-class activists whose attraction to the Aberhart movement was as much based on perceived class interest as was the attraction of rural activists. Social Credit radicalism in the Aberhart period was as much attributable to the attempt by its middle-class leaders to appeal for working-class support as it was to the farm support that it sought.

Social Credit's turn to the right in the forties cannot be dismissed as a mere change in rhetoric. The party's working-class base had collapsed because of the government's shoddy treatment of the unemployed and the closed-mindedness of the cabinet members, especially Aberhart; a mass-based party became a small and relatively passive electoral machine, and the leadership of the government and party abandoned the effort to form a coalition of the popular classes in favour of an increasingly close alliance with monopoly capital. It was a political turn that would kill most political organizations – indeed a more moderate version of the same political turn had killed the political wing of the United Farmers of Alberta. But the Establishment fear of the CCF limited the threat to Social Credit from the traditional right while the new-found prosperity of the province, which allowed the government to spend lavishly on schools and roads, limited the threat from the left. Social Credit, in office after 1944, attempted to curb the growth of the province's trade union movement while the Saskatchewan CCF government promoted unionism and even passed legislation to allow civil servants to unionize despite the lack of an important civil service pressure to do so. Social Credit became the sworn enemy of universal social programs while the CCF became their chief advocate. Alberta's government eschewed a public presence in economic planning while Saskatchewan's government, although timid in the execution of plans, believed firmly in such planning. And while Saskatchewan's CCF pressed for greater government-legislated income equality for citizens, Alberta's Social Credit regime defended the 'trickle-down' theories of the business community. Conway misleads in asserting that Social Credit, like the CCF, 'pursued the notion that a basic social security must be the right of all citizens.' If one omits to define 'a basic social security,' one could state that the right wing of the British Conservative party and the left wing of the British Labour party 'share' such goals; or in the Canadian case, one could simply note that few politicians publicly claim that the poor should be allowed to starve. But what is the point of such broad claims except to obscure the very real differences among parties? Conway does demonstrate similarity in some of the farm legislation of Saskatchewan and Alberta in the period when one boasted a CCF government and the other a Social Credit government, but the social, labour, and economic programs of these two provinces defined the extremes of the spectrum in Canada. If both are simply to be subsumed under the unhyphenated 'populist,' what should we call the Liberal and Conservative parties whose policies were on a continuum between these two 'populist' organizations? The distinction, 'left-wing' populists versus 'right-wing populists,' earlier mentioned, must be retained to demonstrate the profound differences between an organization like the CCF and the post-1940 Social Credit.

While the CCF and Social Credit diverged sharply after 1940, it is true, as noted in chapters 2 and 3 that the early Social Credit movement shared programmatic and rhetorical similarities with the CCF. Naylor is correct to assert that many Prairie voters did not distinguish clearly between the parties; and as Andrews notes about Saskatchewan, rank-and-file party members also de-emphasized the parties' differences.[29] But Naylor and company are incorrect in claiming that only the 'petite-bourgeoisie' were drawn in by the appeal of the new parties. The working class in Alberta, it should be emphasized again, was actively implicated in the spread of Social Credit ideas across the province.

There are, however, key differences in the cross-class character, in the general principles, and in the rhetoric of the early Social Credit and CCF parties that should not be dismissed on the grounds that both parties offered certain common reforms to farmers and workers. The CCF, as a national organization, enjoyed the adherence of all the key non-Communist labour-based parties in the country, including the Independent Labour party in Manitoba, Saskatchewan, and Ontario, the Labour and Socialist parties in British Columbia, and the Canadian Labour party in Alberta.[30] The structural link between the major farm and labour organizations in Saskatchewan defined the character of the CCF in that province even if the numerical strength of both the farmers and their movements made them dominant within that structure. Indeed, the provincial party's connection with the national CCF, in which labour was at least as important as the farmers, also influenced the Saskatchewan CCF's thinking. T.C. Douglas, the first CCF premier, had greater roots in the labour movement than in the farm movement and, as a former MP, was also actively involved with the party's federal organization. The influence of the latter upon his government was apparent in his government's early attempts to draft model labour legislation. Federal party pressures to act quickly in this area in order to impress Ontario workers that the CCF was pro-labour played a key role here.[31]

The Alberta Social Credit alliance of farmers and workers, by contrast with the CCF, was amorphous. Social Credit was not a federation of existing organizations but a coalition of individuals disillusioned with the existing class-based organizations. While CCF leaders had close links with the movements based on social class, Social Credit leaders were mainly lower-middle-class professionals with no clear links either to the movements of the oppressed or to the ruling classes.

The contrast between Social Credit and CCF principles, even if it initially interested only a small percentage of either party's adherents, is important because the leaders held the organizing principles of their parties seriously. After 1940, ideology came to play an important role in Social Credit as Aberhart's eclecticism gave way to a purer form of Douglasism. With Manning's accession to power in 1943, an ideologue of pronounced right-wing views was placed in the position to define the meaning of Social Credit. In the absence by then of a political organization with some independence of and influence upon the government, Manning was able to engineer an increasingly close link between his lower-middle-class government and the richest, most reactionary business interests in Alberta. In Saskatchewan, by contrast, whatever the waffling by Premier Douglas in the face of implacable business hostility and suspicion of government plans, a vibrant party organization and the leaders' rhetorical commitment to social-democratic ideals ensured the emergence of an attitude to governance different from that of the wealthier sister province.[32]

Laclau's view that political discourse speaks to a variety of traditions, of which the 'objective' economic interest of social classes is an important but not all-encompassing part, is quite correct in discussing Social Credit and the CCF. His rather loose use of the term 'populist' does not obscure his point that groups outside the ruling class are open to a variety of political appeals which reflect opposition to the political and economic establishment as oppressors of the 'people.' In the Alberta case, as we have seen, the failure of 'left' forces in the thirties to distance themselves sufficiently from that establishment provided open territory for Social Credit. By the time Social Credit's seduction by that establishment was apparent, the renewed vitality of the Alberta economy and the general political apathy in the province proved sufficient to allow Social Credit to beat back the assault of a re-invigorated left. In Saskatchewan, by contrast, the left remained untested in political office before 1944 and could maintain its integrity with the people in a way that its Alberta counterpart could not. Such emphasis on the 'political' may be disconcerting to those who choose to emphasize pure class phenomena and for whom Saskatchewan and Alberta are therefore of one analytic piece, but several points in its defence should be made. First, as noted, the alliance of class forces represented by the CCF and Social Credit throughout their histories was not the same. Secondly, any analysis that ignores the impact of Alberta's oil wealth after 1947 on the province's social and political organization and assumes that rural Saskatchewan and Alberta remained predominantly the same is simply wrong. Above all, however, it must be emphasized that, as chapters 4 through 6 indicated, the virulence of Social Credit's right-wing turn in the forties cannot be overstated. Any attempt to show basic similarities between Social Credit and the CCF after that time is likely to be as misleading as attempts to conflate communist, fascist, and parliamentary democratic-capitalist regimes on the grounds that similar legislation was passed in certain spheres.

It is useful of course to compare reformist movements in hinterland regions both within Canada and between Canada and other countries, but such comparisons are meaningful only if they are based on close analysis of the regions being compared – not on selective attempts to find similarities (or, for that matter, dissimilarities) in political discourse. Comparisons of class structures form a key part of such contrasts, but such comparisons must go beyond head-counts of members of each social class to include a critical evaluation of the social and economic position of classes, the degree of cohesion and of friction within classes, class consciousness, and the nature of 'class practices,' including the political alliances that cross social class lines.

Conclusion

Although the Social Credit organization is in the late eighties dead as a doornail, the impact of that organization on political thinking in Alberta is enduring. Alberta's Progressive Conservative government, flush with oil royalties in the seventies, seemed to take tentative steps away from the hard right-wing line which Manning had made Alberta's trademark after 1943. But once a recession began in 1982, the Tories rediscovered much of the Manning heritage and found that, particularly in rural Alberta, it still had great resonance. Once again the unions were under siege and universal social programs were attacked. A dispute with the federal government over provincial doctors' rights to charge above prescribed medicare fees reimbursed by the state sounded like a replay of Manning's dispute with Ottawa over hospital fees for patients. Talk of economic planning was eschewed in favour of praises for the market-place; a report prepared by Peter Lougheed during his last term as premier, which suggested a greater state economic role, disappeared quickly from political discussion. The municipalities and school-boards once again found reason to complain about provincial under-funding at a time when provincial taxes were the lowest in the country.

But it would have shocked most of the Social Credit activists of the thirties that such a legacy would be left by their organization. Neither the monetary reformers nor the social reformers who flocked to the Aberhart banner would have recognized Don Getty as a spiritual heir. Some of the more right-wing monetary reformers might have felt kinship with the quasi-fascists who dominated what was left of the Social Credit organization in Alberta by the late eighties; but no doubt the overwhelming majority of those who joined Social Credit clubs in the thirties would have been appalled by the views that, half a century later, would represent 'Social Credit' to Albertans.

Much about Alberta had changed in half a century, and the province's politics reflected a transformed political economy. The economy remained a hinterland economy in which a few staples determined the overall prosperity of its people, but the key staples had changed from agricultural products to petroleum products. The agricultural sector continued to employ far more people than its relative contribution to gross provincial product per capita might suggest, and over-representation in legislative seats of the shrinking rural population gave the farmers a continuing large say in provincial politics. But the demographic and economic changes discussed in chapters 5 and 6 were dramatic and demonstrated that Alberta had become a largely urban province dependent upon the well-being of its oil and gas sector.

Social Credit had begun to transform itself even before the Leduc oil strike of 1947 provided the prosperity that allowed a once-reformist party to survive triumphantly as a born-again reactionary party supporting monopoly capitalism in the name of free enterprise. The discontinuity in Alberta's political tradition marked by the shift in Social Credit thinking after 1940 – and particularly after Manning's accession to power and his redefining of Social Credit objectives – is as sharp as the discontinuity in the province's demographic and economic history. Indeed it bears repeating that, had Alberta not emerged prosperous from the Second World War and then prospered even further with the development of the energy industry, Social Credit dominance as a right-wing Cold War party was unlikely.[1] Social Credit's reform record by 1944 was impressive; yet 30 per cent of Albertans that year voted for parties to the left of Social Credit, indicating their belief that the pace of reform should be faster and their rejection of Social Credit claims that socialists formed part of an international conspiracy.

Only when it became clear after the war that Alberta's prosperity likely had a long lease on life did reform impulses among workers and farmers begin quickly to dissipate. The early history of Social Credit's success is instructive for those anywhere whose aim is to break a particular political mould. Social Credit, by combining charismatic leadership, many opportunities for grass-roots participation (however illusory these proved to be afterwards), and a radical rhetoric with appeal to all groups dispossessed by the Depression, provided a certain model for lower-class unity against 'the interests.' But unlike the CCF, the various Farmer-Labor parties of the American mid-west, or other social-democratic parties, Social Credit had no institutional links with existing farm or labour organizations. Indeed, a common feature of the 'right-populist' organizations seems to be that no such links exist (although one must be careful in the classification of such complex phenomena as Peronism, with its plethora of competing ideologies and class linkages). These organizations in Alberta seemed hopelessly muddled; both the UFA and Labour parties were committed to socialism rhetorically, but in office their leaders proved untrue to party ideals.

This reality provided Aberhart with the opportunity to appear more left-wing than his opponents without espousing a socialist program or talking in social-class terms. He emphasized redistribution of wealth without giving much concern to questions of ownership and control of means of production, distribution and exchange. In office, as noted in chapter 3, Aberhart did deliver in part. But his party's members and supporters, especially in the urban areas, had expected more and learned painfully that the Social Credit leaders, while happy to tilt at windmills when that involved constitutional control of credit, would not alleviate the lot of the unemployed. The 1940 defection of many radicals to the CCF and the refusal of many Social Credit supporters from 1935 to vote almost cost that party the 1940 election. But Social Credit did well in the rural areas, where its attempts to hamstring the farmers' creditors would become part of the political folklore that would maintain the party in office for a generation.

Relatively sure of its rural support, the Social Credit party during the war had moved to the right partly because most of its leaders, other than on the banking issue, did not share the radical views of much of the membership. The rise of the CCF also raised the prospect that if Social Credit emphasized its reformist side, the resurgent united right, which had almost tied Social Credit's popular vote in 1940, might defeat a divided political left. By stridently attacking the CCF from the right and emphasizing to voters that the CCF, rather than the Independents, were the real challengers in the province, Social Credit was able, in 1944, to win the support of many of those to whom the Aberhart party had recently been anathema.

But the move to the right should not be written off as sheer opportunism. Ernest Manning, although appearing to be Aberhart's religious and political devotee, had never really been comfortable with the social-gospel politics that Aberhart somehow managed to reconcile with a stern evangelical profession of individual salvation. Socialism to Manning, as to most ideologues of evangelism, 'de-emphasizes the individual struggle for salvation' and the attainment of grace by placing responsibility for the individual on the shoulders of the state rather than of the individual. Social benefits such as medicare and guaranteed incomes breed idleness and permit 'the evil tendencies of the individual to come to the fore, thereby causing a breakdown of his relationship with God.'[2]

The harsh individualism of the evangelists mixed nicely with the conspiratorial view of social arrangements suggested by Major Douglas to create an anti-socialist brew in which true social reformers were linked with the bankers with about as much reasoning as Hitler's linkage of Bolsheviks, bankers, and Jews. Anti-Semites in Social Credit, whose views followed the master's, were repudiated during the Manning-Strom period, but their manner of reasoning was indeed official ideology. The rights of groups such as workers or farmers to act collectively within society could be harrumphed away by constant invoking of the conspiracy. Hence, the justice or otherwise of collective demands need never be seriously considered.

None the less, the oil-induced prosperity of the province allowed the government to collect revenues per capita well in excess of other Canadian jurisdictions while maintaining the country's least-onerous tax regime. These revenues were spent on health, social, and educational programs as well as on road-building and the building of other infrastructures. While the large quantities of dollars spent have caused many to claim that Social Credit rhetoric and practices were at odds, closer scrutiny of government expenditures tells a different story. Alberta Social Credit was not the Saskatchewan CCF disguised in a cloak of religion and free-enterprise rhetoric. Alberta shunned universal social programs and state-funded health programs without user fees. It resisted attempts by municipalities to reduce the importance of local property taxes in funding education and welfare costs, claiming that local responsibility would be undermined by overly generous provincial funding. The government meanwhile spent almost no money in trying to diversify the economies of the various regions of the province, preferring to use its low taxes, limited regulation of business practices, and anti-union labour legislation to entice profit-seekers. Although Manning, in his last several years of office, appeared finally to develop a concern about poverty in Alberta, he supported only programs that attempted to train the poor to go after job opportunities. Redistribution of existing wealth, which Aberhart had supported in 1935, was now firmly rejected in favour of promotion of economic growth. The solution for poverty for all groups, including native peoples, was to let corporations and individuals make profits that would then be used to expand operations in the province.

Manning's Social Credit party provided no illusions of openness as had the party of Aberhart. Urban and farm radicals left in droves, some for the CCF, some to retreat to political apathy. This exodus left a smaller, largely rural-based, lower-middle-class party that more closely resembled Macpherson's characterization of the party than the earlier party did. But the party was only a cheering gallery for the government, whose leaders were the darlings of the oil companies. Manning, more than any other politician of the post-war period, with the possible exception of Quebec Premier Maurice Duplessis, was proud to extol not only the virtues of capitalism but of large, foreign-owned corporate giants and was pleased to have the sponsorship of rich right-wingers for his white paper and book in 1967.

The buoyancy of the economy from 1947 onwards – and indeed even in the period beginning in 1940, when demand for Alberta's farm products quickly lifted the provincial economy out of the Depression – created a favourable environment for the propagation of 'Manning Social Credit' views. These views had little in common with Douglas Social Credit or the early Aberhart Social Credit, except for a penchant for a conspiratorial outlook of the world. In turn, however, Manning and his associates, as leaders of the government, played an immense role in reshaping political thinking in the province. Oil strikes alone do not change people's perceptions overnight. It was the successful image of the government and the forceful rhetoric of Manning that ensured that Manning's view of reality would take hold among significant elements of all social classes in the province. With little opposition from other political parties, and with certain trade union and farm groups generally pessimistic for many years about the chances of supplanting Social Credit while Manning continued as leader, the government became more and more the only voice heard from Alberta concerning the beliefs of Albertans. Even though no election gave Social Credit as many as six of every ten votes cast, all elections, except notably those in 1940 and 1955, produced lopsided government majorities that limited parliamentary expression of dissent.

Both working-class and middle-class dissent none the less began to emerge clearly in the sixties, and the government was defeated in 1971. But its free-enterprise rhetoric, its view that most programs originating from Ottawa are wrong-headed and socialistic, and above all perhaps its phoney pretence that Albertans speak with one voice have tended to survive. The social changes bubbling under the surface during the later Socred years ensured that not all Albertans would rally to the dubious values which came to dominate government thinking in the early forties. But the Social Credit legacy, despite the generous spirit of Prairie revolt that provided its original animus, was one of obscurantism, xenophobia, and the extolling of greed in the name of religion and liberty.

Notes

Chapter 1

1 According to page opposite title-page of J.R. Mallory, *Social Credit and the Federal Power in Canada* (Toronto: University of Toronto Press 1954)

2 Among studies in the series not dealing with Social Credit were W.L. Morton's *The Progressive Party in Canada*, 1950; D.C. Masters's *The Winnipeg General Strike*, 1952; and Vernon C. Fowke's *The National Policy and the Wheat Economy*, 1957.

3 Harold Schultz's political biography of Aberhart was written mainly from secondary sources because few primary sources were then available to researchers. It none the less formed the basis of several good articles on both Aberhart and Social Credit, viz., 'Portrait of a Premier: William Aberhart,' *Canadian Historical Review*, 45:3 (1964), 185–211; 'Aberhart: The Organization Man,' *Alberta Historical Review*, 7:2 (1959), 19–26; and 'A Second Term: 1940,' *Alberta Historical Review*, 10:1 (1962), 17–26.

4 The best account of the constitutional issues involved and the resultant wrangling in the courts between the federal and Alberta governments is found in Mallory.

5 As indicated by the testimony before the legislature's Agriculture Committee, which held hearings on social credit ideas in 1935 while the United Farmers of Alberta were still in power (John A. Irving, *The Social Credit Movement in Alberta* [Toronto: University of Toronto Press 1959], 163–4)

6 C.B. Macpherson, *Democracy in Alberta: Social Credit and the Party System* (Toronto: University of Toronto Press 1962; first published 1953). Macpherson's analysis was savagely attacked by Seymour Martin Lipset in a review in *Canadian Forum*, 34 (1954), 175–7, 196–8. But his objections seemed to be a priori objections to Marxist language and categories of analysis rather than to substantive features of the argument itself, at least insofar as the argument applied to the province of Alberta.

7 Macpherson, 214

8 David McGinnis, 'Farm Labour in Transition: Occupational Structure and Economic Dependency in Alberta, 1921–1951,' in Howard Palmer, ed., *The Settlement of the West* (Calgary: University of Calgary 1977)

9 Jean Burnet, *Next-Year Country: A Study of Rural Social Organization in Alberta* (Toronto: University of Toronto Press 1951), 147–8

10 John Richards and Larry Pratt, *Prairie Capitalism: Power and Influence in the New West* (Toronto: McClelland and Stewart 1979), 151

11 J. Paul Grayson and Linda Grayson, 'The Social Bases of Interwar Political Unrest in Urban Alberta,' *Canadian Journal of Political Science*, 7:2 (June 1974), 289–313

12 Ibid., 308–9

13 Writes Irving: 'By the beginning of August [1935], mass hysteria had reached such a pitch that UFA speakers found it almost impossible to carry on meetings in many country schools' (317).

14 Ibid., 119

15 Ibid., 120

16 Grayson and Grayson, 309

17 Mallory, 154–61

18 L.P.V. Johnson and Ola MacNutt, *Aberhart of Alberta* (Edmonton: Co-op Press 1970)

19 Francis Richard Swann, 'Progressive Social Credit in Alberta, 1935–1940,' PhD thesis, University of Cincinnati, 1971

20 Lewis H. Thomas, *William Aberhart and Social Credit in Alberta* (Toronto: Copp Clark 1977), 9, 90–1, 130–5, 141–3

21 David Elliott, 'William Aberhart: Right or Left?' in D. Francis and H. Ganzevoort, eds., *The Dirty Thirties in Prairie Canada: 11th Western Canada Studies Conference* (Vancouver: Tantalus Research 1980), 11–31

22 J.L. Finlay, *Social Credit: The English Origins* (Montreal and London: McGill-Queen's University Press 1972)

23 John Laurence Finlay, 'The Origins of the Social Credit Movement.' PhD thesis, University of Manitoba, 1968, 394

24 David R. Elliott and Iris Miller, *Bible Bill: A Biography of William Aberhart* (Edmonton: Reidmore 1987); David R. Elliott, 'Antithetical Elements in William Aberhart's Theology and Political Ideology,' *Canadian Historical Review*, 59:1 (March 1978), 38–58; David Elliott, 'William Aberhart: Right or Left?'

25 Larry Hannant, 'The Calgary Working Class and the Social Credit Movement in Alberta, 1932–35,' *Labour/Le Travail*, 16 (1985), 97–116. After observing that some working-class activists were rewarded for their support of Social Credit with provincial or federal legislative seats, accompanied with legislators' salaries, Hannant observes: 'Such immediate financial rewards might not, however, have been their aim. Considering the circumstances, it is not at all farfetched to think that the RCMP, the Canadian state's provincial police, would sponsor informants in the ranks of newly-founded movements and parties. An RCMP constable working

clandestinely was a member of the CPC from 1922 to 1928 and was the star witness in a 1931 trial which sent eight leaders of the party to jail for several years. During the 1930s, as the Depression created desperate conditions and people cried out for profound social change, the RCMP would have been especially vigilant in seeking to preserve the status quo. Certainly Social Credit would not have been above the RCMP's suspicions' (116).

26 Macpherson, 206–9
27 Barr was twenty-eight years old and executive assistant to Clark when he co-edited a book on western independence: John J. Barr and Owen Anderson, *The Unfinished Revolt: Some Views on Western Independence* (Toronto: McClelland and Stewart 1971), 144.
28 John J. Barr, *The Dynasty: The Rise and Fall of Social Credit in Alberta* (Toronto: McClelland and Stewart 1974), 137, 141, 144–5
29 Barr claims (158) that the league's paid-up membership between elections was 12,000–15,000 during the Manning era. Such figures are challenged in chapter 5 by the league's own files.
30 Barr, 163. Details of the scandals affecting Social Credit in 1955 are provided in chapter 5; further scandals in 1967, minimized by Barr, are discussed in chapter 6.
31 Anderson was executive assistant to Premier Harry Strom when *The Unfinished Revolt* appeared in 1971 (Barr and Anderson, 144).
32 Owen Anderson, 'The Alberta Social Credit Party: An Empirical Analysis of Membership, Characteristics, Participation and Opinion,' PhD thesis, University of Alberta, 1972, 3
33 Ibid., 52–3

Chapter 2

1 Nathan Lasalle Whetten, 'The Social and Economic Structure of the Trade Centres in the Canadian Prairie Provinces with Special Reference to Its Changes 1910–1930,' PhD thesis, Harvard University, 1932, 137
2 David Leadbeater, 'The Development of Capitalism in Alberta,' MA thesis, University of Alberta, 1980, 410
3 C.B. Macpherson, *Democracy in Alberta: Social Credit and the Party System* (Toronto: University of Toronto Press 1962), 16
4 David McGinnis, 'Farm Labour in Transition: Occupational Structure and Economic Dependency in Alberta, 1921–1951,' in Howard Palmer, ed., *The Settlement of the West* (Calgary: University of Calgary Press 1977), 174–86.
5 Macpherson indicates that the census of Canada, 1941, reported 99,732 farms in Alberta (17).
6 Whetten, 137
7 *Census of Canada*, 1931. Following is the occupational breakdown indicated in the census.

Sector	Numbers employed	% of total
Logging, fishing, hunting, trapping	2,649	2.1
Coal mining	8,177	6.3
Other mining	924	0.8
Manufacturing	14,819	11.5
Construction	8,623	6.7
Transportation and communication	14,860	11.5
Trade, commerce, and finance	20,807	16.1
Service	42,010	32.2
Other or unspecified	16,444	12.8

8 Max Foran, *Calgary: An Illustrated History* (Toronto: Lorimer 1978), 180
9 The number of workers per owner/manager, 1931, is indicated in the following table (from *Census of Canada 1931*):

Sector	Number
Coal mining	42.6
Other mining	7.3
Construction	16.2
Manufacturing	12.8
Transportation and communication	70.4
Trade and commerce	2.3

The census data lump owners and managers together, but the removal of managers does not significantly alter the ratio of business owners to workers. The Whetten study indicated that the ratio of workers (129, 313) to business units (9987) was fourteen to one (*Social and Economic Structure of Trade Centres*, 37).
10 The existence of such relations, however, does not imply that workers lacked class consciousness. Bryan Palmer's research on Hamilton workers in the late nineteenth century and Gregory Kealey's parallel research on Toronto workers of the period demonstrate that small factories with paternalistic employers could co-exist with militant unionism and a proud working-class culture. Bryan D. Palmer, *A Culture in Conflict: Skilled Workers and Industrial Capitalism in Hamilton, Ontario, 1860–1914* (Montreal: McGill-Queen's University Press 1979); Gregory S. Kealey, *Toronto Workers Respond to Industrial Capitalism, 1867–1892* (Toronto: University of Toronto Press 1980).
11 The most thorough study of Alberta coal miners is Allan Seager, 'A Proletariat in Wild Rose Country: The Alberta Coal Miners, 1905–1945,' PhD thesis, York University, 1982. See also Allan Seager, 'Socialists and Workers: The Western Canadian Coal Miners, 1900–21,' *Labour/Le Travail*, 16 (1985), 23–59; A. Ross McCormack, *Reformers, Rebels and Revolutionaries: The Western Canadian Radical Movement, 1899–1919* (Toronto: University of Toronto Press 1977),

8–9, 12–13; and Warren Caragata, *Alberta Labour: A Heritage Untold* (Toronto: Lorimer 1979).

12 In 1922, for example, twenty disputes in Alberta, mainly in the coal mines and involving 10,562 workers, cost workers 966,842 days lost. In 1924, a mere nine disputes involving 7146 workers resulted in 1,002,179 lost days of work. David Leadbeater, 'An Outline of Capitalist Development in Alberta,' in David Leadbeater, ed., *Essays on the Political Economy of Alberta* (Toronto: New Hogtown Press 1984), 61.

13 The continuation of labour strife in the 1930s is documented in, among other accounts, the Seager thesis mentioned above as well as Allan Seager, 'A History of the Mine Workers' Union of Canada, 1925–1935,' MA thesis, McGill University, 1977; Frank Paul Karas, 'Labour and Coal in the Crow's Nest Pass: 1925–1935,' MA thesis, University of Calgary, 1972; and Allan Seager, 'The Pass Strike of 1932,' *Alberta History*, 25 (1977), 1–11.

14 Labour legislation throughout Canada before the Second World War is detailed in A.E. Grauer, *Labour Legislation: A Study Prepared for the Royal Commission on Dominion-Provincial Relations* (Ottawa: King's Printer 1939). Employer resistance to minimum wages is discussed in Rebecca Coulter, 'The Working Young of Edmonton 1921–1931,' in Joy Parr, ed., *Childhood and Family in Canadian History* (Toronto: McClelland and Stewart 1982), 143–59.

15 Jack Masson and Peter Blaikie, 'Labour Politics in Alberta,' in Carlo Caldarola, ed., *Society and Politics in Alberta: Research Papers* (Toronto: Methuen 1979), 274

16 On the early history of trade unionism in Alberta, see Alvin Finkel, 'The Rise and Fall of the Labour Party in Alberta, 1917–1942,' *Labour/Le Travail, 16* (1985), 61–96; and Henry C. Klassen, 'The Bond of Brotherhood and Calgary Workingmen,' in Anthony W. Rasporich and Henry C. Klassen, eds., *Frontier Calgary: Town, City and Region, 1875–1914* (Calgary: McClelland and Stewart West 1975), 267–71; and Caragata, 1–68.

17 The impact of high mortgage rates on urban homeowners is discussed in Government of Alberta, *The Case for Alberta, Part 1: Alberta's Problems and Dominion-Provincial Relations* (Edmonton 1938), 325–35. The report notes that 47 per cent of homes in Edmonton and 48 per cent in Calgary are rented. It charges that foreclosures have affected many urban residents, and it notes that both the overall quantity per capita and the size of homes are inferior to Canadian standards as a whole.

On land speculation in the early period of urban development, see John F. Gilpin, 'Urban Land Speculation in the Development of Strathcona (South Edmonton), 1891–1912,' in John E. Foster, ed., *The Developing West: Essays on Canadian History in Honour of Lewis H. Thomas* (Edmonton: University of Alberta Press 1983), 171–99; and Max Foran, 'Land Speculation and Urban Development in Calgary 1884–1912,' in Anthony Rasporich and Henry Klassen, eds., *Frontier Calgary: Town, City and Region 1875–1914* (Calgary: McClelland and Stewart West 1975), 203–20.

18 *The Case for Alberta*, Part 1, 1921

19 V.F. Coe, 'Dated Stamp Scrip in Alberta,' *Canadian Journal of Economics and Political Science*, 4:1 (February 1938), 61

20 E.J. Hanson, 'Public Finance in Alberta since 1935,' *Canadian Journal of Economics and Political Science*, 18:3 (August 1952), 323–4. The politics involved in Alberta railway-building weave throughout Lewis G. Thomas, *The Liberal Party in Alberta: A History of Politics in the Province of Alberta 1905–1921* (Toronto: University of Toronto Press 1959).

21 *The Case for Alberta*, Part 1, 47–9

22 These are Bank of Canada figures quoted in Social Credit Board, *The Records Tell the Story* (Edmonton: the Board 1939), 6.

23 Hanson, 324; *The Case for Alberta*, 91

24 *The Records Tell the Story*, 6; Hanson, 324

25 Provincial income, which in 1927 had been $350 million, fell to $146 million in 1933, thereby seriously reducing the government's potential sources of income (Hanson, 324). The view that indebtedness limited what the government felt it could do is confirmed in Provincial Archives of Alberta, R.G. Reid Interview, 6 October 1969. Many years after the defeat of the UFA government, of which he was the last premier, Reid believed that no more could responsibly have been done by government to help debtors.

26 Annual agreements on division of costs between the federal and provincial governments are found in Public Archives of Canada, Department of Labour Papers, 'Dominion-Alberta Agreements Re Unemployment Relief 1930–40,' Vol. 2138. The most detailed account of federal-provincial wrangling regarding relief is James Struthers, *No Fault of Their Own: Unemployment and the Canadian Welfare State 1914–1981* (Toronto: University of Toronto Press 1983).

27 Donald V. Smiley, ed., *The Rowell-Sirois Report* (Toronto: McClelland and Stewart 1963), 177. Saskatchewan, by contrast, paid more than three and a half times the national average on relief.

28 Caragata, 96. Operation of the camps in Alberta is discussed in Department of Labour Papers, Vols. 2048 and 2060.

29 *Alberta Labour News*, 9 September 1933

30 *Edmonton Journal*, 22 March 1935

31 *Edmonton Journal*, 23 March 1935

32 Howard Palmer observes that 2547 residents were deported from Alberta from 1930 to 1933, mostly as public charges. Most of the deportees were of British descent. In 1932 Edmonton city council, although Labour-led, cut central Europeans without dependants from the relief rolls. Howard Palmer, *Patterns of Prejudice: A History of Nativism in Alberta* (Toronto: McClelland and Stewart 1982), 130–1.

The chairman of the provincial Relief Commission was hostile to foreigners, claiming: 'the unemployed who have been receiving relief, and those who have been demanding it are mainly foreigners. They will never develop into useful citizens.' Howard Palmer, 'Nativism and Ethnic Tolerance in Alberta, 1920–1972,' PhD thesis, York University, 1973, 170.

An excellent piece on the general issue of deportation in Canada is Barbara
Roberts, 'Shovelling Out the "Mutinous,": Political Deportations from Canada
before 1936,' *Labour/Le Travail*, 18 (Fall 1986), 77–110.

33 One constant complaint was the failure to provide cash relief as opposed to
vouchers. Relief officials claimed that the voucher system ensured that welfare
recipients bought food for their children rather than unnecessary items (*Edmonton Journal*, 22 March 1935), but the unemployed protested the paternalism of the
relief departments. The following letter from a mother receiving relief indicates
the indignity felt by those who received vouchers rather than cash. It appeared in
the *Edmonton Journal*, 20 March 1935. '... how does it feel to be a woman on
relief? Standing in a crowd one day, I overheard a woman call relief people cattle,
was it because she is fortunate enough to be a widow of an old civic employee.
In my own case I have worked out hard to keep off relief until my health is gone,
sold nearly all my furniture to try and keep going hoping and praying something
would turn up which never does. We go to a store. Relief goes one side of the
counter, cash the other, so no one will mistake you are on relief. A man and
wife are allowed $3.75. How many luxuries will it buy. I tried to get my little child
to eat porridge which he don't like. I thought I would ask for a package of
cornflakes for him. I pick it up and take it to the counter and was told you can't
have that on relief. One must get an order for boiling beef and most often we get
all the gristle you can't eat. You must not get a copper in change. The only
difference we are from criminals is we are free but I tell you every time i go in a
store I feel like a criminal. Yet my father and two brothers were killed in the war,
they fought that we should all be free. Are we?

'The heads of the relief send stool pigeons round in stores to see what I buy.
Why not give people the cash. If there are a few bargains in any store we could
get them.'

34 See note 13.

35 Of 4054 settlers placed on the land from 1932 to 1940, only 1865 remained on their
land in 1945. 'Province of Alberta, Department of Agricultural Relief Settlement Plan – Summary of Accounts as of March 31, 1945,' in Department of
Labour Papers, Vol. 2106, File 9.0.2.

36 The standard account of the Liberal period in office is the L.G. Thomas book above
mentioned. Members of the first Liberal government are profiled on pages 21–3.

37 Macpherson, 26

38 A biography of Irvine indicating (and perhaps exaggerating) his role in founding
these organizations is Anthony Mardiros, *William Irvine: The Life of a Prairie
Radical* (Toronto: Lorimer 1979).

39 Macpherson, 26; M. Marion Smith, 'The Ideological Relationship between the
United Farmers of Alberta and the Co-operative Commonwealth Federation,'
MA thesis, McGill University, 1967, 5

40 *Alberta Nonpartisan*, 19 June 1919. On the reactions of Prairie farmers generally to
Union government policies, see John Herd Thompson, *The Harvests of War:
The Prairie West 1914–1918* (Toronto: McClelland and Stewart 1978).

41 Mardiros, 57. Macpherson, it should be noted, ignores the economic radicalism of the NPL and implies that the UFA and NPL, because both decried party government, shared essentially the same principles (26).

42 The United Farmers of Alberta decision to enter the political arena is discussed in Macpherson, 44–54. Wood's ideas are detailed in W.K. Rolph, *Henry Wise Wood of Alberta* (Toronto: University of Toronto Press 1950). The rise of the farmers' political movement nationally is detailed in W.L. Morton, *The Progressive Party in Canada* (Toronto: University of Toronto Press 1950).

43 Macpherson, 64

44 William Irvine, *The Farmers in Politics* (Toronto: McClelland and Stewart 1920)

45 Brownlee's connection with the farmers' movement was the legal work he had performed for the UFA and other farmers' organizations. *Canadian Parliamentary Guide*, 1930, 342.

46 Finkel, 'Labour Party in Alberta,' 73, 80

47 Macpherson, 26, 79–81; Carl F. Betke, 'Farm Politics in an Urban Age: The Decline of the United Farmers of Alberta after 1921,' in Lewis H. Thomas, ed., *Essays in Western History* (Edmonton: University of Alberta 1976), 175–89. UFA membership had fallen from 38,000 in 1921 to about 15,000 in 1923 (Macpherson, 64).

48 From the Liberals' fall from power in 1921 to the election of Social Credit in 1935, the party's three provincial leaders were lawyers. Lawyers appear also to have dominated executive positions in the party. Conventions of party members appear to have been held irregularly, mainly when it was necessary to select a new leader. The party held conventions in 1924, 1929, 1932, and 1934; only in the last year was no leadership contest scheduled (Glenbow Alberta Institute, Alberta Liberal Association Records, Box 21, File 120).

49 The province paid out $4 million to the municipalities between 1930 and 1935 for direct relief and spent almost an equal amount on relief works to provide temporary employment to the jobless (*Edmonton Journal*, 5 March 1935). Still, the relief works employees were housed in relief camps and poorly paid, and the percentage of relief costs borne by the province compared with that borne by the municipalities declined throughout the period. Calgary, for example, paid only 32 per cent of its direct relief bill in January 1934, but by February 1935 provincial cuts forced the city to pay 54 per cent of its bill (*Calgary Albertan*, 7 February 1935). It should, however, be noted that both relief rates and minimum wages in Alberta were among the highest in the country (Grauer, *Labour Legislation*, 35, 98).

50 See note 32.

51 For example, the Hunger March of December 1932. See Alvin Finkel, 'Populism and the Proletariat: Social Credit and the Alberta Working Class,' *Studies in Political Economy*, 13 (1984), 109–35.

52 UFA, 1 February 1930, 7

53 UFA, 1 February 1932, 7

54 Significant exceptions were G.G. Coote and Alfred Speakman. Walter Young, *The*

Anatomy of a Party: The National CCF, 1932–61 (Toronto: University of Toronto Press, 1969) 47–8.

55 Finkel, 'Labour Party,' 72

56 Seymour Martin Lipset, *Agrarian Socialism* (Garden City, NY: Anchor 1968), 81; Young, 19

57 The manifesto is reprinted in Young, 304–13.

58 Lipset, 154

59 Francis Richard Swann, 'Progressive Social Credit in Alberta, 1935–1940,' PhD thesis, University of Cincinnati, 1971, 87. Swann quotes Victor Quelch, a Social Credit MP who in a 1959 interview claimed the affiliation with the CCF caused the UFA to lose half its members. He mentions also the opinion of Premier Reid that no more than 15 per cent of the UFA rank-and-file approved the CCF platform. This figure, of course, begs the question why the provincial conventions, which overwhelmingly endorsed affiliation with the CCF, were allegedly so unrepresentative.

60 UFA membership had increased from 13,000 to 17,000 between 1929 and 1931, the years when the radicals consolidated their hold. It then began to drop precipitously in the face of government disinterest in the convention resolutions and the rise of the Social Credit alternative (J.F. Conway, 'To Seek a Goodly Heritage: The Prairie Populist Response to the National Policy,' PhD thesis, Simon Fraser University, 1978, 428–9).

61 According to reports in *Alberta Labor News* and UFA throughout 1933

62 *Canadian Parliamentary Guide*, 1934, 353

63 John Richards and Larry Pratt, *Prairie Capitalism: Power and Influence in the New West* (Toronto: McClelland and Stewart 1979), 54–5

64 Glenbow Alberta Institute, G.G. Coote Papers, File 9, Coote to Premier Reid, 22 February 1935

65 Coote Papers, File 28, W.A. Shields to Coote, 14 September 1935

66 Coote Papers, File 28, R.W. Clow to Coote, 8 August 1935

67 John A. Irving, *The Social Credit Movement in Alberta* (Toronto: University of Toronto Press 1959), 146–7; Macpherson, 94

68 Glenbow Alberta Institute, Henry Spencer Papers, File 3, Spencer to A.P. Waldron, managing ediror, *Western Producer*, 23 June 1937

69 Henry Spencer Papers, Spencer to W.A. Tutti, Douglas Social Credit, British Columbia Section, 7 February 1935; Irving, 150. The support of Spencer and Irvine for monetary reform suggests that Irving is incorrect in claiming 'hostility ... between the Co-Operative Commonwealth Federation and monetary reform factions' (Irving, 69). The major dispute seems to have been over the question of the provincial government's constitutional competence to institute a program of monetary reform.

70 Finkel, 'Labour Party,' particularly 66–7

71 *Edmonton Free Press*, 6 September 1919

72 *Canadian Parliamentary Guide*, 1922

73 The Canadian Labour party platform adopted for Alberta in 1921 claimed the

party's 'ultimate economic aims' were 'the social ownership of the means of wealth production and distribution' and the organizatiion of educational institutions 'so that the function of education would be to prepare for a complete living' (*Alberta Labor News*, 26 November 1921).

74 *Alberta Labor News*, 14 October 1922

75 A debate between communist and main-line spokesmen within the CLP was featured in *Alberta Labor News*, 6 March 1925.

76 *Alberta Labor News*, 16 September 1933. The attitudes and actions of the Labour party leaders are discussed in Finkel, 'Labour Party,' 81–5.

77 Finkel, 'Labour Party,' 88–9

78 On the Hunger March, see Caragata, 105–6; and Finkel, 'Populism and the Proletariat,' 119–20. The 1934 relief strike in Edmonton caused a split among the Labour councillors (Public Archives of Alberta, Edmonton Trades and Labour Council Minutes, 21 May 1934). When the strike was over, the *Alberta Labor News*, while still supportive of the civic administration, observed that many of the unemployed remained bitter against the Labour Party (*Alberta Labor News*, 9 June 1934).

79 *Edmonton Journal*, 20 May 1935

80 *Alberta Labor News*, 19 January 1935

81 The Communists received 5771 votes in the provincial election of 1935, according to *Canadian Parliamentary Guide*, 1937, 391. Since the party followed a policy of giving membership only to those willing and able to carry on regular political work, it is unlikely that a large portion of its voters were also members.

82 Ibid. The Communists received 20 per cent of the vote in Rocky Mountain, the seat which included the coal mines of the Crow's Nest Pass, and 25 per cent of the vote in Willingdon, an east-central farming seat with many east European voters.

83 That, at least, is the argument of Ben Swankey, 'Reflections of a Communist: 1935 Election,' *Alberta History*, 28:4 (Autumn 1980), 30.

84 Two articles by Ben Swankey in *Alberta History* give the Communists' viewpoint on the success of their organizing efforts. These are: 'Reflections of a Communist: The Hungry Thirties,' *Alberta History*, 27:4 (Autumn 1979), 1–12; and 'Reflections of a Communist: 1935 Election,' *Alberta History*, 28:4 (Autumn 1980), 28–36.

85 Public Archives of Canada, Department of Labour files, 'Strikes and Lockouts,' Vol. 353

86 Caragata, 105; Swankey, 'The Hungry Thirties,' 8; Anne B. Woywitka, 'Recollections of a Union Man,' *Alberta History*, 23:4 (Autumn 1975), 17–20; *Alberta Labor News*, 24 December 1932

87 Department of Labour, 'Strikes and Lockouts,' Vol. 359

88 Edmonton Trades and Labour Council Minutes, 21 May 1934; *Edmonton Journal*, 25 March–17 May 1935

89 Caragata, 106; *Edmonton Journal*, 13 May 1935

90 Seager, 'The Pass Strike,' 4–10. Seager notes that the rank-and-file rather than the Communist leadership of the MWUC launched the strike.

91 The meeting featured as speakers British Labour MP Aneurin Bevan and a former minister of justice in Prussia (*Alberta Labor News*, 18 August 1934).

92 Woywitka, 16–17

93 A letter-writer to the *Alberta Labor News*, while remaining personally loyal to the Labour party, indicated why many individuals resented the UFA and the Labour party when the provincial and municipal governments led by these organizations suppressed the Hunger March: '[The Communists'] objective was to demonstrate that in the city of Edmonton with a Labour mayor and Labour council majority and in the province of Alberta with a farmer government in the saddle, unemployed workers and destitute farmers are beaten up if they want to march to the Government buildings to protest their sorry plight. And they succeeded admirably.

'And those who are at the head of the industrial movement in Edmonton are as much to blame as the council. Why did they not protest against the action of the council?...

'Thousands of people watched the demonstrations and what do you suppose they thought as they watched the police clubs descending on the heads of unarmed men and women? They were disgusted, absolutely disgusted. They don't know that the federal government gave orders to stop the hunger march and the local governments danced to the tune, because they are dependent for their finances on the federal government. They blame the local governments for this cowardly action and unless an explanation is coming forth their faith is shattered ... They will assert themselves in the next election.' (*Alberta Labor News*, 24 December 1932)

94 See, for example, Macpherson, 154–9; Irving, 88–93, 171–2.

95 Douglas certainly believed that Aberhart did not understand Social Credit ideas. He wrote Attorney-General J.F. Lymburn that: 'The [Aberhart] proposal appears to contemplate a fixed price regardless of costs, which seems to be assumed as constant, and this price includes something labeled "the unearned increment" which has, however, no relation to that phrase as used in the Social Credit literature. So far from a proposal increasing purchasing power it is a form of taxation which in all probability reduces purchasing power by raising prices ... Generally speaking it would appear upon the face of it that Mr. Aberhart has not grasped that Social Credit involves the *creation* of purchasing power' (Provincial Archives of Alberta, Premiers' Papers, File 1081, Douglas to Lymburn, 1 June 1935).

96 Biographical material on Aberhart is available in David R. Elliott and Iris Miller, *Bible Bill: A Biography of William Aberhart* (Edmonton: Reidmore 1987).

97 Public Archives of Alberta, Calgary Prophetic Bible Conference, 'Bulletin of the Calgary Prophetic Bible Institute,' 1926, 7

98 Ibid. Aberhart's religious activities and ideas are traced carefully in Elliott and Miller, particularly 34–42 and 52–84.

99 William E. Mann, *Sect, Cult and Church in Alberta* (Toronto: University of Toronto Press 1955), 22

100 Irving quotation, 63. See also Irving, 68, 187, 203, 207, 212, 215, 220, 223.

101 Elliott writes: 'contrary to Irving and Mann, Aberhart's support came largely from

the membership of the established churches and from those with marginal religious commitment rather than from the members of sectarian groups.' But he cites only studies of the party membership in the Manning period to prove his point (David R. Elliott, 'Antithetical Elements in William Aberhart's Theology and Political Ideology,' *Canadian Historical Review*, 59:1 [March 1978], 38–58, quotation on 39). See also Larry Hannant, 'The Calgary Working Class and the Social Credit Movement in Alberta, 1932–1935,' *Labour/Le Travail*, 16 (Fall 1985), 97–116.

102 Macpherson, 162
103 Irving, 66–7, 104–5, 125–6
104 Premiers' Papers, File 1125B
105 The platform for the election determined by the two Alberta conventions is reproduced in Alfred J. Hooke, *Thirty Plus Five: I Know, I Was There* (Edmonton: Institute of Applied Art 1971), 66–9.
106 Irving, 141; *Social Credit Chronicle*, 7 December 1934; Hooke, 70
107 *Canadian Parliamentary Guide*, 1935 and 1936; Hannant, 110–13. There were at least thirty farmers in the thirty-nine–person caucus of the UFA in 1935, and the three Labour MLAs (the fourth elected in 1930, a teacher, died a year earlier) were all of working-class backgrounds.
108 This is clear in various issues of *Social Credit Chronicle*, 1934–6. Hannant, 111, provides a social profile of Calgary Social Credit activists, from 1933 to 1935, which indicates that skilled workers constituted 26 per cent of activists, unskilled workers constituted 23 per cent, and retail clerks and office workers provided 15 per cent of the total.
109 *Social Credit Chronicle*, various issues
110 Premiers' Papers, File 1124
111 Irving, 101–3
112 *Social Credit Chronicle*, 12 July 1935
113 *Social Credit Chronicle*, 12 January 1935
114 *Social Credit Chronicle*, 21 September 1934
115 Ibid.
116 *Social Credit Chronicle*, 19 October 1934
117 *Social Credit Chronicle*, 28 September 1934
118 William Aberhart, *Social Credit Manual: Social Credit as Applied to the Province of Alberta* (Calgary: Aberhart 1935), 5
119 Ibid., 7
120 Ibid., 21, 41–3
121 Swann, 21
122 William Aberhart, *Social Credit Manual*, 21
123 Ibid., 55
124 Quoted in Lewis H. Thomas, *William Aberhart and Social Credit in Alberta* (Toronto: Copp Clark 1977), 77.
125 Aberhart, *Social Credit Manual*, 13, 55. Aberhart wrote somewhat incoherently: 'At the present time this great wealth [machinery and natural resources] is being

selfishly manipulated and controlled by one or more men known as the "Fifty Big Shots of Canada" ' (13).

126 *Edmonton Journal*, 5 April 1935

127 Aberhart's 1935 *Manual* (19–21) mentioned twenty-five dollars per person over twenty-one, with five dollars per child; ten dollars per person seventeen or eighteen years old; and fifteen dollars for a nineteen-year-old.

128 Ibid., 13

129 Macpherson, 156; *Social Credit Chronicle*, 17 May 1935. Prices, Aberhart told a large Edmonton audience, would be 'whittled to the bone' (*Edmonton Journal*, 25 May 1935).

130 Douglas's reaction is found in Macpherson, 156. Typical business reaction was that of the Calgary Board of Trade, which complained, as we note further on, of the taxation implications of the Aberhart proposal.

131 Glenbow Archives Institute, Calgary Board of Trade Papers, J.H. Hanna to John Mackay, secretary, Drumheller Board of Trade, 27 May 1935, Box 2, File 13

132 *Edmonton Journal*, 25 July 1935

133 *Edmonton Bulletin*, 26 August 1935

134 *Calgary Herald*, 8 August 1935

135 Calgary Board of Trade Papers, J.H. Hanna to E.C. Gilliatt, managing secretary, Winnipeg Board of Trade, 12 September 1935, Box 2, File 13

136 Joseph A. Boudreau, *Alberta, Aberhart and Social Credit*, Canadian History through the Press Series (Toronto: Holt, Rinehart and Winston 1975), 8–9; Irving, 318

137 *Edmonton Journal*, 3 June 1935

138 As noted in chapter 1, the group that gave Social Credit disproportionate support was the unemployed.

139 Calgary Board of Trade Papers, P.J. Carroll to Hanna, 10 August 1935, Box 2, File 13

140 *Edmonton Journal*, 31 May 1935

141 *Edmonton Bulletin*, 8 August 1935

142 Calgary Board of Trade Papers, Box 1, File 11

143 *Social Credit Chronicle*, 31 August 1934, reported on the successful use of scrip by the town of Raymond. Coe, 'Stamp Scrip,' mentions Vermilion's use of scrip as well (64).

144 Detailed results of the 1935 election are found in *Canadian Parliamentary Guide*, 1936, 395–401, and in Kenneth Wark, *A Report on Alberta Elections 1905–1982* (Edmonton: Government of Alberta 1983), 13, 49–53.

Chapter 3

1 The pressures exerted upon Aberhart at this time were detailed in diaries kept by his executive assistant, Fred Stone. Glenbow Archives Institute, Fred Stone Diary Extracts, 1972, Tape 1, excerpts for 13 November 1935, 22 November 1935. See also Joseph A. Boudreau, *Alberta, Aberhart and Social Credit*, Canadian History through the Press Series (Toronto: Holt, Rinehart and Winston 1975), 50–1.

2 The Douglas-Aberhart controversy is discussed in the Stone Diary, Tape 1, ex-

cerpts for 13 November 1935, 27 December 1935. See also C.B. Macpherson, *Democracy in Alberta: Social Credit and the Party System* (Toronto: University of Toronto Press 1962), 163–5.

3 On the Aberhart government's financial policy, see E.J. Hanson, 'Public Finance in Alberta since 1935,' *Canadian Journal of Economics and Political Science*, 18:3 (August 1952), 323, 325. On the experiment with scrip, see V.F. Coe, 'Dated Stamp Scrip in Alberta,' *Canadian Journal of Economics and Political Science*, 4:1 (February 1938), 60–91.

4 On the insurgency, see Macpherson, 169–77, and J.J. Barr, *The Dynasty: The Rise and Fall of Social Credit in Alberta* (Toronto: McClelland and Stewart 1974), 99–104. On the court decisions, see J.R. Mallory, *Social Credit and the Federal Power in Canada* (Toronto: University of Toronto Press 1954).

5 Glenbow Archives Institute, Calgary Board of Trade Papers, Box 1, File 1, 'Report of Legislative Committee to the Council of the Board of Trade,' 15 April 1936

6 Public Archives of Alberta, Social Credit Board, 'The Records Tell the Story,' (Edmonton: the Board 1939), 23

7 The impact of the change of administration from UFA to Social Credit on teachers and education is explored in Ralph Douglas Ramsay, 'The Alberta Teachers' Alliance as a Social Movement 1918–1936,' MA thesis, University of Calgary, 1978; and in Bernie Ovatt, 'The Papers of William Aberhart as Minister of Education, 1935–1943,' MEd thesis, University of Alberta, 1971.

8 Ovatt, 48

9 Calgary Board of Trade Papers, Box 1, File 2, J.H. Hanna, secretary, Calgary Board of Trade, to Premier J.E. Brownlee, 5 April 1934; Hanna to John Blue, manager-secretary, Edmonton Chamber of Commerce, 3 May 1934

10 An Act for the Establishment of a Department of Trade and Industry and to Prescribe Its Powers and Duties (Assented to 16 April 1934), *Statutes of the Province of Alberta*, 1934, Chap. 33

11 Among the organizations supporting codes, the Alberta branch of the Retail Merchants' Association was prominent. P.W. Abbott, legal representative of 'T. Eaton Company and several others of the larger retail establishments in Edmonton,' to Aberhart, Public Archives of Alberta, Premiers' Papers, File 921A.

12 An Act to Amend and Consolidate the Licensing of Trades and Business Act (Assented to 5 October 1937), *Statutes of the Province of Alberta*, 1937, Third Session, Chap. One

13 Among the boards whose opposition to the bill is recorded in the Premiers' Papers are the boards in Edmonton, Calgary, Red Deer, Medicine Hat, High River, and Lacombe. Premiers' Papers, File 922; F. Ashenhurst, secretary, Alberta Branch, Canadian Manufacturers' Association, to Aberhart, 29 September 1937, Premiers' Papers, File 922.

14 Calgary Board of Trade Papers, Box 1, File 5

15 H.J. Nolan, lawyer with Bennett, Hannah, Nolan, Chambers and Might, to L.A. Cavanaugh (the automobile dealer), 8 November 1938, Calgary Board of Trade Papers, Box 1, File 7

16 *Calgary Albertan*, 9 September 1939; Hanna to W.L. Mackenzie King, 13 January 1938, Calgary Board of Trade Papers, Box 1, File 7
17 An Act Respecting the Marketing of Natural Products and Other Commodities and to Provide for the Regulation Thereof within the Province, *Statutes of the Province of Alberta*, 1939, Chap. 3
18 Calgary Board of Trade Papers, Box 1, File 7
19 *Toronto Globe and Mail*, 25 March 1939
20 John Richards and Larry Pratt, *Prairie Capitalism: Power and Influence in the New West* (Toronto: McClelland and Stewart 1979)
21 Public Archives of Alberta, Alfred Farmilo Papers, Box 1, Item 44, 'A Meeting with Messrs. Glen L. MacLachlan, Powell, Byrne, July 9, 1937'
22 Premiers' Papers, File 1079 'Annual Report of Social Credit Board for 1939, Submitted to the Legislative Assembly of the Province of Alberta, February 1940,' 10–11
23 'The Records Tell the Story,' 14–16
24 A critical account of Métis treatment at the hands of both the UFA and Social Credit is found in Murray Dobbin, *The One-and-a-Half Men: The Story of Jim Brady and Malcolm Norris*, Métis Portraits of the 20th Century (Vancouver: New Star Books 1945). Some indication of the racist attitudes of white settlers in the Métis areas is found in Premiers' Papers, File 725A, Charles Lebos, secretary-treasurer, Lac la Biche Board of School Trustees, to Aberhart, 25 June 1937. Lebos wanted the government to set up a separate 'half-breed' school because the Métis children allegedly were 'lacking in brightness' and carriers of infectious diseases, 'hereditary or otherwise.' The school-board chairman said of the parents: 'most of these people surrounding the village have no initiative and are for the most part immoral, venereal disease in all its ugly stages being prevalent.' The Métis Betterment Act is found in *Revised Statutes of the Province of Alberta*, 1942, Chap. 329.
25 *Edmonton Bulletin*, 22 March 1937; quoted in Boudreau, 67
26 Premiers' Papers, Files 1118, 1124
27 Premiers' Papers, File 1105, 'Minutes of Second Annual Social Credit Convention, Calgary, 13–15 January 1938.'
28 Ibid.
29 Ibid.
30 Ibid.
31 Premiers' Papers, File 1117B. 'Minutes of Third Annual Social Credit Convention, Edmonton, January 1939'; Premiers' Papers, File 1106, 'Minutes of First Annual Social Credit Convention, Edmonton, 1937'
32 Premiers' Papers, File 1117B, 'Minutes of the Fourth Annual Social Credit Convention, 1940'
33 'Minutes of Third Annual Social Credit Convention'
34 'Minutes of First Annual Social Credit Convention'
35 'Minutes of Second Annual Social Credit Convention'
36 Ibid.

37 Premiers' Papers, Files 1014, 1128; *People's Weekly*, 8 February 1936
38 *Western Clarion*, various issues, 1936 and 1937
39 Premiers' Papers, File 1109, W.B. McDowall, president, Castle River Social Credit zone, to Aberhasrt, 1 May 1938
40 *People's Weekly*, 13 June 1936 and 27 June 1936
41 *People's Weekly*, 23 October 1937 and 20 August 1938
42 *People's Weekly*, 26 November 1938
43 Ben Swankey, 'Reflections of a Communist: 1935 Election,' *Alberta History*, 28:4 (Autumn 1980), 36. Swankey notes with reference to the late thirties: 'It was in this period that close relationships were established between the Communist Party and sections of the Social Credit movement including the MLAs which included, for example, Communist support for the election of Orvis Kennedy in an Edmonton by-election in March, 1938, where the victory parade following the election included Leslie Morris, western director of the Communist Party, in its front ranks.'
44 Premiers' Papers, File 1117A, Aberhart to Armand Toupin, secretariat, Ligue du Crédit Social, Hull, Quebec, 13 September 1937. Wrote Aberhart: 'I believe the Communist Party has distributed a large number of these pledges and has been getting them signed and returned to the Alberta Social Credit League ... We need the support of all citizens in the struggle we are now facing, insofar as cooperation with the government is concerned and the expression of their unity of outlook in certain matters. We cannot, however, sacrifice the Social Credit principles in any way to take in those affiliated with other political parties.'
45 Premiers' Papers, File 1115, Ethel Baker to Aberhart, 4 October 1938; Aberhart to Baker, 7 October 1938
46 *People's Weekly*, 26 November 1938
47 Glenbow-Alberta Institute Archives, H.E. Nichols Papers, Box 7, File 42
48 *People's Weekly*, 5 October 1946
49 Nichols Papers, Box 4, File 28
50 Premiers' Papers, File 1004, Provincial Unemployed Married Men's Association to all Social Credit members of the Legislature, n.d.
51 Premiers' Papers, File 1010, Relief Camp Social Crediters to Aberhart, n.d., filed 30 December 1936
52 Premiers' Papers, File 1014, Divisional Conference of Social Credit constituencies of Calgary and Edmonton to Aberhart, 24 April 1937
53 Premiers' Papers, File 1014, A.A. Mackenzie to W.W. Cross, 9 January 1936
54 *People's Weekly*, 24 October 1936
55 Premiers' Papers, File 1011, Fred White, secretary, Calgary TLC, to Aberhart, 4 November 1936. The Provincial Unemployed Married Men's Association joined the Single Unemployed Association in opposing the scheme.
56 *People's Weekly*, 24 October 1936; 26 December 1936
57 Premier's Papers, File 1014, F.J. Buck to W.W. Cross, 24 April 1937, enclosed in W.W. Cross to Aberhart, 24 April 1937
58 Premier's Papers, File 1014, Cross to Aberhart, 24 April 1937

59 Premiers' Papers, File 1017, Sam MacDonald, Evansburg, to Aberhart, 26 March 1939
60 Premiers' Papers, File 1017, A.A. Mackenzie to W.W. Cross, 15 April 1939
61 Premiers' Papers, File 1017, Anonymous to Aberhart, 4 April 1939
62 Premiers' Papers, File 1004, Central Social Credit Club, Calgary, to Aberhart, 3 April 1937
63 Ibid.
64 Premiers' Papers, File 1004, King Edward Social Credit Group #1 to J.A. Maurice, secretary, Social Credit League, 11 March 1937. There can indeed be little doubt that the provincial relief authorities attempted to prevent certain destitute persons from collecting. This was particularly true with regard to 'agitators,' who, in Mackenzie's mind, seemed to include virtually everyone who had ever defied an order in a relief camp. Mackenzie also refused relief to persons who had left the province and then returned. For example, in a letter to his federal counterpart in 1939, he rejected claims for relief from ten men who had returned to Alberta after serving with the Republican forces in Spain even though nine of them had lived in the province for ten years or more before going to Spain. From his point of view, such men had no claim to be provincial residents. He complained to another federal official that these men 'have already endeavoured to disturb the political and social life of the province.' (Public Archives of Canada, Department of Labour Papers, Vol. 2040, File Y1-7-18, A.A. Mackenzie, Alberta Commissioner, Relief and Public Welfare, to Harry Hereford, Dominion Commissioner, Unemployment Relief, 10 February 1939; Hereford to Mackenzie, 15 February 1939; Mackenzie to Hereford, 28 February 1939; Mackenzie to Humphrey Mitchell, Dominion Director of Labour Transference, 7 February 1939)
65 J.W. Hugill, Aberhart's first attorney-general, who resigned from the cabinet in a dispute over the legality of proposed Social Credit legislation, commented: 'Much lip-service was devoted prior to the election, to the abolition of party patronage in the civil service. The sickening result now is that no person can secure employment in the Provincial Government service who is not a subscribing member of a recognized Aberhart social credit group. The number of employees has been increased beyond all reason and necessity. Those suspected of non-adherence to Aberhart's peculiar theology and ideology find their services dispensed with and they have no redress as ostensible servants of the Crown.' (Glenbow Archives, John Hugill Papers, Box 2, File 43; Hugill to D. Morkeberg, Markerville, Alberta, for the information of the Danish ambasssador to Canada, 22 September 1942)
66 In a letter to a Calgary party activist who was making recommendations for positions as labourers, stenographers, and truck operators, Aberhart advised that the activist be careful as to whom he recommended for government positions. 'In my experience or should I say so far as I have been able to ascertain neither the Single or Married Men's Association have been favourable to this Government in any way and in fact have stood back of friend Andy [Andrew Davison, Mayor of Calgary and Independent MLA for Calgary].' (Premiers' Papers, File 1051A, Aberhart to A.F. Van Buren, Calgary, 12 June 1940)

67 Premiers' Papers, File 1079, Social Credit Board to MLAs, 21 May 1938
68 Ibid.
69 Premiers' Papers, File 1113, Lethbridge Constituency Association to Aberhart, 10 November 1937
70 Premiers' Papers, File 1125B, Herbert Clark, secretary-treasurer, Lethbridge constituency organization, to Aberhart, 2 May 1938
71 Premiers' Papers, File 1108, Agnes Halhead, secretary, West End Social Credit Study Group, Calgary, to Aberhart, 12 February 1938
72 Premiers' Papers, File 1108, Aberhart to Halhead, 24 February 1938
73 Premiers' Papers, File 1011, Aberhart to B.W. Birks, Edmonton, 3 November 1936
74 Premiers' Papers, File 1106, 'Minutes of First Annual Social Credit Convention, Edmonton, 1937'
75 Premiers' Papers, File 1105, 'Minutes of Second Annual Social Credit Convention, Calgary, 13–15 January 1938'
76 Premiers' Papers, File 1011, Employment Service to Aberhart, n.d.
77 Ibid.
78 Ibid.
79 Premiers' Papers, File 1011, Unemployed Association of Calgary to Aberhart, 20 November 1939
80 Premiers' Papers, File 1120A, Mrs. D. Gilchrist, Edmonton Constituency Social Credit Association, to Aberhart, 7 June 1940
81 Premiers' Papers, File 1005, R. Williams, secretary-treasurer, Blairmore Local Union No. 7295, District 18, UMWA, to Aberhart, 9 September 1940; Aberhart to Williams, 11 September 1940
82 Premiers' Papers, File 2257C, are filled with complaints to Aberhart from 1935 to 1938 regarding the Workmen's Compensation Board's narrow view of disability and the small claims paid out. Typical was the following letter from A. Rowley, president of the Taber Social Credit group, on 21 January 1937 (Rowley was a miner): '... as the President of our Local of over 100 members I am continually being questioned by these members. What has Aberhart done with these Compensation promises? He sent out his speakers all over the mining districts telling them that the lame, the halt and the blind would get justice.

'Also those who had given their lives for the mining industry and had not been amply provided for because of some slight technical flaw could be found to beat the worker of his just dues, these people would be compensated so said Mr. Low, Mr. Blackmore, Mr. Hansen, Mr. White and Mr. Unwin. Now the cold facts of the hand of law speaks for us in the person of Dr. Victor Wright [Aberhart's selection as chairman of the Workmen's Compensation Board] saying – "I am administering the Act passed in 1918" – and now the miner comes to us with a new worry since you have raised the protection fee to 10 cents per day with no more of a better outlook of getting justice than before. This is certainly heavy payment protection for the blind, the lame and the halt.'

83 Premiers' Papers, File 1055, A. Turner, secretary, Riverdale Social Credit group, to Aberhart, 26 September 1938

84 Premiers' Papers, File 1055, Aberhart to A. Turner, 29 September 1938

85 Judging by letters from constituency associations to Aberhart in Premiers' Papers, Files 1106, 1057, 1125A

86 Macpherson, 126–9

87 Ibid., 214

88 Ibid., 175–7

89 Premiers' Papers, File 1117A

90 *People's Weekly*, 4 September 1937

91 Macpherson, 176

92 *The Rebel*, 5 November 1937. *The Rebel* was a virulent anti–Social Credit newspaper in Calgary in 1937 and 1938.

93 John Hugill Papers, Box 2, File 37, 'Radio Speech 23 September 1937'; John W. Hugill, 'Constitutional Principles (Number One),' pamphlet published by author, Calgary, 1939, Special Collections, University of Alberta

94 In a radio speech in 1939, he referred to Aberhart as a 'supreme dictator.' Hugill Papers, Box 2, File 39, 'Radio Speech 25 April 1939.'

95 Barr, 100–2

96 Alfred J.Hooke, *30 + 5: I Know, I Was There* (Edmonton: Institute of Applied Arts 1971), 70, 84

97 'The Accurate News and Information Bill,' from Lewis H. Thomas, *William Aberhart and Social Credit in Alberta* (Toronto: Copp Clark 1977), 110

98 *Albertan*, 15 January 1936

99 *Albertan*, 24 February 1936

100 Boudreau, 9

101 Of the commission, the Alberta government wrote: 'The Government of Alberta desires to repudiate any responsibility for the Royal Commission which has been set up and for the continuance of its investigation. The Province was not consulted either in regard to the personnel or the terms of reference, and both Saskatchewan and Alberta are without representation on the Commission. In all the circumstances the Government of Alberta has been obliged to withhold its recognition of the Commission.' (Government of Alberta, *The Case for Alberta: Part 1: Alberta's Problems and Dominion-Provincial Relations*, 1938, 3)

102 Ibid.

103 Ibid., 9

104 Government of Alberta, *The Case for Alberta, Part 2: The Urgent Need for Social and Economic Reform*, 1938, 51

105 *Case for Alberta, Part 1*, 130

106 Ibid., 334

107 Public Archives of Canada, Department of Labour Papers, Vol. 2040, File Y1-7-18, W.W. Cross to Norman Rogers, 9 February 1938

108 Ten days after the Supreme Court ruled against the constitutionality of the province's

major social credit bills, Aberhart announced that Social Credit would be running in the Saskatchewan election (Ken Andrews, ' "Progressive" Counterparts of the CCF: Social Credit and the Conservative Party in Saskatchewan, 1935–1938,' *Journal of Canadian Studies*, 17:3 (Fall 1982), 63).

109 Ibid.
110 The Southern Alberta Divisional Conference argued that final selection by a committee 'is not democratic enough.' But the provincial convention referred the motion to the resolutions committee for further study. (Premiers' Papers, File 1105, 'Minutes of Second Annual Social Credit Convention, Calgary, 13–15 January 1938')
111 Andrews, ' "Progressive" Counterparts,' 58
112 Mary Hallett, 'The Social Credit Party and the New Democracy Movement: 1939–1940,' *Canadian Historical Review*, 47:4 (December 1966), 301–2
113 Ibid., 303–4
114 *Edmonton Bulletin*, 30 June 1939
115 Ibid.
116 E.G. Hansell, secretary of the federal Social Credit group, wrote Aberhart: 'With regard to the CCF I understand that they will co-operate with us and with the Herridge movement in order to eliminate conflict in a general election. I understood however that Williams, the CCF leader of Saskatchewan, is not so favourable. I might say we are in a position here to get in touch with Mr. Herridge and also the Secretary and President of the National Council of the CCF should you care to give us any advice along this line.' (Premiers' Papers, File 1055, Hansell to Aberhart, 17 March 1939)
117 Hallett, 311, 315–17, 321–3
118 Macpherson, in particular, emphasizes supposed lemming-like political behaviour of Albertans and its apparent consequences for parliamentary democracy (237–8). Macpherson claims of the UFA and Social Credit period: 'So complete was the predominance of the party in power that there was no need, from its own point of view, to attempt to proscribe other parties' (238).
119 *Canadian Parliamentary Guide*; Kenneth Wark, *A Report on Alberta Elections, 1905–1982* (Edmonton: Government of Alberta 1983), 11–13
120 The general council of the provincial Liberal party decided to leave the question of achieving unity to local Liberal parties. At its meeting 17 June 1939, it resolved: 'To institute an immediate campaign advancing the Liberal platform and policies and a vigorous campaign of the Liberal forces, and the nomination of a Liberal candidate in each constituency.

   'We recommend however that in any constituency where the majority of the Liberals of that constituency desire to cooperate with any other group or groups of political thought in support of some other candidate, the Liberal party in Alberta will support that candidate and the executive is hereby instructed to proceed accordingly.' (Glenbow-Alberta Institute Archives, Alberta Liberal Association Papers, Box 21, File 123.) On Liberal resistance to unity, see also Meir Serfaty,

'Structure and Organization of Political Parties in Alberta, 1935–1971,' PhD thesis, Carleton University, 1977, 82, 89.

121 Serfaty, 120

122 According to Meir Serfaty, when it began operation in Calgary in October 1936 the People's League was virtually an extension of the Board of Trade and the Conservative party (58).

123 In both cities the Civic Government Association provided united right-wing candidates against the Labour ticket.

124 These were the by-elections of 1933 and 1934, mentioned in chapter 2, in which Amelia Turner, the Labour-CCF candidate, was defeated despite garnering more than 40 per cent of the vote each time.

125 *Calgary Herald*, 24 June 1937

126 'Remember they represent banks and mortgage companies not you the people,' thundered a Social Credit pamphlet that outlined the links of People's League leaders with banks and mortgage companies (Premiers' Papers, File 1145, n.d.). One Social Credit publication about the leaders of the Independents was inflammatory enough to earn jail sentences for its authors for inciting violence. Joe Unwin, MLA for Edson, and G.F. Powell, expert adviser to the Social Credit Board, received six month sentences, and Powell, a British immigrant, was subsequently deported.

127 Serfaty, 62, 82; Premiers' Papers, File 1145, Social Credit pamphlet on the League leaders, n.d.

    An example of the conspiratorial or at least secretive behaviour of the rich businessmen of Calgary is found in the Premiers' Papers. A Social Credit supporter had 'accidentally' received a note marked 'extremely confidential' from a Civic Government Association special committee that included former Calgary Board of Trade president L.A. Cavanaugh and flour-mill owner F.E. Spooner, among others. The letter was sent to '90 of the largest taxpayers of this City,' and its explicit goal was to cut the mill rate even if that meant cuts in aid for the needy. After railing about 'those in the City who have no investment at stake who willingly increase City expenditures, knowing that the taxpayer is the one who shoulders the burden,' the letter invited the ninety rich men to a meeting to 'hear how we propose to carry on throughout the year and support the men who will give their time and energy to reducing the mill rate.' The favoured ninety were asked to 'please keep this letter confidential' because 'we want no publicity in connection with this meeting.' The letter itself would serve 'as your identification' to get into the meeting. (Premiers' Papers, File 1068A, sent to Aberhart 23 February 1940. Letter from CGA Special Committee [L.A. Cavanaugh, H.A. Howard, F.E. Osborne, F.L. Irving, E.J. Chambers, W.J. Green, A.D. Cumming, E.T. Critchley, C.E. Carr, A.H. Patrick, F.E. Spooner, W.H.A. Thompson].)

128 Alberta Liberal Association Papers, Box 21, File 123

129 Harold J. Schultz, 'A Second Term: 1940,' *Alberta Historical Review*, 10:1 (Winter 1962), 23

130 Premiers' Papers, File 850A, J.P. Hanna, secretary-treasurer, Calgary Board of Trade, to Aberhart, 2 June 1937

131 Premiers' Papers, File 850A, J.M. Miller, city clerk, Calgary, to Aberhart, 27 January 1938

132 Schultz, 23; Serfaty, 98–101

133 *People's Weekly*, 10 February 1940

134 Aberhart's attitude to the leadership is reflected in a blistering attack in Aberhart Papers, File 1227, Aberhart to A. Orlando, secretary, Cambrian Local Union #7330, District 18, United Mine Workers of America, Wayne, Alberta, 3 March 1939.

135 *Statutes of the Province of Alberta*, Chap. 15, 1938; *People's Weekly*, 12 March 1938. Labour also accused the Board of Industrial Relations, set up by the government to enforce minimum wages and maximum hours, of timidity in defending workers' rights against employers. The minutes of the board's early meetings do indeed suggest a willingness to allow various employers exemptions from minimum wage and maximum hour provisions (Public Archives of Alberta, Board of Industrial Relations Minutes).

136 Alvin Finkel, 'Obscure Origins: The Confused Early History of the Alberta CCF,' in J. William Brennan, ed., *Building the Cooperative Commonwealth: Essays on the Democratic Socialist Tradition in Canada* (Regina: Canadian Plains Research Centre 1985), 109–11

137 *People's Weekly*, 30 March 1940

138 *The Records Tell the Story*

139 David A.A. Finch, 'Turner Valley Oilfield Developments 1914–1945,' MA thesis, University of Calgary, 1985, 31–2

140 For example, the Calgary Board of Trade, in a submission to Aberhart, claimed that British capital destined for the oil industry had been withdrawn 'solely because of the radical ideas on debt reduction expressed and put into effect by the present government' (Premiers' Papers, File 850A, J.P. Hanna, secretary-treasurer, Calgary Board of Trade, to Aberhart, 2 June 1937).

By contrast, the Social Credit organ, *Today and Tomorrow*, claimed early in 1938 that eastern interests supported the Aberhart government's oil policies. Noting that Commonwealth Petroleum had plans to invest ten million dollars in Turner Valley, the paper claimed company president Newton Wylie was positive towards the Alberta government: 'Tremendous praise of Alberta's government for its progressive handling of the vast oil resources in the province is given by Eastern interests, stated Mr. Wylie. Irrespective of political consideration there was no doubt that any misgivings for the future had been cleared away by the policy adopted by the government.' (*Today and Tomorrow*, 6 January 1938)

141 Finch, 133–4

142 Premiers' Papers, File 1050A, A.A. Kelsey, vice-president, Turner Valley Social Credit group, to Aberhart, 24 July 1936; Aberhart to A.L. Clemens, executive member, Okotoks–High River Social Credit constituency, 27 October 1936; Okotoks–High River Social Credit constituency to Aberhart, 2 December 1936

143 Finch, 134
144 Ibid.; *Calgary Herald*, 23 September 1937
145 Premiers' Papers, File 1050A, Report on membership, 31 January 1939
146 *Canadian Parliamentary Guide*
147 Provincial Archives of Alberta, 1940 Social Credit Election Platform
148 Thomas E. Flanagan, 'Ethnic Voting in Alberta Provincial Elections, 1921–1975,' in Carlo Caldarola, ed., *Society and Politics in Alberta: Research Papers* (Toronto: Methuen 1979), 315
149 *Canadian Parliamentary Guide*

Chapter 4

1 L.P.V. Johnson and Ola MacNutt, *Aberhart of Alberta* (Edmonton: Co-op Press 1970), 191
2 Ibid., 197
3 Provincial Archives of Alberta, Alberta Social Credit League Papers, Box 1, Item 1, 'Ritual of the Alberta Monetary Reform Groups Incorporated with the Democratic Monetary Reform Organization of Canada,' 6
4 Ibid., 2
5 Ibid., 6
6 Ibid., 2
7 Ibid., 9
8 Premiers' Papers, File 1089, 16 July 1941. The chamber's views had been asked for by the Auckland Chamber of Commerce, which was concerned about the growth of the Social Credit movement in parts of New Zealand and Australia. These views were then published in Australian newspapers and picked up by Alberta papers. There is no date on the newspaper stories in the premier's papers, but the date on which the premier received copies of the stories is marked 16 July 1941.
9 Ibid.
10 Ibid.
11 Johnson and MacNutt, 184–9
12 Premiers' Papers, File 1129, Aberhart to P.W. McWhirter, Camrose, 15 January 1943
13 Premiers' Papers, File 1117A, 'Social Credit League membership, 18 May 1942.' Four constituencies were indicated as having no paid-up members at that date.
14 Premiers' Papers, File 1117A, Aberhart to Fred Anderson, MLA, 18 May 1942
15 Premiers' Papers, File 1129, Aberhart to P.W. McWhirter, Camrose, 15 January 1943
16 Premiers' Papers, File 1221B, Aberhart to S.W. Cameron, provincial secretary, Alberta Motor Association, Calgary, 2 March 1942
17 Premiers' Papers, File 1051A, G.M. Whicher, president, Calgary Constituency Association, to Aberhart, 1 October 1940
18 Premiers' Papers, File 1051A, Aberhart to Whicher, 2 October 1940

19 Premiers' Papers, File 1068B, Aberhart to Albert Scheerschmidt, Stettler, 16 March 1942. Social Credit groups were often puzzled by the government's reluctance to nationalize oil and hydroelectricity. For example, the vice-president of a Social Credit group had written in 1939: 'I would like to have you tell me why your government do [sic] not take over the resources of the province so the profits from these industries would go into the Provincial Treasury.

I specifically refer to the oil and power companies ... there are many good social crediters who are faced with these questions and I think it would be nice for them to know the why for of these things as there are some parties that are busy telling the people that the Alberta government can do these things but they do not do so because they [the government] are working for the capitalist.' (Premiers' Papers, File 1068A, William Speidel, vice-president, Camrose Social Credit group #574, to Aberhart, 11 November 1939)

20 Premiers' Papers, File 1068B, Aberhart to Albert Scheerschmidt, 16 March 1942

21 Aberhart's co-operation with the federal government extended to a willingness to work closely with the federal Bureau of Public Information, which Ontario Premier Mitchell Hepburn denounced as a political tool of Mackenzie King. Aberhart 'responded positively to all federal appeals for aid in recruiting, war savings, endorsements and the Victory Loan.' (William R. Young, ' "A Highly Intelligent and Unselfish Approach": Public Information and the Canadian West, 1939–45,' *Canadian Historical Review* 52:4 [December 1981], 502)

22 On the Communist Campaign, see Alvin Finkel, *Business and Social Reform in the Thirties* (Toronto: Lorimer 1979), 84.

23 The report of the table officers at the 1940 Alberta Federation of Labour convention noted that 'we express our deepest satisfaction and pleasure' with the province's decision to withdraw its objection to the Unemployment Insurance Act (Alberta Federation of Labour, 'Proceedings of the 23rd Convention of the Alberta Federation of Labour,' Lethbridge, 18 and 19 November 1940, 10).

24 *People's Weekly*, 11 October 1941

25 Provincial Archives of Alberta, Alfred Farmilo Papers, Background Material on Farmilo. Farmilo remained on the board until 1955.

26 Reports of the president and secretary before the 1944 convention of the AFL (Alberta Federation of Labour, 'Proceedings of the 24th Convention of the Alberta Federation of Labour,' Edmonton, 21, 22, and 23 February 1944, 7)

27 Ibid., 11

28 *People's Weekly*, 31 January 1942

29 *Canadian Parliamentary Guide*, 1944, 389

30 Premiers' Papers, File 1079, Social Credit Board to Caucus, 1942 (no further date)

31 Fred White, president of the AFL, while castigating the timidity of the Alberta administration in his address to the 1938 AFL convention, paid tribute to MacLellan for being 'untiring in all his efforts to be of service to our Federation on all measures which have been sponsored by the Federation or been of interest to the

workers of the province' (Alberta Federation of Labour, 'Proceedings of the 22nd Convention of the Alberta Federation of Labour,' 28–30 November 1938, 7).

32 *People's Weekly*, 1 August 1942
33 John A. Irving, *The Social Credit Movement in Alberta* (Toronto: University of Toronto Press 1959), 188
34 *Canadian Parliamentary Guide*, 1941
35 *People's Weekly*, 1 August 1942
36 Glenbow Archives Institute, Alberta CCF Records, Box 5, File 42, William Irvine to David Lewis, 28 June 1944
37 Premiers' Papers, File 1079, R.D. Ansley to Aberhart, 28 May 1942
38 Premiers' Papers, File 1129, Mrs R. Hurlburt to Aberhart, 23 April 1942
39 Premiers' Papers, File 1129, L.D. Byrne to Aberhart, n.d.
40 Premiers' Papers, File 1120A, Bert Sensier, secretary, Crow's Nest Pass Zone, Alberta Social Credit League, Blairmore, to Aberhart, 27 October 1941
41 Premiers' Papers, File 1113, William Wray, acting secretary-treasurer, Central Park Social Credit group, Calgary, to Premier Ernest C. Manning, 23 June 1943
42 For example, before a provincial by-election in Camrose, Aberhart received requests from both Social Crediters and CCFers to allow CCF leader Chester Ronning, who had narrowly lost the seat in the general election, to contest the seat unopposed by a Social Crediter. Aberhart was not supportive. (Premiers' Papers, File 1241, J.E. Liesemer, Didsbury, Alberta, to Aberhart, 26 November 1940; Aberhart to Liesemer, 3 December 1940; G.F. Snyder, Cowley, Alberta, to Aberhart, 30 November 1940)
43 Premiers' Papers, File 1241, Reverend Warwick Kelloway, Calgary, to Aberhart, 22 March 1941
44 Premiers' Papers, File 1241, Aberhart to Liesemer, 3 Dcember 1940
45 C.H. Douglas, *Social Credit* (Hawthorn, Calif.: Omni Publications 1966, [orig. pub. 1935])
46 Louis Even, *Salvation Island* (Ottawa: Regards 1975 [orig. pub. 1938])
47 C.B. Macpherson, *Democracy in Alberta: Social Credit and the Party System* (Toronto: University of Toronto Press 1962), 182–5
48 Lewis H. Thomas, *William Aberhart and Social Credit in Alberta* (Toronto: Copp Clark 1977), 156–7
49 Macpherson, 203
50 David R. Elliott and Iris Miller. *Bible Bill: A Biography of William Aberhart* (Edmonton: Reidmore 1987), 304
51 Ibid., 305
52 Provincial Archives of Alberta, Alberta Social Credit League Papers, Box 2, Tony Cashman, *Ernest C. Manning: A Biographical Sketch* (n.d., but written in 1958, according to *Busy Bee*, Social Credit organ, May–June 1958, 5), 21. The biographical information provided here comes from Cashman.
53 This is implied, in any case, in the correspondence in the Glenbow Archives Institute, Calgary Board of Trade Papers. Fred Stone, Aberhart's sceptical

executive assistant, who regarded both Social Crediters and their philosophy as somewhat bizarre, noted in his diaries that Manning carried much of the weight of the government and was more cautious and placating than other members of the government. Sarcastically, he labelled the future Alberta premier as a 'master of generalities.' (Glenbow Archives Institute: Fred Stone Diaries, Tape 2, 20 January 1936)

54 Premiers' Papers, File 928A, Ernest C. Manning to Miss Agnes Bradley, Edmonton, 30 March 1942

55 Premiers' Papers, File 928A, Aberhart to Thomas Jones, Longview, 26 January 1942; Manning draft for Aberhart (from which the quoted materials are taken), 21 January 1942

56 Premiers' Papers, File 928A, Thomas Jones to Aberhart, 16 January 1942

57 Premiers' Papers, File 1113, Manning to William Wray, acting secretary-treasurer, Central Park Social Credit group, Calgary, 30 June 1943

58 Premiers' Papers, File 1242, Manning to J.B. Hayfield, Bittern Lake, Alberta, 3 February 1944

59 Reported in *Today and Tomorrow*, 'official organ of the Social Credit League,' 16 March 1944

60 *Today and Tomorrow*, 2 March 1944

61 A Communist-led campaign in 1931 for non-contributory unemployment insurance to be financed by a steeply graded income tax (as opposed to the issuance of new money, which was the Social Credit strategy) drew more than 94,000 signatures nation-wide on petitions to Parliament. The small Labour caucus moved that Parliament adopt such a program, but unsurprisingly it was greeted with a lecture from R.B. Bennett about fiscal irresponsibility. (Alvin Finkel, *Business and Social Reform in the Thirties*, 83–4, 162)

62 Extract from J. Vans MacDonald, 'Towards National Socialism,' from *Western Druggist*, June 1943, reprinted in *Today and Tomorrow*, 16 March 1944

63 Reported in *People's Weekly*, 17 April 1943

64 Ibid.

65 *Today and Tomorrow*, 9 March 1944

66 Premiers' Papers, File 1118, 'Social Credit League Membership,' 31 July 1944

67 Premiers' Papers, File 1124, 'Alberta Social Credit League Membership,' 4 April 1938 (includes complete figures on 1937 membership)

68 Edmonton membership had fallen from 1996 to 522, Lethbridge membership from 468 to 40 (Premiers' Papers, File 1118, 'Social Credit League Membership,' 31 July 1944).

69 Premiers' Papers, File 1119, 'Resolutions of the 1944 Social Credit League Convention'

70 E.J. Hanson, 'Public Finance in Alberta since 1935,' *Canadian Journal of Economics and Political Science*, 18:3 (August 1952), 324, 326

71 Social Credit League Papers, Box 3, 'Alberta Provincial Budget Address,' 1 March 1943

72 Meir Serfaty, 'Structure and Organization of Political Parties in Alberta, 1935–71,' PhD thesis, Carleton University, 1977, 113–37
73 *Canadian Parliamentary Guide*, 1945, 382–3
74 *Edmonton Journal* and *Calgary Herald* editorials in July 1944
75 Premiers' Papers, File 1112, copy of letter from Fred A. Schultz, Western Petroleum Operators Ltd., Calgary, to Herbert Greenfield, Calmont Oils, Calgary, 26 July 1944
76 *Today and Tomorrow*, 8 August 1944
77 Alberta Federation of Labour, 'Proceedings of the 23rd Convention of the Alberta Federation of Labour,' Lethbridge, 18 and 19 November 1940, 22
78 The Social Credit convention in 1940 approved a resolution forwarded by the Social Credit Women's Auxiliary, which said that Social Creditors 'are opposed to profiteering out of the sale of armaments and also opposed to profiteering out of the sale of foodstuffs, clothing and the necessities of life.
   'Be it therefore resolved that the conscription of capital and finance must precede any other form of conscription that the exigencies of war may make.' (Premiers' Papers, File 117B, 'Proceedings of Social Credit League Annual Convention,' January 1940)
79 The Social Credit convention has been cited above (note 69). The AFL convention minutes are found in Alberta Federation of Labour, 'Proceedings of the 24th Convention of the Alberta Federation of Labour,' Edmonton, 21–24 February 1944.
80 Ibid., 20
81 Ibid., 36–7
82 David Iwaasa, 'The Japanese in Southern Alberta 1941–45,' *Alberta History*, 24:3 (Summer 1976), 9
83 Under a wartime arrangement made between the provinces and the federal government, corporation and personal income taxes were collected by the senior government, with 5 per cent of the revenue thus collected subsequently returned to the provinces. Other forms of provincial revenue, such as land taxes, liquor taxes, licences, and permits, were still collected by the provinces.
84 *Today and Tomorrow*, 8 August 1944
85 Kenneth Bryden, *Old Age Pensions and Policy-Making in Canada* (Montreal: McGill-Queen's University Press 1974), 93–4
86 Alberta Social Credit League Papers, Box 3, 'Progress in Alberta: 1935–1943,' Social Credit pamphlet, n.d.
87 *Revised Statutes of the Province of Alberta*, 1942, Chap. 77; *Statutes of the Province of Alberta*, 1943, Chap. 7
88 Though the Communists had a change of heart after Social Credit's election in 1935, they had earlier qualified the Social Credit movement as 'fascist' (*Edmonton Journal*, 27 March 1935). CCF attacks, in the form of vitriolic editorials by Elmer Roper and William Irvine, appeared regularly in the pages of the *People's Weekly* during Aberhart's first term. For example, when the government announced its proposed newspaper legislation in 1937, Roper compared Aberhart directly with Hitler. (*People's Weekly*, 4 September 1937)

89 *Canadian Parliamentary Guide*, 1945, 382–3

90 Alberta CCF Papers, Box 5, File 42, Alberta CCF Provincial Office to Margaret Telford, National Office, CCF, 4 November 1944

91 *Today and Tomorrow*, 2 March 1944

92 *People's Weekly*, 20 February 1943. Membership figures from Glenbow Archives Institute, H.E. Nichols Papers, Box 7, File 44; membership had risen to 16,000 by 1944.

93 The early years of the CCL are explored in Irving Martin Abella, *Nationalism, Communism and Canadian Labour: The CIO, the Communist Party and Canadian Congress of Labour, 1935–1956* (Toronto: University of Toronto Press 1973).

94 The 1942 convention of District 18 of the United Mine Workers of America, which included all of Alberta's unionized coal miners, called for the removal of Dr Victor Wright as chairman of the Workmen's Compensation Board and of Farmilo as labour representatve on the board. Farmilo, the miners charged, 'represents only a minority of the organized workers in the province of Alberta,' and his appointment 'has failed to bring about a fair and sympathetic administration for injured workmen.' (Premiers' Papers, File 1227, 'UMWA District 18 Resolutions,' President R. Scott and Secretary-Treasurer A.J. Morrison to Aberhart, 21 January 1942)

95 Alberta CCF Papers, Box 5, File 42, William Irvine, secretary, Alberta CCF, to David Lewis, national secretary, CCF, 2 March 1944

96 Alberta CCF Papers, Box 5, File 42, Alberta Provincial Office, CCF to Margaret Telford, National Office, CCF, 4 November 1944

97 Judging by its impressive electoral performance in constituencies such as Willingdon and Vegreville. In these seats, despite close Social Credit–CCF contests, the LPP gained, respectively, 22 and 17 per cent of the vote. (*Canadian Parliamentary Guide*, 1945, 382)

98 Alberta CCF Papers, Box 5, File 42, William Irvine to David Lewis, 2 March 1944

99 *Canadian Parliamentary Guide*, 1945, 381–2

100 *People's Weekly*, 16 September 1944

101 Morris C. Shumiatcher, 'Alberta Election,' *Canadian Forum*, 24: 284 (September 1944), 127–8. The relative strength of the co-op movement in Saskatchewan to that in Alberta was 210,000 to 120,000 members (Myron Johnson, 'The Failure of the CCF in Alberta: An Accident of History?' MA thesis, University of Alberta, 1974).

102 Elmer Roper response to Shumiatcher, *Canadian Forum*, 24: 285 (October 1944), 161–2

103 Jean Cochran and Pat Kincaid, eds., *Women in Canadian Life: Politics* (Toronto: Fitzhenry and Whiteside 1977), 29, 37, 46–8

104 *Edmonton Free Press*, 17 January 1920

105 *Statutes of the Province of Alberta*, 1930, Chap. 62

106 William Aberhart, *Social Credit Manual: Social Credit as Applied to the Province of Alberta* (1935), 51.

107 Irving, *Social Credit Movement*, 188–90

108 Premiers' Papers, File 650, Government of the Province of Alberta, Department of Agriculture, 'Some reasons for the establishment of women's extension programme,' 10 November 1938

109 Premiers' Papers, File 782, M.W. Robertson, civil service commissioner, to Bill McLean, Edson, 22 March 1941

110 There were no opinion polls carried out that would indicate the extent to which Independent voters in 1940 switched their votes to Social Credit in 1940 and the extent to which 1940 Social Credit supporters provided the base for the Left's large vote gain in 1944. Common sense, however, suggests that there is much truth in the following observations by Elmer Roper after the election: 'By common consent it is established that all the reactionary elements in the province backed the government and although it lost much of the support it had in 1940 it retained enough of it to win when added to the votes which formerly went to the so-called Independents. The government gained about 15,000 votes in all. The Independents lost 85,000. Most of these, probably a minimum of 50,000, went to the government. That means that the government lost at least 35,000 of the votes it got in 1940. This is almost exactly the number of the CCF gain. These are the people who saw through the sell-out. Many of them not only voted for the CCF but became members.' (*People's Weekly*, 19 August 1944)

Chapter 5

1 E.J. Hanson, 'Public Finance in Alberta since 1935,' *Canadian Journal of Economics and Political Science*, 18:3 (August 1952), 322–3

2 Ibid., 322, 324

3 These studies are discussed in chapter 6.

4 John Richards and Larry Pratt, *Prairie Capitalism: Power and Influence in the New West* (Toronto: McClelland and Stewart 1979), 160. The mining sector had provided 11 per cent of value added in 1935; in 1971 it provided 39 per cent. By contrast, during those years, agriculture fell from 54 to 14 per cent. Manufacturing rose modestly from 16 to 20 per cent and construction, aided by the booming energy sector, rose from 14 to 23 per cent.

5 Province of Alberta, *Report of the Royal Commission on Education in Alberta*, 1959, 43. This report included economic data supplied by Eric Hanson, who had been commissioned to prepare a special study on education financing in the province. The report noted: ' ... a high standard of public service has been established in Alberta, largely because of the great increase in revenue from petroleum development. The funds for such development come largely from outside the province and consequently the financial burden of providing services at existing high expenditure levels is met only to the extent of less than half the total expenditure by provincial residents' (43).

6 J.R. Mallory, *Social Credit and the Federal Power in Canada* (Toronto: University of Toronto Press 1954), 162

7 Ed Shaffer, 'The Political Economy of Oil in Alberta,' in David Leadbeater, ed.,

Essays on the Political Economy of Alberta (Toronto: New Hogtown Press 1984), 184

8 *Report of the Royal Commission on Education*, 23–4; *Census of Canada*, 1961. Not only was Alberta becoming more urban, but it was, by 1961, drawing close to the Canadian balance of urban-rural residents. In 1941, when 55.7 per cent of Canadians lived in urban locations (population 1000 or more), only 31.9 per cent of Albertans were urban. In 1961, 63.3 per cent of Albertans were urban as against 69.7 per cent of the Canadian population as a whole. (David Leadbeater, 'The Development of Capitalism in Alberta,' MA thesis, University of Alberta, 1980, 410)

9 C.B. Macpherson, *Democracy in Alberta: Social Credit and the Party System* (Toronto: University of Toronto Press 1962), 10–11; *Census of Canada*, 1961

10 David Monod, 'The End of Agrarianism: The Fight for Farm Parity in Alberta and Saskatchewan,' *Labour/Le Travail*, 16 (1985), 141–2

11 Harry Douglas Trace, 'An Examination of Some Factors Associated with the Decline of the Coal Industry in Alberta,' MA thesis, University of Alberta, 1958; Macpherson, 10: *Census of Canada*, 1961. Wartime subsidies on western coal ended in 1944 (Glenbow Archives Institute, United Mine Workers of America, District 18 Papers, Box 3, File 11, 'Minutes of meeting in the office of the Coal Controller, April 18, 1944').

12 Leadbeater, 'The Development of Capitalism,' 426

13 A.A. Den Otter, 'Railways and Alberta's Coal Problem, 1880–1960,' in A.W. Rasporich, ed., *Western Canada Past and Present* (Calgary: McClelland and Stewart West 1975), 97

14 Provincial Archives of Alberta, Premiers' Papers, File 1905, Industrial Federation of Labour of Alberta submission to Premier, 9 February 1954

15 Premiers' Papers, File 1510, Canadian Manufacturers' Association brief to cabinet, 14 February 1947. The CMA spoke of an 'acute shortage' of skilled workers in the manufacturing and construction sectors.

16 Premiers' Papers, File 1905, Industrial Federation of Labour of Alberta submission to Premier, 9 February 1954

17 Ibid.

18 Premiers' Papers, File 2153, John Ferguson, Department of Industries and Labour, to J.E. Oberholtzer, deputy minister, Department of Industries and Labour, 'Employment Report,' 1 February 1957, 3 June 1957, 4 March 1958

19 There is an extensive literature on the cold war. A good overview is Walter La Feber, *America, Russia and the Cold War, 1945–1971* (New York: Wiley 1972).

20 Macpherson, 207–9

21 *Statutes of the Province of Alberta*, 1946, Chap. 11, An Act Respecting the Rights of Alberta Citizens, assented to 27 March 1946

22 Provincial Archives of Alberta, Alberta Social Credit League Papers, Box 2, 'An Explanation of the Alberta Bill of Rights,' radio addresses by Ernest C. Manning and Lucien Maynard, 17 and 25 April 1946

23 Ibid.

24 *Journals*, Legislative Assembly of Alberta, 10 March 1948

25 Premiers' Papers, File 2161, speech delivered 14 August 1946 on 'Canada's Post-War Outlook.'

26 *Journals*, Legislative Assembly of Alberta, 10 March 1948

27 Ibid.

28 *Busy Bee* (Alberta Social Credit League organ), 1:11 and 1:12 (July–August and September 1957 issues)

29 Howard Palmer, 'Nativism and Ethnic Tolerance in Alberta: 1920–1972,' PhD thesis, York University, 1973, 260

30 Blackmore's views are mentioned in ibid., 284–5. Jaques's views are discussed in David Bercuson and Douglas Wertheimer, *A Trust Betrayed: The Keegstra Affair* (Toronto: Seal 1987), 37–8. Bercuson and Wertheimer analyse the extent of anti-Semitism within the Social Credit movement (34–9).

31 Macpherson, 210–12

32 Premiers' Papers, File 1476, Manning to Major A.H. Jukes, Social Credit provincial president, British Columbia, 20 May 1947

33 Premiers' Papers, File 1476, Manning to Jukes, 20 May 1947; Manning to J.N. Haldeman, chairman, National Social Credit Association, 21 May 1947; Manning to Jukes, 2 October 1947

34 Premiers' Papers, File 1476, Manning to Haldeman, 21 May 1947

35 Macpherson, 212

36 Glenbow-Archives Institute, Norman B. James Papers, File 4, M.L. Krogh, Edmonton, to James, 1 December 1948. Gostick's later activities are detailed in Bercuson and Wertheimer, *A Trust Betrayed*, 39–42

37 *Edmonton Journal*, 22 April 1950

38 Norman B. James Papers, File 4, M.L. Krogh to James, 1 December 1948

39 *Edmonton Journal*, 25 November 1948

40 Dennis Groh, 'The Political Thought of Ernest Manning,' MA thesis, University of Calgary, 1970, 60–1

41 Ibid.

42 According to Jaques, whose Jew-baiting shows up in the quote: 'As for the Communists, they have infiltrated the CBC as they have every other organization. Of course Communists deny this; as Stalin has said, "Words must have no relation to action. Words are one thing, actions another" (such as the "Progressive Labour" Party). I suppose Messrs. Philpott, Davies (Davinsky), Lewis (Lewinstein), M. Halton et al, would deny their Communism, but when people constantly advocate its policies, it's a safe bet they believe in them.' (*Canadian Social Crediter*, 22 March 1945)

43 *Journals*, Legislative Assembly of Alberta, 6 April 1945

44 Ibid.

45 Donald G. Wetherell, 'Some Aspects of Technology and Leisure in Alberta, 1914–1950,' *Prairie Forum*, 11:1 (1986), 55. On censorship between the wars, see David C. Jones, 'The Reflective Value of Movies and Censorship on Interwar Prairie Society,' *Prairie Forum*, 10:2 (Autumn 1985), 383–98.

46 Premier's Papers, File 1371, various letters, including Manning to Miss E. Birch, secretary, United Farmers of Alberta, 22 March 1946, and Beatrice Fernighough, Labour Progressive party, to A.J. Hooke, provincial secretary, 15 March 1946; *People's Weekly*, 18 January 1947 (re AFU opposition), 11 January 1947 (re CCF opposition); Premiers' Papers, File 1512, brief presented by CCL unions, 14 January 1947

47 Premiers' Papers, File 1371, Manning to Birch

48 *People's Weekly*, 11 January 1947

49 Provincial Archives of Alberta, Premier Manning Papers, 1960–8, Box 40, File 405, H.G. Walker, general manager, CBC National Broadcasting (English) to A.J. Hooke, minister of municipal affairs, 4 June 1963 (re *The Blackboard Jungle*)

50 Manning Papers, Box 40, File 405, Manning to George E. Nowlan, minister of national revenue, 26 February 1962 (re *The Wild One*); Manning to Prime Minister John Diefenbaker, 1 March 1962 (re *The Wild One*)

51 *Statutes of the Province of Alberta*, Chap. 76, 1948

52 Premiers' Papers, Vol. 1764, submission of Alberta Federation of Labour to Premier Manning, 1949

53 The strike is dealt with in detail in Monod, 117–43.

54 *People's Weekly*, 5 October 1946

55 Ibid., Glenbow Archives Institute, H.E. Nichols Papers, Box 1, File 1, Nichols to J.S. McLean, Canada Packers, Toronto, 22 December 1947

56 Nichols's own papers reveal that the AFU had been set up with a militant purpose in the late thirties. Its 1939 manifesto declared: 'When the time is opportune and organizational work sufficiently advanced, it is the intention of this organization, when the situation warrants, to initiate a policy of direct action in the way of non-buying of machinery strike and the non-delivery of grain strike, backing up the farmers in Manitoba and Saskatchewan and working in close cooperation with them. In other words, to adopt the same methods as the organized labourers, and withhold our production from the industrial set-up the way they withhold their services from the industrial concerns of whom they work, and a definite, direct way of protest against the lowering of their living standards.' (Nichols Papers, Box 7, File 42)

57 Monod, 138

58 *People's Weekly*, 5 October 1946

59 Premiers' Papers, File 1762, *What Has Been Done for Labour?* (Social Credit election pamphlet), 1948

60 Public Archives of Canada, Canadian Congress of Labour Papers, Vol. 178, File 15, 'Report on the Proceedings of the Canadian Congress of Labour Unions and Labour Councils in Alberta,' 13–15 November 1947

61 *Edmonton Bulletin*, 15 October 1947

62 *People's Weekly*, 18 October 1947

63 Ibid.

64 Ibid.

65 On relations between the Communists and the CCL, see Irving Martin Abella,

Nationalism, Communism and Canadian Labour: The CIO, the Communist Party and Canadian Congress of Labour, 1935–1956 (Toronto: University of Toronto Press 1973).

66 Premiers' Papers, File 1905, C.W. Dean, General Organizer, CCL; J.E. Henderson, General Organizer, CCL; and J. Hampson, Alberta Representative, United Packinghouse Workers of America, to Manning, 27 October 1947

67 Premiers' Papers, File 1512, brief presented by CCL unions, 14 January 1947

68 Warren Caragata, *Alberta Labour: A Heritage Untold* (Toronto: Lorimer, 1979), 140–1

69 Alberta Federation of Labour, 'Proceedings of the 1946 Convention of the Alberta Federation of Labour,' 48–9

70 *Statutes of the Province of Alberta*, Chap. 8, 1947

71 *Statutes of the Province of Alberta*, Chap. 76, 1948

72 Telegrams from labour groups to Manning are in Premiers' Papers, File 1759.

73 *Journals*, Legislative Assembly of Alberta, 31 March 1948

74 CCL Papers, Vol. 37, File 16, Pat Conroy, secretary-treasurer CCL, to Fred Dowling, District Ten Director, United Packinghouse Workers of America, Toronto, 26 July 1948; *People's Weekly*, 15 August 1948

75 The penalties in the 1938 legislation gave no incentive to union leaders to prevent their members from striking since, as the *Edmonton Bulletin* lamented, 'labour unions are not within reach of these penalties [penalties for individuals who defy the Conciliation Act] and that is the weakness, the lamentable and tragic weakness of all labour legislation' (Provincial Archives of Alberta, Department of Labour, Secretary's Files, Box 2, File 470.1; *Edmonton Bulletin*, March 1947).

76 Premiers' Papers, File 1764, submission of Alberta Federation of Labour to Premier Manning, 1949

77 Den Otter, 97

78 Caragata, 132–3; brief of Industrial Federation of Labour of Alberta (CCL) to Government of Alberta, 7 February 1950, Manning Papers, File 1759; Trace, 45, 70

79 Den Otter, 97

80 Throughout the decade of the fifties, there were negligible numbers of strikes and most strikes were of short duration (David Leadbeater, 'An Outline of Capitalist Development in Alberta,' in David Leadbeater, ed., *Essays on the Political Economy of Alberta* [Toronto: New Hogtown Press 1984], 61).

81 Premiers' Papers, File 1905, Robert Atkin, president, and Roy Jamha, secretary-treasurer, Industrial Federation of Labour of Alberta, to Manning, 8 February 1952

82 Ibid.

83 *Canadian Social Crediter*, October 1955

84 Provincial Archives of Alberta, Board of Industrial Relations Papers, Box 4, File 427, 'Minutes of 11 January 1957 Meeting of Board of Industrial Relations'

85 *Calgary Herald*, 29 March 1958; Department of Labour, Secretary's Files, File 481.23, Alberta Federation of Labour brief to Hon. Raymond Reierson, minister of industries and labour, 12 May 1958

86 Department of Labour. This quotation is from an extract of a speech made by John Robinson, minister of industries and labour, in 1948, and included in the AFL brief.
87 In its brief to cabinet in 1960, for example, the AFL observed few niceties and claimed enforcement of the Alberta Labour Act had a total anti-labour bias. The section of the act which prohibited employer interference with the formation of a union, for example, 'has become a big joke.' No penalties had been imposed upon employers under this section though 'there are very few cases' where such interference did not take place whenever unions were mooted in a particular work place. Penalties under the act, claimed the AFL, were only ever assessed against unions. (Premier Manning Papers, Box 81, File 879b, 'Memorandum from Alberta Federation of Labour to Premier and Cabinet Members,' 25 January 1960)

It might be noted that the view of Social Credit's relations with labour presented here is opposite that of John J. Barr in *The Dynasty: The Rise and Fall of Social Credit in Alberta* (Toronto: McClelland and Stewart 1974), 137. Writes Barr: 'During the Manning years, especially after the birth of the N.D.P., labour leaders often publicly lashed the government for "anti-labour" policies; but privately, the same leaders would admit that while there were many changes they desired in specific laws and regulations, on the whole the process of arbiting labour disputes was fairly and impartially administered.' Barr offers not a shred of evidence for this claim, which on the evidence of the late fifties, before the NDP was formed, seems quite fantastic.
88 *Statutes of the Province of Alberta*, 1960, Chap. 54
89 Premiers' Papers, File 1759, submission of Calgary Board of Trade to Board of Industrial Relations, 19 April 1949. The board's observations echoed submissions made earlier by Edmonton's Chamber of Commerce and the provincial branch of the Canadian Manufacturers' Association.
90 Premiers' Papers, File 1904, Alberta Associated Chambers of Commerce and Agriculture to Manning, filed 8 October 1953
91 Glenbow-Alberta Institute, Alberta Liberal Association Papers, Box 35, File 174, 'Edmonton Chamber of Commerce submission to the chairman and members of the Board of Industrial Relations for the Province of Alberta,' 11 January 1956
92 Richards and Pratt, 91
93 Ibid., 55–6, 76
94 Ibid., 57–9; *Statutes of the Province of Alberta*, 1938, Chap. 15, 'An Act for the Conservation of Oil and Gas Resources of the Province of Alberta.'
95 Richards and Pratt, 66, 171
96 Ibid., 66
97 *Statutes of the Province of Alberta*, 1946, Chap. 7, An Act to Incorporate the Alberta Industrial Corporation; *Statutes of the Province of Alberta*, 1945, Chap. 11, An Act to Confirm Order-in-Council No. 1885-44 dated the 6th Day of December 1944 authorizing the execution of certain agreements between the Government of the Province of Alberta and Oil Sands Ltd., and Bitumont Holding Co. Ltd.

98 Premiers' Papers, File 1752B, Horace Mann, vice-president, Electro-Technical Labs, to Manning, 29 February 1952; Manning to Mann, 27 March 1952; J.E. Oberholtzer, deputy minister of industries and labour, to J.L. Robinson, minister of industries and labour, 1 June 1951; Oberholtzer to J.M. Young, general manager, Western Insulation, Vancouver, 15 June 1951; Young to Oberholtzer, 19 June 1951; Oberholtzer to Young, 22 June 1951

99 Alberta Social Credit League Papers, Box 1, Item 5, 'Minutes of the 1960 Alberta Social Credit League convention'

100 Premiers' Papers, File 1857, radio speech of William Irvine, CCF provincial secretary, 26 January 1954

101 *Canadian Social Crediter*, 7:2 (May 1955), 13

102 *Canadian Social Crediter*, 1:1, 5 January 1950

103 Premiers' Papers, File 1753, D.E. Fraser to Manning, 28 January 1950; Alfred Hooke to Manning, 30 October 1951

104 Premiers' Papers, File 2153, Manning to George Mitchell, secretary-treasurer, District Council Number One, International Woodworkers of America, 17 March 1958

105 Premiers' Papers, File 1843, 'Minutes of Social Credit Convention, 1955'

106 *Statutes of the Province of Alberta*, 1957, Chap. 64, An Act to Enable Citizens of Alberta to Participate Directly in the Benefits Arising from the Development of the Oil and Gas Resources of the Province

107 *Statutes of the Province of Alberta*, 1958, Chap. 51, An Act to Provide for Assistance to Municipalities

108 *Statutes of the Province of Alberta*, 1959, Chap. 60, An Act to Amend the Oil and Gas Royalties Dividend Act

109 Premiers' Papers, File 1811, City of Calgary to Manning, 14 January 1986

110 Premiers' Papers, File 1811. Among municipalities writing Manning to endorse Calgary's resolution were Edmonton, Fort Saskatchewan, Lethbridge, Raymond, Wainwright, Grande Prairie, Coleman, Stony Plain, Magrath, Blairmore, Drumheller, Macleod, Leduc, Vegreville, Edson, Strathcona, and Cardston.

111 *Statutes of the Province of Alberta*, 1949, Chap. 86, An Act Respecting the Provision of Assistance in Connection with the Costs of Public Welfare Services

112 *Statutes of the Province of Alberta*, 1958, Chap. 17, An Act to Amend the Public Welfare Act

113 Premiers' Papers, File 1899, 'Government Financing in Alberta Including an Appraisal of Provincial-Municipal Financial Relationships: A Report Prepared for the Union of Alberta Municipalities by the Citizens' Research Institute of Canada,' November 1954

114 The Liberals called for a royal commission on provincial-municipal financing in 1954 (*Journals*, Legislative Assembly of Alberta, 2 March 1954, 25).

115 Premiers' Papers, File 1904, H.E. Pearson, president, Chamber of Commerce, to Manning, 25 January 1952. The chamber claimed that 'Edmonton has special needs for assistance of substantial amount and of pressing character.'

116 Provincial Archives of Alberta, Government Services files, Box 1, File 21,

Government of Alberta, *Report of the Royal Commission on the Metropolitan Development of Calgary and Edmonton*, G. Fred McNally, chairman, 31 January 1956

117 Alberta Social Credit League Papers, Box 3, Item 5, 'Minutes of the Alberta Social Credit League convention, 1960'

118 *Report of the Royal Commission on Education*, 45

119 Kenneth Bryden, *Old Age Pensions and Policy-Making in Canada* (Montreal: McGill-Queen's University Press 1974), 93–7

120 Ibid., 124–5

121 Premiers' Papers, File 1853, radio address by C.E. Gerhart, minister of municipal affairs, 14 April 1952

122 *Statutes of the Province of Alberta*, 1946, Chap. 3, An Act to Provide Health Services for the People of Alberta

123 Premiers' Papers, File 1853, Gerhart address

124 *Busy Bee*, 1:7 (December 1956), 2–3

125 Premiers' Papers, Files 2259A and 2259B, consist mainly of letters from people in need who experienced difficulties in their dealings with municipal welfare officials.

126 Alberta Social Credit League Papers, Box 1, Item 7, 'Opinion Poll Report – Alberta Province November–December 1956.' The report indicated that, while 55 per cent of those polled regarded the government's performance in the education area favourably, 38 per cent did not. Sixty-one per cent of all those polled cited education as an area to which government revenues from oil and gas should be directed.

127 The commission was established by order-in-council 31 December 1957 (*Report of the Royal Commission on Education*, 2).

128 Ibid., 29–30, 37–41

129 Ibid., 39

130 Ibid., 57, 63–4, 129, 132, 136–7, 223–33, 273, 277, 288–91

131 His report is appended to the Royal Commission report.

132 Alberta Social Credit League Papers, Box 1, 'Manning telecasts,' 'Script for telecast,' 9 May 1959

133 *People's Weekly*, 19 August 1944

134 Larry Pratt, 'Grant Notley: Politics as a Calling,' in Larry Pratt, ed., *Essays in Honour of Grant Notley: Socialism and Democracy in Alberta* (Edmonton: NeWest Press 1986), 4

135 David Monod, 'End of Agrarianism.' Monod claims that AFU membership, which reached 31,000 during the 1946 strike, fell to 16,000 by December 1947. A year later, the organization voted to fuse with the UFA.

136 *People's Weekly*, 6 September 1947, 27 September 1947, 29 November 1947

137 Glenbow-Alberta Institute, Alberta CCF Papers, Box 6, File 51. The referendum asked voters if they were 'in favour of the generation and distribution of electricity being conducted by the power company' or 'in favour of the generation and distribution of electricity being made a publicly owned utility administered by the Alberta Government Power Commission.'

138 *Canadian Parliamentary Guide*, 1949
139 The party's membership goal for 1948 was set at 4000 (*People's Weekly*, 24 April 1948). Party records do not indicate membership totals for 1948, but on 31 October 1949 paid-up memberships for 1949 came to 3278, including 225 in Calgary. A year earlier Calgary had 256 paid-up members. (Alberta CCF Files, Box 7, File 71)
140 *Canadian Parliamentary Guide*, 1949. The government took advantage of the CCF-Liberal tie in seats and near-tie in votes to decline to name an official opposition between 1948 and 1952. Prowse and Roper shared the opposition leader's salary. (David Byron, 'The Recognition of Leaders of the Opposition in Alberta, 1905–1983,' *Prairie Forum* 9:1 [Spring 1984], 51)
141 Meir Serfaty, 'Structure and Organization of Political Parties in Alberta, 1935–71,' PhD thesis, Carleton University, 1977, 155. Prowse had sat with the Independents after his election in 1944 as an armed forces representative.
142 Richards and Pratt, 81
143 Ibid., 63
144 *Calgary Herald*, 2 February 1953
145 Judging by the lists of the provincial Liberal Association officers and those of the urban constituency organizations which appear in Glenbow-Alberta Institute, Alberta Liberal Association Papers, Box 13, File 69
146 The poll conducted by Social Credit in 1956 indicated overwhelming support for the provincial government among skilled and unskilled workers as well as farmers. While the government enjoyed significant support from all social groups, opposition support was strongest and indeed almost equal to government support among professionals and owners of businesses. (Owen Anderson, 'The Alberta Social Credit Party: An Empirical Analysis of Membership, Characteristics, Participation and Opinion,' PhD thesis, University of Alberta, 1972, 46)
147 Alberta Liberal Association Papers, Box 15, File 81, radio address by J. Harper Prowse, 10 July 1952
148 Premiers' Papers, File 1853, radio address by C.E. Gerhart, 14 April 1952
149 Premiers' Papers, File 1844, Liberal advertisement, 1955
150 Premiers' Papers, File 1844, Manning radio address, 17 June 1955
151 It had only 1944 paid-up members in 1952 (Alberta CCF Papers, Box 7, File 71).
152 *Canadian Parliamentary Guide*, 1953; Kenneth Wark, *A Report on Alberta Elections 1905–1982* (Edmonton: Goverment of Alberta 1983), 15
153 Premiers' Papers, File 2281B, W.J.C. Kirby (Conservative leader) speech on CFCN, 23 June 1955
154 Premiers' Papers, File 2281B
155 Premiers' Papers, File 2281B, J. Harper Prowse speech on CFCN, 6 June 1955
156 Premiers' Papers, File 2281B, Kirby speech
157 Premiers' Papers, File 1664
158 Bob Hesketh, 'The Abolition of Preferential Voting in Alberta,' *Prairie Forum* 12:1 (Spring 1987), 132

159 Premiers' Papers, File 2281B, include the major election editorials during the 1955 campaign.

160 *Canadian Parliamentary Guide*, 1956; Wark, 15

161 Hesketh, 130

162 The vote totals for the parties were Social Credit, 175,553; Liberals, 117,741; Conservatives, 34,757; CCF, 31,180. Total votes cast were 378,179 (*Canadian Parliamentary Guide*, 1956). The significance of the 1955 election is, to a large degree, missed by John J. Barr in *The Dynasty*. He writes erroneously that 'in 1948 a most unusual thing happened in Alberta: the multi-party system fell into a twenty-year coma' (148). The implication is that it was not until the 1967 election that serious opposition emerged. Clearly, however, more opposition seats were won in 1955 than in 1967 (twenty-four vs ten) and the major opposition party that year won more seats (fifteen vs six) and a larger percentage of the popular vote (31 vs 26 per cent) than the Conservatives did in 1967. Barr also makes light of the impact of the scandals, claiming dubiously that the Manning government was never really tainted by scandals (163).

163 *Report of the Royal Commission Appointed under the Public Inquiries Act, Chapter 139, Revised Statutes of Alberta, 1942*, 6 June 1956 ('Royal Commission to Inquire into Certain Charges, Allegations and Reports Relating to the Conduct of the Business of Government')

164 The government mailed a summary of the commission's findings to every household in the province.

165 *Royal Commission to Inquire into Charges*. Part 2, 167–78

166 Ibid., 178

167 Ibid., 211

168 *Royal Commission to Inquire into Charges*, Part 1, 75–7

169 *Royal Commission to Inquire into Charges*, Part 2, 59–70

170 Ibid., 213–30. Several years later Manning still worried that some MLAs had not learned their lesson about the treasury branches from the 1955 election charges. He wrote the MLAs in 1959: 'Since the Treasury Branches are part of Government it is natural for people requiring loans to seek the favourable influence of Social Credit MLAs in their behalf ... There will, no doubt, be cases in which loans will be declined which may well have proven very satisfactory. However, experience has shown that it is unwise for MLAs to place any pressure on our management to get individual loans approved.' (Premiers' Papers, File 2041, Premiers' Draft to MLAs, 21 October 1959)

171 Premiers' Papers, File 1051A, Aberhart to A.F. Van Buren, Sunshine Auto Camp, Calgary, 12 June 1940

172 Premier Manning Papers, Box 10, File 121B, J.H. Holloway to E.W. Hinman, provincial treasurer, 26 June 1961

173 Ibid.

174 *Statutes of the Province of Alberta*, 1957, Chap. 3, An Act to Incorporate the Alberta Municipal Financing Corporation

175 *Statutes of the Province of Alberta*, 1957, Chap. 60, An Act to Enable Municipali-

ties to borrow from the Alberta Municipal Financing Corporation for and on behalf of Municipal Housing Districts

176 *Statutes of the Province of Alberta*, 1960, Chap. 70, An Act to Amend the Alberta Municipal Financing Corporation Act

177 Alberta Social Credit League Papers, 'Opinion Poll Report (i), 8

178 Ibid., 1–3

179 Ibid., v

180 Ibid., 3

181 A former newsman, Prowse attended law school, beginning in 1953, at the same time that he was opposition leader, causing many to speculate that he was losing interest in politics because he regarded Manning as politically unbeatable. His party's failure to capitalize sufficiently on the scandals to form a government and Social Credit's re-establishment of its former ascendancy after the election added to the collapse of the federal Liberals in Alberta in the elections of 1957 and 1958, reinforcing Prowse's earlier views of Social Credit invincibility. (Meir Serfaty, 'Harper Prowse and the Alberta Liberals,' *Alberta History* 29:1 [Winter 1981], 1–10

182 *Canadian Parliamentary Guide*, 1960

183 Robin Hunter, 'Social Democracy in Alberta: From the CCF to the NDP,' in Larry Pratt, ed., *Socialism and Democracy: Essays in Honour of Grant Notley*, 62–4, 66

184 Alberta Social Credit League Papers, Box 3. The figures are based on membership fee receipts reported in the annual convention minutes.

185 Alberta Social Credit League Papers, Box 1, Item 1, 'Minutes of the Alberta Social Credit League Annual Convention 27 and 28 November 1947'

186 Ibid.

187 Premiers' Papers, File 1461, Mrs Marion Krogh, Edmonton, to Manning, 21 November 1947

188 Premiers' Papers, File 1846B, Resolutions of the 17th Annual Convention of Alberta Social Credit League, 1951

189 Ibid.

190 Hesketh, 131

191 Anderson, 52–3

192 Alberta Social Credit League Papers, Box 1, File 1. The membership fee had been one dollar in 1943 and remained at that level until it was doubled in 1960 for individuals and increased by 50 per cent for a husband and wife joining jointly.

193 The Alberta Social Credit League Papers, interestingly, exclude financial records of the party. But the Premiers' Papers include several references to finances. In Files 1841 and 1842, for example, several entries indicate lavish business donations to Social Credit at election time. In the federal election for 1953, for example, 'the Gas Company' in Calgary provided a donation of three thousand dollars, almost as much as membership fees yielded to the party that year. The previous year, the Motion Picture Operators of the province made a large donation to the provincial electoral fund. The Lethbridge share of this donation, which

was split up among the sixty party candidates, was seventy-five dollars (so, presumably, the total donation was forty-five hundred dollars). Even businessmen who rejected Social Credit monetary policies completely often contributed at election time. For example, R.W. Milner, vice-president and general manager of Alberta Pacific Grain, sent one hundred dollars to the Social Credit federal election campaign fund in 1949, attaching a letter indicating that while he disagreed with Social Credit monetary theories, he was willing to contribute to the party because the league had provided 'an honest administration' in Alberta. (Premiers' Papers, File 1841, H.B. Macdonald, MLA, Calgary, to Manning, 7 August 1953; R.W. Milner, Calgary, to Manning, 3 June 1949; File 1842, Peter Elliott, Manning's executive secretary, to Mrs F. Harvey, Lethbridge, 18 August 1952)

194 *Canadian Social Crediter*, 13 December 1950
195 Dennis Groh, 65
196 *Busy Bee* 1:7 (December 1956), 2
197 Ibid., 4
198 Premiers' Papers, File 1854A, R.C. King, Edmonton, to Manning, 12 February 1948; Manning to King, 15 March 1948
199 Premiers' Papers, File 1881C, 'Federal-Provincial Conference, Preliminary Meeting,' Ottawa, 26 April 1955, 91–6
200 On Social Credit in British Columbia in the fifties, see Walter D. Young, *Democracy and Discontent*, 2d ed. (Toronto: McGraw-Hill Ryerson 1978), 102–5.
201 *Canadian Social Crediter* 7:1 (April 1955)
202 Barr, 133

Chapter 6

1 Provincial Archives of Alberta, Premier Manning Papers, Box 39, File 395(b), Manning to Abe Haider, Saskatoon, Saskatchewan, 6 January 1964
2 Premier Manning Papers, Box 31, File 391, correspondence with various radio evangelists
3 Premier Manning Papers, Box 74, File 802, Manning to Billy Graham, 6 December 1965. Much of the Manning correspondence to Graham in File 802 is addressed, 'Dear Billy.'
4 Premier Manning Papers, Box 39, File 395(b), Maning to Ernest Manthei, Petoskey, Michigan, 6 January 1964
5 Ed Shaffer, 'The Political Economy of Oil in Alberta,' in David Leadbeater, ed., *Essays on the Political Economy of Alberta* (Toronto: New Hogtown Press 1984), 182–4
6 Ibid., 182
7 University of Alberta Library, Government Documents section, Canadian Chamber of Commerce, 'Submission to the Minister of Finance on the Report of the Royal Commission on Taxation,' October 1967; 'Submission by the Algoma Steel Corporation Ltd., August 1967, to Honourable Mitchell Sharp'; 'Submission to the Minister of Finance, the Honourable Mitchell S. Sharp, on the Report of the

Royal Commission on Taxation from the Investment Dealers' Association of Canada,' September 1967

8 University of Alberta Library, Government Documents section, 'Submission by the Government of the Province of Alberta Concerning the Report of the Royal Commission on Taxation,' December 1967, 1-7–8

9 Ibid., VII-4.

10 Premier Manning Papers, Box 41, File 417, Dr J. Donovan Ross, Alberta minister of health, to Honourable J. Waldo Monteith, minister of national health and welfare, 23 November 1962

11 Premier Manning Papers, Box 41, File 418, Manning to Prime Minister Lester Pearson, 31 December 1963

12 *Busy Bee*, 6:4 (July–August 1963), 3

13 Ibid.

14 *Statutes of the Province of Alberta*, 1960, Chap. 86, An Act to Amend the Public Welfare Act. A large portion of the funds for the groups covered in the amended Public Welfare Act was provided by the federal government under the Unemployment Assistance Act of 1956, which placed generous numbers of federal dollars in the hands of the provinces for welfare assistance, 'with the result that on the whole old age supplements have been merged into general welfare programs' (Kenneth Bryden, *Old Age Pensions and Policy-Making in Canada* [Montreal: McGill-Queen's University Press 1974], 125).

15 *Busy Bee* 4:2 (March–April 1961), 3; Premier Manning Papers, Box 31, File 346(a), D.W. Rogers, deputy minister of public welfare, to recipients, 31 August 1960

16 Manning had been made aware, in 1958, of a woman living common-law with a man who provided no support for herself or her children. The chairman of the provincial Pensions Board, asked about her case, wrote flatly: 'In this case, the common-law husband is not registered as being the father of these children, therefore we would have no justification for granting an allowance under the Mother's Allowance Act.' (Premiers' Papers, File 2259, Mrs Florence Sauvé, Calmar, to Manning, 13 July 1958; W.P. Bullock, chairman, Pensions Board, to Peter Elliott, executive secretary to Premier, 18 July 1958)

17 Provincial Archives of Alberta, Premiers' Papers, File 2259B, Sylvia Mears, Drumheller, to Manning, 28 December 1960; K.T. Motherwell, director, Public Assistance branch, to D.W. Rogers, deputy minister of public welfare, 5 January 1961. Mrs Mears claimed in her letter that the welfare authorities told her she would have her children taken away from her if she accepted welfare. Motherwell's letter did not deny this claim.

18 Premier Manning Papers, Box 19, File 205, Mrs L. Forcier, Calgary, to Manning, 12 September 1963; Manning to Forcier, 27 September 1963

19 Premier Manning Papers, Box 19, File 265, include letters from a variety of Albertans who claimed to have been bankrupted by 'co-insurance' charges.

20 Premier Manning Papers, Box 17, File 193(a), Mrs Lillian Fisher, Black Diamond, to Manning, 17 December 1960

21 Ibid., Manning to Fisher, 28 December 1960

22 Premier Manning Papers, Box 74, File 805, D.W. Rogers, deputy minister of public welfare, to Russ Sheppard, executive secretary to Premier Manning, 14 December 1966

23 John J. Barr, *The Dynasty: The Rise and Fall of Social Credit in Alberta* (Toronto: McClelland and Stewart 1974), 144–5

24 Premier Manning Papers, Box 74, File 805, article by Terry Garvin and Heather Robertson, filed December 1966

25 Premier Manning Papers, Box 74, File 805, 'Background Paper – Wabasca, June 1966'; F.C. Colborne, minister of public works, to Manning, 11 August 1966

26 Premier Manning Papers, Box 74, File 805, James Whitford to F.C. Colborne, attachment to Colborne to Manning, 11 August 1966

27 Premier Manning Papers, Box 74, File 805, Whitford to Manning, 19 July 1966

28 A research paper entitled 'Community Opportunity Assessment' was undertaken by the province in conjunction with the federal government 'to analyze social and economic deprivation in seven representative areas,' including the two major cities (Provincial Archives of Alberta, Government Services files, Box 1, File 26, 'A White Paper on Human Resource Development,' March 1967).

29 Premier Manning Papers, Box 41, File 418, Manning to Prime Minister Lester B. Pearson, 31 December 1963, Box 10, File 126, 'Tele-Facts,' 2 November 1965

30 Premier Manning Papers, Box 41, File 418; Manning to Pearson, 31 December 1963; Box 42, File 426(b), 'Frederal-Provincial Conference of the Prime Minister and Premiers July 19–22, 1965, Volume 1,' 45–7

31 Premier Manning Papers, Box 37, File 368, 'Speech given to Annual Convention of the Northwest Electric Light and Power Association,' 5 September 1962

32 Premier Manning Papers, Box 41, File 417, Dr J. Donovan Ross, Alberta minister of health, to Honourable J. Waldo Monteith, minister of national health and welfare, 23 November 1962

33 Premier Manning Papers, Box 41, File 418, Manning to Pearson, 31 December 1963

34 Premier Manning Papers, Box 41, File 418, Dr J. Donovan Ross to Honourable Judy LaMarsh, minister of national health and welfare, 20 December 1963

35 Premier Manning Papers, Box 42, File 426(b), 'Federal-Provincial Conference of the Prime Minister and Premiers,' 19–22 July 1965, Vol. 1, 15–16

36 Premier Manning Papers, Box 40, File 404, Manning to R.T. Bowman, CHWO, Oakville, Ontario, 6 August 1965

37 Premier Manning Papers, Box 40, File 411, 'Proceedings of Third Provincial Premiers' Conference,' Victoria, British Columbia, 6 August 1962, 183–5

38 Premier Manning Papers, Box 42, File 426 (b), 'Federal-Provincial Conference of the Prime Minister and Premiers July 19–22,' July 1965, 1, 25

39 Premier Manning Papers, Box 41, File 421(c), Manning to Pearson, 10 June 1965

40 Premier Manning Papers, Box 31, File 341, Manning to W.O. Twaits, president, Imperial Oil. The generally formal Alberta premier addressed Twaits, 'Dear Bill.'

41 'Submission by the Government of the Province of Alberta Concerning the Report of the Royal Commission on Taxation,' 1-8

42 Ibid., 1-9

43 Canada, *Report of the Royal Commission on Taxation, Volume 1: Introduction, Acknowledgments and Minority Reports* (22 December 1966), 6. The press claimed the commission opinion was that, for tax purposes, 'a dollar is a dollar,' because the commission reported that the base for taxation should be 'the value of the annual net gain or loss in the unit's power, whether exercised or not, to consume goods and services. Such a base would ignore the form of the gain or what was done to obtain the gain.'

44 'Submission by the Government of Alberta,' 1-8

45 Premier Manning Papers, Box 42, File 427A, Manning to Pearson, 28 May 1963

46 Premier Manning Papers, Box 42, File 427A, R.N. Thompson, federal Social Credit leader, to Russ Patrick, Alberta minister of industry and development, 10 July 1963

47 Provincial Archives of Alberta, Alberta Social Credit League Papers, Box 1, 'Opening Statement of the Government of the Province of Alberta to the Federal-Provincial Conference on Constitutional Matters,' 5 February 1968

48 Premier Manning Papers, Box 40, File 404, Manning to Mrs Jean Albersworth, Fairview, Alberta, 18 November 1964

49 The following correspondence makes the point. Raymond Reierson, minister of telephones, to J.W. Hagerman, manager, CKUA, 19 April 1963: ' ... the Executive Council has determined that a return to a non-partisan approach should be made rather than the all-partisan approach taken in the recent federal election.'
    Reierson to Hagerman, 31 May 1963: 'This will confirm our telephone discussion on discontinuing the use of a political news commentator during Federal and Provincial Election Campaigns in future.
    'This is in no way to be construed as a reflection on Mr. Jim Edwards' very able work in this field ... ' (This correspondence is found in Premier Manning Papers, Box 40, File 404.)

50 Premier Manning Papers, Box 44, File 441, Manning to J. Kroeker, Edmonton, 13 July 1965

51 Premier Manning Papers, Box 40, File 41, 'Proceedings, Third Provincial Premiers' Conference,' Victoria, British Columbia, 6 August 1962, 136–7

52 Premier Manning Papers, Box 38, File 3796, R.N. Thompson to Mrs Pearl Johnston, 20 September 1962

53 Premier Manning Papers, Box 38, File 3796, Manning to Johnston, 13 August 1962

54 Philip Mathias, *Forced Growth: Five Studies of Government Investment in the Development of Canada* (Toronto: James Lewis and Samuel 1971)

55 Premier Manning Papers, Box 26, File 294, A.R. Patrick, minister of industry and development, to D.F. Irving, president, Foothills Steel Foundry Division Ltd., Calgary, 17 December 1964

56 Premier Manning Papers, Box 26, File 294, Patrick to Manning, 15 July 1964

57 Premier Manning Papers, Box 37, File 371(c), address in the legislature, 23 February 1965

58 Ibid.

59 Premier Manning Papers, Box 17, File 185(b), Lucien Maynard to Ambrose Holowach, provincial secretary, 13 February 1964; Holowach to Manning, 17 February 1964; *Statutes of the Province of Alberta*, 1964, Chap. 40

60 Barr, 170

61 'White Paper on Human Resources Development,' 25

62 Ibid. 57

63 Ibid.

64 Ibid., 55–7

65 Ibid., 11, 73–4

66 Ibid., 62–4

67 Ibid., 62, 65

68 Ibid., 99

69 The standard study of the Créditiste breakthrough in Quebec in 1962 is Maurice Pinard, *The Rise of a Third Party* (Englewood Cliffs, NJ: Prentice-Hall 1971).

70 Michael B. Stein, *The Dynamics of Right-Wing Protest: A Political Analysis of Social Credit in Quebec* (Toronto: University of Toronto Press 1973), 82, 95

71 *Busy Bee*, March–April 1963

72 *Canadian Social Crediter* 15:8 (August 1963); 15:9 (September 1963)

73 Premier Manning Papers, Box 38, File 381(a), 'A Statement to the Press by R.N. Thompson,' 23 April 1964

74 *Busy Bee*, July–August 1967

75 Ibid.

76 Premier Manning Papers, Box 38, File 377, Manning to Richard Johnston, Vancouver, 6 January 1965

77 Meir Serfaty, 'The Conservative Party of Alberta under Lougheed, 1965–71: Building an Image and an Organization,' *Prairie Forum* 6:1 (Spring 1981), 61

78 Premier Manning Papers, Box 55, File 594, Eldon Wooliams, MP, to Manning, 5 October 1966; Manning to Wooliams, 21 October 1966

79 Alfred J. Hooke, *30 + 5: I Know, I Was There* (Edmonton: Institute of Applied Art 1971), 221

80 Ibid., 252–4

81 Honourable E.C. Manning, *Political Realignment: A Challenge to Thoughtful Canadians* (Toronto: McClelland and Stewart 1967), 11

82 Ibid., 62

83 Ibid., 76

84 *Busy Bee* 8:6 (November–December 1967)

85 Stein, 104. Thompson's views on the Conservatives and conservatism are found in Robert N. Thompson, 'Conservatism in Contemporary Canada,' in *Commonsense for Canadians: A Selection of Speeches Analysing Today's Opportunities and Problems* (Toronto: McClelland and Stewart 1965), 1–11.

86 Thomas E. Flanagan, 'Ethnic Voting in Alberta Provincial Elections,' in Carlo

Caldarola, ed., *Society and Politics in Alberta: Research Papers* (Toronto: Methuen 1979), 317

87 Larry Pratt, 'Grant Notley: Politics as a Calling,' in Larry Pratt, ed., *Socialism and Democracy in Alberta: Essays in Honour of Grant Notley* (Edmonton: NeWest Press 1986), 11

88 Ibid., 5; Jack Masson and Peter Blaikie, 'Labour Politics in Alberta,' in Carlo Caldarola, ed., *Society and Politics in Alberta: Research Papers* (Toronto: Methuen 1979), 275

89 Pratt, 23. See also later material in this chapter on the 1967 election.

90 Premier Manning Papers, Box 46, File 464, 'Submission of the Alberta Federation of Labour to the Premier and Cabinet members,' 22 January 1962

91 Premier Manning Papers, Box 17, File 185(a), M.E. English, executive secretary, Edmonton and District Labour Council, to Manning, 17 April 1964

92 As indicated by the government's own director of personnel in Premier Manning Papers, Box 10, File 121(b), J.N. Holloway to E.W. Hinman, Provincial Treasurer, 26 June 1961. See discussion of this memorandum in chapter 5.

93 Though the government alone ultimately had power to set salaries and working conditions for civil servants in Alberta, a joint council of cabinet members and Civil Service Association members met annually to discuss these issues. According to Roy A. Harrison, executive secretary, CSA, 'Joint Council has operated successfully in the Province of Alberta mainly because both parties have made every endeavour to negotiate in good faith and meetings have been held regularly with full attendance.' (Premier Manning Papers, Box 17, File 184[a], Harrison to Russ Sheppard, executive secretary to Premier Manning, 14 August 1963)

Manning quoted this portion of Harrison's memorandum in a letter sent to Jean Lesage, premier of Quebec, two days later, to explain why Alberta, unlike Quebec, was not considering full-scale union rights for its employees. Despite Harrison's letter, however, the CSA was affiliated with the Canadian Federation of Government Employees Organizations, 'a grouping of the Provincial Government Employees Associations, dedicated to securing collective bargaining rights for public employees.' (Premier Manning Papers, Box 10, File 120[c], 1964 pamphlet of Canadian Federation of Government Employees Organizations)

94 *Statutes of the Province of Alberta*, 1968, Chap. 298, Sections 26–43

95 Provincial Archives of Alberta, Alberta Department of Labour, Research Division, 'A History of Labour and Social Welfare Legislation in Alberta,' 1972

96 Ibid.

97 Premier Manning Papers, Box 10, File 120(b), E.W. Hinman, provincial treasurer, to F.D. Betts, director of personnel, 9 September 1960

98 Premier Manning Papers, Box 7, File 78, A.O. Aalborg, minister of education, 'Foundation Program of School Finance,' April 1961

99 Premier Manning Papers, Box 7, File 74, Glenn Holmes, chairman, Calgary Public School Board, 'Submission to Provincial Cabinet,' 31 May 1965

100 Premier Manning Papers, Box 60, File 648, *Report of Committee Studying Municipal Legislation*, J.C. Hillman, chairman, filed 24 January 1967; 'Submission by

the City of Edmonton to the Standing Committee on Public Affairs, Agriculture and Education,' 5 April 1967; 'Submission by the City of Calgary to the Standing Committee on Public Affairs, Agriculture and Education,' 5 April 1967

101 *Canadian Parliamentary Guide*, 1964

102 *Canadian Parliamentary Guide* 1967

103 Larry Pratt, 'Grant Notley,' 22–3, 27–8

104 Premier Manning Papers, Box 58, File 630, *The Report of the Honourable Mr. Justice W.J.C. Kirby, In the Matter of an Inquiry by a Royal Commission into the Matters Set Out by Order-in-Council 861/67 respecting the Use or Attempted Use by the Honourable Alfred J. Hooke of his Office as a Member of the Executive Council of Alberta, and the Use or Attempted Use by Edgar W. Hinman of his Office as a Member of the Executive Council of Alberta*, October 1968, 1

105 Larry Pratt, 'Grant Notley,' 26–7. Writes Pratt: 'There were in Alberta many social and economic issues crying out for the NDP's attention. The appalling scandal of the province's mental health system, the degradation of Alberta's large, neglected native population, the impact of rapid urbanization on housing, land prices, education and social services, the growth of the public sector and the need to unionize white-collar workers, the impact of farm mechanization and agribusiness in rural Alberta, the underpricing of the province's natural gas and low oil royalties, and the need for an independent industrial strategy – these were the issues of the day which the NDP neglected in its obsession with corruption in high places.'

106 Many of the issues mentioned in note 105 were raised in an NDP provincial election pamphlet found in Premier Manning Papers, Box 55, File 595. In fairness to Pratt, however, the pamphlet restricted itself to generalities whereas NDP charges in the legislature regarding corruption had been detailed to a fault.

107 Premier Manning Papers, Box 55, File 595, 'NDP advertising – A. Cooper,' n.d.

108 Premier Manning Papers, Box 55, File 595, NDP pamphlet

109 Alberta Social Credit League Papers, Box 1, 'Speeches 1967–68,' Manning speech, 20 May 1967

110 For example, when the regulations affecting the oil industry were reviewed in 1961, Manning set up a committee to review these regulations that consisted of representatives of the Canadian Petroleum Association and the Independent Petroleum Association, the two major industry groups, along with government representatives. There were no employee, consumer, or environmentalist representatives – hardly surprising, since Manning's avowed aim was to change the regulations so as to 'give greater incentive for exploration and the discovery of new reserves.' (Premier Manning Papers, Box 37, File 367, Interview of Premier Manning with *Oilweek*, 20 September 1961)

111 Manning speech, 20 May 1967

112 Premier Manning Papers, Box 55, File 595

113 Pratt, 'Grant Notley,' 28

114 *Canadian Parliamentary Guide*, 1968

115 Pratt, 'Grant Notley,' 26

116 There are two biographies of Lougheed that deal with his early career. The more recent, David G. Wood, *The Lougheed Legacy* (Toronto: Key Porter 1985), is unabashed hagiography. Also supportive of its subject but less fawning and more lucid is Allan Hustak, *Peter Lougheed: A Biography* (Toronto: McClelland and Stewart 1979). Both biographies note that Lougheed was part of an independent law partnership when he entered politics in 1965, but that from 1958 to 1962 he served as vice-president, administration, of the Alberta-based mega-corporation, Mannix Company (now Loram Development), whose economic activities spanned construction, oil and gas, equipment sales and service, engineering and consulting, and railway maintenance (Hustak, 50–1; Wood, 35–7).

117 Larry Pratt and John Richards, *Prairie Capitalism: Power and Influence in the New West* (Toronto: McClelland and Stewart 1979), 167–8, 215

118 Serfaty, 59

119 Ibid., 62; Larry Pratt, 'Grant Notley,' 25; Wood, 38

120 Serfaty, 62

121 Premier Manning Papers, Box 55, File 596, A.R. Patrick to Manning, June 1967

122 Premier Manning Papers, Box 55, File 596, Dr J. Donovan Ross to Manning, 22 June 1967

123 Premier Manning Papers, Box 55, File 596, Henry Ruste to Manning, 20 June 1967

124 Premier Manning Papers, Box 55, File 596, A.O. Fimrite to Manning, 27 June 1967

125 Premier Manning Papers, Box 55, File 596, Alfred Hooke to Manning, 29 May 1967

126 Fimrite to Manning, 27 June 1967

127 *Journals of the Legislative Assembly of Alberta*, 27 February 1968, 70

128 Ibid., 4 March 1968, 83

129 Ibid., 27 February 1968

130 Ibid., 27 February 1968

131 Judging by profiles of the twelve new Social Credit members elected in 1967 and of the party's new candidates in 1971. *Busy Bee*, May–June 1967, 5–8; *Insight* (Social Credit organ in 1970 and 1971), 2:1 (March 1971), 12–14.

132 Owen Anderson, 'The Alberta Social Credit Party: An Empirical Analysis of Membership, Characteristics, Participation and Opinion,' PhD thesis, University of Alberta, 1972, 26

133 Judging by the membership figures for the fifties, mentioned in chapter 5, election-year figures for memberships could be two to four times the numbers recorded in years without a provincial election. During the sixties, the flat dollar-per-member fee was replaced by a variety of fees, making it difficult to determine annual memberships from the annual treasurers' reports.

134 Anderson, 161

135 Ibid., 26

136 Ibid., 206

137 Ibid., 18

138 Ibid., 187
139 Premier Manning Papers, Box 55, File 594, Orvis Kennedy to Manning, 8 May 1967
140 Anderson, 212–18
141 Ibid., 46
142 Ibid., 341–53
143 Ibid., 273–4

Chapter 7

1 John J. Barr, *The Dynasty: The Rise and Fall of Social Credit in Alberta* (Toronto: McClelland and Stewart 1974), 163
2 Provincial Archives of Alberta, Premier Manning Papers, Box 58, File 630, *The Report of the Honourable Mr. Justice W.J.C. Kirby, In the Matter of an Inquiry by a Royal Commission into the Matters Set Out by Order-in-Council 861/67 respecting the Use or Attempted Use by the Honourable Alfred J. Hooke of his Office as a Member of the Executive Council of Alberta, and the Use or Attempted Use by Edgar W. Hinman of his Office as a Member of the Executive Council of Alberta,* October 1968, 7
3 Ibid., 84
4 Ibid., 85
5 Ibid., 89
6 Ibid., 302
7 Alfred J. Hooke, *30 + 5: I Know, I Was There* (Edmonton: Institute of Applied Art 1971), 259
8 Ibid.
9 Ibid., 252–5
10 Premier Manning Papers, Box 31, File 346(a), D.W. Rogers, deputy minister, Department of Public Welfare, to R.D. Jorgenson, minister of public welfare, 30 July 1962. Rogers proposed the establishment of a preventive social services program in welfare in this memo, four years before the legislation establishing such a program came into effect.
11 Premier Manning Papers, Box 70, File 764, Government of the Province of Alberta, Department of Public Welfare Social Planning and Development Branch, 'Administration and Policy Guide to the Preventive Social Service Program – Preventive Social Service Act, April 1966.' This document noted: 'In essence, a preventive social service is one designed to develop community awareness and resources, to strengthen and preserve human initiative and to preclude individual and family breakdown. It is any activity which is available to all members of the community on a voluntary basis for the enrichment of their physical, mental and social well-being.'
12 Premier Manning Papers, Box 70, File 764, Alfred J. Hooke, minister of public welfare, to Manning, 20 December 1967

13 Premier Manning Papers, Box 70, File 764, J.E. Oberholtzer, director, Human Resources Development Authority, to Harry Strom, minister of agriculture and chairman of the Human Resources Development Authority, 29 December 1967. This memo observed that at a meeting of the HRDA, chaired by Strom on 28 December 1967, it had been observed that several recommendations of the Advisory Committee on Preventive Social Services were not being followed up by the minister of welfare. It was therefore decided to set up a committee, composed of representatives of Welfare, Health, Youth, and Education, to make recommendations relative to preventive social services. This decision was a transparent attempt to remove Hooke's authority in the area.

14 Barr, *The Dynasty*, 179–80

15 See the discussion of Premier Manning's book, *Political Realignment*, in chapter 6.

16 Barr, *The Dynasty*, 179–80; Hooke 256–8

17 *Insight* (Alberta Social Credit League organ), 1:4 (June–July 1971), 4

18 David G. Wood, *The Lougheed Legacy* (Toronto: Key Porter Books 1985), 71

19 *Insight*, 1:4 (June–July 1971), 4–5

20 *Edmonton Journal*, 19 November 1970

21 Ed Shaffer, 'The Political Economy of Oil in Alberta,' in David Leadbeater, ed., *Essays on the Political Economy of Alberta* (Toronto: New Hogtown Press, 1984), 184

22 *Edmonton Journal*, 19 February 1970

23 Lougheed had raised the property tax issue in his motion of non-confidence on 4 March 1968; he raised it again in his reaction to the first Throne Speech from Strom (*Journals of the Legislative Assembly of Alberta*, 27 February 1968 and 17 February 1969). Though minor changes were made to the Public Welfare Act in 1970, the municipalities continued to pay 20 per cent of welfare costs (*Revised Statutes of the Province of Alberta*, 1970, Chap. 104).

24 John J. Barr, 'Beyond Bitterness,' in John J. Barr and Owen Anderson, *The Unfinished Revolt: Some Views on Western Independence* (Toronto: McClelland and Stewart 1971), 15

25 Ibid., 16

26 Owen Anderson, 'The Unfinished Revolt,' in John J. Barr and Owen Anderson, *The Unfinished Revolt: Some Views on Western Independence* (Toronto: McClelland and Stewart 1971), 42

27 Ibid., 43

28 Ibid., 46

29 *Edmonton Journal*, 13 March 1970

30 Barr, 'Beyond Bitterness,' 29

31 Ibid.

32 Barr, *The Dynasty*, 187; *Edmonton Journal*, 19 November 1970

33 Provincial Archives of Alberta, Research Division, Alberta Department of Labour, 'A History of Labour and Social Welfare Legislation in Alberta,' 1973

34 *Insight* 1:1 (September 1970), 2; 1:2 (November 1970), 9

35 Barr, *The Dynasty*, 188
36 Meir Serfaty, 'The Conservative Party of Alberta under Lougheed, 1965–71: Building an Image and an Organization,' *Prairie Forum* 6:1 (Spring 1981), 67
37 Ibid., 67
38 *Journals of the Legislative Assembly of Alberta*, 6 May 1969
39 Serfaty, 69–70
40 Ibid., 63–5
41 *Insight* 1:2 (November 1970), 8–10
42 *Insight* 1:4 (June–July 1971), 3
43 Provincial Archives of Alberta, Alberta Social Credit League Papers, Box 2, 'Rates and Information' for *Insight*, 'Official Bulletin of Alberta Social Credit League,' n.d. (journal began publication in September 1970)
44 Alberta Social Credit League Papers, Box 3, 'Newsclippings, pre-election 1971'
45 Barr, *The Dynasty* 189–90
46 *Calgary Herald*, 3 August 1971
47 Wood, 73
48 Allan Hustak, *Peter Lougheed: A Biography* (Toronto: McClelland and Stewart 1979), 138
49 *Canadian Parliamentary Guide*, 1972; Kenneth Wark, *A Report on Alberta Elections 1905–1982* (Edmonton: Government of Alberta 1983), 17
50 Larry Pratt, 'Grant Notley: Politics as a Calling,' in Larry Pratt, ed., *Socialism and Democracy in Alberta: Essays in Honour of Grant Notley* (Edmonton: NeWest Press 1986), 28–9, 33–7
51 John Richards and Larry Pratt, *Prairie Capitalism: Power and Influence in the New West* (Toronto: McClelland and Stewart 1979), 215
52 Ibid., 167–8
53 Ed Shaffer, 'Oil, Class and Development in Alberta,' in Larry Pratt, ed., *Socialism and Democracy in Alberta* (Edmonton: NeWest Press 1986), 119–25
54 Larry Pratt, *The Tar Sands: Syncrude and the Politics of Oil* (Edmonton: Hurtig 1976)
55 Alberta Social Credit League Papers, Box 3, 'Newsclippings, pre-election 1971'
56 *Insight* 2:1 (March 1971), 12–14, provided biographies of most of the new Socred candidates.
57 His few speeches in *Alberta Hansard* in 1971 and 1972 indicate a lack of focus or even conviction in his criticisms of government policy.
58 *Edmonton Journal*, 10 November 1971
59 *Insight* 2:1 (March 1971), 12
60 Ernest Watkins, *The Golden Province: A Political History of Alberta* (Calgary: Sandstone Publishing 1980), 213
61 Alberta Social Credit League Papers, Box 2, *Alberta Challenge* (Alberta Social Credit League newspaper), October 1973, 7
62 Ibid., 1
63 Alberta Social Credit League Papers, Box 2, *Social Credit ... on the Move* (Alberta Social Credit League newspaper), 1975, 3

64 *Alberta Challenge*, October 1973, 1

65 *Social Credit ... on the Move*, 1975, 2

66 Watkins, *Golden Province*, 213

67 *Canadian Parliamentary Guide*, 1976; Wark, 17

68 Alberta Social Credit League Papers, Box 2, *New SCene* (Alberta Social Credit League newspaper), 2:1, 1979

69 Alberta Social Credit League Papers, Box 2, Election leaflets, 1979

70 *New SCene* 2:1, 1979

71 Ibid.

72 *Canadian Parliamentary Guide*, 1980; Wark, 18

73 On the rise of western separatism, see Denise Harrington, 'Who Are the Separatists?' in Larry Pratt and Garth Stevenson, eds., *Western Separatism: The Myths, Realities and Dangers* (Edmonton: Hurtig 1981), 23–44.

74 While there are academic writings on the rise of Alberta separatism in general, particularly the articles in the Pratt and Stevenson book cited above, little interest in the flash-in-the-pan Kesler win has been shown, probably because his party's weak showing in the general election later that year – 11 per cent of the provincial vote and no seats – dampened earlier interest.

75 *Edmonton Journal*, various issues, February–May 1982

76 *Canadian Parliamentary Guide*, 1983; Wark, 18

77 David Bercuson and Douglas Wertheimer, *A Trust Betrayed: The Keegstra Affair* (Toronto: Seal 1987), 39

Chapter 8

1 Ghita Ionescu and Ernest Gellner, eds., *Populism: Its Meanings and National Characteristics* (New York: Macmillan 1969), 1

2 John Richards, 'Populism: A Qualified Defence,' *Studies in Political Economy* 5 (Spring 1981), 6

3 Ernesto Laclau, *Politics and Ideology in Marxist Theory* (London: Verso 1979), 174

4 See, for example, Nicos Poulantzas, *Political Power and Social Classes* (London: New Left Books 1975), 76–7, 247–52. Poulantzas's views about political parties are somewhat contradicted by his view that the state apparatus (or what he refers to as the state-ideological apparatuses) enjoys relative autonomy in its relations with the social classes of a society (282, 320).

5 Laclau, 127–8

6 Ibid., 174

7 Steve Stein, *Populism in Peru: The Emergence of the Masses and the Politics of Social Control* (Madison, Wis.: University of Wisconsin Press 1980), 11

8 On Argentina, see G.I. Blanksten, *Peron's Argentina* (Chicago: University of Chicago Press 1974). On Brazil, see Peter Flynn, *Brazil: A Political Analysis* (London: Ernest Benn 1978). A good general history of Latin America, which examines social structures closely, is Benjamin Keen and Mark Wasserman, *A Short History of Latin America*, 2d, ed. (Boston: Houghton Mifflin 1984).

9 Nicos Mouzelis, 'Ideology and Class Politics: A Critique of Ernesto Laclau,' *New Left Review*, 112 (November–December 1978), 50

10 Ibid., 51

11 Ibid.

12 Ibid., 52–3

13 John F. Conway, 'The Prairie Populist Resistance to the National Policy: Some Reconsiderations,' *Journal of Canadian Studies*, 14:3 (Autumn 1979), 78

14 John F. Conway, 'Populism in the United States, Russia and Canada: Explaining the Roots of Canada's Third Parties,' *Canadian Journal of Political Science*, 11:1 (March 1978), 110

15 James Youngdale, *Populism: A Psychohistorical Perspective* (Port Washington, NY: Kennikat Press 1975), 156–73

16 While the Populist parties in southern states were not as racist as the Democrats of the region, 'socially the Populists believed in a fixed inequality of status between the races with moral and intellectual capabilities at its center' (Gerald Gauthier, *Blacks and the Populist Revolt: Ballots and Bigotry in the 'New South'* [Montgomery, Ala.: University of Alabama Press 1977], 133).

17 On Minnesota and the deep south, see Youngdale and Gauthier, respectively. The importance of socialists and of organized labour to the Non-Partisan League in North Dakota is explored in Robert Morlan, *Political Prairie Fire: The Nonpartisan League, 1915–1922* (St Paul: Minnesota Historical Society Press 1985), 24, 31, 65, 360. In an introduction by Larry Remele to the 1985 edition of this work from the fifties, it is mentioned (xii) that recent historiography of the NPL attaches even more importance to the Socialist party presence than Morlan did.

18 Seymour Martin Lipset, *Agrarian Socialism*, 2d ed. (New York: Doubleday 1968), 33–4

19 R.T. Naylor, 'Appendix: The Ideological Foundations of Social Democracy and Social Credit,' in Gary Teeple, ed., *Capitalism and the National Question in Canada* (Toronto: University of Toronto Press 1972), 253

20 Peter R. Sinclair, 'Class Structure and Populist Protest: The Case of Western Canada,' in Carlo Caldarola, ed., *Society and Politics in Alberta* (Toronto: Methuen 1979), 73

21 Peter R. Sinclair, 'The Saskatchewan CCF: Ascent to Power and the Decline of Socialism,' *Canadian Historical Review*, 54 (December 1973), 419–33

22 John W. Bennett and Cynthia Krueger, 'Agrarian Pragmatism and Radical Politics,' in S.M. Lipset, *Agrarian Socialism*, 347–63

23 John F. Conway, 'To Seek a Goodly Heritage: The Prairie Populist Response to the National Policy,' PhD thesis, Simon Fraser University, 1978

24 Ibid., 83

25 Ibid., 88

26 Ibid., 86

27 For example, regarding the experience of the British Labour party, see Ralph Miliband, *Parliamentary Socialism: A Study in the Politics of Labour* (London: Merlin 1973). The West German Social Democrats' moderation in office is ex-

plored in Gerard Braunthal, *The West German Social Democrats 1969–1982: Profile of a Party in Power* (Boulder, Col.: Westview Press, 1983).

28 Walter D. Young, *Democracy and Discontent: Progressivism, Socialism and Social Credit in the Canadian West*, 2d. ed., (Toronto: McGraw-Hill Ryerson 1978), 77; Anthony Mardiros, *William Irvine: The Life of a Prairie Radical* (Toronto: Lorimer 1979), 246–50; Desmond Morton, *The New Democrats 1961– 1986: The Politics of Change* (Toronto: Copp Clark Pitman 1986)

29 Ken Andrews, ' "Progressive" Counterparts of the CCF: Social Credit and the Conservative Party in Saskatchewan, 1935–1938,' *Journal of Canadian Studies*, 17:3 (Fall 1982), 58–74

30 Young, 51–4

31 Glen Makahonuk, 'Masters and Servants: Labour Relations in the Saskatchewan Civil Service, 1905–1945,' *Prairie Forum*, 12:2 (Fall 1987)

32 Premier Douglas's perspective on his government's achievement is contained in L.H. Thomas, ed., *The Making of a Socialist: The Recollections of T.C. Douglas* (Edmonton: University of Alberta Press 1982).

Chapter 9

1 None the less, it should be emphasized that Social Credit's initial sharp right turn occurred *before* Leduc and that the party had lost its mass character several years before the oil strike. There is common sense but a lack of accuracy in the more usual view, expressed by John Richards, whose last statement rings true while his first is simply false: 'I would argue that the arrival of the major oil companies after Leduc completely transformed the movement into a conservative political party whose remaining populism was residual. The survival in office of Social Credit for another two decades is a discomforting fact for anyone on the left to explain. It obviously owes much to the ability of the government to provide public goods out of oil royalties and the replacement of populist mistrust of large scale external capital with an ideology of corporate benevolence.' (John Richards, 'Populism: A Qualified Defence,' *Studies in Political Economy*, 5 [Spring 1981], 26)

2 Dennis Groh, 'The Political Thought of Ernest Manning,' MA thesis, University of Calgary, 1970, 65

Index

THE STATE AND ECONOMIC LIFE

Editors: Mel Watkins, University of Toronto; Leo Panitch, York University

This series, begun in 1978, includes original studies in the general area of Canadian political economy and economic history, with particular emphasis on the part played by the government in shaping the economy. Collections of shorter studies, as well as theoretical or internationally comparative works, may also be included.

1 The State and Enterprise
  Canadian manufacturers and the federal government 1917–1931
  TOM TRAVES

2 Unequal Beginnings
  Agricultural and economic development in Quebec and Ontario until 1870
  JOHN MCCALLUM

3 'An Impartial Umpire'
  Industrial relations and the Canadian state 1900–1911
  PAUL CRAVEN

4 Scholars and Dollars
  Politics, economics, and the universities of Ontario 1945–1980
  PAUL AXELROD

5 'Remember Kirkland Lake'
  The history and effects of the Kirkland Lake gold miners' strike 1941–42
  LAUREL SEFTON MACDOWELL

6 No Fault of Their Own
  Unemployment and the Canadian Welfare State 1914–1941
  JAMES STRUTHERS

7 The Politics of Industrial Restructuring
  Canadian textiles
  RIANNE MAHON

8 A Conjunction of Interests
  Business, politics, and tariffs 1825–1879
  BEN FORSTER

9 The Politics of Canada's Airlines from Diefenbaker to Mulroney
  GARTH STEVENSON

10 A Staple State
  Canadian industrial resources in cold war
  MELISSA CLARK-JONES

11 Women's Work, Markets, and Economic Development in Nineteenth-Century Ontario
  MARJORIE GRIFFIN COHEN